A STUDENT'S GUIDE TO

Textual Criticism
of the Bible

Paul D.
Wegner

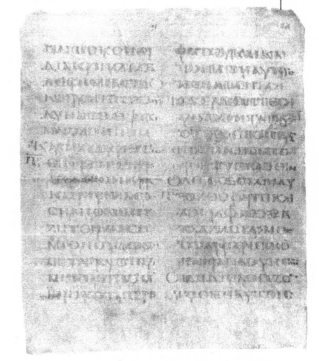

IVP Academic

An imprint of InterVarsity Press
Downers Grove, Illinois

InterVarsity Press
P.O. Box 1400, Downers Grove, IL 60515-1426
World Wide Web: www.ivpress.com
E-mail: email@ivpress.com

InterVarsity Press® is the book-publishing division of InterVarsity Christian Fellowship/USA®, a movement of students and faculty active on campus at hundreds of universities, colleges and schools of nursing in the United States of America, and a member movement of the International Fellowship of Evangelical Students. For information about local and regional activities, write Public Relations Dept., InterVarsity Christian Fellowship/USA, 6400 Schroeder Rd., P.O. Box 7895, Madison, WI 53707-7895, or visit the IVCF website at <www.intervarsity.org>.

All Scripture quotations, unless otherwise indicated, are the author's own translation.

See pages 311-313 for further permissions credits.

Design: Kathleen Lay Burrows

Images: Codex Petropolitanus (6th century), page from Gospel of Matthew: The Pierpont Morgan Library/Art Resource, NY
manuscript: Erich Lessing/Art Resource, NY

ISBN 978-0-8308-2731-2

Printed in the United States of America ∞

Library of Congress Cataloging-in-Publication Data

Wegner, Paul D.
  A student's guide to textual criticism of the Bible; its history,
  methods, and results / Paul D. Wegner.
    p. cm.
  Includes bibliographical references and indexes.
  ISBN 0-8308-2731-5 (pbk.: alk. paper)
  1. Bible—Criticism, Textual. I. Title.
  BS471.W44 2004
  220.4'046—dc22

                                                                            2004008463

P	22	21	20	19	18	17	16	15	14	13	12	11	10
Y	29	28	27	26	25	24	23	22	21	20			

To

Professor R. E. Clements:

a gentleman,

scholar,

mentor

and friend

To

Professor R. E. Clements,

a gentleman,

scholar,

mentor

and friend

Contents

Abbreviations

ABD	*Anchor Bible Dictionary.* Edited by David N. Freedman. 6 vols. New York, 1992.
AJSL	*American Journal of Semitic Languages and Literature*
AOS	American Oriental Studies
b.	Babylonian Talmud
BA	*Biblical Archaeologist*
BANE	*The Bible and the Ancient Near East: Essays in Honor of William Foxwell Albright.* Edited by George E. Wright. Garden City, 1961; reprint, Winona Lake, 1979.
BAR	*Biblical Archaeology Review*
BASOR	*Bulletin of the American Schools of Oriental Research*
B. Bat.	*Baba Batra*
BibRev	*Bible Review*
BHK	*Biblia Hebraica.* Edited by Rudolf Kittel. Stuttgart, 1905-1906, 1925^2, 1937^3, 1951^4, 1973^{16}.
BHS	*Biblia Hebraica Stuttgartensia.* Edited by Karl Elliger and Wilhelm Rudolph. Stuttgart, 1984.
Bib	*Biblica*
BJRL	*Bulletin of the John Rylands University Library of Manchester*
B.M.	British Museum
BT	*Bible Translator*
CBQ	*Catholic Biblical Quarterly*
CBP	Chester Beatty Papyri
CHB	*The Cambridge History of the Bible.* Edited by Peter R. Ackroyd et al. 3 vols. Cambridge, 1963.
CMHB	*Canon and Masorah of the Hebrew Bible. An Introductory Reader.* Edited by Sid Z. Leiman. Library of Biblical Studies. New York, 1974.
CRINT	Compendia rerum iudaicarum ad Novum Testamentum
CSCO	*Corpus scriptorum christianorum orientalium.* Edited by Jean B. Chabot et al. Paris, 1903-.
DJD	Discoveries in the Judaean Desert
Ebr (Hébr)	Hebrew
EJ	*Encyclopaedia Judaica.* 16 vols. Jerusalem, 1971.
Eus. *HE*	Eusebius. *Historia ecclesiastica (Ecclesiastical History).*

ET	English translation
GBS:OTS	Guides to Biblical Scholarship: Old Testament Series
HDB	*A Dictionary of the Bible.* Edited by James Hastings et al. Revised by Frederick C. Grant and Harold H. Rowley. 4 vols. New York, 1963.
HE	*Historia ecclesiastica*
HSM	Harvard Semitic Monographs
HSS	*Harvard Semitic Studies*
HTR	*Harvard Theological Review*
HUCA	*Hebrew Union College Annual*
IBR	Institute for Biblical Research
IDB	*The Interpreter's Dictionary of the Bible.* Edited by George A. Buttrick. 4 vols. Nashville, 1962.
IDBSup	*Interpreter's Dictionary of the Bible: Supplementary Volume.* Edited by Keith R. Crim. Nashville, 1976.
IOSCS	International Organization for Septuagint and Cognate Studies
IEJ	*Israel Explorational Journal*
ISBE	*International Standard Bible Encyclopedia.* Edited by Geoffrey W. Bromiley et al. Rev. ed. 4 vols. Grand Rapids, 1979-1988.
JAOS	*Journal of the American Oriental Society*
JBL	*Journal of Biblical Literature*
JBS	Jerusalem Biblical Studies
JGRCJ	*Journal of Greco-Roman Christianity and Judaism*
JJS	*Journal of Jewish Studies*
JNSL	*Journal of Northwest Semitic Languages*
JPS	Jewish Publication Society
JQR	*Jewish Quarterly Review*
JSOT	*Journal for the Study of the Old Testament*
JSS	*Journal of Semitic Studies*
JTS	*Journal of Theological Studies*
LCL	Loeb Classical Library
lit.	literally
LXX	Septuagint
m.	Mishnah
Meg.	Megillah
Migne, PG	*Patrologiae cursus completus. Series Graeca.* Edited by Jacques-Paul Migne. 162 vols. Paris, 1857ff.
Mm[Mas.M]	Masorah magna
Mp	Masorah parva
ms(s)	manuscript(s)
MT	Masoretic Text

NCBC	New Century Bible Commentary
n.d.	no date
Ned.	Nedarim
NICOT	New International Commentary on the Old Testament
NIDOTTE	*New International Dictionary of Old Testament Theology and Exegesis*
NovTSup	Novum Testamentum Supplements
OBO	Orbis biblicus et orientalis
Occ	Occidental (Western)
Or(.)	Oriental (Eastern)
OTL	Old Testament Library
OTS	Oudtestamentische Studien
PO	Patrologia orientalis
PSBA	*Proceedings of the Society of Biblical Archaeology*
PWCJS	Proceedings of the World Congress of Jewish Studies
QHBT	*Qumran and the History of the Biblical Text.* Edited by Frank M. Cross and Shemaryahu Talmon. London, 1975.
RB	*Revue biblique*
RevQ	*Revue de Qumrân*
SBL	Society of Biblical Literature
SBLMasS	Society of Biblical Literature Masoretic Studies
SBLSCS	Society of Biblical Literature Septuagint and Cognate Studies
SBT	Studies in Biblical Theology
ScrHier	*Scripta hierosolymitana*
SCS	Septuagint and Cognate Studies
SD	Studies and Documents
SNTSMS	Society for New Testament Studies Monograph Series
SP	Samaritan Pentateuch
SPB	Studia postbiblica
TOTC	Tyndale Old Testament Commentaries
TynBul	*Tyndale Bulletin*
UBS	United Bible Society
VK	Van Kampen Collection (The Scriptorium)
VT	*Vetus Testamentum*
VTSup	Vetus Testamentum Supplements
WBC	Word Biblical Commentary
WTJ	*Westminster Theological Journal*
ZAW	*Zeitschrift für die alttestamentliche Wissenschaft*

List of Figures, Tables and Maps

Preface

Students often ask, "Is the Bible we have today accurate?" or "How accurate is the biblical text?" A response is almost impossible without discussing questions of textual criticism. This book is written to provide both the basics of textual criticism and the background needed to answer questions regarding the accuracy of the Bible. In my experience of teaching biblical Greek, Hebrew and Bible introduction courses, students repeatedly find textual criticism in both the Old and New Testaments difficult to understand. Several scholarly books discuss in detail the process and technical problems of textual criticism. More recently several simplified works have also appeared on either Old Testament or New Testament textual criticism. This book, however, is a practical, step-by-step approach for the beginning student and layperson who wishes to have a broad working knowledge of both Old and New Testament textual criticism.

Questions of textual criticism are often first encountered simply by reading the notations "some ancient versions read . . ." or "some of the oldest manuscripts do not contain these verses" that appear in the margins of various modern Bible translations. For example:

> 1 Samuel 6:19 (Hebrew Bible). "And He struck down the men of Bethshemesh because they looked into the Ark of the LORD and He struck down the people *50,070 men* and the people mourned because the LORD struck down the people with a great slaughter."

In this case the phrase in italics ("50,070 men") is translated as "70 men" in several of the modern translations (e.g., NIV, NRSV, NLT, ESV). However, many Hebrew manuscripts and ancient versions (e.g., Septuagint [hereafter LXX], Latin Vulgate, Syriac Peshitta) contain the reading "50,070 men." Modern translations, therefore, deal with this passage differently:

NIV: "seventy men." Note: "A few Hebrew manuscripts; most Hebrew manuscripts and Septuagint *50,070*."

NASB: "50,070 men." No note.

NLT: "seventy men." Note: "As in a few Hebrew manuscripts; most Hebrew manuscripts and Greek versions read *50,070 men*. Perhaps the text should be understood to read *the Lord killed 70 men and 50 oxen.*"

NRSV: "seventy men." Note: "Heb *killed seventy men, fifty thousand men.*"

The question is, How many people were actually killed after looking into the ark? The majority of Hebrew manuscripts and the Greek text record 50,070. Why then do several modern translations say that only 70 men were killed? Which reading is correct?

> Luke 11:4. "And forgive us our sins, as we ourselves also forgive those who are indebted to us. And lead us not into temptation."

Some translators believe the last sentence should be similar to that found in the Lord's Prayer as recorded in Matthew 6:9-13 and thus add the phrase "but deliver us from evil [or the evil one]." Once again, modern translations handle this in a variety of ways:

> NIV: "and lead us not into temptation." Note: "Some manuscripts *temptation but deliver us from the evil one.*"
>
> NASB: "And lead us not into temptation." No note.
>
> NLT: "and lead us not into temptation." Note: "Some manuscripts add additional portions of the Lord's Prayer as it reads in Matt 6:9-13."
>
> NRSV: "and lead us not into temptation." Note: "Other ancient authorities add *but rescue us from the evil one* (or *from evil*)."

These differences and their notations often confuse the reader and raise questions regarding the accuracy of the text. This book discusses these issues and is specifically directed to someone who is new to the field of textual criticism or who is having difficulty understanding this area. It is intended to be a guide, introducing the reader to the questions, processes and tools of textual criticism. For the student who wishes to proceed further, bibliographies for each area of textual criticism are also included.

The scriptural citations are my own translations of the *Biblia Hebraica Stuttgartensia* (1984) or the United Bible Societies' *The Greek New Testament* (4th rev. ed.), unless otherwise noted.

I wish to thank Dr. Michael W. Holmes for reading a preliminary draft of the chapters on New Testament textual criticism. A special thanks also to Joe Gordon, Diane Hakala and Mitch Miller for their varied assistance during the writing process, and to my wife, Cathy, for reading over several preliminary drafts of this book.

PART I

Introductory Material

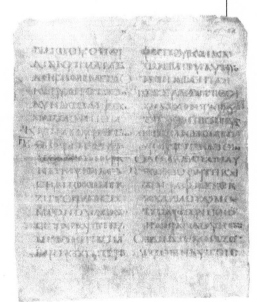

I

Introduction to Textual Criticism

This chapter sets forth the aim of this book and the definition, purpose, goal and importance of textual criticism. It describes the differences between Old Testament and New Testament textual criticism and defines the term *variant reading*.

The job of the textual critic is very similar to that of a detective searching for clues as to the original reading of the text. It is reminiscent of the master detective Sherlock Holmes who could determine a number of characteristics of the suspect from the slightest of clues left at the crime scene. In our case the "crime scene" is the biblical text, and often we have far fewer clues to work from than we would like. Yet the job of the textual critic is extremely important, for we are trying to determine the exact reading of a text in order to know what God has said and expects from us. This book describes the basic principles involved in the process of determining the most reliable reading of the text. Let's begin our journey with a definition of textual criticism.

1.1 Definition of Textual Criticism

It can be difficult for today's student, who photocopies, sends faxes and reads hundreds of pages for assignments, to appreciate how painstaking a task it was to copy a book before the introduction of movable type. In reading any version of the Bible today, it is essential to understand that its books underwent many centuries of hand copying before the appearance of the printing press in the fifteenth century A.D.

Unfortunately no original manuscripts (called "autographs") of any of the biblical books have been recovered, and since no extant manuscripts agree with each other in every detail, textual criticism is necessary to resolve questions of variation. Alfred E. Housman, a text critic of classical works, observes

Figure 1.1 A scribe at work. At the end of an Armenian manuscript of the Gospels, a scribe describes his hard-working conditions, saying that his ink had frozen and that his fingers were still stiff due to the cold of the snowstorm (Bruce M. Metzger, *The Text of the New Testament*, 3rd ed. [New York: Oxford University Press, 1992], p. 18). Another scribe graphically describes the harsh effects of his painstaking job: "Writing bows the back, thrusts the ribs into one's stomach, and fosters a general debility of the body" (Ibid., pp. 17-18). [Bibliothèque nationale de France]

that textual criticism is based on "common sense and the use of reason."[1] Briefly stated, *textual criticism is the science and art that seeks to determine the most reliable wording of a text.*[2] It is a science because specific rules govern the evaluation of various types of copyist errors and readings, but it is also an art because these rules cannot rigidly be applied in every situation. Intuition and common sense must guide the process of determining the most plausible reading. Informed judgments about a text depend on one's familiarity with the types of copyist errors, manuscripts, versions and their authors. It is a complex process with few shortcuts, but one that can be learned through systematic effort.

1.2 Importance of Textual Criticism

The importance of textual criticism is threefold. First and foremost, it attempts to establish the most reliable reading of the text. Second, in cases where a definitive reading is impossible to determine, it can help to avoid dogmatism. Third, it can help the reader better understand the significance of marginal readings that appear in various Bible translations. Textual criticism is not a matter of making negative comments or observations about the biblical text; instead it is the process of searching through the various sources of the biblical texts to determine the most accurate or reliable reading of a particular passage. It can, in fact, actually lead to increased confidence in the reliability of the biblical texts. Bruce K. Waltke notes that in the *Biblia Hebraica Stuttgartensia* (the most recent critical edition of the Hebrew

---

[1]Alfred E. Housman, "The Application of Thought to Textual Criticism," *Proceedings of the Classical Association* 18 (1922): 67.

[2]See P. Kyle McCarter, *Textual Criticism: Recovering the Text of the Hebrew Bible*, GBS:OTS (Philadelphia: Fortress, 1986), p. 18.

Bible; hereafter *BHS*) approximately one textual note appears for every ten words; thus 90 percent of the text is without significant variation.[3] According to Shemaryahu Talmon, even the errors and textual variations that exist "affect the intrinsic message only in relatively few instances."[4] Similarly in the New Testament, the fourth edition of the United Bible Societies' (hereafter UBS) *Greek New Testament* text notes variants regarding approximately 500 out of 6,900 words, or only about seven percent of the text.[5] Textual criticism, therefore, mainly concerns itself with this small portion of the biblical text called "variant readings." A variant reading is any difference in wording (e.g., differences in spelling, added or omitted words) that occurs among manuscripts.

Sir Frederic Kenyon (d. August 1952), a renowned New Testament text critic of the twentieth century, summarized the overall favorable result of New Testament textual criticism:

> It is reassuring at the end to find that the general result of all these discoveries and all this study is to strengthen the proof of the authenticity of the Scriptures, and our conviction that we have in our hands, in substantial integrity, the veritable Word of God.[6]

Many things have changed in the area of textual criticism over the last five decades since Kenyon. Further examination of the manuscripts from the Dead Sea area have revolutionized the study of Old Testament textual criticism, and more Greek manuscripts or fragments are now available for New Testament studies (i.e., manuscripts from St. Catherine's Monastery presently number 301; one of the newest manuscripts published, $\mathfrak{P}^{116}$, is a fragment of Hebrews 2:9-11 and 3:3-6).[7] Even though we have more evidence today than any previous generation, the issues of textual criticism have become more complex than ever. Still there are relatively few significant variants in the Bible, and among these variants there is very little difference in meaning and content. To help put this into perspective it is commonly said that no theological doctrine or is-

---

[3]Bruce K. Waltke, "Old Testament Textual Criticism," in *Foundations for Biblical Interpretation*, ed. David S. Dockery, Kenneth A. Matthews and Robert Sloan (Nashville: Broadman, 1994), p. 157. See also Bruce K. Waltke, "Textual Criticism of the Old Testament and Its Relationship to Exegesis and Theology," in *New International Dictionary of Old Testament Theology & Exegesis*, vol. 1, ed. Willem A. VanGemeren (Grand Rapids: Zondervan, 1997), esp. pp. 64-66.

[4]Shemaryahu Talmon, "Old Testament Text," *CHB* 1:161.

[5]The textual appendix of this Greek text only notes passages where there are significant questions regarding the text.

[6]Frederic G. Kenyon, *The Story of the Bible*, 2nd ed. (London: John Murray, 1964), p. 113.

[7]Amfilochios Papathomas, "A New Testimony to the Letter of the Hebrews," *JGRCJ* 1 (2000): 18-24.

sue hinges on a textual variant,[8] and that there are more differences between the various English translations of the New Testament than among the Greek manuscripts.[9]

1.3 Differences Between Old Testament and New Testament Textual Criticism

Old Testament textual criticism differs from New Testament textual criticism for two principal reasons: (1) the time period during which Old Testament manuscripts were copied is much greater, and (2) they have different starting points. It is no surprise that the history of transmission for the Old Testament is much longer than the New Testament's, but there are also other issues that make their histories significantly different.

1.3.1 Old Testament Transmissional History

If Moses, traditionally dated to the fifteenth century B.C., wrote any of the biblical texts, then some Old Testament texts may have been copied for over three thousand years.[10] The earliest extant copy of any part of the Old Testament is of two verses from the book of Numbers inscribed on silver amulets dated to the seventh century B.C. (see pp. 140-42). The next oldest texts, dated to the third century B.C., come from the Dead Sea area (e.g., 4QSam[b] [4Q52] and 4QJer[a] [4Q70]).[11] There are very few extant, early manuscripts or fragments of the Old Testament, but in contrast, there are about ninety-three manuscripts or manuscript fragments of the New Testament that are dated within three hundred years after the New Testament was written.[12] This does not even take into account the numerous quotations from early church fathers.

Until 1947 one of the oldest, accessible complete Hebrew manuscripts was Codex Leningradensis (Leningrad Public Library Ms. B 19[A]), dated to A.D. 1008, though portions of other biblical books were available from possibly 100 to 150 years earlier (e.g., British Museum Codex OR. 4445 [of the Pentateuch; dated to about A.D. 820-850]; Codex Cairensis [dated to about A.D. 895]).[13] But

---

[8]Waltke, "Textual Criticism of the Old Testament," p. 65; Bruce M. Metzger, *The Text of the New Testament: Its Transmission, Corruption, and Restoration*, 3rd ed. (New York: Oxford University Press, 1992), p. 112.

[9]Paul D. Wegner, *The Journey from Texts to Translations* (Grand Rapids: Baker, 1999), p. 213. See also David A. Black, *New Testament Textual Criticism: A Concise Guide* (Grand Rapids: Baker, 2001), p. 13.

[10]Bruce K. Waltke and Michael O'Connor, *An Introduction to Biblical Hebrew Syntax* (Winona Lake, Ind.: Eisenbrauns, 1990), p. 4.

[11]Frank M. Cross, "The Oldest Manuscripts from Qumran," *JBL* 74 (1955): 147-72.

[12]Kurt Aland and Barbara Aland, *The Text of the New Testament*, trans. Erroll F. Rhodes (Grand Rapids: Eerdmans, 1979), chart on p. 81.

[13]The Aleppo Codex dates to about A.D. 930, but was not accessible until more recently.

DEAD SEA SCROLLS

Since 1947 at least 900 manuscripts have been found in caves along the western shore of the Dead Sea. The largest number of these manuscripts were at a site commonly known as Qumran, leading them to be referred to as the Qumran scrolls. From Cave 4 came over 500 documents, many of which were either simply fragments or unreadable (see fig. 1.2). The manuscripts are generally dated between 250 B.C. to A.D. 135. About one quarter are portions of biblical texts.[a] Some of the biblical books were represented by a great number of copies (e.g., the book of Isaiah had twenty-one different manuscripts), whereas Esther and possibly Nehemiah were not represented at all. It is uncertain whether the omission of the books of Esther and Nehemiah was intentional or accidental.[b]

---

[a]James C. VanderKam, *The Dead Sea Scrolls Today* (Grand Rapids: Eerdmans, 1994), p. 31.
[b]Most scholars believe that Ezra and Nehemiah were considered one book at this time based on the following information: (1) In *Contra Apion* 1:8 (dated to A.D. 93-95) Josephus states there are twenty-two canonical books. (2) Jubilees 2:23 refers to twenty-two canonical books (dated between 170-140 B.C.). (3) 4 Ezra 14:44-46 says there are twenty-four canonical books (dated to the first century A.D.). In order to arrive at twenty-two canonical books we must combine the following books: (1) Judges and Ruth, (2) 1-2 Samuel, (3) 1-2 Kings, (4) Jeremiah and Lamentations, (5) the Twelve Minor Prophets (generally called The Book of the Twelve), (6) Ezra and Nehemiah, and (7) 1-2 Chronicles. To achieve twenty-four canonical books Judges and Ruth as well as Jeremiah and Lamentations are considered separate books.

---

in the middle of the twentieth century things began to change and the number of early manuscripts of the Old Testament increased significantly, largely due to the discovery of manuscripts in the Judean Desert (commonly called the Dead Sea Scrolls).

The discovery of the Dead Sea Scrolls revolutionized the field of Old Testament textual criticism because for the first time Hebrew manuscripts (or at least fragments) from at least as early as the first century B.C. were available for most of the Old Testament.[14] Nevertheless, most of the earliest extant Hebrew manuscripts are still a significant distance from the autographs of the Old Testament.

Not only is there a significant difference in the number of early manuscripts but also the transmissional history is different. Throughout the history of the Old Testament the Israelites appear to have had a group of scribes

---

[14]James C. VanderKam, *The Dead Sea Scrolls Today* (Grand Rapids: Eerdmans, 1994), p. 31.

Figure 1.2. Cave 4 at Qumran in which approximately 400 to 600 ancient manuscripts were found [Paul D. Wegner]

or priests dedicated to the job of preserving and maintaining their sacred Scriptures. This was often not the case for the New Testament manuscripts since the Christian church was persecuted during much of its early history, and manuscript copies made by professional scribes were very expensive. Many early New Testament manuscripts were copied by believers who desired to have their own copy of these precious works. Thus there are more manuscripts from this early transmissional period of the New Testament, though they may also be more flawed since they were not made by professional scribes. Sometimes they only had a few verses written on whatever material was available (e.g., potsherds, scraps of papyrus or parchment). The following picture is an ostracon (piece of broken pottery) from the seventh century A.D. found in Upper Egypt with an inscription of Luke 22:70-71, sometimes referred to as "the poor man's Bible."

Figure 1.3. The "poor man's Bible," an ostracon of Luke 22:70-71 from the seventh century A.D. [Institut Français d'archéologie orientale]

1.3.2 Different Starting Points

Largely because of the lack of early Old Testament manuscripts (in contrast to the plethora of New Testament manuscripts) and the differences in the transmissional process between the Old and New Testament manuscripts, the text critics of each of the testaments have been led to different starting points. James Barr explains it well:

> With a non-uniform text [e.g., the New Testament] we may find variant readings, and textual discussion begins from the variant readings, even if all of them "make sense." With a text of high uniformity [e.g., the Old Testament], however, textual discussion will more frequently begin from the feeling that there is a "difficulty"; the procedure will be more independent of the existence of variant readings.[15]

This makes the task of Old Testament text critics more subjective than that of their New Testament counterparts. P. Kyle McCarter notes the additional difficulty that a text may be corrupt even though it remains clear and easy to understand:

> A copyist who inadvertently strays from his text is much more likely to write something familiar to himself—something he frequently writes—than something unfamiliar. It is the nature of scribal error that it tends to produce the ordinary, commonplace, or "easy" reading. Corrupt texts, therefore, very often read quite smoothly.[16]

This leads us to our next question, namely, what is the goal or aim of textual criticism?

1.4 Goal of Textual Criticism

Since no autographs are available today of either the Old or New Testaments, the general task of the text critic is to get back as close as possible to those autographs. This is no easy task, for textual criticism is also affected by higher-critical matters, such as how and when a text reached its final form.

1.4.1 Goal of Old Testament Textual Criticism

It is difficult to know when the composition of a biblical book was completed and the transmission of the text began. This is complicated further by the possibility that these two processes may overlap to some extent. It was once thought possible to recover the *ipsissima verbs* ("actual words") of the inspired writer and that these were the original autographs of Scripture. However, today most scholars recognize that it is impossible to trace the formation of any of the

---

[15]James Barr, *Comparative Philology and the Text of the Old Testament: With Additions and Corrections* (Winona Lake, Ind.: Eisenbrauns, 1987), p. 4.

[16]McCarter, *Textual Criticism*, p. 14.

Old Testament books and that most have undergone later modifications.[17] Just three examples will suffice to indicate that even the most conservative scholars must allow for some modification of the original texts. (1) In Genesis 14:14, the city of Laish (Judg 18:29), or Leshem (Josh 19:47), is called "Dan" before its name was ever changed to "Dan," and no manuscript evidence suggests a different reading.[18] It is most likely that an editor later changed it so that his readers would understand which city was being indicated. (2) Deuteronomy 34 records the death of Moses, and verse 10 even states that "since that time [i.e., the death of Moses] no prophet has arisen in Israel like Moses," which implies that this chapter must have been written sometime after Moses' death. Jewish tradition holds that Joshua wrote this chapter.[19] Others suggest a Deuteronomistic editor.[20] But when was it added to the rest of Deuteronomy? Because all of the Hebrew manuscripts contain this chapter, it must have been added fairly early and then maintained by the scribes. (3) The phrase "and within yet sixty-five years Ephraim will be shattered from being a people" in Isaiah 7:8 has puzzled scholars for years since it does not appear to fit the context, even though its information is correct. Esarhaddon (680-669 B.C.) or Ashurbanipal (= Osnappar, 669-627 B.C.) came through approximately sixty-five years after the time of Isaiah 7 and deported more people from Israel (cf. Ezra 4:2, 9-10).[21] The most likely explanation is that this phrase was added by an editor or copyist sometime later (perhaps when these events happened), but once again no textual evidence suggests that this phrase was a later addition to the text. Since these parts appear in all the extant Hebrew manuscripts and ancient versions, they must have been put into the text fairly early and apparently were part of the authoritative text maintained by the scribes. Thus our understanding of the final form of the text must include at least these types of modifications of the text.

---

[17]Bruce K. Waltke, "Aims of Old Testament Textual Criticism," *WTJ* 51 (1989): 93. See also Michael Fishbane, *Biblical Interpretation in Ancient Israel* (Oxford: Clarendon, 1985), pp. 44-88.

[18]Derek Kidner, *Genesis: An Introduction and Commentary*, TOTC (Downers Grove, Ill.: InterVarsity Press, 1967), p. 16; Bruce K. Waltke and Cathi J. Fredricks, *Genesis. A Commentary* (Grand Rapids: Zondervan, 2001), pp. 232; Claus Westermann, *Genesis 12-36. A Commentary*, trans. John J. Scullion (Minnneapolis: Augsburg, 1985), p. 201.

[19]b. B. Bat. 14b and Ibn Ezra (Joseph H. Hertz, ed., *The Pentateuch and Haftorahs. Hebrew Text English Translation and Commentary* [London: Soncino, 1972], p. 916. Josephus believed that Moses himself wrote this chapter (*Antiquities of the Jews*, 4.8.48).

[20]Andrew D. H. Mayes, *Deuteronomy*, NCBC (Grand Rapids: Eerdmans, 1979), pp. 47, 413-14.

[21]Joseph Blenkinsopp, *Isaiah 1-39: A New Translation with Introduction and Commentary*, AB 19 (New York: Doubleday, 2000), p. 229; Brevard S. Childs, *Isaiah*, OTL (Louisville, Ky.: Westminster John Knox, 2001), p. 65; Ronald E. Clements, *Isaiah 1-39*, NCBC (Grand Rapids: Eerdmans, 1980), p. 85; J. Alec Motyer, *Isaiah: An Introduction and Commentary*, TOTC (Downers Grove, Ill.: InterVarsity Press, 1999), p. 76; John N. Oswalt, *The Book of Isaiah 1-39*, NICOT (Grand Rapids: Eerdmans, 1986), pp. 201-2; Hans Wildberger, *Isaiah 1-12: A Commentary*, trans. Thomas H. Trapp (Minneapolis: Fortress, 1991), p. 302.

Table 1.1. Perceived Goals of Old Testament Textual Criticism

Goal	Description	Scholars
1. Restore the original composition	The goal is to recover the author's *ipsissima verba*, "to establish the text as the author wished to have it presented to the public."	Most older textual critics, Harrison[a]
2. Restore the final form of the text (most modern textual critics)	The goal is to recover the *ipsissima verba* of the final redactor, assuming that the book has gone through some evolutionary process to get to this final form.	Brotzman,[b] Deist,[c] Würthwein[d]
3. Restore the earliest attested form	The goal is to recover the earliest attested form of the text for which there are actual textual witnesses. Generally the text in view is from the second century B.C., and conjectural emendations are not allowed.	Hebrew University Bible Project, UBS Hebrew Old Testament Text Project
4. Restore accepted texts (plural)	The goal is to recover the texts as they were accepted by particular religious communities. Each text may differ according to the authoritative standard of its particular community.	James Sanders, Brevard Childs (though he centers on the MT text accepted by the Jews)
5. Restore final texts (plural)	The goal is to recover the final form of the text. In some books or pericopes this may mean that there are several equally valid texts of the Old Testament that need to be restored.	Emanuel Tov,[e] Bruce K. Waltke[f]
6. Restore all various "literary editions" of the Old Testament	The goal is not to just reproduce the MT, but to restore all the "literary editions" of the various writings that can be discerned in the evolution of the Hebrew Bible (e.g., the LXX, SP, MT, as well as all others represented at Qumran and other places).	Eugene Ulrich[g]

[a]Roland K. Harrison, *Introduction to the Old Testament* (Grand Rapids: Eerdmans, 1969), p. 259.

[b]Ellis R. Brotzman, *Old Testament Textual Criticism: A Practical Introduction* (Grand Rapids: Baker, 1994), pp. 124, 129.

[c]Ferdinand E. Deist, *Toward the Text of the Old Testament* (Pretoria: Kerkboekhandel Transvaal, 1978), p. 24.

[d]Ernst Würthwein, *The Text of the Old Testament. An Introduction to the Biblia Hebraica,* trans. Erroll F. Rhodes, 2nd ed. (Grand Rapids: Eerdmans, 1995), p. 105.

[e]Emanuel Tov, *Textual Criticism of the Hebrew Bible,* 2nd ed. (Minneapolis: Fortress, 2001), p. 171.

[f]Waltke, "Old Testament Textual Criticism," p. 175.

[g]Eugene Ulrich, "Multiple Literary Editions: Reflections Toward a Theory of the History of the Biblical Text," in *Current Research and Technological Developments on the Dead Sea Scrolls: Conference on the Texts from the Judaean Desert, Jerusalem, 30 April 1995,* ed. Donald W. Perry and Stephen D. Ricks, Studies on the Texts of the Desert of Judah 20 (Leiden: Brill, 1996), pp. 78-105. Ulrich disagrees significantly with Tov: "Thus the target of 'textual criticism of the Hebrew Bible' is not a single text. The purpose or function of textual criticism is to reconstruct the history of the texts that eventually become the biblical collection in both its literary growth and its scribal transmission; it is not just to judge individual variants in order to determine which were 'superior' or 'original.' The 'original text' is a distracting concept for the Hebrew Bible" (pp. 98-99).

Table 1.1 summarizes and augments the history of what scholars believe to be the goal of Old Testament textual criticism as described in an article by Bruce K. Waltke.[22]

1.4.1.1 Final form or forms of the Old Testament text. Several modern scholars have adopted the goal of determining the final form or the final attested form of the text,[23] but even the ability to do this has been questioned. Both Emanuel Tov and Bruce Waltke have argued that there may be several original forms of a biblical text,[24] an idea based primarily on divergent readings of parallel passages in the Old Testament (e.g., 2 Sam 22 // Ps 18; 2 Kings 18:13-20:19 // Is 36-39; Is 2:2-4 // Mic 4:1-3; Ps 14 // Ps 53; Ps 40:13-17 [MT 14-18] // Ps 70) and the existence of divergent manuscripts. Tov states:

> These parallel sources are based on ancient texts which already differed from each other before they were incorporated into the biblical books, and which underwent changes after they were transmitted from one generation to the next as part of the biblical books. Hence, within the scope of the present analysis, these parallel texts, which are found in all biblical witnesses, including 𝔐 [MT], are of particular interest. The differences between these parallel texts in 𝔐, as well as in other texts, *could* reflect very ancient differences created in the course of the copying of the biblical text, similar to the differences known from a comparison of ancient scrolls and manuscripts.[25]

To argue for two separate textual traditions based on the differences in these parallel passages is only one of the possible answers. Table 1.2 examines the differences in the text of the MT between Isaiah 2:2-4 and Micah 4:1-3 in more detail.

Out of 272 consonants in Micah 4:1-3 there are only thirty that are different from those in Isaiah 2:2-4, or about 11 percent of the letters. The differences between these consonants can be grouped in the following ways: several (12 consonants) are different because the words are out of order; some (25 consonants) use a different but similar word; one consonant adds a final *nûn;* one consonant uses a plural verb instead of a singular, and one adds a whole phrase (11 consonants). It is difficult to know why these texts are so similar and yet contain differences. These differences may indicate two original sources or one source

---

[22]Waltke, "Aims of Old Testament Textual Criticism," pp. 93-108. See also Al Wolters, "The Text of the Old Testament," in *The Faces of Old Testament Studies: A Survey of Contemporary Approaches,* ed. David W. Baker and Bill T. Arnold (Grand Rapids: Baker, 1999), pp. 31-32.

[23]Deist, *Towards the Text of the Old Testament,* p. 24; Brevard S. Childs, *Introduction to the Old Testament as Scripture* (Philadelphia: Fortress, 1979), pp. 96-97.

[24]Emanuel Tov, *Textual Criticism of the Hebrew Bible* (Minneapolis: Fortress, 1992), pp. 12-13; Waltke, "Old Testament Textual Criticism," pp. 174-76.

[25]Tov, *Textual Criticism,* p. 12.

Table 1.2. Isaiah 2:2-4 and Micah 4:1-3 Compared

Isaiah 2:2-4	Micah 4:1-3
וְהָיָה בְּאַחֲרִית הַיָּמִים	וְהָיָה בְּאַחֲרִית הַיָּמִים
נָכוֹן יִהְיֶה הַר בֵּית־יְהוָה	יִהְיֶה הַר בֵּית־יְהוָה
בְּרֹאשׁ הֶהָרִים וְנִשָּׂא מִגְּבָעוֹת	נָכוֹן בְּרֹאשׁ הֶהָרִים וְנִשָּׂא הוּא מִגְּבָעוֹת
וְנָהֲרוּ אֵלָיו כָּל־הַגּוֹיִם:	וְנָהֲרוּ עָלָיו עַמִּים:
וְהָלְכוּ עַמִּים רַבִּים וְאָמְרוּ	וְהָלְכוּ גּוֹיִם רַבִּים וְאָמְרוּ
לְכוּ וְנַעֲלֶה אֶל־הַר־יְהוָה	לְכוּ וְנַעֲלֶה אֶל־הַר־יְהוָה
אֶל־בֵּית אֱלֹהֵי יַעֲקֹב	וְאֶל־בֵּית אֱלֹהֵי יַעֲקֹב
וְיֹרֵנוּ מִדְּרָכָיו וְנֵלְכָה בְּאֹרְחֹתָיו	וְיוֹרֵנוּ מִדְּרָכָיו וְנֵלְכָה בְּאֹרְחֹתָיו
כִּי מִצִּיּוֹן תֵּצֵא תוֹרָה	כִּי מִצִּיּוֹן תֵּצֵא תוֹרָה
וּדְבַר־יְהוָה מִירוּשָׁלָ͏ִם:	וּדְבַר־יְהוָה מִירוּשָׁלָ͏ִם:
וְשָׁפַט בֵּין הַגּוֹיִם	וְשָׁפַט בֵּין עַמִּים רַבִּים
וְהוֹכִיחַ לְעַמִּים רַבִּים	וְהוֹכִיחַ לְגוֹיִם עֲצֻמִים עַד־רָחוֹק
וְכִתְּתוּ חַרְבוֹתָם לְאִתִּים	וְכִתְּתוּ חַרְבֹתֵיהֶם לְאִתִּים
וַחֲנִיתוֹתֵיהֶם לְמַזְמֵרוֹת	וַחֲנִיתֹתֵיהֶם לְמַזְמֵרוֹת
לֹא־יִשָּׂא גוֹי אֶל־גּוֹי חֶרֶב	לֹא־יִשְׂאוּ גּוֹי אֶל־גּוֹי חֶרֶב
וְלֹא־יִלְמְדוּ עוֹד מִלְחָמָה:	וְלֹא־יִלְמְדוּן עוֹד מִלְחָמָה:

that has been intentionally modified or unintentionally corrupted resulting in two distinct readings—either explanation is plausible,[26] as is the case for many of the parallel passages in the Hebrew Bible.[27] But a problem like the LXX version of the book of Jeremiah, which is arranged differently and is one-eighth shorter than the MT, cannot be accounted for merely by different copyists of the same text.[28] A fragment of a scroll of the book of Jeremiah found at Qumran (4QJer[b] [4Q71]) dated by paleography to the first half of the second century B.C. contains characteristics similar to the LXX,[29] suggesting that there were different versions of the Hebrew texts known at this time.[30] However, it is not

---

[26]See Oswalt's discussion on Isaiah 2:2-4 and the parallel passage in Micah 4:1-3 in his *Book of Isaiah Chapters 1-39*, p. 115.

[27]Genesis 10:1-29 // 1 Chronicles 1:4-24; 2 Samuel 22 // Ps 18; 2 Samuel 23:8-39 // 1 Chronicles 11:11-41; Psalm 14 // Psalm 53; Ezra 2 // Nehemiah 7:6-72; Jeremiah 52 // 2 Kings 24:18-25:30; Isaiah 36:1—38:8 // 2 Kings 18:13—20:11; Psalm 40:13-17 // Psalm 70; Psalm 57:8-11 // Psalm 108:1-5; 1 Samuel 31:1-7 // 1 Chronicles 10:1-14; 2 Samuel 1:1-10 // 1 Chronicles 11:1-3; 2 Samuel 6:1-11 // 1 Chronicles 13:6-14; 2 Samuel 5:11-25 // 1 Chronicles 14:1-17.

[28]The two forms of the book of Jeremiah are difficult to assess (see discussion by John A. Thompson, *The Book of Jeremiah*, NICOT [Grand Rapids: Eerdmans, 1980], pp. 117-20), but the literary strata suggested by Tov are not convincing: Joshua 20:1-6; Joshua 24:33 (LXX); Ezekiel 7:3-9; 1 Samuel 16-18; Proverbs 24-31 (primarily order); Numbers 10:34-36 (primarily order).

[29]See the discussion on these fragments by Karen H. Jobes and Moisés Silva, *Invitation to the Septuagint* (Grand Rapids: Baker, 2000), pp. 173-77.

[30]John G. Janzen, *Studies in the Text of Jeremiah*, HSM 6 (Cambridge, Mass.: Harvard University Press, 1973), pp. 173-84; Tov, *Textual Criticism*, pp. 186-97; Waltke, "Aims of Old Testament Textual Criticism," p. 105. Qumran scrolls are generally named in the following order: (1) number of the cave where the manuscript was found, (2) place of origin (i.e., Q = Qumran),

known how the different versions originated or if they were both seen as equally authoritative. Recent work on the shorter version of Job in the LXX has suggested that in some cases the copyist/editor intentionally shortened a Hebrew text similar to the proto-MT in order to make it more appealing to his Hellenistic audience.[31] Is it also possible that early Jews in Alexandria used the LXX because they could understand the Greek, but they knew that the Hebrew text behind it was the more authoritative text?

1.4.1.2 Fluidity of the Old Testament text. It appears that the Old Testament text was somewhat fluid (or subject to change) until about the first century A.D., as seen in the increasing number of *matres lectionis* (i.e., letters used to indicate vowels to aid in pronunciation of the text) added by the scribes, the interchange of similar words and the various forms of the text in existence by the second century B.C. One reasonable explanation for the addition of *matres lectionis* is that following the return from the Babylonian Exile the Jews needed extra help in understanding Hebrew since they had grown accustomed to Aramaic (e.g., see Nehemiah 8:8; 13:24). Following the Exile, when there were multiple sites of worship and learning for the Jews (i.e., Babylon and Palestine), it is plausible that variants of the Hebrew text may have developed because it was harder to keep strict control over the copying of Scripture.

However, any amount of fluidity makes the text critic's task more difficult

Table 1.3. Hebrew Text Timeline

				Vowel points were added (5th-8th centuries)			
400 B.C.	200 B.C.	0	A.D. 200	A.D. 400	A.D. 600		A.D. 800
Proto-MT (c. at least 300 B.C.)			Unified text (proto-MT) (c. A.D. 100)				Codex Or 4445 (c. 820-850)
	LXX (c. 250-150 B.C.)						Codex
	SP (c. 200 B.C.)			Latin Vulgate (c. 400)			Cairensis
	Qumran Mss. (250 B.C.–A.D. 50)			Syriac Peshitta (c. 5th century, but may contain earlier elements)			(c. 895)

(3) whether the text is written in ancient script (e.g., "paleo"), (4) abbreviated name of the biblical book, and (5) a superscript letter indicating its place in the series of manuscripts that have been found. Hence 1QIsa[a] means the scroll was found in Cave 1 at Qumran and contains the book of Isaiah, first copy.

[31]Peter J. Gentry, *The Asterisked Materials in the Greek Job*, SBLSCS 38 (Atlanta: Scholars Press, 1995), pp. 386-87. See also: Peter J. Gentry, "The Septuagint and the Text of the Old Testament," IBR lecture, San Antonio, Texas, November 20, 2004, p. 5.

MATRES LECTIONIS

Certain Hebrew consonants (i.e., primarily ה [h] = "a" vowel, ו [w] = "o" or "u" vowels, and י [y] = "e" or "i" vowels) were added to the text in order to indicate a vowel sound. Vowel points were not inserted in the Hebrew text until about A.D. 500-800, and continued to be added to the text until about A.D. 1000; they have been used to determine the date of certain texts. For example, the proto-MT has fewer *matres lectionis* than most of the manuscripts from Qumran and thus the Qumran texts are generally dated after the text of the proto-MT. The following example illustrates the differences:

Isaiah 40:1 (supposed proto-MT) נחמו נחמו עמי יאמר אלהיכם

Isaiah 40:1 (MT) נַחֲמוּ נַחֲמוּ עַמִּי יֹאמַר אֱלֹהֵיכֶם

Isaiah 40:1 (4QIsaᵃ)

The texts above are alike except where *matres lectionis* are included to help indicate which vowel to use, even where the final letter is added to show the pronominal suffix should be pronounced (e.g., *kema*, not *kem*). Note the arrows above point out the *matres lectionis* that have been added to the text.

---

since there are more options to choose from (i.e., it is hard to determine the earliest form of a text if it continued to change).

In one sense an established text makes the text critic's task easier because there is a standard against which to judge, as was the case from about the first to the fifteenth centuries A.D. But the problem with a unified text is that earlier and possibly even more accurate variations may have been removed by those who determined which text to retain. Is it possible then to determine a form of the Old Testament text that preceded the form in the first century A.D.? In some cases, yes, as the following illustration indicates.

The *BHS* of Genesis 4:8 can be translated very literally as: "And Cain said to Abel his brother, and when they were in the field then Cain rose up over Abel his brother and killed him." An obvious element missing from this verse is what Cain said to Abel. Several ancient versions or recensions (SP; LXX; Peshitta; Vulgate), as well as some Hebrew manuscripts include the phrase,

Table 1.4. Variations in Old Testament Text

BHS	Some Hebrew Manuscripts; SP; LXX; Peshitta; Vulgate
Genesis 4:8 וַיֹּאמֶר קַיִן אֶל־הֶבֶל אָחִיו וַיְהִי בִּהְיוֹתָם בַּשָּׂדֶה וַיָּקָם קַיִן אֶל־הֶבֶל אָחִיו וַיַּהַרְגֵהוּ "And Cain said to Abel his brother, and it came about when they were in the field then Cain rose up over Abel his brother and killed him."	Each version has a reading similar to: "And Cain said to Abel his brother, 'Let us go out into the field'; and it came about when they were in the field then Cain rose up over Abel his brother and killed him."

"Let us go out into the field," which appears to be necessary for the meaning of the text. These sources may have included this phrase to smooth out the translation. However, it seems more reasonable that originally the phrase was in the text, but at some point in the copying process it was omitted from the MT (i.e., BHS; possibly because the eye of the scribe jumped from אָחִיו right to וַיְהִי both of which have several similar consonants).

1.4.1.3 A complex goal. Although evidence of the earliest stages of the transmission of the Old Testament is extremely scarce, it is nevertheless a reasonable goal to attempt to determine the earliest form of the canonical text.[32] Waltke urges Old Testament text critics to "resist the temptation to lower their sights from the high ideal of recovering final text(s) that emerged in Israel before prophecy ceased in Israel."[33] It is appropriate to ask which of the texts we know to have existed before the first century A.D. (e.g., Dead Sea Scrolls, LXX, SP) most likely reflect the original form of the Hebrew text. For example, did Deuteronomy 27:4 originally contain a prescription of worship at Mt. Ebal as the MT states or at Mt. Gerizim as the SP has it?[34] Is the MT correct in saying that the Israelites spent 430 years in Egypt (Exodus 12:40) or are the LXX and SP correct that this period included the time spent in both Egypt and Canaan? Waltke concludes his discussion on the aim of Old Testament textual criticism as follows:

> The text critic's aim will vary according to the nature of the book. If a book had

---

[32]Tov currently argues that the preferred goal of Old Testament textual criticism is: "to aim at the one text or different texts which was (were) accepted as authoritative in (an) earlier period(s)" (*Textual Criticism*, p. 288).

[33]Waltke, "Aims of Old Testament Textual Criticism," p. 101.

[34]There is no question that differing theological considerations affected the reading of this passage. See James A. Montgomery, *The Samaritans: The Earliest Jewish Sect* (Philadelphia: Winston, 1907), p. 35.

but one author, then the critic will aim to restore his original composition; if it be an edited text, then he will seek to recover the final, canonical text. If he turns up more than one final text, he will turn his data over to the literary and canonical critic to determine whether the text is in process of developing into a final canonical text or whether it existed in more than one canonical form.[35]

What I take issue with in Waltke's statement is whether there ever was more than one authoritative form of the text. A biblical book may have gone through some modification on its way to its final, authoritative form, and there may be times when we can identify these changes (e.g., "Dan" in Genesis 14:14; Isaiah 7:8b), but the goal of the Old Testament text critic is to determine the final, authoritative form, which then was maintained by the scribes and was later recorded in the canon. This position assumes Adam van der Woude's contention that there has always been a relative "uniformity" of the textual tradition in the religious circles around the temple, even amidst the "plurality" that developed before the turn of the century.[36] This goal pushes to an even earlier period than Waltke's phrase "if it be an edited text then he will seek to recover the final, canonical text" (which we assume he dates about 300 B.C.). The final form of the text that later became canonical may not be obtainable in every case, nevertheless it is a plausible goal in the vast majority of the cases (over 90 percent), especially given the number of materials discovered in the twentieth century.

Figure 1.4. 𝔓[52] a section of the Gospel of John 18:31-33 dated to the early second century A.D. [John Rylands University Library]

1.4.2 Goal of New Testament Textual Criticism

1.4.2.1 The current debate. As with the Old Testament, the traditional goal of New Testament textual criticism to recover the text of the autographs has been questioned significantly by recent scholars. Were there several editions

---

[35]Waltke, "Aims of Old Testament Textual Criticism," pp. 107-8.

[36]Adam S. van der Woude, "Pluriformity and Uniformity: Reflections on the Transmission of the Text of the Old Testament," in *Sacred History and Sacred Texts in Early Judaism: A Symposium in Honour of Adam S. van der Woude*, ed. Jan N. Bremmer and Florentino García Martínez (Kampen: Kok Pharos, 1992), pp. 151-69.

of some of the New Testament books? Or did Paul make multiple copies of some of his letters?[37] Eldon Jay Epp provides several lines of evidence that he believes may point in the direction of multiple forms of New Testament books (he calls this *multivalence* of the original texts): (1) our present Gospels used preexisting sources or precanonical versions, (2) some have suggested that the book of Acts has come down to us in two differing textual streams, and (3) the doxology in Romans 16:25-27 appears in some manuscripts in Romans 14:23, causing some scholars to suggest that the book may have had a shorter and a longer form.[38] However, whether this is enough evidence to posit multiple forms of the biblical text is questionable, and it has the appearance of an endless hunt for supposed sources, as has been the case with Pentateuchal source criticism.

Bart Ehrman takes a somewhat different direction and suggests that when an early scribe changed a text to provide a more orthodox theological viewpoint, he may then have created a new original text.[39] This raises several questions: What happens if the new alteration becomes popularly accepted by the church as the more authoritative text? Is the other virtually lost except as a variant of the text? Do we have two original texts? Ehrman raises a plausible viewpoint, but we have very little evidence that the early church was trying to fortify theological positions rather than trying to maintain an accurate text. There is, in fact, a somewhat similar example in 1 Timothy 3:16, where the Greek word ὅς, "he, or the one who is," has been changed to θεός, "God," making the text much stronger theologically. However, the editors of the UBS Greek text suggest (based at least partially on the manuscript evidence) that this theologically stronger variant is a later reading. Ehrman and others suggest that these changes were made very early in the transmission of the text. While it is difficult to know what happened in the first hundred years of the history of transmission, there is little convincing evidence for such changes. The early church seems to have taken great care to monitor er-

---

[37]See the discussion by Michael W. Holmes, "Reasoned Eclecticism in New Testament Textual Criticism," in *The Text of the New Testament in Contemporary Research: Essays on the Status Quaestionis*, ed. Bart D. Ehrman and Michael W. Holmes, Studies and Documents 46 (Grand Rapids: Eerdmans, 1995), pp. 353-54.

[38]Eldon Jay Epp, "Issues in New Testament Textual Criticism: Moving from the Nineteenth Century to the Twenty-First Century," in *Rethinking New Testament Textual Criticism*, ed. David Allan Black (Grand Rapids: Baker, 2002), p. 73.

[39]Bart D. Ehrman, *The Orthodox Corruption of Scripture: The Effect of Early Christological Controversies on the Text of the New Testament* (New York: Oxford University Press, 1993); cf. his "The Text as Window: New Testament Manuscripts and the Social History of Early Christianity," in *The Text of the New Testament in Contemporary Research: Essays on the Status Quaestionis: A Volume in Honor of Bruce M. Metzger*, Studies and Documents 46 (Grand Rapids: Eerdmans, 1995), pp. 361-79.

rant theology and their sacred texts (e.g., their controversies with Gnostics, docetists and Marcion). To give some idea of the authority and reverence that these sacred words engendered, one need only look at quotations from the early church fathers. For example, in a letter to the Corinthians (c. 95), Clement of Rome states: "Take up the epistle of the blessed Paul the Apostle" (*1 Clement* 47:1),[40] which implies that they had in their possession an authoritative letter from Paul.

Other scholars have also questioned the accuracy of the transmission process in the first century of the church. Helmut Koester states that "whatever evidence there is indicates that not only minor, but also substantial revisions of the original texts have occurred during the first hundred years of the transmission."[41] Some even argue that the text should not be viewed as a fixed autograph but rather as a "moving stream"[42] or a "living text."[43] Surely these views overstate the case, whereas the traditional view has much to substantiate it. While questions as to the original text surface in some places, a substantial amount of the New Testament text remains unquestioned and most likely represents the text of the original autographs or very close to it. While the writers of New Testament Scriptures were still alive it is unlikely that people could have changed their writings without their authors pointing out such discrepancies. Paul sometimes requested that his letters be circulated to other churches (Col 4:16), and thus the autographs must have been copied almost immediately; this would make it unlikely that others could modify the text without some traces of the originals existing. The early church also had a great reverence for these works (2 Tim 3:16; 2 Pet 1:20-21) and their authors (2 Pet 3:15-16), so it is doubtful that they would change their writings (see also Rev 22:18-19).

1.4.2.2 The goal. A plausible goal for New Testament textual criticism is the recovery of the original readings of the text or in some cases it may be necessary to identify the earliest possible readings.[44] It may not always be possible to know for certain that we have an original reading, but remember there is only about 6 percent of the Greek text that is in question. Bruce M. Metzger states it this way:

---

[40]Kirsopp Lake, *The Apostolic Fathers with an English Translation*, LCL (Cambridge, Mass.: Harvard University Press, 1976), 1:88-89.

[41]Helmut Koester, "The Texts of the Synoptic Gospels in the Second Century," in *Gospel Traditions in the Second Century: Origins, Recensions, Text and Transmission*, ed. William L. Peterson, Christianity and Judaism in Antiquity 3 (Notre Dame, Ind.: University of Notre Dame Press, 1989), p. 37.

[42]J. Neville Birdsall, "The New Testament Text," in *CHB* 1:377.

[43]David C. Parker, *Living Text of the Gospels* (Cambridge: Cambridge University Press, 1997).

[44]Eldon J. Epp, "Textual Criticism (NT)," *ABD* 6:412.

Although in very many cases the textual critic is able to ascertain without residual doubt which reading must have stood in the original, there are not a few other cases where he can come only to a tentative decision based on an equivocal balancing of probabilities. Occasionally none of the variant readings will commend itself as original, and he will be compelled either to choose the reading which he judges to be the least unsatisfactory or to indulge in conjectural emendation. In textual criticism, as in other areas of historical research, one must seek not only to learn what can be known, but also to become aware of what, because of conflicting witnesses, cannot be known.[45]

In some cases New Testament manuscripts date to within fifty to one hundred years after their autographs. For example, Rylands Papyrus 457 ($\mathfrak{P}^{52}$) is

---

ABUNDANCE OF MANUSCRIPTS

There are over 5,400 manuscripts of New Testament passages and books.[a] By comparison there are relatively few manuscripts of other ancient writings, as noted below:

Thucydides, *History of the Peloponnesian War* (c. 460-400 B.C.)	Only 8 extant mss, the earliest being c. A.D. 900, plus a few fragments from the 1st century A.D.
Julius Caesar, *Gallic War* (composed 58-50 B.C.)	Several extant mss, but only 9 or 10 of good quality; the oldest is about 900 years after Julius Caesar.
Livy, *Annals of the Roman People* (59 B.C.-A.D. 17)	Only 35 of the original 142 books have survived; 20 extant mss; only 1 ms (containing fragments of books 3-6) is as old as the fourth century A.D.
Tacitus, *Histories and Annals* (c. A.D. 100)	Only 4.5 of the original 14 books of *Histories* and 10 (with portions of 2 more) of the 16 books of *Annals* survived in 2 mss dating from the ninth and eleventh centuries A.D.

---

[a]F. F. Bruce, *The New Testament Documents: Are They Reliable?* 5th ed. (Downers Grove, Ill.: InterVarsity Press, 1960), pp. 16-17.

---

[45]Metzger, *Text of the New Testament*, p. 246.

thought to be dated to about A.D. 125 to 150, and the Gospel of John ranges anywhere from A.D. 40 to 110;[46] the interval between its authorship and extant manuscript evidence is thus very short. Given the reverence that the early church had for the New Testament and its authors, it would seem that they would try to maintain it as accurately as possible.

The difficulty facing the New Testament text critic is weighing the numerous copies of the New Testament books and their variant readings. Eldon J. Epp explains how these variant readings may have originated:

> An apostolic letter or a portion of a gospel would be read in a worship service; visiting Christians now and again would make or secure copies to take to their own congregations, or the church possessing it might send a copy to another congregation at its own initiative or even at the request of the writer (cf. Col 4:16); and quite rapidly numerous early Christian writings—predominately those that eventually formed the NT—were to be found in church after church throughout the Roman world. Naturally, the quality of each copy depended very much on the circumstances of its production; some copies must have been made in a rather casual manner under far less than ideal scribal conditions, while others, presumably, were made with a measure of ecclesiastical sanction and official solicitude, especially as time passed.[47]

The plethora of New Testament manuscripts is a great benefit when trying to determine the original reading of the New Testament, for it is easier to sift through and evaluate the various extant readings than to emend texts with no evidence. Therefore the goal of New Testament textual criticism is to determine the most plausible original reading out of a large body of evidence.

Further Reading

Old Testament Textual Criticism

Albrektson, Bertil. "Textual Criticism and the Textual Basis of a Translation of the Old Testament." *BT* 26 (1975): 314-24.

Barrick, William D. "Current Trends and Tensions in Old Testament Textual Criticism." *BT* 35 (1984): 301-8.

Brotzman, Ellis R. *Old Testament Textual Criticism. A Practical Introduction.* Grand Rapids: Baker, 1994.

Deist, Ferdinand E. *Towards the Text of the Old Testament.* Translated by Walter K. Winkler, 2nd ed. Pretoria: Kerkboekhandel, 1981.

———. *Witnesses to the Old Testament: Introducing Old Testament Textual Criticism.* The Literature of the Old Testament 5. Pretoria: Kerkboekhandel, 1988.

Goshen-Gottstein, Moshe H. "The Textual Criticism of the Old Testament:

---

[46]Robert Kysar, "John, the Gospel of," *ABD* 3:918.
[47]Epp, "Textual Criticism (NT)," 6:415.

Rise, Decline, Rebirth." *JBL* 102 (1983): 365-99.

Klein, Ralph W. *Textual Criticism of the Old Testament: The Septuagint after Qumran.* GBS:OTS. Philadelphia: Fortress, 1974.

McCarter, P. Kyle. *Textual Criticism: Recovering the Text of the Hebrew Bible.* GBS:OTS. Philadelphia: Fortress, 1986.

Orlinsky, Harry M. "The Textual Criticism of the Old Testament." In *BANE.* See pp. 113-32.

Payne, David F. "Old Testament Textual Criticism: Its Principles and Practice." *TynBul* 25 (1974): 99-112.

Roberts, Bleddyn J. *The Old Testament Text and Versions.* Cardiff: University of Wales Press, 1951.

———. "The Textual Transmission of the Old Testament." In *Tradition and Interpretation,* pp. 1-30. Edited by George W. Anderson. Oxford: Clarendon, 1979.

Talmon, Shemaryahu. "The Old Testament Text." In *CHB* 1:159-99. (Reprinted in *QHBT,* pp. 1-41).

Thomas, D. Winton. "The Textual Criticism of the Old Testament." In *The Old Testament and Modern Study,* pp. 238-59. Edited by Harold H. Rowley. Oxford: Clarendon, 1951.

Thompson, John A. "Textual Criticism, OT." *IDBSup.* See pp. 886-91.

Tov, Emanuel. "The Text of the Old Testament." In *Bible Handbook.* Vol. 1. *The World of the Bible,* pp. 156-86. Edited by Adam S. van der Woude. Translated by Sierd Woudstra. Grand Rapids: Eerdmans, 1986.

———. *Textual Criticism of the Hebrew Bible.* Minneapolis: Fortress, 1992.

Waltke, Bruce K. "Aims of Old Testament Textual Criticism." *WTJ* 51 (1989): 93-108.

———. "Old Testament Textual Criticism." In *Foundations for Biblical Interpretation,* pp. 156-86. Edited by David S. Dockery, Kenneth A. Matthews and Robert Sloan. Nashville: Broadman, 1994.

———. "The Textual Criticism of the Old Testament." In *Biblical Criticism: Historical, Literary, and Textual,* pp. 47-65. Edited by Roland K. Harrison et al. Grand Rapids: Zondervan, 1978. Also found in *Expositor's Bible Commentary,* 1:211-28. Edited by Frank E. Gaebelein. Grand Rapids: Zondervan, 1979.

Weingreen, Jacob. *Introduction to the Critical Study of the Text of the Hebrew Bible.* New York: Oxford University Press, 1982.

Würthwein, Ernest. *The Text of the Old Testament: An Introduction to the Biblia Hebraica.* Translated by Erroll F. Rhodes. 2nd ed. Grand Rapids: Eerdmans, 1995.

New Testament Textual Criticism

Aland, Kurt, and Barbara Aland. *The Text of the New Testament.* Translated by Erroll F. Rhodes. Grand Rapids: Eerdmans, 1987.

Black, David A. *New Testament Textual Criticism.* Grand Rapids: Baker, 1995.

Colwell, Ernest C. "Text and Ancient Versions of the New Testament." In *Interpreter's Bible* 1:72-83. Nashville: Abingdon, 1952.

Elliott, James K. *A Bibliography of Greek New Testament Manuscripts.* SNTSMS 62. Cambridge: Cambridge University Press, 1989.

———. "Can We Recover the Original New Testament?" *Theology* 77 (1974): 338-53.

———. "In Defense of Thoroughgoing Eclecticism in New Testament Textual Criticism." *ResQ* 21 (1978): 95-115.

———. "Rational Criticism and the Text of the New Testament." *Theology* 75 (1972): 338-43.

Epp, Eldon J. "The Eclectic Method in New Testament Textual Criticism: Solution or Symptom? *HTR* 69 (1976): 211-57.

———. "Textual Criticism." *ABD* 6:412-35.

———. "Textual Criticism." In *The New Testament and Its Modern Interpreters,* pp. 75-126. Edited by Eldon J. Epp and George W. MacRae. The Bible and Its Modern Interpreters 3. Philadelphia: Fortress; Atlanta: Scholars Press, 1989.

———. "The Twentieth Century Interlude in New Testament Textual Criticism." *JBL* 93 (1974): 386-414.

Epp, Eldon J., and Gordon D. Fee, eds. *New Testament Textual Criticism.* Oxford: Clarendon, 1981.

Fee, Gordon D. "Rigorous or Reasoned Eclecticism—Which?" In *Studies in New Testament Language and Text,* pp. 174-97. Edited by James K. Elliott. NovTSup 44. Leiden: Brill, 1976.

Greenlee, J. Harold. *Introduction to New Testament Textual Criticism.* Rev. ed. Peabody, Mass.: Hendrickson, 1995.

Kenyon, Frederic G. *Handbook of the Textual Criticism of the New Testament.* 2nd ed. London: Macmillan, 1912.

———. *The Text of the Greek Bible.* Revised by Arthur W. Adams. 3rd ed. London: Duckworth, 1975.

McReynolds, Paul R. "Establishing Text Families." In *The Critical Study of Sacred Texts,* pp. 97-113. Edited by Wendy D. O'Flaherty. Berkeley Religious Studies Series. Berkeley: Graduate Theological Union, 1979.

Metzger, Bruce M. *Annotated Bibliography of the Textual Criticism of the New Testament 1914-1939.* SD 16. Copenhagen: Munksgaard, 1955.

———. *The Early Versions of the New Testament: Their Origin, Transmission, and Limitations.* Oxford: Oxford University Press, 1977.

———. *The Text of the New Testament: Its Transmission, Corruption, and Restoration.* 3rd ed. New York: Oxford University Press, 1992.

Robertson, Archibald T. *An Introduction to the Textual Criticism of the New Testament.* Nashville: Abingdon, 1925.

Scrivener, Frederick H. A. *A Plain Introduction to the Criticism of the New Testament.* Edited by Edward Miller. 4th ed. 2 vols. London: George Bell, 1894.

2

Transmissional Errors
Occurring in the Bible

This chapter describes types of errors that commonly occurred in the transmission of texts, with examples from Hebrew and Greek texts. It covers both unintentional changes (homophony, haplography, dittography, etc.) and intentional changes (substituting more common words for rare words, additions or glosses, harmonization, etc.).

We have all carefully typed or hand copied written information only to find in checking it over that there are multiple mistakes. In a similar way the text of the Bible has undergone centuries of hand copying by scribes who were prone to human error. Even in the case of the Old Testament, where for a significant period of its textual history well-trained scribes copied the text following strict precautionary rules, changes to the text were made, both unintentionally and intentionally. The writing materials themselves sometimes facilitated errors; most had rough surfaces on which the details of particular letters could be lost. Greek and possibly Hebrew[1] were written in *scriptio continua* (without breaks between words), with little if any punctuation. It is important, therefore, in determining the most plausible reading of a text to understand the types of errors that may have been incorporated in the transmissional process.

2.1 Unintentional Changes

2.1.1 Mistaken letters

One of the most common errors made by copyists was the confusion of similar

---

[1]Emanuel Tov, *Textual Criticism of the Hebrew Bible*, 2nd ed (Minneapolis: Fortress, 2001), pp. 208-9; Alan R. Millard, " 'Scriptio Continua' in Early Hebrew—Ancient Practice or Modern Surmise?" *JSS* 15 (1970): 2-15; Joseph Naveh, "Word Division in West Semitic Writing," *IEJ* 23 (1973): 206-8.

letters. Just as in English *u* and *v* can sometimes look alike because of poor pen-manship, so, for example, in Hebrew square script the ד (*d, dālet*) and ר (*r, rēš*) may easily be confused. The Greek uncial letters C (sigma), O (omicron), and Θ (theta) can also sometimes look very similar.

- **Old Testament example.** Genesis 10:4 cites a race known as the "Dodanim" (דֹּדָנִים, *dōdānîm*), but 1 Chronicles 1:7 calls them the "Rodanim" (רֹדָנִים, *rōdānîm*). The name "Rodanim" is generally preferred as a reference to the Rhodians of the Asia Minor coastline.[2]

- **New Testament example.** Some uncial manuscripts may have confused OC ("the one who is" א*, A*) and ΘC ("God"; א[2], A[c]) in 1 Timothy 3:16.

2.1.2 Homophony

The substitution of similar sounding words. In English "it's" is often mistakenly written for "its," or "there" for "their." Several Hebrew letters (e.g., א [*'alep*] and ע [*'ayin*], ת [*tāw*] and ט [*tēt*], ס [*sāmek*] and שׂ [*śîn*]) cannot be distinguished by sound alone, so that errors of homophony could have been incorporated into the text during periods of oral trans-mission or when one person read the text to several scribes who transcribed it (which may have happened at Qumran). Greek too has similar sounding

Figure 2.1. A portrait of a girl with a writing tablet [Museo Archeologico Nazionale, Naples, Italy/ HIP/Art Resource, NY]

letters (e.g., α [*alpha*] and o [*omicron*], and o [*omicron*] and ω [*omega*]).

- **Old Testament example.** In Isaiah 9:2 (ET 3) the word לֹא (*lō'*, "not"; "Thou hast multiplied the nation, [and] *not* increased the joy" [KJV]) was appar-ently incorrectly substituted for the word לוֹ (*lô*, "to him" or "to it"; "You shall multiply the nation, You shall increase their gladness [lit. 'gladness to it']" [NASB]). The Masoretes recognized the problematic negative particle in

---

[2]Victor P. Hamilton, *The Book of Genesis: Chapters 1-17*, NICOT (Grand Rapids: Eerdmans, 1990), p. 334; Derek Kidner, *Genesis: An Introduction and Commentary*, TOTC (Downers Grove, Ill.: InterVarsity Press, 1967), p. 106; Nahum M. Sarna, *Genesis* בְּרֵאשִׁית, JPS Torah Commentary (New York: Jewish Publication Society, 1989), p. 71.

this verse and noted in the *Masorah parva* (cf. pp. 109-10) that it should be translated instead as לֹו (*lô*, "to it"). This change agrees with the Peshitta and Targum Jonathan.

- **New Testament example.** There are two similar sounding readings of Romans 5:1— ἔχομεν ("we have" א[1], B[2], F, etc.) and ἔχωμεν ("we shall have" א*, A, B*, C, etc.).

Figure 2.2. Ancient writing materials. Drawing from an old Bible. [Paul D. Wegner]

2.1.3 Haplography

The omission of a letter or word, which is usually due to a similar letter or word in the context. For instance, "occurence" is a common misspelling of "occurrence." An omission can easily happen when, in copying a text, one's eye skips ahead to another word or line with the same word or letter. This tendency is compounded when there are no spaces between words or punctuation marks, which certainly was the case for Greek texts and may have been true of Hebrew as well.

- **Old Testament example.** People from the tribe of Benjamin are referred to as בְּנֵי בִנְיָמִן (*bĕnē binyāmin*, "sons of Benjamin") nine times out of ten in the Old Testament, but in Judges 20:13 they are simply called בִּנְיָמִן (*binyāmin*). The Masoretes apparently thought that the text suffered from haplography since they inserted pointing for the word "sons" (בְּנֵי, *bĕnē*) without including the consonants.

As noted above the Masoretes, who maintained the Hebrew text from about A.D. 500–1100, sometimes would make notations in the marginal Masorahs or leave the text unpointed when they questioned it for some reason. Notice that the second line merely has the vowel points for בְּנֵי, *bĕnē* in the *BHS* text:

וְעַתָּה תְּנוּ אֶת־הָאֲנָשִׁים בְּנֵי־בְלִיַּעַל אֲשֶׁר בַּגִּבְעָה וּנְמִיתֵם וּנְבַעֲרָה רָעָה

מִיִּשְׂרָאֵל וְלֹא אָבוּ ְ בִּנְיָמִן לִשְׁמֹעַ בְּקוֹל אֲחֵיהֶם בְּנֵי־יִשְׂרָאֵל

"'Now, give up the men, the sons of Beliyaʿal (worthless fellows) who are in Gibeah, that we may kill them and remove (the) evil from Israel.' But the *sons* of Benjamin were not willing to listen to the voice of their brothers, the sons of Israel." (Judges 20:13)

- **New Testament example.** Some manuscripts of John 1:13 read ἐγενηθησαν (P⁷⁵, A, B* Δ Θ) while others read ἐγεννήθη (itᵇ, Irenaeusˡᵃᵗ, Tertullian, Origenˡᵃᵗ½ , etc.); both mean "were born" though they come from two different roots, γεννάω and γίνομαι, respectively.

The following pictures illustrate how difficult it would be to copy some of these early texts:

Figure 2.3. The Isaiah Scroll from Qumran Cave 4. Notice that there are no vowel points or punctuation marks, and the final letters are very rare. [John C. Trever]

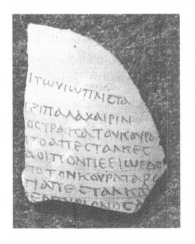

Figure 2.4. An early Greek ostracon dated to about A.D. 160. Notice that there are no divisions between words and no punctuation marks. [Paul D. Wegner]

2.1.4 Dittography

A letter or word that has been written twice rather than once. For example, in English *latter* might mistakenly be written for *later*. This mistake is easily made, especially when copying a group of letters that are very similar.

- **Old Testament example.** In Jeremiah 51:3a the word יִדְרֹךְ (*yidrōk*, "he drew [a bow]") appears twice, consecutively; the Masoretes, recognizing the mistake, left the second יִדְרךְ (*ydrk*) unvocalized. The Hebrew text of Jeremiah 51:3a reads as follows in the MT:

  אֶל־יִדְרֹךְ הַדֹּרֵךְ יִדְרךְ קַשְׁתּוֹ "Let not the archer bend *bend* his bow."[3]

  ↑

- **New Testament example.** Dittography may have occurred in Mark 3:16 where the words ἐποίησεν τοὺς δώδεκα ("and he appointed the twelve") appears to be repeated from verse 14.

2.1.5 Metathesis

A reversal in the order of two letters or words. This is a common typographical error; for example, "urn" for "run," "dog" for "god," or "nay" for "any."

- **Old Testament example.** Deuteronomy 31:1 of the MT reads וַיֵּלֶךְ מֹשֶׁה (*wayyēlek mōšeh*, "And Moses *went*"), but a manuscript from Qumran (4QDtn) has וַיְכַל מֹשֶׁה (*wykl mšh*, "And Moses *finished*"). The difference between the two readings is that the letters ל (*lāmed*) and כ (*kap*) have switched positions.

- **New Testament example.** In John 1:42 the name Ἰωάννου (*Iōannou*, "of John"; 𝔓⁶⁶,⁷⁵, ℵ, etc.) is read as Ἰωνᾶ (*Iōna*, "of Jonah") in some manuscripts (A, B², etc.) which suggests both metathesis and the removal of some letters.

2.1.6 Fusion

Incorrect word division that results in two words being joined as one. An illustration in English would be, "the man held his handout" (rather than *hand out*).

- **Old Testament example.** Fusion probably appears in the MT of Leviticus 16:8, "And Aaron shall cast lots for the two goats, one for the LORD and the other lot for Azazel (לַעֲזָאזֵל, *la'ăzā'zēl*)" (see also vv. 10, 26). Medieval rabbis identified Azazel as a hairy desert demon,[4] but why would Aaron give

---

[3]This verse is difficult to translate. It reads this way in the Peshitta, Vulgate and Targum, but other readings have been suggested (e.g., "Let not him who bends his bow bend it" [NASB]).
[4]For a good discussion of this view see Gordon J. Wenham, *The Book of Leviticus*, NICOT (Grand Rapids: Eerdmans, 1979), pp. 233-34.

one of the goats to a demon? It makes more sense to divide the name in two, לַעֲזָאזֵל (*lā'ēz 'ōzēl*, "for the goat of departure [or 'going away']," referring to the goat that is led off into the desert. This reading is supported by the LXX and Vulgate.

- **New Testament example.** In Mark 10:40 ἀλλ' οἷς ("but for whom"; A, B², etc.) is read as ἄλλοις "for others" in some manuscripts (א, B*, D, etc.).

2.1.7 Fission

One word that has incorrectly been separated into two. For example, "Jennifer is a *grand child*" can be a mistake of fission that should read "Jennifer is a *grandchild*."

- **Old Testament example.** Fission may appear in Hosea 6:5c where the MT reads וּמִשְׁפָּטֶיךָ אוֹר יֵצֵא (*ûmišpāṭeykā 'ôr yēṣē'*, "and your judgments, light goes forth"), but the LXX reads καὶ τὸ κρίμα μου ὡς φῶς ἐξελεύσεται, "and my judgment goes forth like light." The latter suggests a Hebrew reading of וּמִשְׁפָּטִי כָאוֹר יֵצֵא (*ûmišpāṭi kě'ôr yēṣē'*), wherein the *kāp* is joined to the following word.[5]

- **New Testament example.** A few manuscripts of Romans 7:14 split the word οἴδαμεν "we know" (B², D², etc.) into οἶδα μὲν, ("on the one hand I know"; 33, ℓ 833, etc.).

2.1.8 Homoioteleuton and Homoioarkton

Homoioteleuton is an omission caused by two words or phrases that end similarly. *Homoioarkton* is an omission caused by two phrases that begin similarly. Sometimes these are called parablepsis, meaning "oversight" or "faulty seeing." This can happen with numbers as well as words. For instance, in copying the numbers 523, 432, 600, 446, 732, it would be easy for the eye to skip from 432 to 732 because of their like endings, leaving out the two numbers in between.

- **Old Testament example.** In 1 Samuel 14:41, a portion is missing from the MT that appears in other versions. The LXX reads:

  And Saul said, "O Lord, God of **Israel,** *why have you not answered your servant this day? If the iniquity is in me or in my son Jonathan, O Lord, God of Israel, give Urim(?); but if this iniquity is in thy people* **Israel**, give Thummim(?)."

The words in italics do not appear in the MT, perhaps because the eyes of the scribe jumped from the first occurrence of the word *Israel* to the third, omitting the words in between.

---

[5]Douglas Stuart, *Hosea-Jonah*, WBC (Waco, Tex.: Word, 1987), p. 99.

- **New Testament example.** In 1 John 2:23 the phrase τὸν πατέρα ἔχει ("has the father") (א, B, C, etc.) appears twice, causing a copyist's eyes to skip from the first to the second and omit the intervening words ὁ ὁμολογῶν τὸν υἱόν καὶ ("the one who confesses the Son also") (vg^{ms}, bo^{ms}).

2.1.9 Other Omissions or Additions

Other changes occur, sometimes due to vowel pointings, sometimes possibly because abbreviations were misinterpreted[6] and sometimes for no apparent reason.

- **Old Testament example.** In 1 Samuel 13:1 the number of years that Saul reigned in Jerusalem appears to be left out. This is why various modern translations differ in the translation at this verse:

  NASB: "Saul was *forty* years old when he began to reign, and he reigned *thirty-two* years over Israel."

  NIV: "Saul was thirty years old when he became king, and he reigned over Israel forty-two years."

  KJV: "Saul reigned one year; and when he had reigned two years over Israel . . ."

  The first two translations acknowledge that the ages have fallen out and supply the missing information using logical deduction. However, the King James Bible just translates it as if nothing has fallen out of the text.

- **New Testament example.** Some of the better manuscripts (𝔓^{46}, א*, B*, etc.) omit the phrase ἐν Ἐφέσῳ ("in Ephesus") in Ephesians 1:1.

2.2 Intentional Changes

Evidence suggests that the Hebrew text was somewhat flexible until the first century A.D. when it became unified. Following the first century A.D., the scribes' primary desire was to retain this text. The scribes clearly had a great reverence for the text; therefore it is reasonable to assume that any changes were an attempt to improve or clarify the text, with no intention of corrupting it. The Jewish nation believed the Scriptures were a living book with continuing relevance, prompting scribes occasionally to update or expand the text to make it more readily understandable.

- **Old Testament example.** In Genesis 14:14 the MT says that Abraham chased the kings who captured his nephew Lot as far as "Dan," but ac-

---

[6]See Godfrey R. Driver, "Abbreviations in the Masoretic Text," *Textus* 1 (1960): 112-31; and his, "Once Again Abbreviations," *Textus* 4 (1964): 76-94; cf. Michael Fishbane, "Abbreviations, Hebrew Texts," *IDBSup*, pp. 3-4.

cording to Joshua 19:47 and Judges 18:29 the city was not named Dan until many years later. It is plausible that a later scribe realizing that the city was now called Dan, changed the text in Genesis 14:14 to reflect this new name.

- **New Testament example.** It appears that ἀμήν ("amen") was added to some manuscripts (אֲ, 436, 2464, K, L, P, etc.) in 1 Peter 5:14 possibly in order to make it more similar to the ending of 2 Peter.

In their zealousness to preserve Scripture, scribes had a tendency to include everything in the text (e.g., glosses, marginal notes, insertions) rather than omit anything; thereby expanding the text in some places. The New Testament appears to have experienced less flexibility in the transmissional process, but it is still plausible that copyists made modification to certain texts.

Since the transmission of Scripture occurred over such a long period of time and under such diverse conditions, it is possible that many intentional changes may never be detected, or if detected, the original wording may never be determined. Intentional changes are much more controversial—not everyone agrees on specific examples, but the following give an indication of the purpose of intentional changes.

Figure 2.5. A modern Jewish scribe [Jewish Chronicle Archive/HIP/ Art Resource, NY]

Figure 2.6. A correction made to the text of Romans 15:30 in $\mathfrak{P}^{46}$ by a later scribe [P. Mich. Inv. 6238, Special Collections Library, University of Michigan]

2.2.1 Changes in Spelling or Grammar

Over time, scribes apparently tended to update archaic language so that the text could be better understood.

- **Old Testament example.** The MT of Psalm 11:1d reads נוּדוּ הַרְכֶם צִפּוֹר (*nûdiw harkem ṣippôr*, "flee to your mountain a bird"). But the LXX (Psalm 10:2) reads μεταναστεύου ἐπὶ τὰ ὄρη ὡς στρουθίον ("flee to the mountain like a bird"). The latter appears to follow an original Hebrew reading of נוּדִי הַר כְּמוֹ צִפּוֹר (*nûdî har kĕmô ṣippôr*), that includes the archaic Hebrew form כְּמוֹ (*kĕmô*), meaning "like, as." It is quite plausible that a scribe was confused by the archaic form.[7]

- **New Testament example.** In Matthew 1:7-8 the name *Asaph* ('Ασάφ) is found in several older manuscripts ($\mathfrak{P}^{1vid}$, ℵ, B, etc.), but later copyists apparently believed they were correcting the text by changing it to *Asa* ('Ασά), the king of Judah (1 Kings 15:9-24) (L, W, Δ, etc.).

2.2.2 Clearing Up Other Difficulties

Since the biblical text was intended to be read and understood by people through many millennia, it is reasonable that copyists may have modified unclear phrases, rare words or even words used in an unusual way so that they could be more easily understood.

- **Old Testament example.** In Isaiah 39:1 the MT uses the word חָזַק (*ḥāzaq*) with the unusual meaning "to get well, recuperate," but the first Isaiah Scroll found at Qumran (1QIsaᵃ) has חָיָה (*ḥāyâ*, "to live, revive, recuperate"), which is the more common word.

- **New Testament example.** The composite quotation from Malachi 3:1 and Isaiah 40:3 in Mark 1:2-3 is sometimes attributed to "Isaiah the prophet" in earlier manuscripts (ℵ, B, etc.), but some later copyists modified it to ἐν τοῖς προφήταις ("in the prophets") (A, W, etc.).

2.2.3 Harmonization

Harmonization is the modification of one passage to make it agree with another. This appears more commonly in the New Testament, especially in the Gospels where there are several similar accounts of a story.

- **Old Testament example.** The editors of the *BHS*³ suggest adding the phrase וַיַּרְא אֱלֹהִים כִּי־טוֹב ("and God saw that it was good") to Genesis 1:7,

---

[7]For other examples see P. Kyle McCarter, *Textual Criticism: Recovering the Text of the Hebrew Bible*, GBS:OTS (Philadelphia: Fortress, 1986), pp. 51-57.

which would make a similar structure to that found in verses 4, 10, 12, 18, 21, 31 and correspond to verse 8 in the LXX.

- **New Testament example.** A variant of the phrase in John 19:20, ἦν γεγραμμένον Ἑβραϊστί, Ῥωμαιστί, Ἑλληνιστί ("It was written in Hebrew, in Latin, in Greek"), was added to Luke 23:38 in some manuscripts (C^3, W, Δ, etc.).

2.2.4 Euphemistic Changes

A euphemism is the substitution of a milder term for a more unpleasant or offensive one, but sometimes changes were made simply to smooth out the grammar or help the text to sound better.

- **Old Testament example.** The divine name בַּעַל (*ba'al*, "Baal") was sometimes replaced with the word בֹּשֶׁת (*bōšet*, "shame"; 1 Chron 8:33; 9:39: אֶשְׁבָּעַל [*'ešbā'al*, "man of Baal"; compare the parallel verses in 2 Sam 2:8-12: אִישׁ־בֹּשֶׁת [*'išbōšet*, "man of shame"]; 1 Chron 8:34; 9:40: מְרִיב בָּעַל [*měrib bā'al*, "Baal is (my/our) advocate(?)"] = 2 Sam 4:4: מְפִיבֹשֶׁת [*měpibōšet*, "from before shame"]).[8] A plausible explanation for this change is that the Baal cult posed a significant active threat to Yahwism when the books of Samuel were written, so the author substituted a euphemism for the offensive name Baal. By the Chronicler's time, however, the Baal cult had become less of a threat and he was able to employ the name.

- **New Testament example.** Several scribes appear to have had difficulty copying the phrase "your Father, who sees what is done in secret, will reward you" (Matthew 6:4, 6) without adding the phrase ἐν τῷ φανερῷ ("in the open" or "openly"; L, W, Δ, etc.); or the word γραμματέων ("scribes") without adding καὶ Φαρισαίων ("and Pharisees"; Mt 27:41; D, W, etc.).

2.2.5 Theological Changes

Some changes apparently were made for theological reasons, either because God (or someone else) was placed in an unfavorable light or the text seemed irreverent. Modifications removed the offending words or phrase.

- **Old Testament example.** It seems that Genesis 18:22 originally read "and God remained standing before Abraham." However, the phrase "to stand before someone" later came to denote subservience to that person. Scribes therefore rearranged the sentence order out of reverence for God.

- **New Testament example.** In Luke 2:41, 43, the words οἱ γονεῖς αὐτοῦ ("his

---

[8]Gillis Gerleman, *Synoptic Studies in the Old Testament* (Lund: Gleerup, 1948), p. 23.

parents") have been changed to "Joseph and Mary" (v. 41) in some manuscripts (1012, It), or "Joseph and his mother" (A, C, Ψ, etc.), possibly to safeguard the doctrine of the virgin birth of Jesus.

2.2.6 Additions and Glosses

There are several apparent instances of additions, glosses (explanatory notes) or further explanations of difficult words and phrases in the biblical text. These notes may have been originally written into the text or were later incorporated from marginal notes. In the New Testament especially, these additions are sometimes conflations, combining two or more readings.

- **Old Testament example.** In Genesis 7:6b a phrase appears to have been added to clarify an unusual word וְהַמַּבּוּל הָיָה מַיִם עַל הָאָרֶץ (wĕhammabbûl hāyâ mayim ʿal hāʾāreṣ, literally, "and the flood was water upon the earth"). The unusual word מַבּוּל (mabbûl, "flood") is clarified by the phrase מַיִם עַל הָאָרֶץ (mayim ʿal hāʾāreṣ, cf. 6:17).[9]

- **New Testament example.** Some manuscripts of Luke 24:53 add the word ἀμήν ("amen") at the end of the verse which suggests that some thought a Gospel should end this way (see mss of Matthew 28:20; A^2, Δ, Θ, etc.).

Generally it is easier to spot an unintentional change—they are a more predictable result of the copying process. An intentional error, on the other hand, is much more difficult to determine. Bruce Metzger observes, "scribes who thought were more dangerous than those who wished merely to be faithful in copying what lay before them."[10] Intentional errors are much harder to detect and correct since it is generally difficult to know why the changes were made. Sometimes scribes even reintroduced a previously corrected error, as Metzger points out:

> In the margin of codex Vaticanus at Heb. i.3 there is a curiously indignant note by a rather recent scribe [perhaps from the thirteenth century] who restored the original reading of the codex, φανερῶν, for which a corrector had substituted the usual reading, φέρων: "Fool and knave, can't you leave the old reading alone and not alter it!" (ἀμαθέστατε καὶ κακέ, ἄφες τὸν παλαιόν, μὴ μεταποίει).[11]

Intentional errors were likely introduced into the text when the copyist thought that a word was misspelled, contained a theological mistake or appeared not to correspond to another biblical passage.

---

[9]See also Joshua 2:15; 20:3, as explained by McCarter, *Textual Criticism*, p. 33.
[10]Bruce M. Metzger, *The Text of the New Testament: Its Transmission, Corruption, and Restoration*, 3rd ed. (New York: Oxford University Press, 1992), p. 195.
[11]Ibid., pp. 195-96.

Table 2.1. Summary of Transmissional Errors

Unintentional Changes

Error	*Definition*	*Example*
Mistaken letters	Confusion of similar letters	*d* written for *b*
Homophony	Substitution of similar sounding words	*there* for *their*
Haplography	Omission of a letter or word usually due to a similar letter or word in context	*occurrence* written incorrectly as *ocurrence*
Dittography	A letter or word that has been written twice rather than once	*latter* written for *later*
Metathesis	Reversal in order of two letters or words	*dog* written for *god*
Fusion	Incorrect word division that results in two words being joined as one	*hand out* written as *handout*
Fission	Incorrect word division that results in one word being written as two	*grandchild* written as *grand child*
Homoioteleuton	An omission caused by two words or phrases that end similarly	"God of Israel ... thy people Israel"
Homoioarkton	An omission caused by two words or phrases that begin similarly	"David said ... David believed"
Other omissions	Any other omissions	The number of years omitted from 1 Sam 13:1

Intentional Changes

Error	*Example*
Changes in spelling or grammar	*Asaph* (Ἀσάφ) in Mt 1:7-8 is sometimes changed to *Asa* (Ἀσά), the king of Judah (1 Kings 15:9-24).
Clearing up difficulties	"Isaiah the prophet" in Mk 1:2-3 is sometimes modified to ἐν τοῖς προφήταις ("in the prophets").
Harmonization	Dan (Gen 14:14) is mentioned by that name before its name was changed to Dan (Josh 19:47; Judg 18:29).
Euphemistic changes	The divine name בַּעַל (*baʿal*, "Baal") was sometimes replaced with the word בֹּשֶׁת (*bōšet*, "shame"; 1 Chron 8:33; 9:39, אֶשְׁבַּעַל [*'ešbāʿal*, "man of Baal"]; compare the parallel verses in 2 Sam 2:8-12, אִישׁבֹּשֶׁת [*'išbōšet*, "man of shame"]).
Theological changes	Genesis 18:22 originally read "and God remained standing before Abraham." However, the phrase "to stand before someone" later came to denote subservience to that person. Scribes therefore rearranged the sentence order out of reverence for God.
Additions and glosses	Some manuscripts of Luke 24:53 add the word ἀμήν "amen") at the end of the verse.

Further Reading

Old Testament

Brotzman, Ellis R. *Old Testament Textual Criticism: A Practical Introduction.* Grand Rapids: Baker, 1994.

Klein, Ralph W. *Textual Criticism of the Old Testament: The Septuagint after Qumran.* GBS:OTS. Philadelphia: Fortress, 1974.

McCarter, P. Kyle. *Textual Criticism: Recovering the Text of the Hebrew Bible.* GBS:OTS. Philadelphia: Fortress, 1978.

Payne, David F. "Old Testament Textual Criticism: Its Principles and Practice." *TynBul* 25 (1974): 99-112.

Talmon, Shemaryahu. "Aspects of the Textual Transmission of the Bible in Light of Qumran Manuscripts." *Textus* 4 (1964): 95-132. Reprinted in *QHBT*, pp. 226-63.

Tov, Emanuel. "Criteria for Evaluating Textual Readings—The Limitations of Textual Rules." *HTR* 75 (1982): 429-48.

———. *Textual Criticism of the Hebrew Bible.* Minneapolis: Fortress, 1992.

Weingreen, Jacob. *Introduction to the Critical Study of the Text of the Hebrew Bible.* New York: Oxford University Press, 1982.

Würthwein, Ernst. *The Text of the Old Testament. An Introduction to the Biblia Hebraica.* Translated by Erroll F. Rhodes. 2nd ed. Grand Rapids: Eerdmans, 1995.

New Testament

Aland, Kurt, and Barbara Aland. *The Text of the New Testament. An Introduction to the Critical Editions and to the Theory and Practice of Modern Textual Criticism.* Translated by Erroll F. Rhodes. Grand Rapids: Eerdmans, 1987.

Birdsall, J. Neville. "The New Testament Text." In *CHB* 1:308-77.

Black, David A. *New Testament Textual Criticism.* Grand Rapids: Baker, 1995.

Comfort, Philip W. *Early Manuscripts & Modern Translations of the New Testament.* Grand Rapids: Baker, 1990.

Fee, Gordon D. "The Textual Criticism of the New Testament." In *The Expositor's Bible Commentary,* 1:419-33. Edited by Frank E. Gaebelein. Grand Rapids: Zondervan, 1979.

Finegan, Jack. *Encountering New Testament Manuscripts: A Working Introduction to Textual Criticism.* Grand Rapids: Eerdmans, 1974.

Greenlee, J. Harold. *Introduction to New Testament Textual Criticism.* 2nd ed. Peabody, Mass.: Hendricksons, 1996.

———. *Scribes, Scrolls, and Scripture. A Student's Guide to New Testament Textual Criticism.* Grand Rapids: Eerdmans, 1985.

Holmes, Michael W. "Textual Criticism." In *New Testament Criticism & Interpretation,* pp. 101-36. Edited by David A. Black and David S. Dockery. Grand Rapids: Zondervan, 1991.

Metzger, Bruce M. *Chapters in the History of New Testament Textual Criticism.*
New Testament Tools and Studies 4. Grand Rapids: Eerdmans, 1963.

―――. *The Text of the New Testament. Its Transmission, Corruption, and Restoration.* 3rd ed. New York: Oxford University Press, 1992.

―――. *A Textual Commentary on the Greek New Testament.* 2nd ed. Stuttgart: Deutsche Bibelgesellschaft, 1994.

3

Transmission of the Biblical Texts

This chapter describes the transmission of the biblical texts, as far as their history is known. After the Old and New Testament texts reached their finalized forms, they were copied and maintained throughout their history. This chapter describes this process and lays the foundation for the rest of the book.

It is hard for us who commonly own multiple copies of the Bible to understand that for much of the Old and New Testaments' history individuals rarely owned even a part of a Bible. In Old Testament times the sacred scrolls were kept in the temple and generally were handled and read only by the priests and possibly the Levites. By New Testament times the entire collection of books that made up the Bible would have been very expensive, and much of the New Testament circulated as individual books or letters. A low literacy rate was also a factor during much of the time of the transmission of Scriptures. Still these works were maintained and handed down through many generations. Understanding some of this history will provide a better foundation for textual criticism.

3.1 The Old Testament Text

If Moses, living in the fifteenth century B.C., wrote or collected any of the Pentateuch, then some Old Testament texts would have been transmitted for more than three thousand years before we received them in our modern translations. This naturally leads to such crucial questions as, Who copied these texts through the millennia? What did they look like? How were they maintained? Are the texts we have today an accurate reflection of the original texts? Each of these questions will be examined in this chapter. There are no original manuscripts (or *autographa*) of the Old Testament—any extant manuscript is a copy of an earlier one. The word *manuscript* derives from a Latin word meaning "that which is written by hand." Until the invention of the printing press in the fifteenth century, all books were copied by hand.

3.1.1 The Old Testament Text Prior to 400 B.C.

Since there is so little evidence concerning this early period, we are left with several significant questions. First, in what language(s) were the earliest biblical manuscripts written? Bruce Waltke and Michael O'Connor believe that Moses wrote in some form of Hebrew, but they also point out that several languages of the period were fairly similar:

> A variety of related languages and dialects, more or less closely related to Hebrew, were recorded at the time Hebrew scriptures were being written. The Iron Age (1200-500 B.C.) forms a convenient watershed in the history of Syro-Palestinian languages, though the significance of the year 1200 should not be exaggerated: the earliest Biblical Hebrew had a great deal in common with Ugaritic and Amarna Canaanite.[1]

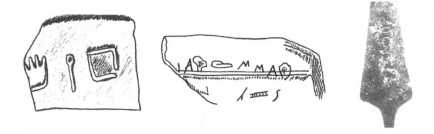

Figure 3.1. (1) Drawing of a potsherd from Gezer, (2) a plaque from Shechem and (3) a photo of a dagger from Lachish with inset of inscription [Israel Antiquities Authority]

Some of these early Semitic alphabetic inscriptions go back to the early second millennium (e.g., graffiti from the turquoise mining area of Serbit el-Khadim in the Sinai Peninsula [c. 1475 B.C.], inscription from Byblos [c. 2000 B.C.], a potsherd from Gezer [c.1800-1650 B.C.])[2] and have striking similarities to paleo (early)-Hebrew (e.g., they are an alphabetic language, have similar vocabulary, and a similar script, see fig. 3.1).

Thus the earliest biblical texts were probably written in paleo-Hebrew script,[3] though there are no actual extant Hebrew texts that predate about 800

---

[1]Bruce K. Waltke and Michael O'Connor, *An Introduction to Biblical Hebrew Syntax* (Winona Lake, Ind.: Eisenbrauns, 1990), pp. 3, 8.

[2]See Paul D. Wegner, *The Journey from Texts to Translations* (Grand Rapids: Baker, 2000), pp. 79-81.

[3]See Ernst Würthwein, *The Text of the Old Testament: An Introduction to the Biblia Hebraica*, trans. Erroll F. Rhodes, 2nd ed. (Grand Rapids: Eerdmans, 1995), p. 3; Emanuel Tov, *Textual Criticism of the Hebrew Bible*, 2nd ed. (Minneapolis: Fortress, 2001), pp. 218-20; David Diringer, "The Biblical Scripts," in *CHB* 1:12.

Figure 3.2. Seal found at Megiddo carved in jasper: "Belonging to Shema, servant of Jeroboam" (c. 786-746 B.C.) [Israel Antiquities Authority]

B.C. (e.g., seal of Jeroboam II, c. 786-746 B.C., see fig. 3.2; Hezekiah's tunnel inscription, c. 701 B.C.; silver amulets, c. mid-seventh century B.C.)—the earliest extant texts are written in this script.

The changeover from paleo-Hebrew to square (or Aramaic) script took place between the fifth and third centuries B.C.[4] and would probably have been hastened by the Jewish exile in Babylon, where Aramaic was the common language.[5] Knowing about the similarities between specific letters in both paleo-Hebrew and square script can help identify and date certain copying mistakes. For example, the *wāw* and the *yôd* were very similar in the Hebrew square script written at Qumran, but they are not as similar in paleo-Hebrew script (see figure 3.3).

Paleo-Hebrew Script	Square Script
  wāw *yôd*	ו י *wāw* *yôd*
	Qumran Text *wāw* *yôd* *wāw*

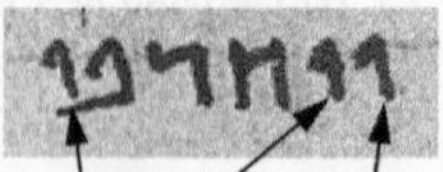

Figure 3.3. Differences between paleo-Hebrew script and square script

Second, did the Israelites originally use *scripto continua* (continuous writing) without spaces between words?[6] On the one hand, we have early Aramaic correspondence that includes spaces and sometimes even markers between words; the paleo-Hebrew inscription at the end of Hezekiah's Tunnel shows

[4]William F. Albright, *The Archaeology of Palestine*, rev. ed. (Harmondsworth, Middlesex: Penguin, 1960), pp. 149-50; Frank M. Cross, "The Oldest Manuscripts from Qumran," *JBL* 74 (1955): 147-72 (repr. in *QHBT*, pp. 147-76); Frank M. Cross, "The Development of the Jewish Scripts" in *BANE*, pp. 133-202.
[5]Franz Rosenthal, *A Grammar of Biblical Aramaic*, Porta Linguarum Orientalium (Wiesbaden: Otto Harrassowitz, 1974), pp. 5-6.
[6]Tov, *Textual Criticism*, pp. 208-9; Alan R. Millard, " 'Scriptio Continua' in Early Hebrew—Ancient Practice or Modern Surmise?" *JSS* 15 (1970): 2-15; Joseph Naveh, "Word Division in West Semitic Writing," *IEJ* 23 (1973): 206-8.

dots between words (see fig. 3.4).[7] However, these are not biblical scrolls and they date to a time significantly later than when the earliest biblical manuscripts would have appeared. On the other hand, the earliest proto-Canaanite or paleo-Hebrew inscriptions do not ordinarily evince word divisions.

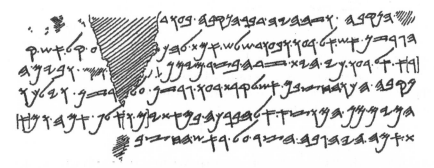

Figure 3.4. The paleo-Hebrew inscription at the end of Hezekiah's Tunnel, discovered in 1880 by some schoolboys. Notice the dots between words.[8]

The earliest extant portion of a biblical text appears without spaces and is written on silver amulets, but amulets may not have been treated with the same reverence as biblical manuscripts. Evidence indicates that at least from the time of the Dead Sea Scrolls, biblical texts were written with spaces between the words to aid in the reading of the text, though some of these scrolls have unclear word divisions. Sometimes an incorrect word division can cause problems in the transmission of the Old Testament. For example in Amos 6:12 the Hebrew reads literally as:

Do horses run on rocky crags?
Does one plow with oxen? [אִם־יַחֲרוֹשׁ בַּבְּקָרִים]
But you have turned justice into poison,
and the fruit of righteousness into bitterness.

The second question in this verse does not seem to fit the context: the an-

---

[7]Roland K. Harrison describes the importance of the Lachish ostraca, which are dated to approximately the early sixth century, as follows: "The latter are of value for the textual critic because of the incidence of scribal errors, the use of the *scriptio defectiva* rather than the fuller forms of the Massoretic tradition, the presence of the dot as a word-divider, and the fact that the language of the ostraca is to all intents and purposes the kind of classical Hebrew familiar from the Old Testament writings" (*Introduction to the Old Testament* [Grand Rapids: Eerdmans, 1969], p. 246).

[8]Klaas A. D. Smelik, *Writings from Ancient Israel: A Handbook of Historical and Religious Documents*, trans. Graham I. Davies (Edinburgh: T & T Clark, 1991), p. 70.

swer to the first question is no (horses may fall if they run on rocky crags), but the answer to the second is yes (plowing is commonly done with oxen). The editors of the RSV have divided the Hebrew words slightly differently and translated it "Does one plow the sea with oxen?" (אִם־יַחֲרוֹשׁ בַּבְּקָר יָם). The only difference between these two translations is that the Hebrew word for "oxen," בַּבְּקָרִים (babběqārîm), is divided into the two words "oxen" (בְּקָר, běbāqār) and "sea," (יָם, yām), and the word is repointed. The latter translation is preferred in that the Hebrew word for "oxen" is a collective noun not requiring the plural, and it anticipates a negative answer like its parallel unit.

Third, what material were the early manuscripts written on? It is likely that the biblical texts were written on papyrus or leather scrolls.[9] These materials were extremely perishable in the semi-arid land of Palestine and thus required constant copying by the priests or scribes. Jeremiah 36:2 gives some indication as to the writing process when God tells Jeremiah to "Take for yourself a scroll and write on it all the words that I have spoken to you." Scrolls were limited in length by their bulk and manageability, but they continued to be used in synagogues even after the codex (a manuscript bound in book form) was introduced for private use in the second century A.D.[10]

Our final question, Who maintained these biblical texts in this early period? does not have a definitive answer. It appears that initially the Old Testament texts were copied by priests, Levites or scribes, who reverenced and maintained them as records of Israel's early history and their relationship to Yahweh. Waltke and O'Connor make an interesting point:

> That no other Israelite writings, such as the Book of Yashar (e.g., 2 Sam 1:18) or the Diaries of the Kings (e.g., 2 Chr 16:11), survive from this period indirectly suggests the determination of the scribes to preserve the books that became canonical. The foes of Hebrew Scripture sometimes included audiences who sought to kill its authors and destroy their works (cf. Jeremiah 36). From the time of their composition, however, they capture the hearts, minds and loyalties of the faithful in Israel who kept them safe often at risk to themselves. Such people must have insisted on the accurate transmission of the text.[11]

Even from a very early period there is evidence that some books of Scripture were treated with reverence and were thought to be authoritative (Ex 17:14-16; 24:3-4, 7). The stone tablets upon which the Lord inscribed the Ten Commandments were stored in the ark of the Covenant (Ex 25:16, 21; Deut 10:2-5; 1 Kings 8:9; Heb 9:4), a sacred place. The law of Moses was to be taught

---

[9]Würthwein, *Text of the Old Testament*, pp. 4-9; Donald Wiseman, "Books in the Ancient Near East and in the Old Testament," in *CHB* 1.30-32.

[10]Ernst Sellin, *Introduction to the Old Testament* (Nashville: Abingdon, 1968), p. 492.

[11]Waltke and O'Connor, *Introduction to Biblical Hebrew Syntax*, p. 16.

to the priests and commanded to be publicly read aloud every seven years so that the Israelites would not forget God's laws (Deut 31:9-11); it was to be stored alongside the ark of the covenant (Deut 31:24-26); and nothing was to be added to or deleted from its words (Deut 4:2; 12:32). The Old Testament also mentions written forms of prophetic oracles (2 Chron 21:12; Is 30:8; Jer 25:13; 29:1; 30:2; 36:1-32; 51:60-64; Ezek 43:11; Dan 7:1; Hab 2:2) and histories recorded by prophets (1 Chron 29:29; 2 Chron 9:29; 12:15; 13:22; 20:34; 26:22; 32:32; 33:18-19), but the first reference to a collection of biblical books (בַּסְּפָרִים, *bassĕpārîm*) is in Daniel 9:2, which states: "in the first year of his [Darius II] reign, I, Daniel, understood from the books, according to the word of the LORD to Jeremiah the prophet, the number of years for the desolation of Jerusalem would be seventy years." This passage indicates that in Daniel's time the book of Jeremiah was part of a larger collection of books that he considered authoritative.[12]

3.1.2 The Old Testament Text 400 B.C. to A.D. 100

Sometime toward the beginning of this period the Old Testament canon was completed, as Roland K. Harrison explains:

> In all its essentials the canon was most probably complete by about 300 B.C., and while discussion concerning certain component parts was continued well into the Christian era, the substance of the canon as it existed a century and a half after the time of Ezra and Nehemiah remained unaffected by these controversies.[13]

From about 500 B.C. to A.D. 100 an influential group of teachers and interpreters of the Law called *sopherim*, "scribes," arose to preserve Israel's sacred traditions, the foundation of the nation.[14] The Babylonian Talmud (*Qidd.* 30a) says, "The ancients were called *soferim* because they counted [*sfr*] every letter in the Torah."

3.1.2.1 Preserving the text. Hebrew manuscripts copied before the first century A.D. show two tendencies on the part of the scribes: they preserved the accuracy of the text, and at the same time were willing to revise or update the text.[15] One of the best examples of the preserving of the text is found in the textual tradition from Qumran, which follows the proto-MT and contains the majority of the manuscripts (35 percent according to Tov).[16] These manu-

---

[12]Harrison, *Introduction to the Old Testament*, p. 266. See also Wegner, *Journey from Texts to Translations*, pp. 99-116.

[13]Harrison, *Introduction to the Old Testament*, p. 286. See also the prologue to Ecclesiasticus (dated to about 132 B.C.) and the LXX.

[14]Emanuel Tov, "The Text of the Old Testament" in *The World of the Bible*, ed. Adam S. van der Woude, trans. Seird Woudstra (Grand Rapids: Eerdmans, 1986), p. 160. See also Sirach 38:24—39:15.

[15]Waltke and O'Connor, *Hebrew Syntax*, pp. 16-17.

[16]Tov, *Textual Criticism*, p. 115.

scripts are very similar to manuscripts of the MT from about A.D. 1000. Emanuel Tov states:

> As a rule, the scribes treated 𝔐 [MT] with reverence, and they did not alter its orthography and morphology as did the scribes of the 𝔪 [SP] . . . and of many of the Qumran scrolls. . . . Since 𝔐 contains a carefully transmitted text, which is well-documented in a large number of copies, and since it is reflected in the rabbinic literature as well as in the Targumim and many of the Jewish-Greek revisions of 𝔊 [LXX], it may be surmised that it originated in the spiritual and authoritative center of Judaism (later to be known as that of the Pharisees), possibly in the temple circles. It was probably the temple scribes who were entrusted with the copying and preserving of 𝔐. Though this assumption cannot be proven, it is supported by the fact that the temple employed correctors (מגיהים, *maggihim*) who scrutinized certain scrolls on its behalf. . . . The fact that all the texts left by the Zealots at Masada (dating until 73 CE) reflect 𝔐 is also important.[17]

I agree with Tov that the MT originated with the spiritual and authoritative center of Judaism, and by the end of this period there was a unified tradition of this text that appears to have been accepted universally by Judaism. Even the Christians, who often used the LXX in everyday life, understood that the LXX was based on an authoritative Hebrew source (e.g., see Justin Martyr's debates with Typho).

3.1.2.2 Revising the text. At the same time the scribes were preserving the text, they also revised it in at least three different ways: (1) sometime during this period the change from paleo-Hebrew to Assyrian square script occurred (see earlier discussion); (2) the orthography (i.e., spelling) and archaic forms of the proto-MT were beginning to be updated; and (3) corrections were made (as suggested in texts from the Dead Sea area, e.g., 4QIsaᵃ). William F. Albright states: "A principle which must never be lost sight of in dealing with documents of the ancient Near East is that instead of leaving obvious archaisms in spelling and grammar, as later became the fashion in Greece and Rome, the scribes generally revised ancient literary and other documents periodically. This practice was followed with particular regularity by cuneiform scribes."[18] These tendencies are not contradictory—the scribes assigned to Scriptures a high degree of authority and upheld them with great reverence, but their desire was for readers to understand them. This care in copying corresponds well with the copying practices throughout the ancient Near East as Albright also

---

[17]Tov, *Textual Criticism*, p. 28.
[18]William F. Albright, *From the Stone Age to Christianity*, 2nd ed. (Baltimore: John Hopkins Press, 1957), p. 79.

points out: "The prolonged and intimate study of the many scores of thousands of pertinent documents from the ancient Near East proves that sacred and profane documents were copied with greater care than is true of scribal copying in Graeco-Roman times."[19]

The Egyptian pyramid texts, which were copied meticulously even though they were never to be seen by human eyes, also demonstrate this type of care in the copying process.[20] Kenneth Kitchen quotes the boast of an Egyptian scribe dating to about 1400 B.C.: "[The book] is completed from its beginning to its end, having been copied, revised, compared and verified sign by sign."[21] The sacred Scriptures, which the Israelites believed came from God through their forefathers and prophets, were maintained with similar or greater care.

However, one type of revision that the scribes felt was necessary to accurately preserve the text was the addition of *matres lectionis* ("mothers of reading"), which did not affect the meaning or pronunciation of the word but helped to clarify which form of the word the author intended. In the earliest phase of its development Hebrew was written only with consonants, but possibly as early as the ninth century B.C. the consonants ה (*hē*), י (*yôd*) and ו (*wāw*) were added to some words to indicate three classes of long vowels (see earlier discussion).[22] These long vowels sometimes were used as case endings to signify the grammatical function of words, but they always aided in the proper pronunciation of the text.[23] As the language continued to develop, scribes used the *matres lectionis* more extensively, which increased the certainty as to how the text should be translated. David Freedman has dated the form of the proto-MT, which was maintained in the MT, to between the third and second century B.C., based on its orthography (primarily the number of *matres lectionis*);[24] both the Samaritan Pentateuch and the Qumran materials use more *matres lectionis*. Once the proto-MT became unified in the first century A.D., further additions of *matres lectionis* were not permitted. During the fifth to ninth centuries, another system to facilitate proper pronunciation was developed that used vowel points in the text. Several different pointing systems appeared in various scribal schools, but in time the Tiberian point-

---

[19]Ibid., pp. 78-79.

[20]Ibid., p. 79; Waltke and O'Connor, *Introduction to Biblical Hebrew Syntax*, p. 17.

[21]Kenneth A. Kitchen, *Ancient Orient and the Old Testament* (Chicago: InterVarsity Press, 1966), p. 140.

[22]Waltke and O'Connor, *Hebrew Syntax*, pp. 17-18.

[23]See Frank M. Cross and David N. Freedman, *Early Hebrew Orthography: A Study of the Epigraphic Evidence*, AOS 36 (New Haven, Conn.: American Oriental Society, 1952), pp. 45-60, 65-70.

[24]David N. Freedman, "The Massoretic Text and the Qumran Scrolls: A Study in Orthography," *Textus* 2 (1962): 87-102 (repr. in *QHBT*, pp. 196-211).

ing system gained general acceptance.[25]

Evidence from about the mid-third century B.C. on suggests that there were several centuries during which a variety of texts of the Old Testament existed simultaneously (e.g., at least, proto-MT, LXX, SP and possibly other forms suggested by the manuscripts found in the Dead Sea area).[26] However, there has been significant discussion as to how the proto-MT arose as well as the variety of other forms (see table 3.1).

Paul de Lagarde (1827-1891) argued that all the Hebrew texts derive from one original manuscript (a single copy *[ein einziges Exemplar]*; see fig. 3.5).[27] He reasoned that since all Masoretic manuscripts have some specific characteristics in common (e.g., the *puncta extraordinaria*, dots above letters considered questionable by scribes), they must be dependent on one another, and therefore it is possible to retrieve the original text. By the time of Paul Kahle (1875-1964), the number of known manuscripts had increased and several divergent text types had been identified. Kahle argued that there were many vulgar texts (*Vulgärtexte,* or corrupted texts) that were standardized into an official text (see fig. 3.5).[28] In the mid-1950s two other scholars, William F. Albright and Frank M. Cross, began to develop a third view, arguing for the possibility of local recensions/text types/families.[29] This theory reduced the textual witnesses to three text types from different areas: Palestine (SP, MT of Chronicles, several Qumran texts), Babylon (MT) and Egypt (LXX; see figure 3.6).[30]

---

[25]Even as late as Codex Reuchlinianus (A.D. 1105) another pointing system (not Tiberian) was used. Scholars disagree as to whether it was pre-Masoretic (Alexander Sperber, *Codex Reuchlinianus with a General Introduction: Masoretic Hebrew,* Corpus Hebraicorum Medii Aevi 2/1 [Copenhagen: Munksgaard, 1956], intro.), post-Masoretic (Shelomo Morag, "The Vocalization of Codex Reuchlinianus: Is the 'Pre-Masoretic' Bible Pre-Masoretic?" *JSS* 4 [1959]: 229, 237), or a Tiberian pointing system not accepted by the Masoretes (Moshe H. Goshen-Gottstein, "The Rise of the Tiberian Bible Text," in *Biblical and Other Studies,* ed. Alexander Altmann [Cambridge, Mass.: Harvard University Press, 1963], pp. 113-14; Würthwein, *Text of the Old Testament,* pp. 21-28).

[26]Tov, *Textual Criticism,* pp. 160-63.

[27]Paul de Lagarde, *Anmerkungen zur griechischen Übersetzung der Proverbien* (Leipzig: Brockhaus, 1863), pp. 3-4.

[28]Paul Kahle, "Untersuchungen zur Geschichte des Pentateuchtextes," *Theologische Studien und Kritiken* 38 (1915): 399-439.

[29]William F. Albright, "New Light on Early Recensions of the Hebrew Bible," *BASOR* 140 (1955): 27-33; Frank M. Cross, "The Evolution of a Theory of Local Texts," in *Qumran and the History of the Biblical Text,* ed. Frank M. Cross and Shemaryahu Talmon (Cambridge, Mass.: Harvard University Press, 1975), pp. 306-20; Frank M. Cross, *The Ancient Library of Qumran and Modern Biblical Studies,* rev. ed. (Grand Rapids: Baker, 1980), pp. 188-94; Frank M. Cross, "The History of the Biblical Text in the Light of Discoveries in the Judean Desert," *HTR* 57 (1964): 218-99; Frank M. Cross, "The Contribution of the Qumran Discoveries to the Study of the Biblical Text," *IEJ* 16 (1966): 81-95.

[30]Frank M. Cross, "The Contribution of the Qumran Discoveries to the Study of the Biblical Text," reprinted in *Qumran and the History of the Biblical Text,* ed. Frank M. Cross and Shemaryahu Talmon (Cambridge, Mass.: Harvard University Press, 1975), pp. 278-92.

Table 3.1. Chart of Various Views Accounting for Textual Diversity

Scholar	Date	Description
Paul de Lagarde (Göttingen)	1827-1891	The MT started out as one original copy and all the manuscripts can be traced back to this original. Thus all the various extant manuscripts are deviations or copies of a single original manuscript.
Paul Kahle (Oxford)	1875-1964	There were many divergent manuscripts that were at some point standardized into an official text.
William F. Albright (Johns Hopkins University), Frank M. Cross (Harvard University)	Albright (1891-1971) Cross (1921-)	There may have been an original authoritative text, but it was copied and maintained in three different areas thus giving rise to three local recensions, text types or text families. These recensions originated from Palestine (SP, MT of Chronicles, some Qumran mss), Babylon (MT) and Egypt (LXX).
Shemaryahu Talmon (Hebrew University)	(1920-)	The Hebrew text had a diversity of forms, and the three text types are only a remnant of a much greater diversity in early Judaism that was subsequently lost. The three recensions were retained because they were protected by religiously cohesive social groups: the LXX by the Christians, the SP by the Samaritans and the MT by rabbinic Judaism.[a]
Emanuel Tov (Hebrew University)	(1941-)	There was not one original authoritative text, but there may have been several authoritative forms of a biblical book. He questions the recensions, or text families, and argues instead that the various manuscripts are related to each other "in an intricate web of agreements, differences, and exclusive readings."[b] He recognizes five different groups among the Qumran manuscripts: (1) mss following "Qumran practice" (20 percent); (2) proto-Masoretic mss (60 percent); (3) pre-Samaritan mss (5 percent); (4) Ur-LXX mss (5 percent); and (5) nonaligned mss (15 percent [sic 105%]).
Eugene Ulrich (University of Notre Dame)	(1938-)	Similar to Talmon, emphasizing a great diversity of biblical texts by late Second Temple times, but these arose from a succession of "literary editions" of books (or parts of books) as temporary stages in evolution toward the final canonical form. Each new literary edition was produced by a creative editor responding to a new religious situation, and thus the distinction between literary development of the text and textual transmission is blurred.[c]

[a]Shemaryahu Talmon, "The Textual Study of the Bible—A New Outlook," in *Qumran and the History of the Biblical Text*, ed. Frank M. Cross and Shemaryahu Talmon (Cambridge, Mass.: Harvard University Press, 1975), pp. 321-400.
[b]Emanuel Tov, *Text-Critical Use of the Septuagint*, JBS 3 (Jerusalem: Simor, 1981), p. 274.
[c]Eugene Ulrich, "Pluriformity in the Biblical Text, Text Groups, and Questions of Canon," in *The Madrid Qumran Conference: Proceedings of the International Congress on the Dead Sea Scrolls, Madrid, 18-21 March 1991*, ed. Julio T. Barrera and Luis V. Montaner (Leiden: Brill, 1992), pp. 37-40; Eugene Ulrich, "Multiple Literary Editions: Reflections Toward a Theory of the History of the Biblical Text," in *Current Research and Technological Developments on the Dead Sea Scrolls: Conference on the Texts from the Judaean Desert, Jerusalem, 30 April 1995*, ed. Donald W. Perry and Stephen D. Ricks, Studies on the Texts of the Desert of Judah 20 (Leiden: Brill, 1996), pp. 78-105.

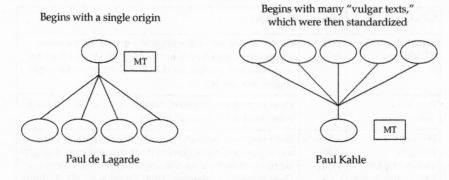

Figure 3.5. Paul de Lagarde's and Paul Kahle's understandings of the origin of the Masoretic Text

Cross went on to argue that the SP became a divergent sectarian recension around 100 B.C., whereas the proto-MT went on to become the standard text of the rabbis around A.D. 100. While the idea of local textual traditions is helpful in explaining the diversity among the related manuscripts, the Qumran scrolls seem to indicate greater similarities between some of these so-called text types than the concept suggests. But it is likely that there was significant interaction between these geographical areas so that similarities may be accounted for by similar *Vorlagen* or the revisions that certain texts underwent. This type of correction and interaction can be observed in the Isaiah Scroll from Qumran where corrections are made right in the text. Still, the Albright and Cross model has been challenged by several scholars;[31] most recently Emanuel Tov has questioned both the notion of an Ur-text that gave rise to the divergent text types as well as the grouping of Qumran texts into fixed text types. He has argued instead that the Qumran manuscripts are related to one another in an intricate web of agreements, differences and exclusive readings.[32] Tov believes that the Qumran manuscripts reveal five different groups (four of which were unknown prior to the Qumran discoveries) distinguished on the basis of the content of their variants.[33]

Tov's arguments have not ruled out the possibility of an original text that

---

[31]Bruce K. Waltke, *Prolegomena to the Samaritan Pentateuch* (Ph.D. diss., Harvard University, 1965); Shemaryahu Talmon, "The Textual Study of the Bible—A New Outlook," in *QHBT*, pp. 321-400; Emanuel Tov, *The Text-Critical Use of the Septuagint in Biblical Research* (Jerusalem: Simor, 1981); Emanuel Tov, "A Modern Textual Outlook Based on the Qumran Scrolls," *HUCA* 53 (1982): 11-27.

[32]Tov, *Text-Critical Use of the Septuagint*, p. 274.

[33]Emanuel Tov, "Groups of Biblical Texts Found at Qumran," in *Time to Prepare the Way in the Wilderness* (Leiden: Brill, 1995), pp. 85-102; Tov, *Textual Criticism*, p. 114.

LOCAL TEXT FAMILIES

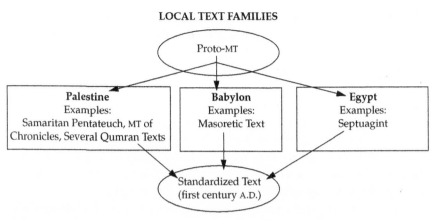

Figure 3.6. William F. Albright and Frank M. Cross's view of the origin of the Masoretic Text

was copied and maintained in different areas, and in time began to look significantly different. But even this would also demand a certain amount of interaction and influences between geographical areas, which corresponds with what we know about trade and interaction among the different geographical areas in the ancient Near East. In fact, it is possible that when the manuscripts were brought to Qumran in the second century B.C., one of the things the Qumran scribes began to do was to compare and correct them (as can be seen in 1QIs[a]). There is still much we do not know about the interaction that took place in the development of the Hebrew texts, but the possibility of an autograph seems to be implied in several Old Testament passages (Ex 17:14-16; 24:3-4, 7; 25:16, 21; Deut 31:9-11, 24-26; Josh 8:35, etc.). Also Adam S. van der Woude argues for a uniform tradition:

> There was always a relative uniformity of textual tradition in the religious circles around the temple in Jerusalem. This means that there was a basically uniform tradition *besides* a pluriform tradition in Palestine Judaism in the last centuries B.C., in the sense that only the proto-Masoretic textual tradition was passed on in Jerusalem, whereas elsewhere also biblical manuscripts circulated which bore close resemblance to the text of the Septuagint or the Samaritan Pentateuch or differed in other respects from the proto-Masoretic tradition.[34]

---

[34] Adam S. van der Woude, "Pluriformity and Uniformity: Reflections on the Transmission of the Text of the Old Testament," in *Sacred History and Sacred Texts in Early Judaism: A Symposium in Honour of Adam S. van der Woude*, ed. Jan N. Bremmer and Florentino García Martínez (Kampen: Kok Pharos, 1992), pp. 151-69. A more popular version of this article is found in Adam S. van der Woude, "Tracing the Evolution of the Hebrew Bible," *BibRev* 11 (1995): 42-45. See also Tov, *Textual Criticism*, p. 28; and Lawrence H. Schiffman, *Reclaiming the Dead Sea Scrolls* (Philadelphia: Jewish Publication Society, 1994), pp. 171-73.

Al Wolters states: "If these scholars are right, the MT represents a textual tradition that can lay claim to a much higher degree of legitimacy than the other ancient witnesses to the Hebrew Bible."[35]

While certain texts appear to have been favored in certain geographical locations, this does not demand that text types developed in those locations. However, constant copying will cause these texts to have similarities. Because of the movement of manuscripts and the importance of these works to the Jews, it is reasonable to assume that scribes were constantly comparing texts and attempting to improve their readings. But this occurred only within certain parameters since each of the text groups have what appear to be preferred readings that were not accepted into the other manuscripts.

Until about sixty years ago very little was known about the Hebrew text prior to A.D. 800—the only extant works that could shed light were the SP, the LXX and the Nash Papyrus. Since then the discovery of the Dead Sea Scrolls has provided a great number of manuscripts dated between 250 B.C. and A.D. 50.

3.1.3 The Old Testament Text from About A.D. 100 to 500

There is a significant difference between the varied textual traditions found at Qumran dating between the third and first centuries B.C., and the minimal deviations in the Hebrew texts from Masada (just prior to A.D. 73), the caves at Naḥal Ḥever (late first century A.D.), and Wadi Murabbaʿat (written before the Bar Kochba Revolt in A.D. 132-135). It is uncertain as to how this unified text came about, but the traditional view has been that during the first century A.D. a strong movement emerged in Judaism to establish a unified, authoritative text of the Hebrew Bible. This text was dependent on earlier traditions that were available to the Jewish scribes at that time, but variants and differences in the text were removed. Once the scribes had a unified, authoritative text, they were meticulous to ensure that the Hebrew text did not become corrupted. Scholars have used the following arguments to substantiate this view:[36]

All the extant Hebrew texts indicate a text very similar to the proto-MT with few

---

[35] Al Wolters, "The Text of the Old Testament," in *The Face of Old Testament Studies: A Survey of Contemporary Approaches,* ed. David W. Baker and Bill T. Arnold (Grand Rapids: Baker, 1999), p. 31.

[36] Dominique Barthélemy, "Text, Hebrew history of," *IBDSup,* pp. 881-82; Frank M. Cross, *The Ancient Library of Qumran and Modern Biblical Studies,* 3rd ed. (Minneapolis: Fortress, 1961), pp. 171ff.; George Fohrer, *Introduction to the Old Testament* (Nashville: Abingdon, 1968), pp. 489-501; Moshe Greenberg, "The Stabilization of the Hebrew Bible Reviewed in the Light of the Biblical Materials from the Judaean Desert," *JAOS* 76 (1956): 157-167; Shemaryahu Talmon, "The Old Testament Text," *CHB* 1:159, 168-69; Waltke, "Textual Criticism," p. 57; Würthwein, *Text of the Old Testament,* pp. 13-16.

variations (Nash Papyrus, Masada mss, Naḥal Ḥever mss, and Wadi Murabba'at mss).

There are a few passages from rabbinic literature that suggest the rabbis had various forms of the Hebrew text which they weighed to establish a standardized text:

> Three Codices [of the Pentateuch] were in the Court of the Temple, Codex *Meon*, Codex *Zaatute* and Codex *Hi*. In one the reading was מעון *refuge* [Deut. XXXIII 27], and in the other two Codices read מעונה [with the final *He*], the reading of the two was accepted and that of the one Codex was rejected. One Codex read זעטוטי [= ζητητής] *enquires of* [Exod. XXIV 5] and the other two Codices read נערי *young men of*, the reading of the two Codices was accepted and that of the one Codex was rejected. In one Codex the reading היא [with a *Yod*] occurred nine times and in the other two Codices it occurred eleven times, the reading of the two Codices was accepted and that of the one Codex was rejected.[37]

Several passages from rabbinic literature suggest that certain scribes were paid from the temple funds to correct manuscripts (*TB Keth.* 106a; *TJ Sheq.* IV.3) and that temple scrolls were used to check manuscripts (*TJ Sanh.* II.6).

There was a desire to provide a consistent standard for debates between Christians and Jews in the first century A.D. (see Justin Martyr *Dialogue* 68). Hillel the Elder needed a standardized text on which to base his seven rules of biblical hermeneutics (*Rabbi Nathan* 37A). Even though Josephus (c. A.D. 37-100) in the late first century A.D. is surely exaggerating, there may be a kernel of truth in his statements:

> But that our forefathers took no less, not to say even greater, care that the nations I have mentioned in the keeping of their records—a task which they assumed to their chief priests and prophets—and that down to our own time these records have been, and if I may venture to say so, will continue to be, preserved with scrupulous accuracy. (Josephus *Contra Apion* 1.29)[38]

Later Josephus states:

> We have given practical proof of our reverence for our own Scriptures. For, although such long ages have now passed, no one has ventured either to add, or

---

[37]Christian D. Ginsburg, *Introduction to the Massoretico-Critical Edition of the Hebrew Bible* (New York: KTAV, 1966), pp. 408-9. (*TJ Ta'an.* IV.2; *Soferim* VI.4). Bertil Albrektson points out that the various traditions concerning this account (*TJ Ta'an.* IV.2; *Soferim* VI.4; *Aboth de R. Nathan*, B. 46; and *Sifre* 2, 356) contain significant differences. See Jacob Z. Lauterbach, "The Three Books Found in the Temple at Jerusalem," *JQR* n.s. 8 (1917-1918): 385-423; and Shemaryahu Talmon, "The Three Scrolls of the Law that were found in the Temple Court," *Textus* 2 (1962): 14-27.

[38]Henry St. John Thackeray, *Josephus with an English Translation*, LCL (Cambridge, Mass.: Harvard University Press, 1961), 1:174-75.

remove, or to alter a syllable; and it is instinct with every Jew, from the day of his birth to regard them as the decrees of God, to abide by them, and, if need be, cheerfully to die for them. (Josephus *Contra Apion* 1.37-42)[39]

Albrektson, however, argues convincingly against this view. First, he suggests that the reason the manuscripts from Murabba'at all belonged to the same text type may be because they were associated with "the followers of the rebel leader Bar Kochba, who was closely connected with the master of "normative" Judaism, R. Aqiba.[40] Second, the MT has numerous inconsistencies and copyist errors, such as haplography, dittography and erroneous word divisions, that should not appear if, in fact, there had been a careful comparison of manuscripts and textual traditions.[41] He attributes this unity of the text in the first century A.D. to political and socioreligious factors of the time. Albrektson argues that the Pharisees, the only group to survive the destruction of the second temple, maintained the proto-MT.[42] He raises good questions concerning the commonly held view of a purposeful standardization of the Hebrew text in the first century A.D. He has not, however, substantially supported a plausible alternative view. Moshe Greenberg argued that the standardization of the Hebrew text took place much earlier in the second century B.C. by scribes within reach of Jerusalem who were able to critically evaluate the various manuscripts and textual variants and thus were able to exclude the proto-SP and the Hebrew *Vorlage* of the LXX.[43] Adam S. van der Woude agrees and states:

> Albrektson is right in assuming that the textual tradition of the Hebrew Bible which won the day was used by the Pharisees. But this still leaves at least one question unanswered. If, as he supposes, the textual tradition supported by the Pharisees prevailed after 70 AD, it must have existed before that. But in view of the pluriformity of the textual traditions of the Old Testament which can still be observed in Qumran, we still have to explain how and why the Pharisees had an essentially uniform textual tradition before the catastrophe of 70 AD.
>
> We can infer that the standardization of the proto-Masoretic text of the Hebrew Bible had basically already taken place in certain Jewish circles before 70 AD not only from the discoveries of the biblical writings at Masada, but also from the fact that "normative" Judaism had rejected the textual tradition of the Septuagint at an early stage.[44]

Van der Woude argues that a unified textual tradition goes back at least as

---

[39]Ibid., 1:177-81.

[40]Albrektson, "Reflections," p. 58.

[41]Ibid., pp. 59-62; Wolters, "Text of the Old Testament," p. 29.

[42]Tov, *Textual Criticism*, p. 195; Albrektson, "Reflections," pp. 49-65.

[43]Moshe Greenberg, "The Stabilization of the Text of the Hebrew Bible Reviewed in Light of the Biblical Materials from the Judaean Desert," *JAOS* 76 (1956): 157-67.

[44]Woude, "Pluriformity and Uniformity," pp. 160-61.

far as the second century B.C. He then goes further and proposes an additional theory be considered: there may have always been a relatively uniform text in the religious circles of Jerusalem.[45] He explains its development as follows:

> The standardization of the proto-Masoretic tradition should be thought of as a process, in which readings regarded as erroneous were gradually expurgated, sporadic changes were made in the text for theological reasons, and manuscripts which did not meet the requirement of the standardized text were removed in the course of time. . . . The event of 70 AD at most precipitated the final phase in the proto-Masoretic textual tradition, but did not bring about the process of standardization as such.[46]

It still seems somewhat unclear whether the text was intentionally standardized, gradually expurgated or only one of the textual traditions maintained. Whatever the case, it is plausible that some variant readings may have been lost or virtually eliminated in the process. From at least the first century A.D. onward the proto-MT was generally copied by well-trained, professional scribes who were meticulous in their work. Jewish writings mention that the temple employed correctors *(meggihim)* who scrutinized the scrolls to safeguard their precision.[47]

From about A.D. 100 to 300 a second group of scribes arose, called the Tannaim *(tānnāîm)*, or "repeaters" (i.e., teachers), who began copying their traditions shortly after the beginning of the Christian era. Sometime during the talmudic period (100 B.C. to A.D. 400), which overlaps the periods of the Sopherim, Tannaim and Amoraim, meticulous rules were developed to preserve the Old Testament text in synagogue scrolls:

1. Only parchments made from clean animals were allowed; these were to be joined together with thread from clean animals.

2. Each written column of the scroll was to have no fewer than forty-eight and no more than sixty lines whose breadth must consist of thirty letters.

3. The page was first to be lined, from which the letters were to be suspended.

4. The ink was to be black, prepared according to a specific recipe.

5. No word or letter was to be written from memory.

6. There was to be the space of a hair between each consonant and the space

---

[45]Ibid., p. 163. He says that Tov comes close to this position when he says: "Although . . . textual plurality was characteristic for all of Palestine, it appears that in temple circles there existed a preference for one textual tradition, i.e., the texts of the Masoretic family" (see Tov, *Textual Criticism*, p. 191).

[46]Woude, "Pluriformity and Uniformity," p. 162.

[47]*b. Kethub.* 106a states, "*Maggihim* of books in Jerusalem received their fees from the temple funds"; cf. *b. Pesah.* 112a (Tov, *Textual Criticism*, pp. 28, 32, 190).

of a small consonant between each word, as well as several other spacing rules.

7. The scribe must wash himself entirely and be in full Jewish dress before beginning to copy the scroll.

8. He could not write the name Yahweh with a newly dipped brush, nor take notice of anyone, even a king, while writing this sacred name.[48]

Later an entire tractate was devoted to the proper procedure for preparing a sacred scroll and included even more rules intended to assure an accurate text.[49]

A third group of scribes who preserved the Hebrew texts from about A.D. 200 to 500 were called the Amoraim (amôrāîm), or "expositors." During this period, the Talmud (from לָמַד, lāmad, "to study") began to be formed, containing further expositions on the stipulations included in the Mishnah and the Gemara (a commentary on the Mishnah). The Amoraim were centered in two areas, Babylonia and Palestine, giving rise to two Talmuds, the Babylonian and the Palestinian. Some form of verse divisions for the Hebrew text are known from this early period (even though Babylonian and Palestinian traditions differ),[50] as well as paragraph and liturgical divisions. Rabbinic tradition indicates that by this time scribes realized that the text was in need of some minor corrections, many of which are noted in *Biblia Hebraica Stuttgartensia* (afterward *BHS*), either in the Masorah or in the text.

3.1.4 The Old Testament Text from About A.D. 500 to 1000

Around the end of the fifth century A.D., a fourth group of scribes called the Masoretes inherited the scribal traditions and carried on the work of preserving the text. Their diligent labors from about A.D. 500 to 1000 helped to preserve the Hebrew text that we have today, the Masoretic Text. These scribes were extremely careful and treated the text with great reverence. Their meticulous notes regarding the text of the Old Testament helped maintain a remarkably accurate text for about a thousand years.

3.1.4.1 Masoretic notations. Though these scribes appear to have inherited a unified text, they also had questions regarding the reading of some passages. As we noted above, scribes of this period had both tendencies to preserve the text as well as to revise the text; once the text was unified, however, the ability to revise it was greatly hampered. Thus they developed special notations to in-

---

[48]Frederic G. Kenyon, *Our Bible and the Ancient Manuscripts*, rev. ed. (New York: Harper, 1958), pp. 78-79; Samuel Davidson, *Introduction to the Old Testament* (Edinburgh: T & T Clark, 1856), p. 89.

[49]*b. Masseketot Sopherim* (mid-eighth century tractate); Abraham Cohen, ed., *The Minor Tractates of the Talmud*, 2 vols. (London: Soncino, 1965), 1:211-324.

[50]Würthwein, *Text of the Old Testament*, p. 21.

dicate questions concerning the text without changing the consonantal text. Exactly when these notations were added is still unknown.

- *Kethib and Qere readings.*[51] A frequent notation in the MT (848 to 1,566 times, depending on the manuscript) denotes scribal questions concerning a specific word in the MT. Rather than change the consonantal text (i.e., the *kĕṯîb,* "what was written"), they indicated the preferred reading (i.e., the *qĕrê,* "what is to be read") in the margin (marked with a ק underneath) and marked on the word in the text the vowel pointing of the *qĕrê.*

- *Special points (puncta extraordinaria).* Fifteen times in the MT small diamonds appear over letters or words to indicate reservations (either textual or doctrinal) about the reading. A good example is found on the words "and Aaron" (וְאַהֲרֹן, *wĕ'ahărōn*) in Numbers 3:39.

כָּל־פְּקוּדֵי הַלְוִיִּם אֲשֶׁר פָּקַד מֹשֶׁה וְאַהֲרֹן עַל־פִּי יְהוָה
לְמִשְׁפְּחֹתָם כָּל־זָכָר מִבֶּן־חֹדֶשׁ וָמַעְלָה שְׁנַיִם וְעֶשְׂרִים אָלֶף:

"All the numbered men of the Levites whom Moses *and Aaron* numbered according to the mouth of the LORD by their families, every male from a month old and upwards, (were) 22,000." (literal translation)

The scribes apparently questioned the originality of the phrase "and Aaron," since both verses 16 and 42 state that Moses (no mention of Aaron) numbered the people.

- *Suspended letters (litterae suspensae).*[52] Four times in the MT, letters are suspended above the line (נ *[n]* in Judges 18:30 and ע [ʿ] in Job 38:13, 15 and Ps 80:14 [ET 80:13]) and all MT manuscripts agree in marking them. A good example is the *nûn* in Judges 18:30:

וַיָּקִימוּ לָהֶם בְּנֵי־דָן אֶת־הַפָּסֶל וִיהוֹנָתָן בֶּן־גֵּרְשֹׁם בֶּן־מְנַשֶּׁה
הוּא וּבָנָיו הָיוּ כֹהֲנִים לְשֵׁבֶט הַדָּנִי עַד־יוֹם גְּלוֹת הָאָרֶץ:

---

[51]See James Barr, "A New Look at Kethibh-Qere," *OTS* 21 (1981): 19-37; Harry M. Orlinsky, "The Origin of the Kethib-Qere System—A New Approach," VTSup 7 (1960): 184-92; Tov, *Textual Criticism,* pp. 60-63; Tov, "Text of the Old Testament," p. 162; Israel Yeivin, *Introduction to the Tiberian Masorah,* ed. and trans. E. J. Revell, SBLMasS 5 (Missoula, Mont.: Scholars Press, 1980), pp. 52-59; Wegner, *Journey from Texts to Translations,* pp. 173-75; Würthwein, *Text of the Old Testament,* pp. 17-18.

[52]See Tov, *Textual Criticism,* p. 57; Yeivin, *Introduction to the Tiberian Masorah,* p. 47; Wegner, *Journey from Texts to Translations,* p. 173; Würthwein, *Text of the Old Testament,* p. 19; *b. Baba Bathra* 108b. The great Jewish expositor Rashi (1040-1105) argued: "Because of the honour of Moses was the *Nun* written so as to alter the name. The *Nun,* however is suspended to tell thee that it is not Manasseh, but Moses" (Ginsburg, *Introduction to the Masoretico-Critical Edition,* p. 336).

"The sons of Dan set up for themselves the graven image and Jonathan the son of Gershom, the son of *Manasseh*, he and his sons were priests for the tribe of the Danites unto the day of the Exile of the land."

The suspended *nûn* is commonly thought to have been added to spare Moses (מֹשֶׁה, *mōšeh*) the embarrassment of having a relative who set up the graven images at Dan, an action that would be more fitting of a relative of Manasseh (מְנַשֶּׁה, *mĕnaššeh*), a wicked king born several hundred years later.

- *Inverted nuns (nun inversum).*[53] Nine times an inverted *nûn* occurs in the MT (before Num 10:35; after Num 10:36; and in Ps 107:21-26, 40). These are probably scribal signs that indicate the scribes thought the verses to be out of order.

- *Special letters.*[54] There are large letters written in most manuscripts of the MT that indicate important details; for example, the first letter of a book (Gen [בְּרֵאשִׁית], Prov [מִשְׁלֵי], Song [שִׁיר], Chron [אָדָם]) or a section (Eccles 12:13 [סוֹף]); the middle letter of the Pentateuch (Lev 11:42 [גָּחוֹן]); and the middle verse of the Pentateuch (Lev 13:33 [וְהִתְגַּלָּח]).

- *Sebirin.*[55] There are numerous *sebirin* found in various manuscripts (70 to 200 cases, Tov; about 350 cases, Ginsburg) that are indicated by the word סְבִיר, "that which is supposed" (a passive participle of the Aramaic word סְבַר, "to suppose") in the marginal notes. Tov states: "The Masoretic terminology is therefore: סבירין ומטעין, 'it has been suggested wrongly.'"[56] *Sebirin* indicate words or forms of words that appear difficult in the context that are nevertheless correct and should not be changed (e.g., Gen 19:8 הָאֵל, "these," *sebirin* הָאֵלֶּה [more common form of "these"]; Jer 48:45 אֵשׁ יָצָא, "fire goes forth [masculine form]" *sebirin* יָצְאָה [feminine form]).

- *Corrections by the scribes (tiqqune sopherim,* תקוני ספרים, "scribal correc-

---

[53]See Sid Z. Leiman, "The Inverted *Nuns* at Numbers 10:35-36 and the Book of Eldad and Medad," *JBL* 93 (1974): 348-55; Tov, *Textual Criticism*, pp. 54-55; Yeivin, *Introduction to the Tiberian Masorah*, pp. 46-47; Würthwein, *Text of the Old Testament*, p. 17; Ginsburg, *Introduction to the Massoretico-Critical Edition*, pp. 341-45.

[54]See Bleddyn J. Roberts, *The Old Testament Text and Versions. The Hebrew Text in Transmission and the History of the Ancient Versions* (Cardiff: University of Wales Press, 1951), p. 31; Tov, *Textual Criticism*, pp. 57-58; Yeivin, *Introduction to the Tiberian Masorah*, pp. 47-48.

[55]Ginsburg, *Introduction to the Massoretico-Critical Edition*, pp. 187-96; Tov, *Textual Criticism*, p. 64; Würthwein, *Text of the Old Testament*, p. 16; Yeivin, *Introduction to the Tiberian Masorah*, pp. 62-64.

[56]Tov, *Textual Criticism*, p. 64.

tions").[57] There are at least eighteen of these corrections in the MT that remove words the scribes considered objectionable or inappropriate. A good example is in Genesis 18:22; because the phrase "to stand before someone" came to mean "to stand in subservience to someone," the statement "but the LORD remained standing before Abraham" was seen as disrespectful to God. The scribes, therefore, changed the order to "but Abraham remained standing before the LORD" and noted in the margin that here a correction had been made by the scribes (see also Num 11:15; 12:12; 1 Sam 3:13).

- *Scribal omissions* (*itture sopherim,* עטורי ספרים, "scribal omissions").[58] The Babylonian Talmud (*Ned. 37b*) mentions five places where a *wāw* had been left off a word (four times off the word אחר, Gen 18:5; 24:55; Num 31:2; Ps 68:26 and once off of משפטיך, Ps 36:7).

These notations indicate how important it was to the scribes to retain a unified text, while still being able to question certain readings that may have been corrupted in the process of hand-copying.

3.1.4.2 Masoretic families. There were two major venues of Jewish scholarship during this period, one in Babylon and one in Palestine. Following the Islamic conquest of Palestine in A.D. 638, Tiberias once again revived and became the chief center for Jewish textual studies.[59] From about A.D. 500 to 800 the Masoretes added vowel points, accents and the Masorahs (to help safeguard the text from error) as well as many scribal corrections.

In the early half of the tenth century two notable Masoretic families flourished in Tiberias, the Ben Asher and Ben Naphtali families. It was once thought that these two families maintained significantly different textual traditions, but more likely they represent only one textual tradition with minor variations.[60] There are only eight minor differences between the consonantal texts of these two families, though they also differ as to word division and vo-

---

[57]William E. Barnes, "Ancient Corrections in the Text of the OT (*Tikkun Sopherim*)," *JTS* 1 (1899-1900): 387-414; Ginsburg, *Introduction to the Massoretico-Critical Edition*, pp. 347-67; Tov, *Textual Criticism*, pp. 64-65; Würthwein, *Text of the Old Testament*, pp. 17-18; Yeivin, *Introduction to the Tiberian Masorah*, pp. 49-51.

[58]Tov, *Textual Criticism*, p. 67; Würthwein, *Text of the Old Testament*, p. 19; Yeivin, *Introduction to the Tiberian Masorah*, p. 57.

[59]Solomon Grayzel, *History of the Jews*, rev. ed. (Philadelphia: Jewish Publication Society, 1968), pp. 248-49; Max L. Margolis and Alexander Marx, *A History of the Jewish People* (Philadelphia: Jewish Publication Society of America, 1934), p. 266.

[60]Goshen-Gottstein, "Rise of the Tiberian Bible Text," p. 112. Würthwein notes: "This close relationship is also attested by Mishael, who mentions more than four hundred instances where Ben Asher and Ben Naphtali stand in agreement, apparently against other Masoretes" (*Text of the Old Testament*, p. 25).

calization.[61] Eventually, the Ben Naphtali tradition died out and the Ben Asher tradition was maintained as the superior text.

3.1.5 The Hebrew Text After A.D. 1000

The Masoretes hand copied the Hebrew text for over one thousand years before the invention of the printing press, and yet it has remained extremely accurate. Every copy of the Hebrew Scriptures was a monumental task, and the Masoretes prided themselves on retaining the accuracy of the Hebrew text. One of the Masoretic schools in Alcalá, Spain, was so well known for producing accurate manuscripts that for almost a century after the printing press was introduced the hand-printed manuscripts from this school still vied with those produced by the printing press. Some of these manuscripts from this period are still valuable for textual criticism and are described later in this book. There are also about three thousand Hebrew manuscripts of the Tiberian tradition, which date from the twelfth century A.D. on.[62] In 1488 the first complete Hebrew Bible was printed and in 1516-1517 the first Rabbinic Bible appeared. Later, in 1524-1525, the Second Rabbinic edition was published; it was edited by a Hebrew Christian named Jacob ben Ḥayyim. This text included the rabbinic notes for the Hebrew text which are the main reason the text retained such accuracy over centuries of copying.

The proto-Masoretic and later Masoretic tradition has a long history, and has enjoyed a privileged status, as Wolters points out:

> Our survey of late-twentieth-century scholarship on the ancient versions and the Samaritan Pentateuch has revealed a paradoxical situation with respect to the MT and its antecedents. On the one hand its status is that of only one of a number of textual traditions, and on the other it seems to have had a privileged position. Not only does it appear to preserve an older stage of the text than the Samaritan Pentateuch, but it seems to have been regarded, from the first century B.C. onward, as a standard against which the LXX should be corrected, and as the appropriate point of departure for new translations, notably the Targums, the Peshitta, and the Vulgate. There is certainly no dispute that after about A.D. 100 the proto-Masoretic text is regarded in Jewish circles as uniquely authoritative.[63]

3.2 The New Testament Text

In some senses the history of the transmission of the New Testament manuscripts is significantly different than the Old Testament, since it was influenced by the history of the early Christian church. The early church was persecuted

---

[61]Würthwein, *Text of the Old Testament*, p. 24; Yeivin, *Introduction to the Tiberian Masorah*, pp. 142-43.

[62]Würthwein, *Text of the Old Testament*, pp. 24-25.

[63]Wolters, "The Text of the Old Testament," pp. 28-29.

for much of its history and thus the transmission of the New Testament texts often lacked much of the care and precision that the Old Testament received. Still the early church held the New Testament texts with the same reverence and authority as the Old Testament (cf. 2 Pet 3:15-16). An examination of the history of the transmission of the New Testament will provide a foundation for our study in New Testament textual criticism.

3.2.1 The New Testament Text Prior to A.D. 100

While there are no autographs of the New Testament, several papyrus fragments date to the second century ($\mathfrak{P}^{32}$, $\mathfrak{P}^{46}$, $\mathfrak{P}^{52}$, $\mathfrak{P}^{64[+67]}$, $\mathfrak{P}^{66}$). $\mathfrak{P}^{52}$ is a fragment of the Gospel of John dated to the early second century, possibly only about fifty to seventy-five years after the book was written. The earliest New Testament manuscripts were written in an uncial script, somewhat similar to our capital letters, on papyrus (see 2 Jn 12), but by the third century, parchment or vellum was beginning to take over as the preferred medium of writing because it provided a better contrast to ink (see 2 Tim 4:13). Some of the shorter New Testament books could have been written on a single piece of papyrus (e.g., 2 and 3 Jn, Jude), but longer works would have been in the form of scrolls (e.g., Matthew, Mark).

Some New Testament material, such as the Gospel traditions, would initially have been circulated orally, whereas Paul's letters would have been written and sent to their recipients. The autographs were either written by their authors or dictated to scribes (or amanuenses; see Rom 16:22; 2 Thess 3:17). Once the letters were written, they were delivered to their respective churches by friends or travelers going to that destination. For example, Tychicus, one of Paul's friends and faithful brother, delivered Paul's letters to the Ephesians (Eph 6:21-22), to the Colossians (Col 4:7-9) and possibly to Titus (Tit 3:12).

Paul sometimes encourages the recipients of his letters to circulate them among the other churches (Col 4:16), and thus the autographs would at times have been copied almost immediately and sent off to other churches. It is unlikely that a professional scribe would be hired to copy these letters since the cost generally would have been prohibitive. Most likely someone from the various recipient churches would copy the autographs and send them on to the next church. Bruce Metzger explains: "In the early years of the Christian Church, marked by rapid expansion and consequent increased demand by individuals and by the congregations for copies of the Scriptures, the speedy multiplication of copies, even by non-professional scribes, sometimes took precedence over strict accuracy of detail."[64] This may explain the large number

---

[64]Bruce M. Metzger, *Manuscripts of the Greek Bible: An Introduction to Greek Palaeography* (New York: Oxford University Press, 1981), p. 21.

of New Testament manuscripts, and why there are generally more mistakes in New Testament manuscripts than in copies of the Old Testament. Most if not all of the New Testament books were completed by A.D. 100, after which began the copying process.

3.2.2 *The New Testament Text After A.D. 100*

During the beginning of the second century A.D., the Christians introduced a new form of written text called the codex, which is very similar in form to our modern books, being bound on the left side of the page.[65] $\mathfrak{P}^{52}$ is written on both sides, suggesting that it was part of a codex rather than a scroll. To date, there are only about five known New Testament manuscripts or fragments written on papyrus dated to the second century, but since the early church was often persecuted it is surprising that any of the manuscripts have survived. In A.D. 64 Nero charged the Christians with setting Rome on fire and persecuted them as traitors. In 303 Diocletian ordered all sacred Scriptures of the Christians to be burned, but soon Emperor Constantine halted their persecution and declared freedom of religion throughout the Roman Empire in the Edict of Milan (313). The Christian church grew so fast during this period that Constantine requested fifty new copies of the Scriptures from Eusebius for the churches of Constantinople. From the fourth century on it was the task of monks to study and make copies of Scripture.

The manuscripts went through several different styles of writing following A.D. 100, including uncial, cursive and minuscule. Uncial script was commonly used between the first and about the sixth century A.D., though it did continue into the tenth or eleventh centuries. For several centuries these uncial texts were written with no breaks between words. This could lead to mistakes (e.g., see Mark 10:40 where the letters ΑΛΛΟΙΣΗΤΟΙΜΑΣΤΑΙ can be read as ἀλλ' οἷς ἡτοίμασται, "but [it is for] those whom it has been prepared," or less likely ἄλλοις ἡτοίμασται, "but [it is for] others whom it has been prepared"). Codex Sinaiticus (fourth century) and Codex Alexandrinus (fifth century) do not have divisions between words, but by the sixth century, and possibly because of the use of cursive writing, divisions began to appear between words.

Only about one hundred of the early uncial manuscripts written on papyrus have survived, but more written on parchment (c. 266) date from the fourth to the tenth centuries. Cursive script, which can be likened to modern English cursive writing, was used from about the third to ninth centuries. Cursive could be written much more quickly since the letters are connected and often simplified, as noted by Metzger: "For daily use this way of writing [uncial script] took too

---

[65]Colin H. Roberts and Theodore C. Skeat, *The Birth of the Codex* (London: Oxford University Press, 1983), p. 61.

much time, and at an early date cursive writing developed from the uncial and continued to be used concurrently with it. Besides being more convenient, cursive letters were often simplified as well as combined when the scribe would join two or more together without lifting his pen (ligature)."[66] The third type of writing, minuscule script, is similar to cursive script only smaller; it eventually predominated from the ninth century to about the fifteenth century, when the printing press was invented. This easy-to-write smaller script saved valuable space on the parchment, which probably had become much more expensive. At present there are about 2,754 New Testament minuscule manuscripts.

At some early point the New Testament scribes also developed a system of abbreviations for common words to save space. This goes back at least as far as about A.D. 200 ($\mathfrak{P}^{46}$ from the Chester Beatty collection) but apparently continued on into the minuscule manuscripts also. The following table shows fifteen of the most commonly abbreviated words:

Table 3.2 Commonly Abbreviated Words in New Testament Manuscripts

Greek Words	Meaning	Nominative Abbreviation	Genitive Abbreviation
θεός	God	ΘΣ/θς	ΘΥ/θυ
κύριος	Lord	ΚΣ/κς	ΚΥ/κυ
Ἰησοῦς	Jesus	ΙΣ/ις	ΙΥ/ιυ
Χριστός	Christ	ΧΣ/χς	ΧΥ/χυ
υἱός	son	ΥΣ/υς	ΥΥ/υυ
πνεῦμα	spirit	ΠΝΑ/πνα	ΠΝΣ/πνς
Δαυ(ε)ίδ	David	ΔΑΔ/δαδ	
σταυρός	cross	ΣΤΣ/στς	ΣΤΥ/στυ
μήτηρ	mother	ΜΗΡ/μηρ	ΜΗΣ/μης
πατήρ	father	ΠΗΡ/πηρ	ΠΤΣ/πτς
Ἰσραήλ	Israel	ΙΗΛ/ιηλ	
σωτήρ	salvation	ΣΗΡ/σηρ	ΣΡΣ/σρς
ἄνθρωπος	man	ΑΝΟΣ/ανος	ΑΝΟΥ/ανου
Ἰερουσαλήμ	Jerusalem	ΙΛΗΜ/ιλημ	
οὐρανός	heaven	ΟΥΝΟΣ/ουνος	ΟΥΝΟΥ/ουνου

---

[66]Metzger, *Manuscripts of the Greek Bible*, p. 21.

Generally the abbreviations include the first and the last letter of the word; the latter is necessary to indicate the declension, or part of speech, of the word. The use of cursive script allowed for more possible mistakes to be made in the copying process since it is harder to distinguish the letters, and the use of abbreviations led to word mix-ups. Few if any punctuation marks were added to the earliest manuscripts (e.g., $\mathfrak{P}^{46}$ and $\mathfrak{P}^{66}$, both dated to about A.D. 200, include occasional punctuation marks); but more were added by scribes during the sixth and seventh centuries. Verse divisions were a very late development; in fact, the first English Bible to contain verse divisions was the Geneva Bible, translated by William Whittingham in 1560.

Parchment and leather were sometimes cleaned and rescraped for reuse, which resulted in a manuscript called a "palimpsest," from the two Greek words πάλιν (*palin*, "again") and ψάω (*psaō*, "to scrape"). About 20 percent of extant New Testament manuscripts are palimpsests (e.g., Codex Ephraemi is a fifth-century New Testament manuscript that was erased and reused in the twelfth century for thirty-eight sermons or treatises of Ephraem, a fourth-century Syrian church father).

In time the church developed a lectionary system for the Old and New Testaments that enabled the entire Bible to be read in the course of several years. At first, notations were made in later uncial manuscripts that indicated the order in which texts were to be read, beginning with Easter and continuing throughout the year. Later, presumably for the convenience of readers who most likely did not own their own Bible, lectionaries included the text of the biblical passages to be read during worship services. The earliest extant lectionaries come from about the tenth century and have become another source for determining the most accurate readings of the New Testament.

3.2.3 The Transmission Process

The transmission process is certainly more complicated than is often thought: New Testament manuscripts were likely taken from one place to another; some were destroyed in wars; others were hidden; some may have been "corrected" by copyists who compared them to other manuscripts; and they were copied over a long period of time. Gordon Fee describes the earliest period of textual transmission as follows:

> Much of the difficulty stems from the work of the earliest Christian copyists. In a time when the majority of people were illiterate and when Christianity periodically underwent severe persecution, there were probably few professionally trained scribes in the service of the church. Moreover, seldom were the scribes possessed by the spirit of the scribes of the later times who worked according to

the instructions of the Lord given in Deuteronomy 12:32: "Thou shalt not add thereto, nor diminish therefrom." In fact, the opposite seems to have been true of the scribes in the first two centuries.[67]

As scribes inadvertently and sometimes intentionally introduced errors into their copies, a ripple effect would result: copies of their copies would pass on these errors as well as new ones. Unless these manuscripts were compared with others and "corrected," mistakes would be retained. In principle, manuscripts can be compared and arranged into textual clusters based on similarity of mistakes. While not all scholars agree with this general description of the transmission process, Michael Holmes encapsulates the following foundational principles that are generally accepted:[68]

1. Every manuscript's textual tradition or text-form contains evidence of corruption.

The various manuscripts demonstrate a progression from a rather undisciplined or less accurate copying process from the latter first and early second centuries, to more disciplined and stable textual traditions in the fifth century. There is little evidence to suggest intentional "recensional" activity (i.e., a scribe intentionally alters the text to make it correspond more closely to his or her own views), but most variants in manuscripts appear to be the result of unintentional mistakes or scribes who intentionally attempted to "correct" a text.

2. It is reasonable to assume that a greater quantity of later manuscripts will be discovered than earlier ones due to the perishability of writing materials, the number of manuscripts made and the possibility of their destruction (e.g., Tischendorf found monks burning old manuscripts to keep themselves warm during one of his visits to St. Catherine's monastery). Thus the transmission process has been shaped by external circumstances, such as wars, persecution, the rise of Islam and the politics of the Byzantine Empire.

3. Some late manuscripts may be copies of much earlier manuscripts (i.e., a later copyist may have had access to an early manuscript). It appears possible to reconstruct at least some stages of the transmission process (e.g., family 1 and family 13 demonstrate significant textual similarities); this helps us to understand the broader picture of the transmission of the text.

Sometimes cross-contamination was the result of seemingly random events, as Michael Holmes explains:

---

[67]Gordon D. Fee, "Textual Criticism of the New Testament," in *Studies in the Theory and Method of New Testament Textual Criticism*, ed. Eldon J. Epp and Gordon D. Fee, Studies and Documents (Grand Rapids: Eerdmans, 1993), p. 9.

[68]Michael W. Holmes, "A Case for Reasoned Eclecticism," in *Rethinking New Testament Textual Criticism*, ed. David A. Black (Grand Rapids: Baker, 2002), pp. 92-97.

For example, an influential church leader (such as John Chrysostom) supplies, or someone in a centrally located and/or better-supplied scriptorium (in Constantinople, for example) chooses—perhaps for reasons having nothing to do with textual character; such as greater legibility, layout, format, or arrangement of text, or simply because it was close at hand—a manuscript as an exemplar from which to make new copies and a standard against which to correct existing ones; and as a result the Bibles in use in the area(s) influenced by that leader or scriptorium begin to reflect the textual character (whatever it happens to be) of the selected model.[69]

The transmission process then was not always consistent, nor did it necessarily follow well-defined principles.

In some senses the history of the New Testament is similar to that of the Old Testament in that during the second century there may have been competing forms of the New Testament (e.g., Marcion had a reduced canon from the orthodox church). More recently, Bart Ehrman has suggested that the New Testament may have been established by the interaction of several competing groups of early Christians that had very different beliefs (e.g., Ebionites, Marcionites).[70] But from early church history we are able to see that the early Christians fended off those who held heretical beliefs and were able to maintain the text of the New Testament. As far as we know, Marcion and those who held different canons or texts were offshoots and did not represent mainstream Christianity. This situation can be compared to Jewish scribes who maintained the proto-MT against competing versions of the Old Testament in the early first century A.D.

Further Reading

Old Testament

Ackroyd, Peter R., and C. F. Evans, eds. *The Cambridge History of the Bible.* Vol. 1, *From the Beginnings to Jerome.* Cambridge: Cambridge University Press, 1970.

Black, Matthew. "The Biblical Languages." In *CHB* 1:11-29.

Brotzman, Ellis R. *Old Testament Textual Criticism: A Practical Introduction.* Grand Rapids: Baker, 1994.

Diringer, David. "The Biblical Scripts." In *CHB* 1:1-10.

Driver, Godfrey R. *Semitic Writing from Pictograph to Alphabet.* Revised by S. A. Hopkins. London: Oxford University Press, 1976.

Ewert, David. *From Ancient Tablets to Modern Translations: A General Introduction to the Bible.* Grand Rapids: Zondervan, 1983.

---

[69]Holmes, "Reasoned Eclecticism," pp. 92-97.

[70]Bart Ehrman, *Lost Christianities: The Battles for Scripture and the Faiths We Never Knew* (Oxford: Oxford University Press, 2000).

Payne, David F. "Old Testament Textual Criticism: Its Principles and Practice." *TynBul* 25 (1974): 99-112.

Roberts, Bleddyn J. *The Old Testament Text and Versions: The Hebrew Text in Transmission and the History of Ancient Versions.* Cardiff: University of Wales Press, 1951.

Smelik, Klaas A. D. *Writings from Ancient Israel,* translated by Graham I. Davies. Louisville, Ky.: Westminster/John Knox, 1991.

Talmon, Shemaryahu. "Aspects of the Textual Transmission of the Bible in Light of Qumran Manuscripts." *Textus* 4 (1964): 95-132. Reprinted in *QHBT*, pp. 226-63.

Tov, Emanuel. *Textual Criticism of the Hebrew Bible.* Minneapolis: Fortress, 1992.

Waltke, Bruce K. "The Textual Criticism of the Old Testament." In *Biblical Criticism: Historical, Literary, and Textual,* pp. 47-65, edited by Roland K. Harrison et al. Grand Rapids: Zondervan, 1978. (Also found in *Expositor's Bible Commentary,* edited by Frank E. Gaebelein, 1:211-28. Grand Rapids: Zondervan, 1979.)

———. "Textual Criticism of the Old Testament and Its Relation to Exegesis and Theology." In *NIDOTTE* 1:51-67.

Waltke, Bruce K. and Michael O'Connor. *An Introduction to Biblical Hebrew Syntax.* Winona Lake, Ind.: Eisenbrauns, 1990.

Wegener, George S. *Six Thousand Years of the Bible,* translated by M. Shenfield. London: Thames & Hudson, 1963.

Wegner, Paul D. *The Journey from Texts to Translations.* Grand Rapids: Baker, 2000.

Yeivin, Israel. *Introduction to the Tiberian Masorah.* SBLMasS 5. Missoula, Mont.: Scholars Press, 1980.

New Testament
Black, David A., ed. *Rethinking New Testament Textual Criticism.* Grand Rapids: Baker, 2002.

Bruce, Frederick F. *The Books and the Parchments.* 3rd ed. Westwood, N.J.: Revell, 1963.

Comfort, Philip W. *Early Manuscripts and Modern Translations of the New Testament.* Grand Rapids: Baker, 1990.

Fee, Gordon D. "The Textual Criticism of the New Testament." In *Expositor's Bible Commentary,* 1:419-33, edited by Frank E. Gaebelein. Grand Rapids: Zondervan, 1979.

Gelb, Ignace J. *A Study of Writing.* Chicago: University of Chicago Press, 1952.

Greenlee, J. Harold. *Scribes, Scrolls, and Scripture: A Student's Guide to New Testament Textual Criticism.* Grand Rapids: Eerdmans, 1985.

Kenyon, Frederic G. *Our Bible and the Ancient Manuscripts,* edited by A. W. Adams. 5th ed. New York: Harper, 1958.

Metzger, Bruce M. *Manuscripts of the Greek Bible: An Introduction to Palaeography.* New York: Oxford University Press, 1981.

———. *The Text of the New Testament: Its Transmission, Corruption, and Restoration.* 3rd ed. New York: Oxford University Press, 1992.

PART II

Old Testament
Textual Criticism

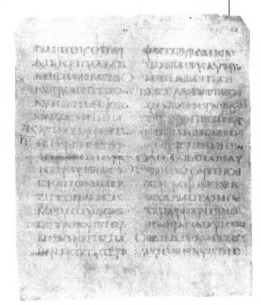

Old Testament Textual Criticism

4

A Brief History of Old Testament Textual Criticism

This chapter provides a brief history of Old Testament textual criticism from the Dead Sea Scrolls and the Septuagint to its present state. Most modern Old Testament text critics consider it preferable to make a diplomatic edition (i.e., from an early, extant Hebrew manuscript) and include a textual apparatus compiling variants from different sources.

When holding the modern Old Testament text in our hands, it is difficult to comprehend all the lives and talent dedicated to preparing it for more than three thousand years. A high regard for Scripture, devotion to detail and providence have preserved over the millennia a text that is remarkably reliable, something more recently confirmed by some of the Dead Sea Scrolls. We will now turn briefly to a history of Old Testament textual criticism from its earliest stages to gain a frame of reference from which to work.

4.1 Dead Sea Scrolls

Until the discovery of the Dead Sea Scrolls, the oldest, extant Hebrew manuscripts of any significant portion of the Old Testament was from the ninth century A.D. Things changed drastically, however, with the discovery of manuscripts in the caves around Qumran in 1947. From these caves we now have somewhere around 900 manuscripts in varying degrees of preservation dated between the third century B.C. and the first century A.D.[1]

Several manuscripts from the Dead Sea area indicate corrections to the texts, which are placed within the margins or between the lines. Some have suggested that these changes were made based merely on the preferences of

---

[1] James C. VanderKam, *The Dead Sea Scrolls Today* (Grand Rapids: Eerdmans, 1994), pp. 16-32; John J. Collins, "Dead Sea Scrolls," *ABD* 2:86.

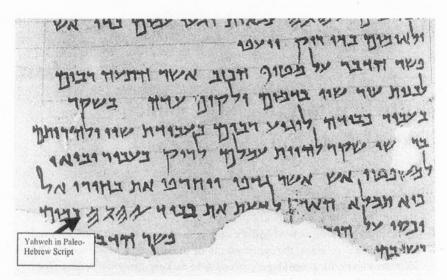

Figure 4.1. A page from the Habakkuk Commentary dated to the second century B.C. and found in Cave 4 at Qumran. Notice the name Yahweh is printed in paleo-Hebrew script. [John C. Trever]

the Qumran scribes (possibly for theological or grammatical reasons),[2] but even a cursory glance at the Isaiah Scroll from Qumran (1QIsᵃ) argues against this possibility since there are many changes that do not appear to show any consistent rationale (e.g., switching from Yahweh to Adonai and then back again in the following lines). More likely, these corrections indicate proofreading changes or that the texts were modified based on different readings in various manuscripts. It is fairly well accepted among scholars that the Dead Sea Scrolls give evidence that at least three textual traditions were prevalent about the third century B.C.: one following the SP (pre-Samaritan Pentateuch or "harmonizing text"), one the LXX (a supposed Hebrew original behind the text of the LXX) and one the proto-MT (the consonantal base text that was later developed and maintained by the medieval Masoretes).[3] However, Emanuel Tov argues for at least five textual tradi-

[2]Emanuel Tov, *Textual Criticism of the Hebrew Bible* (Minneapolis: Fortress, 1992), pp. 259-65; Arie Rubinstein, "The Theological Aspect of Some Variant Readings in the Isaiah Scroll," *JJS* 6 (1955): 187-200; Ernest Würthwein, *The Text of the Old Testament: An Introduction to the Biblia Hebraica*, trans. Erroll F. Rhodes, 2nd ed. (Grand Rapids: Eerdmans, 1995), p. 33.

[3]Frank M. Cross, "The Evolution of a Theory of Local Texts," in *Qumran and the History of the Biblical Text*, ed. Frank M. Cross and Shemaryahu Talmon (Cambridge, Mass.: Harvard University Press, 1976), pp. 306-20; Frank M. Cross, *The Ancient Library of Qumran and Modern Biblical Studies*, 3rd ed. (Minneapolis: Fortress, 1995); Philip W. Skehan, "The Biblical Scrolls

tions: the three mentioned previously plus nonaligned texts and texts written according to "Qumran practice."[4] It is the latter group of texts, which Tov calls "Qumran practice," that appears to give the best evidence for some type of textual criticism occurring at Qumran, for they contain numerous corrections.

Therefore it is reasonable to conclude that the scribes at Qumran may have modified their texts because they were aware of other traditions or manuscripts of the Old Testament. This possibility is also suggested by several of the Qumran texts themselves. For example, the Isaiah Scroll (1QIsᵃ) includes a significant number of corrections to the text, the majority of which bring its readings into closer harmony with the MT's readings, but several additions actually go the other way, suggesting that the text being followed may have had a different reading (e.g., Isaiah 8:16 adds את *['t]*; Isaiah 11:4 adds יומת רשע *, ywmt rsʿ*; Isaiah 44:3 adds כן, *kn*). An interesting example is found in Isaiah 3:17-18:

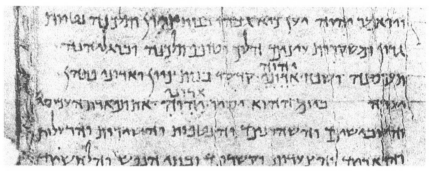

Figure 4.2. Textual variants from Qumran (Isaiah 3:17-18) [John C. Trever]

In the third line (fig. 4.2), dots appear below the MT reading אדוני (*'dwny*, "the Lord") and the alternate reading יהוה (*yhwh*, "Yahweh") appears above it. But in the fourth line the readings are reversed: dots appear below the word יהוה (*yhwh*) and the reading from the MT appears above it. Dots placed above (Is 7:16; 35:10; 36:4, 7; 41:20) or below (Is 34:17; 40:7) a letter, word or phrase may indicate similar changes. Other markings in the first Isaiah Scroll point to some degree of textual criticism being carried on at this early period. These markings include the following:

from Qumran and the Text of the OT," *BA* 28 (1965): 99; Joseph T. Milik, *Ten Years of Discovery in the Wilderness of Judea*, trans. John Strugnell (Naperville, Ill.: Alec R. Allenson, 1959), pp. 20-31.
[4]Tov, *Textual Criticism*, pp. 114-17, 155-63.

- Letters appearing above the line (Is 1:1-3, 7, 11, 24; see fig. 4.3)

- One word crossed out and another written in (see fig. 4.4)

- A word squeezed in sideways in the margin (Is 35:9; 37:9; 38:21-22; 40:8; see fig. 4.5)

If these markings are the result of text critical work at Qumran, then they may be the earliest extant evidence for this type of activity.[5]

Figure 4.3 Textual variants from Qumran (Isaiah 1:1-3) [John C. Trever]

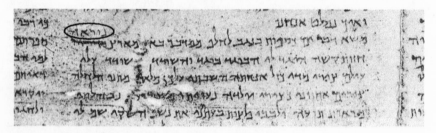

Figure 4.4 Textual variant from Qumran (Isaiah 21:1) [John C. Trever]

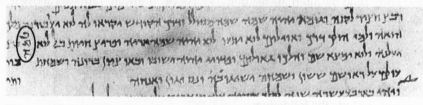

Figure 4.5 Textual variant from Qumran (Isaiah 35:9) [John C. Trever]

---

[5]There is certainly evidence that suggests corrections or editorial work occurred before this time; e.g., Genesis 14:14 contains the name "Dan" before the city was even called Dan (see Josh 19:47; Judg 18:29), but even the earliest Hebrew texts and the ancient versions have this reading.

4.2 Septuagint (LXX)

Before the discoveries of the Dead Sea Scrolls it was reasonable to use the LXX and other ancient versions of the Bible as primary evidence for the text of the Old Testament. This was because extant evidence for these ancient versions preceded evidence for the MT by four hundred years or more in most cases. The LXX was commonly used to provide evidence for readings that diverged from the MT, and these readings were given priority since there was no other comparative evidence by which to question them. However, the discovery of the Dead Sea Scrolls and more recent studies have challenged this thinking in several ways. First, recent studies have shown that the proto-MT underlies a significant portion of the readings in the LXX. Al Wolters has correctly stated:

> Since 1970 a number of volumes have appeared in the Göttingen edition of the LXX, accompanied by an impressive series of auxiliary studies. As this hitherto most comprehensive and reliable edition of the LXX nears completion, scholars have begun to realize that its textual base shows much greater affinity to the MT than was previously assumed. For one thing, the study of the translation technique employed in many books of the LXX has made clear that Greek renderings that used to be taken as evidence of a non-Masoretic *Vorlage* can in many cases be explained as reflecting a Hebrew text that is identical with the MT.[6]

Scholars are beginning to realize that often what was commonly thought to be a distinct reading of a Greek text that went back to a Hebrew *Vorlage* can now be better understood as a translator's free rendering of the proto-MT. Second, even the Old Greek texts (i.e., what is thought to be the original Greek text of the LXX) have apparently undergone revisions and recensions that have brought them into greater conformity to the proto-MT (e.g., the *kaige* recension appears to be dated to the mid-first century B.C., indicating clear revisions toward the proto-MT).[7] Third, since the discovery of the Dead Sea Scrolls it is no longer possible to assume that the distinctive readings of the LXX are necessarily older than the proto-MT since evidence for the proto-MT can be shown to be just as early as, if not earlier than, the LXX.

4.3 A Unified Text by the First Century A.D.

The Dead Sea scrolls indicate a significant variety of textual traditions by about the third century B.C., and it appears that the scribes were allowed some flexibility in modifying the texts (e.g., the addition of *matres lectionis*, glosses [clarifying additions], modifying archaic words). However, after the mid-first

---

[6]Al Wolters, "The Text of the Old Testament," in *The Face of Old Testament Studies: A Survey of Contemporary Approaches*, ed. David W. Baker and Bill T. Arnold (Grand Rapids: Baker, 1999), pp. 23-24.

[7]Tov, *Textual Criticism*, pp. 25, 30; Wolters, "Text of the Old Testament," pp. 24-25.

century A.D. things had significantly changed and modifications were no longer permitted, as evidenced by the consistency of the manuscripts from Masada (prior to 73 A.D.), from the caves at Naḥal Ḥever (latter first century A.D.) and Wadi Murabbaʿat (prior to the Bar Kochba Revolt in 132-35 A.D.). Bruce Waltke also points to rabbinic evidence that suggests unification of the text transpired during the first century A.D.:

> Indeed, the seven rules of biblical hermeneutics, compiled by Hillel the Elder at the time of Herod, demanded an inviolable, sacrosanct, authoritative text. Moreover, Justin's complaint against Trypho the Jew that the rabbis had altered the venerable LXX to remove an essential arm from the Christian propaganda also demonstrates that the rabbis desired an authoritative text.[8]

Justin's complaint regarding the Greek translations of Aquila (A.D. 120), Symmachus (A.D. 180) and Theodotion (A.D. 180) was primarily aimed at their translation of עַלְמָה (ʿalmâ, LXX παρθένος, parthenos, usually "virgin") as νεᾶνις (neanis, "young woman") in Isaiah 7:14.

Justin Martyr said to Trypho (a Jewish scholar) concerning Isaiah 7:14:

> But I am far from putting reliance in your teachers, who refuse to admit that the interpretation made by the seventy elders who were with Ptolemy [king] of the Egyptians is a correct one; and they attempt to frame one another. And I wish you to observe, that they have altogether taken away many Scriptures from the translations effected by those seventy elders who were with Ptolemy.[9]

What is interesting about this quote from Justin Martyr is that the proto-MT apparently was not merely changed to נַעֲרָה (naʿărâ, "young girl, woman"), which suggests that they were not free to modify the Hebrew text at will but were able to retranslate the LXX.

Because of the meticulous work of the scribes, there was very little variation among MT manuscripts from the first to the fifteenth centuries A.D., when movable print began to be used for Bible translations. During the process of the unification of the textual tradition, however, certain readings were necessarily chosen over others, and thus some type of text-critical work established a unified tradition. Little is said about how this unified tradition arose. Some variants may have been maintained in the *Kethib/Qere* notes in the marginal Masorah, but a unified authoritative text was easier to maintain than flexible or multiple texts. Some readings that were not chosen may have been the originals, and it is up to the Old Testament text critic today to attempt to retrieve these early readings where possible.

---

[8]Bruce K. Waltke, "The Textual Criticism of the Old Testament," in *Biblical Criticism: Historical, Literary, and Textual*, ed. Roland K. Harrison et al. (Grand Rapids: Zondervan, 1978), p. 57.
[9]Justin Martyr *Dialogues of Justin* 68, Ante-Nicene Fathers, ed. Alexander Roberts and James Donaldson (Grand Rapids: Eerdmans, 1987), 1:234.

4.4 Origen's Hexapla

The debates between Christians and Jews compelled Origen to compile one of the earliest and most important examples of Old Testament textual criticism, the Hexapla (A.D. 230-245). His reason for making the Hexapla is clearly stated in a letter responding to Julius Africanus (c. 240): "I make it my endeavor not to be ignorant of their [LXX's] various readings, lest in my controversies with the Jews I should quote to them what is not found in their copies, and that I may make some use of what is found there, even although it should not be in our Scriptures."[10] The six-column arrangement of texts enabled one to see the relationship of the Hebrew text to the various Greek versions of the time (see pp. 192-95). Ernst Würthwein points out the purpose of the Hexapla:

> The Hebrew text stands in first place as the original, and the sequence of the version corresponds to their relationship to the original, priority going to Aquila as the most literal. The primary interest of the Alexandrian scholar was to link 𝕾 to the original Hebrew text with the help of the other more literal versions.[11]

This monumental work apparently was destroyed in the Arab invasions of the early seventh century A.D., but readings from the Hexapla can be found in various manuscripts that were copied before the work was destroyed (e.g., G [Codex Sarravianus], M [Codex Coislianus], 86 and 88).

4.5 Latin Vulgate

Jerome translated the Old Testament into Latin about A.D. 390-405, apparently using a base text that was a form of the Hebrew text. Ernst Würthwein notes the limitations of Jerome's translation:

> As there were no dictionaries or grammars in his day, his most important aids were the Greek versions of the Septuagint, Aquila, Symmachus, and Theodotion, and any information he could obtain from the Jewish side. As a result he kept very much along traditional lines, and the influences of the resources mentioned above are clearly observable in his work.[12]

Still, Jerome understood the difficulties of the translation process, for he states:

> Translation . . . is a difficult, almost impossible, art to master. Languages vary so in their order of words, in their individual metaphors, and in their native idioms. The translator is thus faced with a choice between a literal, word-for-

---

[10]Origen *Origen to Africanus* 5, in Frederick Crombie, "The Writings of Origen," in *Ante-Nicene Christian Library: Translations of the Writings of the Fathers Down to A.D. 325*, ed. Alexander Roberts and James Donaldson (Grand Rapids: Eerdmans, 1991), 4:387.

[11]Würthwein, *Text of the Old Testament*, p. 57.

[12]Ibid., pp. 92-93.

Figure 4.6. St. Jerome (c.345-420) studying Scripture by Domenico Ghirlandaio (1448-1494) [Chiesa di Ognissanti, Florence, Italy/Scala/Art Resource, NY]

word rendering (which is certain to sound absurd and so be a travesty of the original) and something very much freer (in which case he is liable to be accused of being unfaithful).[13]

Jerome chose primarily a sense-for-sense translation method for Old Testament in the Latin Vulgate, though in some places he is slavishly literal.[14] Since there is no record of what Hebrew text Jerome used and because he chose to translate in a sense-for-sense rather than a literal manner, some scholars question the Vulgate's usefulness to textual criticism.[15] It is apparent that he weighed the accuracy of his sources and based his translation on a Hebrew text, often correcting the Old Latin and Greek texts. Thus in some sense Jerome used principles of textual criticism to produce the Latin Vulgate, even though it is unclear how he decided which text to use.

Hendly F. D. Sparks makes an interesting and helpful comment:

---

[13]*Praefationi in chronicon Eusebii a Graeco Latine redditum et continuatum.* See also: Hendly F. D. Sparks, "Jerome as Biblical Scholar," *CHB*, 1:522.

[14]Sparks, "Jerome as Biblical Scholar," 1:525-26.

[15]Friedrick Stummer, *Einführung in die lateinische Bibel: Ein Handbuch für Vorlesungen und Selbstunterricht* (Paderborn: Schöningh, 1928), p. 123; Würthwein, *Text of the Old Testament,* p. 97.

In spite of his grasp of text-critical principles and his constant censure of the Latin and Greek biblical texts of his day, Jerome found but little amiss with the current Hebrew text. This text, so far as we can see, was substantially the same as our own standard Massoretic text; and it is, therefore, to us all the more surprising that it never seems seriously to have occurred to him, either that it might have been at one time only one of several competing texts, or that it might be in any degree corrupt. The reason presumably was that, whereas Jerome's Latin and Greek manuscripts differed repeatedly and widely among themselves, his Hebrew manuscripts did not. In other words, except in the merest handful of passages, and then only in unimportant details, they posed no obvious textual problems.[16]

4.6 Masoretes

During the time of the Masoretes (A.D. 500-1100), traditions regarding the reading of the text and its pointing were established and recorded. They diligently made meticulous notes regarding the text, from recording the number of letters used in the book to indicating its middle letter, as H. Wheeler Robinson observed: "Everything countable seems to be counted."[17] Thus the textual criticism from this period basically maintained the traditional Hebrew text. Two notable families of scribes from Tiberias in Palestine, the Ben Asher and Ben Naphtali families, vied with each other in copying and preserving the authoritative Hebrew text. Eventually the Ben Asher tradition won out— two of the oldest extant manuscripts of the MT, the Cairo Codex of the Prophets (both former and latter prophets, A.D. 895) and the Aleppo Codex (complete Old Testament, A.D. 930), come from the Ben Asher family.

4.7 Printed Hebrew Bibles

Shortly after the invention of movable print, a poor edition of the Hebrew text of Psalms appeared in 1477, most likely from Bologna, Spain. In 1488, Abraham ben Hayyim of Bologna was enlisted to produce the first printed Old Testament with vowel

Figure 4.7 Printing press (old wood cut)

---

[16]Sparks, "Jerome as Biblical Scholar," 1:532.

[17]H. Wheeler Robinson, "The Hebrew Bible," in *The Bible in Its Ancient and English Versions*, ed. H. Wheeler Robinson, 2nd ed. (London: Oxford University Press, 1954), p. 29.

points and accents. In 1516-1517 the first Rabbinic Bible (Old Testament with Masorahs and several Jewish commentaries, e.g., Rashi, Kimḥi) was published in Venice by Daniel Bomberg. With the help of Jacob ben Ḥayyim, Bomberg published the Second Rabbinic Bible (1524-1525), which became the standard MT for about four hundred years.[18] These printed editions are significant to Old Testament textual criticism because they combined several manuscripts in order to produce a single text with the best readings available at the time.

Figure 4.8. Brian Walton's London Polyglot (1654-1657) [Paul D. Wegner]

4.8 Polyglot Bibles

The polyglot versions, published from the beginning of the sixteenth century onward, were the next advance in Old Testament textual criticism. Cardinal Ximenes, archbishop of Toledo, produced the Complutensian Polyglot Bible in 1514-1517. The scribes at Toledo had access to some of the earliest extant Hebrew manuscripts, and this Bible was based largely on a critical examination of these manuscripts. The Hebrew text does not include accents and the vowel points are unreliable, but the consonantal text is sound. The next to appear was the Antwerp Polyglot (1569-1572), published by Christophe Plantin at Antwerp (Belgium) and paid for by King Philip II of Spain. Its Hebrew text derived from the Complutensian Polyglot and the Second Rabbinic Bible of Jacob ben Ḥayyim. The

---

[18]Nahum H. Sarna, "Bible Text," *EJ* 4:831-35; Waltke, "Textual Criticism of the Old Testament," p. 63.

Paris Polyglot (1629-1645), published by Guy M. leJay, was essentially the same as the Antwerp Polyglot, with the addition of the SP and its Targums, the Peshitta and an Arabic version with a Latin translation. Nine years later Brian Walton produced the London Polyglot Bible (1654-1657), which included seven columns of text: the Hebrew text with a Latin interlinear translation, the SP (only in the first volume), a Targum, the LXX, the Vulgate, the Peshitta and the Old Syriac, all with their Latin translations.

The text followed those of Jacob ben Hayyim (Second Rabbinic Bible) and Johann Buxtorf (sixth Rabbinic Bible).[19] These works are useful in comparing the various readings of the versions but do not provide any significant variants of the Hebrew manuscripts.

4.9 Hebrew Editions with Textual Apparatuses

Not until 1720 did a text of the Hebrew Bible appear with a textual apparatus that recorded the most important readings of five manuscripts at Erfurt as well as nineteen printed manuscripts. This edition, published by Johann Heinrich Michaelis (1668-1738), a German pietist, was called *Biblia Hebraica ex aliquot manuscriptis et compluribus impressis codicibus. . . .*[20] About fifty years later another Hebrew text was published with a massive textual apparatus. This work was produced by Benjamin Kennicott (1718-1783), canon of Christ's Church, Oxford, in 1776-1780 and was called *Vetus Testamentum Hebraicum cum variis lectionibus.*[21] Without vowel points or accents, it records variants from 615 manuscripts, 52 editions of the Hebrew text and 16 manuscripts of the SP.[22] In 1784-1788 Giovanni B. de Rossi, an Italian scholar, published *Variae lectiones Veteris Testamenti . . . ,*[23] which compiles variant readings in the consonantal text from 1,475 manuscripts and editions (intro., p. xlv). This work was more comprehensive and accurate than Kennicott's, but neither is of much value to Old Testament textual criticism, as Würthwein explains:

> The actual value of both Kennicott's and de Rossi's collections of variants of these editions for the recovery of the original text is very small. Apart from orthographic differences and simple scribal errors (such as haplography, dittography, inversion of consonants), the variants they record are concerned with the use of the plural or singular with collective nouns, the addition or omission of such words as כֹּל [kōl] or ו [wāw], the interchange of prepositions with similar meanings or of words with synonymous expressions. . . . This certainly demonstrates

---

[19] Thomas H. Darlow and Horace F. Moule, *Historical Catalogue of the Printed Editions of Holy Scripture in the Library of the British and Foreign Bible Society* (London: Bible House, 1903), 2.715.

[20] Michaelis's Hebrew text was printed in Halle by Magdeburg in 1720.

[21] Kennicott's Hebrew text was printed in Oxford by Clarendon in 1776-1780.

[22] Würthwein, *Text of the Old Testament*, p. 40.

[23] De Rossi's text was printed in Parma by Regio typographeo in 1784-1788.

the lack of any absolute uniformity in the transmission of the text, such as is assumed by the theory of single archetype. But what is lacking is variants of any real significance for the meaning of the text, such as are found in New Testament manuscripts. These collections of variants provide scarcely any help in dealing with corrupt passages.[24]

The disappointing outcome of these works led to a declining interest in Old Testament textual criticism so that no further works of this nature have been forthcoming.

Seligmann Baer, aided by Franz Delitzsch, prepared an eclectic text of the MT (except for Exodus to Deuteronomy), drawing the preferable readings from various sources. This work, *Textum Masoreticum accuratissime expressit e fontibus Masorae codicumque varie illustravit* (1869-1895),[25] did not meet with a favorable response. The Dead Sea Scrolls had not yet been discovered and the medieval Hebrew manuscripts that it used reflected a unified Masoretic tradition and furnished few significant variations.[26] Recently there has been a revived interest in producing an eclectic edition by Oxford University Press, called *The Oxford Hebrew Bible*, with Ronald Hendel as editor in chief.[27]

4.10 Diplomatic Editions

Diplomatic editions reproduce a particular *textus receptus* (lit. "received text," or a form of the MT) of the original Hebrew text, in contrast to an eclectic edition that attempts to reconstruct the original reading of the Old Testament text by combining the most accurate readings in one text. The first edition of the *Biblia Hebraica* (BHK^1) was published in Leipzig, Germany, in 1906 by the German Bible Society (Deutsche Bibelgesellschaft) and edited by Rudolph Kittel. It used the Hebrew text of the Second Rabbinic Bible (1524-1525) edited by Jacob ben Hayyim. A second edition of the BHK^2 was published in 1913 and contained only minor corrections. Not everyone was happy with these editions—largely because they used an eclectic Hebrew text and contained many emendations in the textual apparatus. Roland Harrison notes the criticisms of the textual apparatus:

> The first important scholar to criticize this curious situation was C. C. Torrey, who made a scathing attack on the methods used to amass this apparatus. Torrey's views were shared by Montgomery, who in his *Critical and Exegetical Commentary on the Book of Daniel* (1927) ignored the apparatus completely. These opinions were also elaborated by Margolis, who made it clear that the Kittel critical

---

[24]Würthwein, *Text of the Old Testament*, pp. 40-41.

[25]Baer's text was printed in Leipzig by Bernhardi Tauchnitz.

[26]Paul Kahle, cited in Hans Bauer and Pontus Leander, *Historische Grammatik der hebräischen Sprache* (Hildesheim: Olms, 1965), p. 90; Paul Kahle, *Der hebräische Bibeltext seit Franz Delitzsch, Franz Delitzsch-Vorlesungen 1958* (Stuttgart: Kohlhammer, 1961), pp. 11-16.

[27]To see developments in *The Oxford Hebrew Bible*, see <http://ohb.berkeley.edu/>.

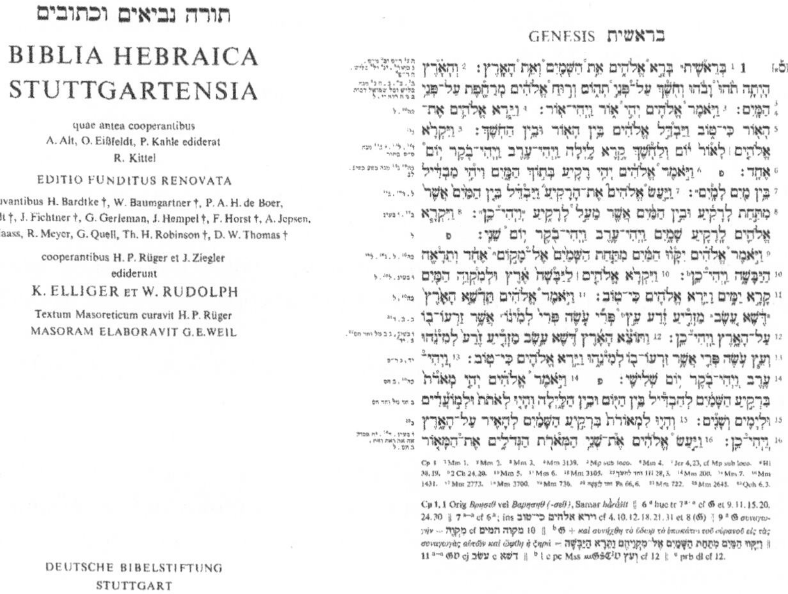

תורה נביאים וכתובים

BIBLIA HEBRAICA
STUTTGARTENSIA

quae antea cooperantibus
A. Alt, O. Eißfeldt, P. Kahle ediderat
R. Kittel

EDITIO FUNDITUS RENOVATA

adjuvantibus H. Bardtke †, W. Baumgartner †, P. A. H. de Boer,
O. Eißfeldt †, J. Fichtner †, G. Gerleman, J. Hempel †, F. Horst †, A. Jepsen,
F. Maass, R. Meyer, G. Quell, Th. H. Robinson †, D. W. Thomas †

cooperantibus H. P. Rüger et J. Ziegler
ediderunt

K. ELLIGER ET **W. RUDOLPH**

Textum Masoreticum curavit H. P. Rüger
MASORAM ELABORAVIT G. E. WEIL

GENESIS בראשית

DEUTSCHE BIBELSTIFTUNG
STUTTGART

Figure 4.9. *BHS* **title page and page of Genesis 1:1-16 [American Bible Society]**

apparatus was completely unreliable for scholarly purposes. Orlinsky also took the same stand in 1934, and has continued his criticism of this collection of material since that time. Ziegler and Katz have been equally forthright in their warnings as to the complete inadequacy of the Kittel apparatus.[28]

Christian D. Ginsburg prepared an edition of the MT for the British and Foreign Bible Society (1908 and following; new ed. 1920) that is essentially the text of Jacob ben Ḥayyim with a textual apparatus collating variant readings from more than seventy manuscripts and nineteen editions published before 1524, though most are from the thirteenth century or later. Würthwein critiques this work:

> Although this edition has a certain importance as a collection of Masoretic material, its value is lessened by the unevenness of the material, which was gathered almost haphazardly, and the absence of any attempt to weigh or group it. By far the majority of the variants are trivial, and do not affect the sense or the interpretation of the text. Variants in early versions are very rarely noticed.[29]

---

[28]Roland K. Harrison, *Introduction to the Old Testament* (Grand Rapids: Eerdmans, 1969), p. 251.
[29]Würthwein, *Text of the Old Testament*, pp. 41-42.

This work was followed by BHK^3, edited in 1929-1937 by Rudolf Kittel and Paul Kahle, and published in Stuttgart, Germany. It was a significant improvement using a new Hebrew base text and a new textual apparatus, but it still significantly depended on emendations. The Hebrew text was not that of the Second Rabbinic Bible as in earlier editions, but the Codex Leningradensis (Ms. B19[A]) dated A.D. 1008 from what appears to be the Ben Asher tradition. The editors had hoped to use the Aleppo Codex, but it was not available.[30]

Following this work, in 1958 Norman H. Snaith prepared for the British and Foreign Bible Society another edition based primarily on Ms. Or. 2626-2628 from the British Museum. This manuscript was copied in Lisbon in 1482 and also reflects the Ben Asher tradition.

The most recent complete critical edition of the MT is BHS (1967-1977), edited by Karl Elliger and Wilhelm Rudolph. Its base text is again the Codex Leningradensis (Ms. B19[A]); it contains a new presentation of the Masorah and a new apparatus incorporating evidence from the Dead Sea Scrolls. The textual apparatus no longer has separate apparatuses for minor and significant variants, and a considerable number of conjectures without textual support have been removed.

A new edition of the Biblia Hebraica (titled Biblia Hebraica Quinta) is in process, and one fascicle containing the Megilloth (e.g., Ruth, Song of Solomon, Ecclesiastes, Lamentations and Esther) has already appeared. It is a diplomatic edition of the Codex Leningradensis (Ms. B19[A]) largely because the Aleppo Codex is incomplete. The editors have chosen to make a diplomatic edition for the following reasons: (1) too little is known about the history of the development of the Hebrew Bible and the various textual traditions to construct an accurate eclectic text; (2) one would have to choose a particular point in the development of the Hebrew Bible's history to construct an eclectic text, and at present there is no consensus which would be the best point for the reconstruction; and (3) to be adequate an eclectic text would need to present all variants found in surviving witnesses, and the editors believed that would be beyond the limits of a one-volume Hebrew text.[31]

Another major critical edition of the Hebrew Bible is being produced that uses the Aleppo Codex (tenth century) as its base text and is called The Hebrew University Bible Project (described in detail on pp. 112-13). It contains four apparatuses with no conjectural readings or evaluations of the merits of the readings. So far only Jeremiah, Isaiah and Ezekiel have been published.

Another important project that has been in progress for over thirty years is

---

[30]Rudolf Kittel and Paul Kahle, BHK, p. xxix.
[31]Biblia Hebraica Quinta, ed. Adrian Schenker et al. (Stuttgart: Deutsche Bibelgesellschaft, 2004), pp. VIII-IX.

called the Hebrew Old Testament Text Project and is sponsored by the United Bible Societies (UBS). The goal of this project is to make a text-critical commentary on the Old Testament. An initial report was published in 1973-1980;[32] however, the committee is still in the process of making a much more detailed final report; three volumes have already appeared.[33] Wolters describes this work:

> These massive volumes are a monument to careful text-critical scholarship and embody a wealth of information about the history of the biblical text and its interpretation. Although the body of the work is devoted to assessing the divergences from the MT that have been accepted in the major contemporary Bible versions, there are also extensive essays by Barthélemy on the history of Old Testament textual criticism and on the whole range of witnesses to the Old Testament text. . . . The committee took as its goal the recovery of phase 2, essentially the proto-Masoretic text. . . . With impressive erudition, Barthélemy discusses hundreds of emendations to the MT that have been proposed and accepted in the modern commentaries and translations and finds most of them wanting. In volume 2, out of eight hundred emendations that were examined, only seventy-eight are found to be probable, and most of these do not materially affect the sense [see P. Dion, review of *Critique textuelle*, vol. 2, in *JBL* 107 (1988): 738]. In short, these volumes constitute a massive vindication of the traditional Hebrew text.[34]

4.11 Present State of Old Testament Textual Criticism

Most scholars today have abandoned any attempt to develop an eclectic Hebrew text (combining the best readings from each of the Hebrew manuscripts, similar to the United Bible Society's text of the New Testament). In the case of the Old Testament text, scholars have argued that the literary history is very complicated and far too little of it is known. Some scholars have suggested that different versions of part or all of some books may have coexisted or that there may have been different stages in the literary development of a book (e.g., Jeremiah and Ezekiel both have shorter and longer forms).[35] Tov states: "Large-scale differences between the textual witnesses show that a few books and parts of books were once circulated in different formulations representing dif-

---

[32]*Preliminary and Interim Report on the Hebrew Old Testament Text Project*, 5 vols. (New York: United Bible Societies, 1973-1980).

[33]Dominique Barthélemy, ed., *Critique textuelle de l'Ancien Testament*, vol. 1, *Josué, Juges, Ruth, Samuel, Rois, Chroniques, Esdras, Néhémie, Esther*; vol. 2, *Isaïe, Jérémie, Lamentations*; vol. 3, *Ezéchiel, Daniel et les Douze Prophètes*, OBO 50 (Fribourg: Editions universitaires; Göttingen: Vanderhoeck & Ruprecht, 1982, 1986, 1992).

[34]Wolters, "The Text of the Old Testament," p. 36.

[35]Tov, *Textual Criticism*, pp. 177-97; Bruce K. Waltke, "Old Testament Textual Criticism," in *Foundations for Biblical Interpretations*, ed. David S. Dockery, Kenneth A. Matthews and Robert Sloan (Nashville: Broadman, 1994), pp. 174-76.

ferent literary stages, as a rule one after the other, but possibly also parallel to each other."[36] The situation is complicated even further by the fact that we do not know when the development, modification and compilation of the books ceased.[37] In addition, for the vast majority of Old Testament books the oldest extant text was copied at least several hundred years after it was first written.

It is therefore considered preferable to choose a particular extant manuscript of the Old Testament (a *textus receptus*) and add a textual apparatus, noting where the text differs from other readings.[38] The assumption is that it is better to produce a known form of the Old Testament than to attempt a hypothetical eclectic text that may never have existed. Thus recent diplomatic editions of the Old Testament use the Codex Leningradensis (dated to A.D. 1008; *BHK, BHS*) or the Aleppo Codex (dated A.D. 930; The Hebrew University Bible Project) as the *textus receptus* and note variants in a critical apparatus.

Further Reading

Ginsburg, Christian D. *Introduction to the Massoretico-Critical Edition of the Hebrew Bible.* New York: KTAV, 1966.

———. *Historical Catalogue of the Printed Editions of Holy Scripture in the Library of the British and Foreign Bible Society.* 2 vols. London: Bible House, 1903.

Kahle, Paul. *The Cairo Geniza.* 2nd ed. Oxford: Clarendon, 1959.

Klein, Ralph W. *Textual Criticism of the Old Testament: The Septuagint after Qumran.* GBS:OTS. Philadelphia: Fortress, 1974.

McCarter, P. Kyle. *Textual Criticism: Recovering the Text of the Hebrew Bible.* GBS:OTS. Philadelphia: Fortress, 1986.

Roberts, Bleddyn J. *The Old Testament Text and Versions.* Cardiff: University of Wales Press, 1951.

———. "The Textual Transmission of the Old Testament." In *Tradition and Interpretation,* edited by George W. Anderson. Oxford: Clarendon, 1979. See pp. 1-30.

Sarna, Nahum H. "Bible Texts." *EJ* 4:831-35.

Talmon, Shemaryahu. "The Old Testament Text." In *CHB* 1.159-99. Reprinted in *QHBT,* pp. 1-41.

———. "Synonymous Readings in the Textual Traditions of the Old Testament." *ScrHier* 8 (1961): 335-83.

Thompson, John A. "Textual Criticism, OT." *IDBSup.,* pp. 886-91.

Tov, Emanuel. *Textual Criticism of the Hebrew Bible.* Minneapolis: Fortress Press, 1992.

---

[36]Tov, *Textual Criticism,* p. 177.
[37]Carl E. Armerding, *The Old Testament and Criticism* (Grand Rapids: Eerdmans, 1983), p. 99.
[38]Emanuel Tov, "The Text of the Old Testament," in *Bible Handbook,* vol. 1, *The World of the Bible,* ed. Adam S. van der Woude, trans. Sierd Woudstra (Grand Rapids: Eerdmans, 1986), p. 156.

————. "The Text of the Old Testament." In *Bible Handbook*. Vol. 1, *The World of the Bible*, pp. 156-90, edited by Adam S. van der Woude. Translated by Sierd Woudstra. Grand Rapids: Eerdmans, 1986.

Waltke, Bruce K. "The Textual Criticism of the Old Testament." In *Biblical Criticism: Historical, Literary, and Textual*, pp. 47-65, edited by Roland K. Harrison et al. Grand Rapids: Zondervan, 1978. Reprinted in *Expositor's Bible Commentary*, 1:211-28, edited by Frank E. Gaebelein. Grand Rapids: Zondervan, 1979.

Würthwein, Ernst. *The Text of the Old Testament: An Introduction to the Biblia Hebraica*, pp. 1-104, translated by Erroll F. Rhodes. 2nd ed. Grand Rapids: Eerdmans, 1995.

Yeivin, Israel. *Introduction to the Tiberian Masorah*. SBLMS 5. Missoula, Mont.: Scholars Press, 1980.

Excursus 1: *Modern Diplomatic Editions of the Hebrew Bible*

The present Hebrew Bible is called the Masoretic Text (MT) because it was pre-served by the Masoretes (possibly from מָסַר, *māsar*, "to hand down") from about A.D. 500 to 1100. The Masoretes were a group of scribes who copied and maintained the traditions of the Hebrew text that had been passed down to them. Technically the MT is a group of closely related manuscripts whose name derives from the apparatus called the Masorah attached to it. Tov says: "This apparatus, which was added to the consonantal base, developed from earlier traditions in the seventh to the eleventh centuries—the main developments occurring in the beginning of the tenth century with the activity of the Ben Asher family in Tiberias."[1] The MT includes the consonantal text, scribal nota-tions (e.g., vowel points, accents) and the Masorah. Modern editions of the MT (e.g., *BHS, BHQ* and the Hebrew University Bible Project) also include textual apparatuses that note different readings between the manuscript used for the MT and the other traditions, texts and versions. Each of these will be discussed in more detail below.

The present Hebrew text of the Old Testament is based on the Masorah, the purpose of which is to ensure the accuracy of the transmission of the text.[2] Rabbi Akiba described "tradition" (מָסוֹרֶת, *massôret*) as "a fence about the Law."[3] The Masoretic material was translated orally at first, but as it continued to grow it was increasingly recorded along with the text. The sacredness of the biblical text and the importance of following the laws in order to be approved by Yahweh required that the text be preserved accurately. Since so much rested on the accuracy of their Scriptures and the ability to transfer these laws to later generations, it is easy to see why the Masoretes took such care in establishing rules for its transmission. That biblical manuscripts have been copied for thou-sands of years with only minor variations suggests that the Masorah was quite successful in preserving the text.

---

[1] Emanuel Tov, *Textual Criticism of the Hebrew Bible*, 2nd ed. (Minneapolis: Fortress, 2001), p. 22.
[2] See Gérard E. Weil, "La nouvelle édition de la Massora (BHK) et l'histoire de la Massorah," in *Congress Volume: Bonn 1966*, VTSup 9 (Leiden: Brill, 1963), pp. 266-84.
[3] See *m. 'Abot* 3:14. Rabbi Akiba predated the Masorah by five centuries and thus used the word in the sense of "tradition," not in its later technical sense. Also there is some question whether Rabbi Akiba was referring to the oral Law or to the written Law, but the saying still indicates the rabbinic view of the importance of the tradition.

GENESIS בראשית

Masorah Parva
This part of the masorah often notes orthographic peculiarities and was intended to help scribes ensure textual accuracy. Most note how many times a particular form occurs, or when there is a kethib/qere reading.
How to use it: First, locate the circulus found over or between words in the text and follow it over to the side margin where the notation appears about that word or phrase (if between words).

Masorah Magna
This part of the masorah is used in conjunction with the Masorah parva and generally provides lists of where the particular forms mentioned in the Masorah parva are found.
How to use it: Match the numbers of each note to the small numbers on the side.

[ᴳ] 1 ¹ בְּרֵאשִׁ֖ית בָּרָ֣א אֱלֹהִ֑ים אֵ֥ת הַשָּׁמַ֖יִם וְאֵ֥ת הָאָֽרֶץ׃ ² וְהָאָ֗רֶץ
הָיְתָ֥ה תֹ֙הוּ֙ וָבֹ֔הוּ וְחֹ֖שֶׁךְ עַל־פְּנֵ֣י תְה֑וֹם וְר֣וּחַ אֱלֹהִ֔ים מְרַחֶ֖פֶת עַל־פְּנֵ֥י
הַמָּֽיִם׃ ³ וַיֹּ֥אמֶר אֱלֹהִ֖ים יְהִ֣י א֑וֹר וַֽיְהִי־אֽוֹר׃ ⁴ וַיַּ֧רְא אֱלֹהִ֛ים אֶת־
הָא֖וֹר כִּי־ט֑וֹב וַיַּבְדֵּ֣ל אֱלֹהִ֔ים בֵּ֥ין הָא֖וֹר וּבֵ֥ין הַחֹֽשֶׁךְ׃ ⁵ וַיִּקְרָ֨א
אֱלֹהִ֤ים ׀ לָאוֹר֙ י֔וֹם וְלַחֹ֖שֶׁךְ קָ֣רָא לָ֑יְלָה וַֽיְהִי־עֶ֥רֶב וַֽיְהִי־בֹ֖קֶר י֥וֹם
אֶחָֽד׃ פ ⁶ וַיֹּ֣אמֶר אֱלֹהִ֔ים יְהִ֥י רָקִ֖יעַ בְּת֣וֹךְ הַמָּ֑יִם וִיהִ֣י מַבְדִּ֔יל
בֵּ֥ין מַ֖יִם לָמָֽיִם׃ ⁷ וַיַּ֣עַשׂ אֱלֹהִים֮ אֶת־הָרָקִיעַ֒ וַיַּבְדֵּ֗ל בֵּ֤ין הַמַּ֙יִם֙ אֲשֶׁר֙
מִתַּ֣חַת לָרָקִ֔יעַ וּבֵ֣ין הַמַּ֔יִם אֲשֶׁ֖ר מֵעַ֣ל לָרָקִ֑יעַ וַֽיְהִי־כֵֽן׃ ⁸ וַיִּקְרָ֧א
אֱלֹהִ֛ים לָֽרָקִ֖יעַ שָׁמָ֑יִם וַֽיְהִי־עֶ֥רֶב וַֽיְהִי־בֹ֖קֶר י֥וֹם שֵׁנִֽי׃ פ
⁹ וַיֹּ֣אמֶר אֱלֹהִ֗ים יִקָּו֨וּ הַמַּ֜יִם מִתַּ֤חַת הַשָּׁמַ֙יִם֙ אֶל־מָק֣וֹם אֶחָ֔ד וְתֵרָאֶ֖ה
הַיַּבָּשָׁ֑ה וַֽיְהִי־כֵֽן׃ ¹⁰ וַיִּקְרָ֨א אֱלֹהִ֤ים ׀ לַיַּבָּשָׁה֙ אֶ֔רֶץ וּלְמִקְוֵ֥ה הַמַּ֖יִם
קָרָ֣א יַמִּ֑ים וַיַּ֥רְא אֱלֹהִ֖ים כִּי־טֽוֹב׃ ¹¹ וַיֹּ֣אמֶר אֱלֹהִ֗ים תַּֽדְשֵׁ֤א הָאָ֙רֶץ֙
דֶּ֚שֶׁא עֵ֣שֶׂב מַזְרִ֣יעַ זֶ֔רַע עֵ֣ץ פְּרִ֞י עֹ֤שֶׂה פְּרִי֙ לְמִינ֔וֹ אֲשֶׁ֥ר זַרְעוֹ־ב֖וֹ
עַל־הָאָ֑רֶץ וַֽיְהִי־כֵֽן׃ ¹² וַתּוֹצֵ֨א הָאָ֜רֶץ דֶּ֠שֶׁא עֵ֣שֶׂב מַזְרִ֤יעַ זֶ֙רַע֙ לְמִינֵ֔הוּ
וְעֵ֧ץ עֹֽשֶׂה־פְּרִ֛י אֲשֶׁ֥ר זַרְעוֹ־ב֖וֹ לְמִינֵ֑הוּ וַיַּ֥רְא אֱלֹהִ֖ים כִּי־טֽוֹב׃ ¹³ וַֽיְהִי־
עֶ֥רֶב וַֽיְהִי־בֹ֖קֶר י֥וֹם שְׁלִישִֽׁי׃ פ ¹⁴ וַיֹּ֣אמֶר אֱלֹהִ֗ים יְהִ֤י מְאֹרֹת֙
בִּרְקִ֣יעַ הַשָּׁמַ֔יִם לְהַבְדִּ֕יל בֵּ֥ין הַיּ֖וֹם וּבֵ֣ין הַלָּ֑יְלָה וְהָי֤וּ לְאֹתֹת֙ וּלְמ֣וֹעֲדִ֔ים
וּלְיָמִ֖ים וְשָׁנִֽים׃ ¹⁵ וְהָי֤וּ לִמְאוֹרֹת֙ בִּרְקִ֣יעַ הַשָּׁמַ֔יִם לְהָאִ֖יר עַל־הָאָ֑רֶץ
וַֽיְהִי־כֵֽן׃ ¹⁶ וַיַּ֣עַשׂ אֱלֹהִ֔ים אֶת־שְׁנֵ֥י הַמְּאֹרֹ֖ת הַגְּדֹלִ֑ים אֶת־הַמָּא֣וֹר

Cp 1 ¹Mm 1. ²Mm 2. ³Mm 3. ⁴Mm 3139. ⁵Mp sub loco. ⁶Mm 4. ⁷Jer 4,23, cf Mp sub loco. ⁸Hi 38,19. ⁹⁻²Ch 24,20. ¹⁰Mm 5. ¹¹Mm 6. ¹²Mm 3105. ¹³לחשך Hi 28,3. ¹⁴Mm 200. ¹⁵Mm 7. ¹⁶Mm 1431. ¹⁷Mm 2773. ¹⁸Mm 3700. ¹⁹Mm 736. ²⁰לבקעה Ps 66,6. ²¹Mm 722. ²²Mm 2645. ²³Qoh 6,3.

Cp 1,1 Orig Βρησιθ vel Βαρησηθ (-σεθ), Samar *bārāšit* ‖ 6 ᵃ huc tr 7ᵃ⁻ᵃ cf ᴳ et 9.11.15.20. 24.30 ‖ 7 ᵃ⁻ᵃ cf 6 ᵃ; ins וירא אלהים כי־טוב cf 4.10.12.18.21.31 et 8 (ᴳ) ‖ 9 ᵃ ᴳ συναγω-γήν cf מקוה המים 10 ‖ ᵇ ᴳ ÷ καὶ συνήχθη τὸ ὕδωρ τὸ ὑποκάτω τοῦ οὐρανοῦ εἰς τὰς συναγωγὰς αὐτῶν καὶ ὤφθη ἡ ξηρά = וַיִּקָּוּוּ הַמַּיִם מִתַּחַת הַשָּׁמַיִם אֶל־מִקְוֵיהֶם וַתֵּרָא הַיַּבָּשָׁה ‖ 11 ᵃ⁻ᵃ ᴳᴹ cj עֵשֶׂב c דֶּשֶׁא ‖ ᵇ l c pc Mss ᴹᴳˢ²ᵀᵛ וְעֵץ cf 12 ‖ ᶜ prb dl cf 12.

Textual Notes: This part of the MT contains textual information from the editors of the *BHS* to help determine the most accurate reading of the text.

Figure E1.1. The Biblia Hebraica Stuttgartensia (1967-77, 1983). [American Bible Society]

Figure E1.2. Cover page from the Codex Leningradensis dated to c. A.D. 1008 (Fol. 474r) [National Library of Russia]

BHK, BHS and *BHQ* all contain the Masorah represented in the text of the Leningrad Public Library Ms. B 19^A (A.D. 1008), which is a complete Ben Asher manuscript.[4] Textual notes also appear at the bottom of the pages of the critical editions of the MT that compare it to other extant Hebrew manuscripts and versions. The Masorah and textual notes are written in Aramaic, not Hebrew, and are greatly abbreviated. Still, with proper guidance and careful explanation, the information of the Masorah can greatly add to one's knowledge of the MT. The Western Masoretes divided the Masorah into two main parts: the marginal Masorah and the final Masorah.

1 Marginal Masorah (Masora marginalis)

Written within the margins of the text, the marginal Masorah records details on how words were to be written or read, or how often words or phrases occur. Over time these notations became so numerous that the Masoretes were obliged to record them in other Masoretic handbooks. The marginal Masorah

---

[4]This manuscript has now been published in a facsimile edition (*Biblia Hebraica Leningraden-sia*, ed. Aron Dotan [Peabody, Mass.: Hendrickson, 2000]).

furnishes a wealth of information comprising two parts: the masorah parva and masorah magna.

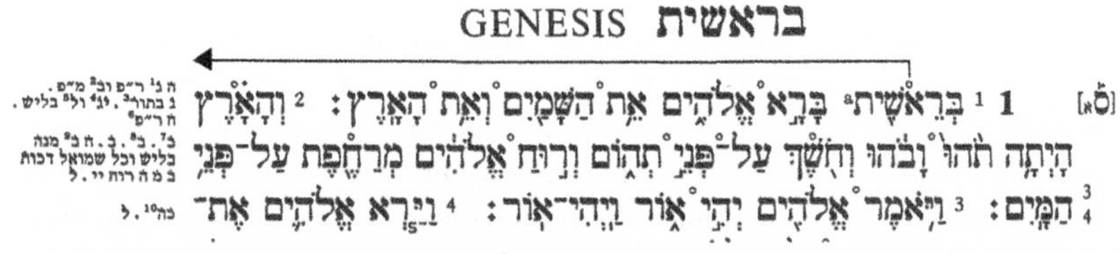

GENESIS בראשית

הָאָרֶץ וְאֵת הַשָּׁמַיִם אֵת אֱלֹהִים בָּרָא בְּרֵאשִׁית 1

Figure E1.3. *Masorah parva* (Genesis 1). The first circulus refers to the first reading in the margin with the notation that the word בְּרֵאשִׁית (*běrēšît*) occurs ה (5 times) in the Old Testament; ג (3 times) ר'' פ (at the head [beginning] of a verse) and ב (2 times) מ'' פ (in the middle of the verse). [American Bible Society]

1.1 Masorah parva (Mp)

The *masorah parva*[5] (sometimes called *masorah qĕtannâ*, "little Masorah") is written along the outer margin of the text. The *masorah parva* primarily concerns Hebrew orthography (the rules and conventions of spelling), including the number of occurrences of orthographic peculiarities, combinations of words, *qere* forms and some scribal corrections, variants among parallel passages and special details (e.g., a verse that contains all the letters of the Hebrew alphabet, the middle letter of a book, the shortest verse).[6] As Tov explains:

> Since the purpose of the Masorah was to ensure the precise transmission of the biblical text, it focused on the aspect most problematic for scribes, that is, orthography. The Masoretes and their followers described in various treatises the rules of the biblical orthography and they wrote marginal notes—in Aramaic—on the *exceptions* to these rules. Their main attention was directed toward the question of how many times a certain orthography occurred in a given biblical book or in the Bible as a whole.[7]

---

[5]See Israel Yeivin, *Introduction to the Tiberian Masorah*, ed. and trans. Ernest J. Revell, SBLMS 5 (Chico, Calif.: Scholars Press, 1980), pp. 64-74.

[6]The standard for determining which words should appear in the *Masorah parva* is delineated in the following Masoretic handbook: Elias Levita, *Massoreth ha-Massoreth* (Venice, 1538), reprinted as *Massoreth ha-Massoreth*, ed. Christian D. Ginsburg (London: Longmans, Green, Reader & Dyer, 1867), which was reprinted as *Massoreth ha-Massoreth*, ed. Christian D. Ginsburg (New York: KTAV, 1968). An example of a rule in this work states: "There is no noun to be found in the whole Bible, with *Cholem* as the last vowel, which is not written *plene*, with the *mater lectionis Vav*, except in a few instances which deviate from this rule, as I shall explain in the following section" (pp. 146-47). This means that the word אֵפוֹד (*ʾēpôd, plene* spelling) would not be written as אֵפֹד without being noted in the *masorah parva*.

[7]Tov, *Textual Criticism*, p. 73.

The number of occurrences refers to the exact form of a particular word or phrase (i.e., with particular vowel points or accents). The value of the *masorah parva* to textual criticism is that it is much more specific than a concordance, but Tov cautions that it may not always be correct:

> In the use of the *Massora parva* it is well to bear in mind that the notes are often neither consistent nor accurate. One reason for this is that the *Massora parva* was initially transmitted with its companion manuscript but later also separately or even copied in other manuscripts. Thus not one but several Massora texts were in circulation. The invention of the art of printing increased the confusion because the Second Rabbinic Bible, which would later become the *textus receptus*, contained an eclectic *Massora parva*, composed by Ben Hayyim from various sources.[8]

1.2 Masorah magna. The *masorah magna* is actually a book of lists indicating where specific forms occur that are cited in the *masorah parva*.

GENESIS בראשית

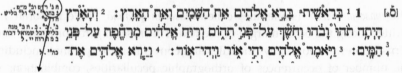

Cp 1   ¹Mm 1.   ²Mm 2.   ³Mm 3.   ⁴Mm 3139.   ⁵Mp sub loco.   ⁶Mm 4.   ⁷Jer 4,23, cf Mp sub loco.   ⁸Hi 38,19.   ⁹2 Ch 24,20.   ¹⁰Mm 5.   ¹¹Mm 6.   ¹²Mm 3105.   ¹³וחד לחשך Hi 28,3.   ¹⁴Mm 200.   ¹⁵Mm 7.   ¹⁶Mm 1431.   ¹⁷Mm 2773.   ¹⁸Mm 3700.   ¹⁹Mm 736.   ²⁰וחד לַיָּצָא Ps 66,6.   ²¹Mm 722.   ²²Mm 2645.   ²³Qoh 6,3.

Figure E1.4. *Masorah magna* (Genesis 1). The small numbers in the *masorah parva* (side of the page) correspond to the same numbers in the *masorah magna* (bottom of the page). The first superscript number 1 in the *masorah parva* corresponds to the superscript number 1 in the *masorah magna* and states that it is the first list in the *masorah magna*. If we went to that list it would include the three places that the word בְּרֵאשִׁית (*běrē'šît*) occurs at the beginning of the verse. The second superscript number indicates the second list in the *masorah magna* recording the two places where בְּרֵאשִׁית (*běrē'šît*) occurs in the middle of the verse. On that same page superscript number 7 is interesting in that the *masorah parva* says that the phrase תֹהוּ וָבֹהוּ (*tōhû wābōhû*, "formless and void") occurs only here and in Jeremiah 4:23; then it says compare that place also (cf. Mp sub loco). [American Bible Society]

2 Final Masorah (*Masorah finalis*)

This Masorah, a compilation of lists too large for the *masorah parva* and the *masorah magna*, is collected in what are sometimes called Masoretic handbooks. One of these is an alphabetical list of words that occur only twice, one without the ו (*wāw*, meaning "and") and the other with it. This collection, called *Okhla weOkhla*

---

[8]Tov, *World of the Bible*, p. 161.

after its first entry (אָכְלָה, *'oklâ* [1 Sam 1:9] and וְאָכְלָה, *wĕ'oklâ* [Gen 27:19]), was published by Salomon Frensdorff and contains 374 separate lists.[9] Part of the final Masorah is commonly recorded at the end of the book divisions in the Leningrad Public Library Ms. B19[A] and thus is recorded in *BHS* (and also in *BHK*).[10] It indicates the care and precision of the Masoretes, who even counted the letters of the MT to ensure their works were accurate. For example, part of the information included at the end of the Pentateuch (i.e., after Deuteronomy) is:

סכום הפסוקים של ספר	(the total of the verses which are to the book)
תשע מאות	(900)
וחמשים וחמשה:	(55)
ה נ ץ	(955)
וחציו ועשית על־פי	(the middle of it [the book], namely, ועשית על פי is at Deuteronomy 17:10)
וסדרים לא	(the number of *sederim* [divisions] in Deuteronomy is 31)
סכום הפסוקים של תורה	(the total of the verses which are in the Torah [or Pentateuch])
חמשת אלפים	(5,000)
ושמונה מאות	(800)
וארבעים	(40)
וחמשה:	(5)
הקּ מה	(5,845)
כל סדרי תורה	(all the *sederim* of the Torah)
מאה וששים ושבעה:	(167)
קסז	(167)
סכום התיבות של תורה	(the total number of words in the Torah)
תשעה ושבעים אלף	(79,000)
ושמונה מאות	(800)
וחמשים	(50)
וששה	(6)
סכום אותיות של תורה ארבע מאות אלף	(the total number of letters which are in the Torah are 400,000)
ותשע מאות וארבעים וחמשה	(945)

---

[9]The *Okhla weOkhla* was first published in Hanover by Hahn'sche hofbuchhandlung in 1864. It was reprinted in Tel Aviv by Sion in 1968.

[10]These notes are found after Genesis, Exodus, Leviticus, Numbers, Deuteronomy, Joshua, Judges, 2 Samuel, 2 Kings, Isaiah, Jeremiah, Ezekiel, Hosea, Joel, Amos, Obadiah, Jonah, Micah, Nahum, Habakkuk, Zephaniah, Haggai, Zechariah, Malachi (includes cumulative information about the twelve prophets), Job, Psalms, Proverbs, Ruth, Song of Songs, Ecclesiastes, Lamentations, Esther, Daniel, Nehemiah (cumulative information for both Ezra and Nehemiah) and 2 Chronicles.

3 Description of the Textual Apparatus

Copies of the MT known as diplomatic editions contain a copy of one tradition of the MT along with a textual apparatus that compares it to other forms of the MT as well as other texts and versions. To date, there are two major diplomatic editions: the Hebrew University Bible Project and *Biblia Hebraica Stuttgartensia* (*BHS*). Both provide insights into the Hebrew text, but for our purposes the best tool is *BHS* since it contains the whole MT. A description of each edition follows.

3.1 The Hebrew University Bible Project

The basic text for this work is the Aleppo Codex, which comes from the Ben Asher tradition and is dated to the first part of the tenth century. At present only three biblical books have appeared: Moshe H. Goshen-Gottstein, ed., *The Hebrew University Bible: The Book of Isaiah*, 2 vols. (Jerusalem: Magnes, 1975, 1981); Chayim Rabin et al., eds., *The Hebrew University Bible: The Book of Jeremiah* (Jerusalem: Magnes, 1997); and Moshe H. Goshen-Gottstein and Shemaryahu Talmon, eds., *The Hebrew University Bible: The Book of Ezekiel* (Jerusalem: Magnes, 2004). This work has four separate apparatuses that divide the textual evidence according to the nature of the witnesses. The first apparatus compiles evidence from the ancient versions, including the Arabic translation of Saadia Gaon, LXX, Vulgate, Peshitta, Targum Jonathan and MT. The second apparatus contains Hebrew texts from the Second Temple period (516 B.C.-A.D. 70), namely, rabbinic literature and texts from the Judean Desert. The third apparatus includes textual witnesses from medieval codices (none dating earlier than A.D. 800) that highlight consonantal differences. The fourth apparatus collates evidence from the medieval codices concerning differences in vocalization and accents. The textual notes have the following characteristics:

- They do not contain emendations.

- The editors do not take any position as to the comparative value of the various readings.

- The readings are sometimes designated by various grammatical categories, such as *num* (= *numerus*), meaning "number" when the witnesses interchange singular and plural forms.[11]

---

[11]Tov, *Textual Criticism*, p. 378.

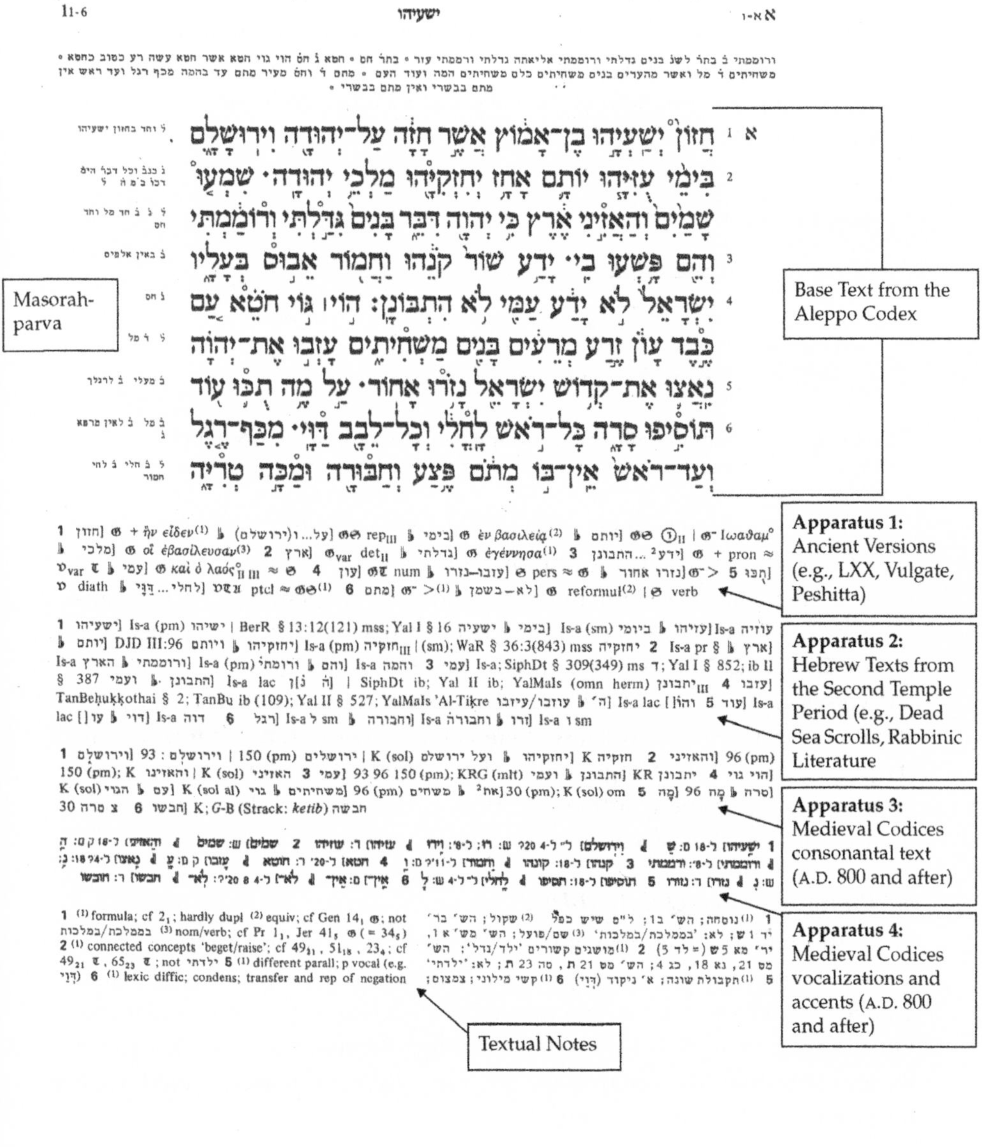

11-6   ישעיהו   א ו-א

ורומפמתי בֿ בתֿ לשֿג בנים גדלתי ורומפמתי אליאתה נדלתי ורומפמתי עזר • בתֿ חם • חמא גֿ חםֿ הוי גוי חטא אשר חטא עשה רע כסוב כחםא •
משחיתים רֿ סל ואשר מתעריםבנים משחיתים כלם משחיתים המה וצדר העם • מהם וֿ וחםֿ מעיר מתם עד בהמה מכף רגל ועד ראש אין
מתם בבשרי ואין מתם בבשרי • ·

	א 1 חֲזוֹן יְשַׁעְיָהוּ בֶן־אָמוֹץ אֲשֶׁר חָזָה עַל־יְהוּדָה וִירוּשָׁלָ‍ם
Masorah-parva	2 בִּימֵי עֻזִּיָּהוּ יוֹתָם אָחָז יְחִזְקִיָּהוּ מַלְכֵי יְהוּדָה שִׁמְעוּ
	שָׁמַיִם וְהַאֲזִינִי אֶרֶץ כִּי יְהוָה דִּבֵּר בָּנִים גִּדַּלְתִּי וְרוֹמַמְתִּי
	3 וְהֵם פָּשְׁעוּ בִי יָדַע שׁוֹר קֹנֵהוּ וַחֲמוֹר אֵבוּס בְּעָלָיו
	4 יִשְׂרָאֵל לֹא יָדַע עַמִּי לֹא הִתְבּוֹנָן הוֹי גּוֹי חֹטֵא עַם
	כֶּבֶד עָוֹן זֶרַע מְרֵעִים בָּנִים מַשְׁחִיתִים עָזְבוּ אֶת־יְהוָה
	5 נִאֲצוּ אֶת־קְדוֹשׁ יִשְׂרָאֵל נָזֹרוּ אָחוֹר עַל מֶה תֻכּוּ עוֹד
	6 תּוֹסִיפוּ סָרָה כָּל־רֹאשׁ לָחֳלִי וְכָל־לֵבָב דַּוָּי מִכַּף־רֶגֶל
	וְעַד־רֹאשׁ אֵין־בּוֹ מְתֹם פֶּצַע וְחַבּוּרָה וּמַכָּה טְרִיָּה

Base Text from the Aleppo Codex (label at right)

Apparatus 1: Ancient Versions (e.g., LXX, Vulgate, Peshitta)

Apparatus 2: Hebrew Texts from the Second Temple Period (e.g., Dead Sea Scrolls, Rabbinic Literature)

Apparatus 3: Medieval Codices consonantal text (A.D. 800 and after)

Apparatus 4: Medieval Codices vocalizations and accents (A.D. 800 and after)

Textual Notes

(Apparatus 1)
1 חזון] 𝔊 + τοῦ εἰδεῖν(1) ‖ [על...ו(ירושלם)] 𝔊 rep‖ [בימי 𝔊‖ ἐν βασιλεία(2) ‖ [יותם 𝔊‖ ⓵II ‖ Ἰωαθαμ‖ [מלכי] 𝔊‖ οἱ ἐβασίλευσαν(3) 2 [ארץ] var det‖ [גדלתי] 𝔊 ἐγέννησα(1) ‖ [ירד...התבונן] 𝔊 + pron ‖ [עמי 𝔊‖ καὶ ὁ λαός‖III ‖ 4 [עון] num ‖ [עזבו-נזרו] 𝔊 pers ‖ 𝔊‖ 5 < [חפו ‖ [נזרו אחור] 𝔊‖ 6 [מתם] 𝔊 ptcl ‖ 𝔊(1) ‖ [לא-בשמן] 𝔊 reformul(2) ‖ verb‖ [לחלי...דני] 𝔊‖ עצמ‖ diath

(Apparatus 2)
1 ישעיהו] Is-a (pm) | עוזיהו Is-a | BerR § 13:12(121) mss; Yal I § 16 | ישעיה Is-a (sm) | בימי Is-a‖ [ביומ‖ | בימו‖] Is-a (pm) | יותם DJD III:96 | ויתם Is-a pr § | WaR § 36:3(843) mss | יחזקיה‖III | [יחזקיהו Is-a (sm) | 2 [הארץ Is-a (pm) | וירומפמתי] Is-a (pm) | [והם Is-a | והם 3 [עמי Is-a; SiphDt § 309(349) ms | Yal I § 852; ib I‖ | יתבונן‖III 4 [עזבו § 387 | [התבונן] Is-a lac II | SiphDt ib; Yal II ib; YalMals (omn herm) TanBeḥukkothai § 2; TanBu ib (109); Yal II § 527; YalMals 'Al-Tiḳre | [עוד Is-a | והול 5 [ועור Is-a lac | דוה‖ | דוי Is-a sm 6 [רגל] Is-a sm | וחברה וחבורה] Is-a | [זרו Is-a sm

(Apparatus 3)
1 וירושלם] 93 : וירושלים | ועל ירושלם K | חזקיה K | חזקיהו 2 [והאזיני 96 (pm) | 150 (pm) | ירושלים K (sol) | 150 (pm); K (sol) והאזיני | K | האזיני 3 [עמי 93 96 150 (pm); KRG (mlt) ועמי | [התבונן KR יתבונן | [הוי גוי 96 (pm) | K‖ סרה ‖ K (sol) הבי | גוי K (sol al) | [אחֿ 30 (pm); K (sol) om 5 [פה 96 (pm) | משחים‖ | [סרה K; G-B (Strack: *ketib* חבשו) | חברה 6 [חבשו K; 30 סרה ‖

(Apparatus 4)
1 (1) formula; cf 2₁; hardly dupl (2) equiv; cf Gen 14₁ ‖ not ‖ (1)נוסח‖; הש׳ בר׳‖ (2) שקול ‖ (3)‖ nom/verb; cf Pr 1₁, Jer 41₈ (𝔊 = 34₈) ‖ 'בכפלכום/בכפלכות‖ (3) שם/פועל‖ (4) פש א ל‖ 2 (1) connected concepts 'beget/raise'; cf 49₂₁, 51₁₈, 23₄; cf 49₂₁, 65₂₃ ‖ not ‖ ילדהו 5 (1) different parall; p vocal (e.g. דְוָי ‖ 6 (1) lexic diffic; condens; transfer and rep of negation ‖

Figure E1.5. The Hebrew University Bible Project [Brill Academic Publishers]

3.2 Biblia Hebraica Stuttgartensia (BHS)

This work is based on the Masoretic tradition found in Codex Leningradensis B19[A] (even in places where the text is known to be wrong, for example, Gen 4:18; Is 2:15; Jon 3:6) and includes the *masorah parva* and the *masorah magna*.[12] The Codex Leningradensis B19[A] is a complete manuscript from the Ben Asher tradition dated to A.D. 1008 (see p. 97). The editors of *BHS* have compiled a textual apparatus at the bottom of the page that includes both the variant readings as well as their evaluations.

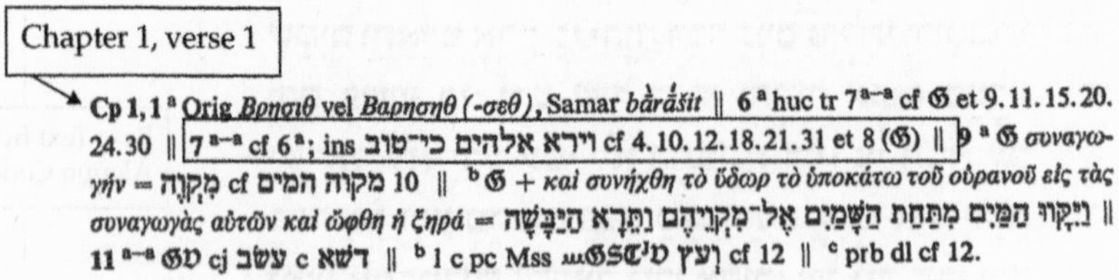

Chapter 1, verse 1

➤ Cp 1,1 ᵃ Orig *Βρησιθ* vel *Βαρησηθ (-σεθ)*, Samar *bårášit* ‖ 6 ᵃ huc tr 7ᵃ⁻ᵃ cf 𝔊 et 9.11.15.20. 24.30 ‖ 7 ᵃ⁻ᵃ cf 6ᵃ; ins וירא אלהים כי־טוב cf 4.10.12.18.21.31 et 8 (𝔊) ‖ 9 ᵃ 𝔊 συναγω- γήν = מִקְוֵה cf מקוה המים 10 ‖ ᵇ 𝔊 + καὶ συνήχθη τὸ ὕδωρ τὸ ὑποκάτω τοῦ οὐρανοῦ εἰς τὰς συναγωγὰς αὐτῶν καὶ ὤφθη ἡ ξηρά = וַיִּקָּוּ הַמַּיִם מִתַּחַת הַשָּׁמַיִם אֶל־מְקְוֵיהֶם וַתֵּרָא הַיַּבָּשָׁה ‖ 11 ᵃ⁻ᵃ 𝔊𝔙 cj c עשׂב dשׂא ‖ ᵇ l c pc Mss 𝔪𝔊𝔖𝔙 וְעֵץ cf 12 ‖ ᶜ prb dl cf 12.

Figure E1.6. *Biblia Hebraica Stuttgartensia* apparatus [American Bible Society]

In figure E1.6 the phrase from Genesis 1:7 indicated by "7a-a" means that the editors are identifying the phrase found in verse seven from letter "a" to letter "a" (equaling the entire phrase) in order to comment on it. "Cf" means compare verse 6a. The editors of the *BHS* then suggest adding ("ins") the phrase וירא אלהים כי־טוב ("and God saw that it was good"), as found in (cf) verses 4, 10, 12, 18, 21, 31 and in verse 8 of the LXX (𝔊). The text critic should use caution here because there is no evidence from Hebrew manuscripts to suggest this change, and the Septuagint is known for harmonizing texts (or changing the wording of certain verses to make them correspond more closely to other texts).

3.3 Biblia Hebraica Quinta (BHQ)

The forthcoming fifth edition of the *Biblia Hebraica* will have significant similarities to the earlier editions (e.g., it is a diplomatic edition with Codex Leningradensis as a base text, the structure and style is largely the same, and it provides the editors' decisions on certain readings). Because much has changed in the area of textual criticism over the last thirty years, the masorah and textual notes will have to be entirely reworked.

---

[12]*Biblia Hebraica Stuttgartensia*, ed. Karl Elliger and Wilhelm Rudolph (Stuttgart: Deutsche Bibelgesellschaft, 1977).

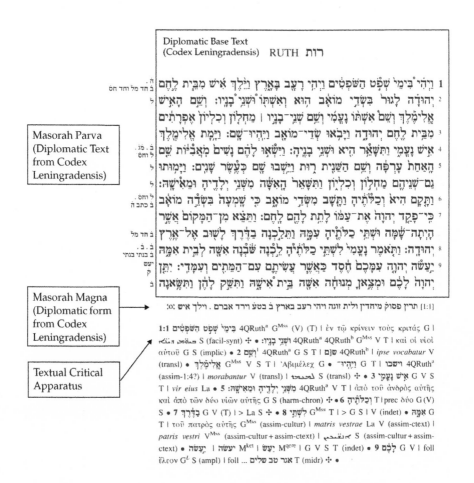

Masorah Parva
(Diplomatic Text
from Codex
Leningradensis)

Masorah Magna
(Diplomatic form
from Codex
Leningradensis)

Textual Critical
Apparatus

Figure E1.7. *Biblia Hebraica Quinta*, Ruth 1:1-9. The textual apparatus on Ruth 1:1, first contains the lemma from the base text (M^L; בִּימֵי שְׁפֹט הַשֹּׁפְטִים); then the witnesses that agree with this reading (4QRuth^a [one of the mss of Ruth from Qumran], G^Mss [reading of more than one manuscript of the Old Greek], V [Latin Vulgate], T [Targum] I [separator line]); then appears the first reading that differs from the base text (ἐν τῷ κρίνειν τοὺς κριτάς G [sigla of witnesses attesting this reading] I [separator line]); another reading appears next that differs from the base text [Syriac text] S [Syriac]; next appear the notations "facil-synt" (facilitation of the syntax, "simplifying the syntax") and "+" (symbol indicating that the commentary section has a discussion of this variant) and finally "•" (marks the end of the discussion of the variant). [German Bible Society]

Table E1.1. Major Abbreviations for the *BHS* and *BHQ*

BHS	Manuscript	BHQ
𝕸	Samaritan Pentateuch	Smr
𝕸ᵀ	Samaritan Pentateuch Targum	Smrᵀ
α′	Aquila	α′
ε′	Origen's Quinta Text	ε′
θ′	Theodotion	θ′
ο εβρ′	Origen's Hebrew Text	εβρ′
σ′	Symmachus	σ′
𝖆	Arabic Version	
𝖆	Ethiopic Version	
Arm	Armenian Version	
Bo	Bohairic Version	Bo
Ed(d)	Kennicott, de Rossi and Ginsburg (compilation of Hebrew variants)	
Eus	Eusebius of Caesarea	
𝕲	Septuagint	G
𝕲*	Septuagint original handwriting	G*
𝕲ᴬ	Codex Alexandrinus (LXX)	
𝕲ᴮ	Codex Vaticanus (LXX)	
Hier	Hieronymus (Jerome)	Hie
𝖃	Coptic version	
𝕷	Latin version	La
L	Codex Leningradensis	Mᴸ
𝔐	Masoretic Text	M
Orig	Origen	
𝕼	Qumran	
𝖘	Syriac version	S
Sa	Sahidic version	Sa
𝕿	Targum	T
Ter	Tertullian	
𝖛	Vulgate (Latin)	V
Vrs	Multiple versions	Vᴹˢˢ

BHS	Meaning	BHQ
	abbreviation	abbr
acc	accent	
add	addition	+
akk	Akkadian	
al	others	
alit	otherwise	
	amplification	ampl
	Aramaic	aram
	assimilation	assim
c	with	
cet	the rest, others	
cf	*confer,* compare	cf
cj	connect, conjunction	cj
cod(d)	codex(es)	
	commentary	comm
	conflation	confl
	conjecture	conjec
cp	chapter	cp
crrp	corruption	crrp
dl	delete	
dttg	dittography	ditt
dub	doubtful	
	emendation by scribe	em scr
	error	err

Table 4.1. *continued*

etc	*et cetera*	
exc	they have dropped out	
excr	extraordinary	
	facilitation (simplification)	facil
fin	finish	
	fragmentary	frag
frt	perhaps	
gl	gloss	
hpgr	haplography	hapl
	harmonization	harm
hpleg	*hapax legomenon* (occurs only once)	
	homoioarcton (homoioarkton)	homarc
	homoioteleuton	homtel
id	------ (the same)	
	illegible	illeg
	making implicit	implic
inc	uncertain	
	insert	
	insufficient data for conclusion	insuf
	interpretation	interp
	interpolation	interpol
invers	reverse order	
item	otherwise	
K	kethib	ket
l	read	
	lacuna (hole in manuscript)	lacun
leg	to read	
marg	marginal, in the margin	
m cs	because of meter	
	metathesis	metath
Ms(s)	Hebrew manuscripts	ms(s)
pc Mss	a few Hebrew manuscripts (3-10)	
nonn Mss	some Hebrew manuscripts (11-20)	
mlt Mss	many Hebrew manuscripts (20+)	
om	omit	om
p	part	
par	parallel	par
plur	plural	pl
prb	probably	
prp	propose	
Q	qere	qere
	restoration	rest
	stylistic	styl
	substitution	substi
Tiq soph	correction by the scribes	tiq soph
Tr	transpose	transp
Var	various	
	verse(s)	v(v)
	version(s)	vrs(s)
	end of case in apparatus	•
	end of case but with same lemma	○
+	add	+
>	greater than	>
<	less than	
| |	separates readings	| |
( )	lacuna	( )
*	original handwriting	*
	further discussion in commentary	+

Further Reading

Editions of the Masorah

The Second Rabbinic Bible.

Frensdorff, Salomon, ed. *Okla weOkhla*. Hanover: Hahn'sche hofbuchhandlung. 1864. Reprint, Tel Aviv: Sion, 1968.

————. *The Massorah Magna*. Part 1, *Massoretic Dictionary or the Massorah in Alphabetic Order*. Hanover: Hahn'sche hofbuchhandlung. 1876. Reprint, New York: KTAV, 1968.

Ginsburg, Christian D. *The Massorah Compiled from Manuscripts*. 4 vols. London and Vienna: Georges Brög, 1880-1905.

Weil, Gérard E., ed. *Massorah Gedolah iuxta codicem Leningradensem B 19a*. Vol. 1, *Catalogi*. Rome: Pontifical Biblical Institute, 1971. (A diplomatic edition of the Leningradensis B19^A manuscript and the best resource available today.)

See also the actual texts: Aleppo Codex, *BHK, BHS* and *BHQ*.

Other Works

Albright, William F. "New Light on Early Recensions of the Hebrew Bible." *BASOR* 140 (1955): 27-33. Reprinted in *QHBT*. See pp. 140-46.

Barr, James. "A New Look at Kethibh-Qere." *OTS* 21 (1981): 19-37.

Blau, Ludwig. "The Extraordinary Points in the Pentateuch." *JQR* 19 (1907): 411-19.

Brotzman, Ellis R. *Old Testament Textual Criticism: A Practical Introduction*. Grand Rapids: Baker, 1994. See esp. pp. 97-106.

Cross, Frank M. "The Contributions of the Qumran Discoveries to the Study of the Biblical Text." *IEJ* 16 (1966): 81-95. Reprinted in *QHBT*. See pp. 278-92.

————. "The Evolution of a Theory of Local Texts." In *QHBT*. See pp. 306-20.

Dotan, Aron. "Massorah." *EJ* 16:1401-82.

Freedman, David N. "The Massoretic Text and the Qumran Scrolls: A Study in Orthography." *Textus* 2 (1962): 87-102. Reprinted in *QHBT*. See pp. 196-211.

Ginsburg, Christian D. *Introduction to the Massoretico-Critical Edition of the Hebrew Bible*. Repr. New York: KTAV, 1966. See pp. 9-107, 183-96, 308-67.

————. *The Massoreth Ha-Massoreth of Elias Levita*. 2nd ed. New York: KTAV, 1968.

Greenberg, Moshe. "The Stabilization of the Text of the Hebrew Bible in Light of the Biblical Materials from Qumran." *JAOS* 76 (1956): 157-67. Reprinted in *CMHB*. See pp. 298-326.

Rüger, Hans P. *An English Key to the Latin Words and Abbreviations and the Symbols of Biblia Hebraica Stuttgartensia*. Stuttgartensia: German Bible Society, 1985. In Scott, William R. *A Simplified Guide to the BHS*. Berkeley, Calif.: BIBAL, 1987.

Scott, William R. *A Simplified Guide to BHS.* Berkeley: BIBAL, 1987.

Skehan, Patrick W. "The Biblical Scrolls from Qumran and the Text of the Old Testament." *BA* 28 (1965): 87-100. Reprinted in *QHBT.* See pp. 264-77.

Sperber, Alexander. "Problems of the Masora." *HUCA* 17 (1942-43): 293-394.

Talmon, Shemaryahu. "Aspects of the Textual Transmission of the Bible in the Light of the Qumran Manuscripts." *Textus* 4 (1964): 95-132. Reprinted in *QHBT.* See pp. 226-63.

―――. "The Old Testament Text." In *CHB* 1.159-99. Reprinted in *QHBT.* See pp. 1-41.

Tov, Emanuel. "A Modern Textual Outlook Based on the Qumran Scrolls." *HUCA* 53 (1982): 11-27.

Waltke, Bruce K. "The Textual Criticism of the Old Testament." In *Biblical Criticism: Historical, Literary, and Textual,* edited by Roland K. Harrison et al. Grand Rapids: Zondervan, 1978. See pp. 47-65.

Weil, Gérard E. "Qere-kethibh." *IDBSup.* See pp. 716-23.

―――. "Prolegomena." In *BHS.* See esp. pp. XIII-XVII.

Wonneberger, Reinhard. *Understanding BHS: A Manual for the Users of the Biblia Hebraica Stuttgartensia.* Rome: Biblical Institute Press, 1984. See esp. pp. 61-73.

Würthwein, Ernst. *The Text of the Old Testament: An Introduction to the Biblia Hebraica,* translated by Erroll F. Rhodes. 2nd ed. Grand Rapids: Eerdmans, 1995. See esp. pp. 13-28.

Yeivin, Israel. *Introduction to the Tiberian Masorah.* Edited and translated by Ernest J. Revell. BLMS 5. Chico, Calif.: Scholars Press, 1980.

5

Determining the Most Plausible Original Reading

This chapter provides a step-by-step procedure for determining the most plausible reading of an Old Testament text. First, the chapter discusses where to start and where to look for evidence. Next, it differentiates between internal and external evidence. Then it introduces how to weigh the evidence in order to determine the most plausible reading.

Before going camping, some preliminary decisions will make the whole trip smoother. First, where are you going? Second, how long are you staying? Third, what kind of equipment will you need? Similarly, in Old Testament textual criticism it is helpful to lay some groundwork before we start. Where are we going, or what is the goal?

The goal of Old Testament textual criticism is to try to work back as closely as possible to the final form of the text that was maintained by the scribes and later canonized. This would be the point where literary development (and other higher critical issues) ended and the copying process began. However, anyone who has worked with literary materials knows that the process is never quite this clear-cut and that these two processes very likely overlap to some extent. Second, how long are we staying? This refers us to some guidelines to help determine how much food or how many clothes we need to bring. The primary guideline for Old Testament textual criticism is, which reading will most likely give rise to the others? This will help us work back to the most plausible original reading. And finally, what equipment will we need? As we learned in the previous chapter, the most suitable text to begin with is the *Biblia Hebraica Stuttgartensia (BHS)*—its textual notes provide much of the evidence necessary to determine the proper reading of the text. Because these notes sometimes contain Hebrew, Greek, Latin or even Syriac translations, dictionaries for these languages will also be helpful.

5.1 Where Do We Start?

The first step in Old Testament textual criticism is to determine where errors appear in the text, but this is not always easy because some errors may read quite smoothly. A New Testament text critic can begin with the variant readings of a text. Old Testament textual criticism, however, is more subjective because of the high uniformity of the text, as James Barr explains: "textual discussion will more frequently begin from the feeling that there is a 'difficulty'; the procedure will be more independent of the existence of variant readings."[1]

The best way to identify possible errors in the Old Testament text is to look for problems in translation, apparent textual corruptions or textual variations (e.g., various MT readings [Qumran texts, *Kethib/Qere* readings, other Hebrew mss., etc.], SP, LXX, Latin Vulgate and Syriac Peshitta) to see where they differ and then try to determine why. Modern diplomatic texts (*BHS, BHQ,* Hebrew University Bible Project) have already done much of this work in their textual apparatuses.

To be effective, textual criticism should include the following steps: (1) collect evidence from various sources, including the MT tradition, recensions and ancient versions, (2) evaluate both internal and external evidence, (3) determine the most plausible reading, and (4) suggest a conjectural reading only when the attested readings do not make sense. We will work through each of these steps.

5.2 Collecting the Evidence

The job of the text critic requires the perceptivity of a private detective in piecing together the steps that led up to the present text. We must carefully examine every piece of evidence before drawing a final conclusion. Evidence comes from the following sources (see fig. 5.1).

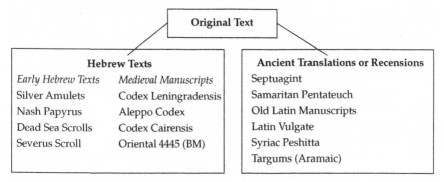

Figure 5.1. Sources of the Original Hebrew Text

---

[1] James Barr, *Comparative Philology and the Text of the Old Testament: With Additions and Corrections* (Winona Lake, Ind.: Eisenbrauns, 1987), p. 4.

5.2.1 Examining the Masoretic Tradition

The MT is a good place to begin since it derives from the longest and, to date, most reliable tradition overall. The first step is to determine the most accurate text of the MT; it has a number of forms, each of which varies slightly from the others. Most modern critical editions of the MT (e.g., *BHS, BHQ*, Hebrew University Bible Project) are diplomatic editions (i.e., reproductions of one known codex of the MT—often the Codex Leningradensis, dated to A.D. 1008) that reproduce the text exactly, even when it is known to be wrong (e.g., see textual notes for Psalm 5:10[c] where the editors note that the accent is incorrectly placed [יַחְלִיקוּן] יַחֲלִיקוּן instead of יַחֲלִיקוּן] and Psalm 20:9[a] where a *daghesh* is added for no apparent reason [קָמְנוּ instead of קַמְנוּ]). Generally modern critical editions of the MT have already compared the MT traditions and provide a summary of the pertinent information in their textual appara-

Table 5.1. Sources of the Original Hebrew Text

1. Codex Cairensis (A.D. 895)
2. Leningrad (formerly St. Petersburg) Codex of the Prophets (A.D. 916)
3. Aleppo Codex (first half of the tenth century)
4. British Museum Codex of the Pentateuch (950)
5. Codex Leningradensis B19[A] (1008)
6. Codex Reuchlinianus of the Prophets (1105)
7. Erfurt Codices: E1 (fourteenth century); E2 (thirteenth century); E3 (before 1100)
8. Hebrew Codices from the Cairo Geniza (sixth to fourteenth centuries)
9. Daniel Bomberg (first Rabbinic) Bible (1416-1417)
10. Complutensian Polyglot (1522)
11. Second Rabbinic Bible of Jacob ben Ḥayyim (1524/1525)
12. London Polyglot (1654-1657)
13. Works collecting variant readings from many of the medieval texts are:

    a. Johann H. Michaelis, *Biblia Hebraica ex aliquot manuscriptis et compluribus impressis codicibus . . .* (Halle: Magdeburg, 1720)

    b. Benjamin Kennicott, *Vetus Testamentum Hebraicum cum variis lectionibus*, 2 vols. (Oxford: Clarendon, 1776-80)

    c. Giovanni B. de Rossi, *Variae Lectiones Veteris Testamenti . . .* , 4 vols. (Parmae: Ex Regio typographeo, 1784-1788)

    d. Christian D. Ginsburg, *The Old Testament, Diligently Revised According to the Massorah and the Early Editions with the Various Readings from MSS and the Ancient Versions*, 4 vols. (London: Trinitarian Bible Society, 1926)

tuses. Books by Michaelis, Kennicott, de Rossi and Ginsburg are commonly referenced since they collate variant readings from many Hebrew medieval texts (see pp. 164-65).

The textual apparatus indicates any corrections or variations from this standard text. For the most part the MT is very stable and a comparison of various manuscripts of the MT provides few variants of any consequence. In general, any significant variations in manuscripts arose before the text became unified or from traditions other than the MT (e.g., LXX, Qumran texts, SP, Vulgate, Syriac); they should be carefully examined. The preceding list (see table 5.1), while not complete because there are over three thousand Hebrew manuscripts, provides a significant number of the MT sources arranged in chronological order. It would be difficult, if not impossible, to check all of these sources, but *BHS* has already examined most of them (as well as the versions) in its textual apparatus. The list is provided for two reasons: (1) ease of access to their names if it becomes necessary to consult the Hebrew sources, and (2) to engender an appreciation for the detailed work that has gone into *BHS* and other critical editions.

Example. An example of a corruption from the Codex Leningradensis that can be corrected merely by looking at other copies of the MT is found in Genesis 2:18:

וַיֹּאמֶר יְהוָה אֱלֹהִים לֹא־טוֹב הֱיוֹת הָאָדָם לְבַדּוֹ אֶעֱשֶׂהּ־לּוֹ עֵזֶר כְּנֶגְדּוֹ׃

"And the LORD God said, 'It is not good for the man to be alone, I will make *(her)* for him a help(er) corresponding to him.'"

In this case, the *daghesh* (dot) in the final *hê* of this word leads to an awkward translation (i.e., see translation above in italics); the textual note on this passage suggests this is a mistake found in the Codex Leningradensis, but many Hebrew manuscripts do not include the *daghesh*. In this example one need go no further; the best reading of the MT is a suitable reading for the text; in other cases, however, it may be necessary to also compare variant readings from other sources.

5.2.2 *Examining Other Sources*

The past century has provided an amazing wealth of material for the Old Testament textual critic, and as many sources as possible should be examined. It is probably best to arrange the source material into primary sources (i.e., those written in Hebrew) and secondary sources (i.e., those written in some other language) so that we have some method for beginning to evaluate them. Table 5.2 contains the most important sources.

Table 5.2. The Primary and Secondary Sources

Primary Sources (Hebrew mss)	Secondary Sources (other languages)
Silver Amulets	Samaritan Pentateuch
Nash Papyrus	Greek Versions or Recensions
Dead Sea Scrolls (202 mss)	Septuagint
Psalms (36 mss) [Psalms Scroll]	Aquila
Deuteronomy (29 mss)	Symmachus
Isaiah (21 mss) [Isaiah Scroll]	Kaige-Theodotion
Habakkuk Commentary	Origin's Hexapla
Tefillin and Mezuzoth from Judean Desert	Hesychius
Severus Scroll (R. Meir's Torah)	Lucian
About 3,000 MT manuscripts	Post-Hexaplaric Revisions
	Aramaic Targums
	Syriac Versions
	Peshitta
	Syro-Hexapla
	Latin Versions
	Old Latin
	Latin Vulgate
	Coptic Versions
	Sahidic
	Akhmimic
	Bohairic
	Ethiopic Version
	Armenian Version
	Arabic Versions

Example: In Genesis 2:2 it is necessary to examine other sources beyond the MT, which reads:

וַיְכַל אֱלֹהִים בַּיּוֹם הַשְּׁבִיעִי מְלַאכְתּוֹ אֲשֶׁר עָשָׂה
וַיִּשְׁבֹּת בַּיּוֹם הַשְּׁבִיעִי מִכָּל־מְלַאכְתּוֹ אֲשֶׁר עָשָׂה:

"And God finished on the seventh day all his work which he did and he rested
on the seventh (day) from all his work which he did."

The editors of the *BHS* point out that while all the Hebrew manuscripts indicate this reading, the SP, LXX and the Syriac Peshitta read that God finished
his work on the sixth day instead of the seventh. Since later it is said that God

rested on the seventh day from the work that he had done, it seems reasonable that his work was actually completed on the sixth day. It is possible that a Jewish audience would have considered the resting as part of the work of creation, but it seems more likely that the versions are correct in seeing the resting as a separate element from the work of creation. Thus we have an example where other witnesses may suggest a more plausible reading of a passage.

5.3 Evaluating the Internal and External Evidence

This is where skill, knowledge and balance on the part of the text critic are needed to determine the most plausible reading of a text. Intuition and common sense must guide the text critic; at the same time, informed judgments must be based on familiarity with types of copyist errors, manuscripts, versions and their authors. Bruce Metzger quips, "To teach another to become a textual critic is like teaching another to become a poet."[2] While natural talent is certainly a factor, the skills and rules related to textual criticism can be honed and sharpened by regular interaction with the texts. The following guidelines can help the Old Testament textual critic to evaluate the evidence:

- Determine the reading that would most likely give rise to the other readings.

- Carefully evaluate the weight of the manuscript evidence.

- Determine if the reading is a secondary reading or a gloss.

- Determine which reading is most appropriate in its context.

This first guideline is foundational to all the others, and common sense will provide the best guidance when trying to determine the most plausible reading of the text. Tov considers these types of rules to be subjective and valuable in only a small percentage of readings that need to be evaluated. He admits, however, that they are more helpful in the evaluation of some external witnesses.[3] Tov seems to favor this last guideline:

> The quintessence of textual evaluation is the selection from the different transmitted readings of the one reading . . . which is the most appropriate to its context. Within the process of this selection, the concept of the "context" is taken in a broad sense, as referring to the language, style, and content of both the immediate context and of the whole literary unit in which the reading is found.[4]

---

[2]Bruce M. Metzger, *The Text of the New Testament: Transmission, Corruption, and Restoration,* 3rd ed. (New York: Oxford University Press, 1992), p. 211.
[3]Emanuel Tov, *Textual Criticism of the Hebrew Bible,* 3rd ed. (Minneapolis: Fortress, 2001), pp. 293-311.
[4]Ibid., p. 309.

Each of the rules can be shown to have weaknesses. In the end common sense and an understanding of Hebrew words, grammar and style are the best tools for the Old Testament text critic. These guidelines may nevertheless be useful under certain circumstances and thus are helpful to know.

Once a corruption or significant variant has been identified, the next step is to evaluate both internal evidence (i.e., examining the passage or broader context of the passage) and external evidence (i.e., examining other sources containing this passage) to aid in determining the most plausible reading.

Example. Ruth 4:4 contains a variant that can probably be resolved by carefully examining both the internal and the external evidence:

וַאֲנִי אָמַרְתִּי אֶגְלֶה אָזְנְךָ לֵאמֹר קְנֵה נֶגֶד הַיֹּשְׁבִים וְנֶגֶד זִקְנֵי עַמִּי
אִם־תִּגְאַל גְּאָל וְאִם־לֹא יִגְאַל הַגִּידָה לִּי וְאֵדְעָ כִּי אֵין זוּלָתְךָ
לִגְאוֹל וְאָנֹכִי אַחֲרֶיךָ וַיֹּאמֶר אָנֹכִי אֶגְאָל׃

"So I myself said I will reveal (in) your hearing saying, 'Acquire (it) before the ones sitting (here), even before the elders of my people. If *you* will redeem (it) redeem (it), but if *he* will not redeem (it) tell me so I will know for there is no one but *you* to redeem (it) and I am after *you*.' And he said, 'I will redeem (it).'"

Most Hebrew manuscripts read וְאִם־לֹא יִגְאַל , "but if *he* will not redeem (it)," whereas some Hebrew manuscripts, the LXX, the Latin Vulgate and the Syriac Peshitta appear to derive from a Hebrew *Vorlage* that reads וְאִם־לֹא תִגְאַל , "but if *you* will not redeem (it)," a wording that makes more sense in the context. The latter reading is supported as follows: (1) the context (internal evidence) suggests that Boaz is speaking to his relative (the second person form is used just prior to this) in the presence of the elders of the city; and (2) there is significant support from some of the Hebrew manuscripts and the other ancient versions (external evidence). However, it is also possible that since this transaction is being witnessed by the elders of the city, confirmation that he will not redeem the field would probably have to come from them and thus the third person form may be correct. Jack Sasson argues that the MT vividly pictures Boaz addressing the elders.[5] It is also easy to see why some of the Hebrew manuscripts and other ancient witnesses would have changed the form to the second person to smooth out the reading. This variant is more difficult than it may appear at first sight—in weighing both readings it is necessary to examine both internal and external evidence to reach to a final decision.

---

[5]Jack M. Sasson, *Ruth. A New Translation with a Philological Commentary and a Formalist-Folklorist Interpretation*, Johns Hopkins Near Eastern Studies (Baltimore: Johns Hopkins, 1979), p. 118.

5.3.1 Internal Evidence

Internal evidence includes the types of changes described in chapter two (e.g., haplography, dittography, metathesis), as well as any evidence derived from the structure of the text itself (e.g., common sentence structures, word usages, or literary structures, such as ellipsis [i.e., omission of an implied word or phrase], alphabetic acrostic, chiasm [i.e., inverted sequence or crossover of parallel words or phrases—a b b' a' pattern]; see table 5.3).

Table 5.3. Internal Evidence

Problems with the pointing or word divisions of the Hebrew Text	Certain characteristics of the authors or editors
Transmissional corruptions	Special meanings of words
Scribal changes	
Linguistic or literary structures or patterns	

Questions of spelling or word usage, for example, may be resolved by examining spelling or usage in the rest of the book or in comparable genres of the Old Testament. The following questions may be useful in unraveling a difficult reading:

- Is there any evidence of transmissional corruption (e.g., metathesis, haplography, fusion; see pp. 44-50)? Corruptions of this type are fairly easy to spot and may reasonably resolve a problem passage.

- Is it plausible that a scribe purposely or inadvertently changed the text (e.g., omission, changes for euphemistic reasons, archaic usage; see pp. 50-55)?

- Do any linguistic forms or literary structures of the passage help determine the original reading of the text? For example, the editors of *BHS* suggest including the following phrase in Genesis 1:6 because a similar pattern appears in verses 4, 10, 12, 18, 21, 31: וַיַּרְא אֱלֹהִים כִּי־טוֹב, *wayyarĕ' 'ĕlōhîm kî-ṭôb*, "And God saw that it was good."

One should exercise caution in this case, however, because the only textual evidence for this insertion is from the LXX, which is known for harmonizing texts.

5.3.2 External Evidence

When a difficult passage is not resolved by merely examining the internal evidence, the text critic must turn to external evidence of manuscripts and versions outside the MT. However, James Barr notes potential problems in using the versions for textual criticism:

> The scholar cannot use the ancient versions as if they were actual Hebrew texts.

The translators may have misunderstood the original Hebrew, so that their version is not a good, but a very bad, guide to what the original text said. Finding a difficult passage in Hebrew, they may have just guessed at the sense. They may not have translated literally, but have given a rough paraphrase of what was said. They may be literal at one place but paraphrastic at another; and in some versions, like the LXX, the translating techniques differed from book to book, and even between sections of books.[6]

Because evidence for the Old Testament text comes from many different sources and languages, the weight of the manuscript evidence must be carefully evaluated. This evaluation is based on five factors: language of the witness, date of the witness, reliability of the witness, provenance (origin/source) and purpose of the witness, and interdependence of the witnesses.

5.3.2.1 *Language of the witness.* Old Testament text critics are becoming much more sophisticated in their evaluation of the ancient versions. They carefully examine each version to determine the standard deviation of an author in word usage (i.e., comparing how consistently an author translated a specific Hebrew word into another language), grammar and sentence structure. Through this type of in-depth comparison they can determine specific translation characteristics and how close a given version is to its *Vorlage* (i.e., manuscript from which the scribe was copying). Nevertheless, caution should be exercised here since the translator may not have always followed or even understood the *Vorlage*. Thus we must still consider texts written in Hebrew to be of primary importance.

5.3.2.2 *Date of the witness.* The general principle to follow is that the more times a text has been copied, the greater the possibility for corruption. Exceptions to this principle are based on the skill of the copyists in preserving their *Vorlage* or the method of the copyist. For example, the copyist of 1QIsa[a] apparently was not merely interested in copying the Hebrew text but added *matres lectionis* and other changes to render the text more understandable to his readers. Because of this, as Tov has noted, the text of 1QIsa[a] differs more from the MT than do some of the later medieval manuscripts.[7] Despite this, however, it is noteworthy that the vast majority of changes are in orthography (i.e., how the words are spelled) and do not affect the meaning of the text.

Because the text of the proto-MT became highly unified during the first century A.D., texts before this date may contain variant readings that were removed during this time period. Some of these early traditions, such as the LXX and Dead Sea Scrolls, may provide important evidence concerning the original reading of the text. This is one reason why the Dead Sea Scrolls, most of which date from before the first century A.D., are important to textual criticism.

---

[6]Barr, *Comparative Philology*, p. 2.
[7]Tov, *Textual Criticism*, p. 301.

5.3.2.3 Reliability of the witness. Reliability of a manuscript is based on how close a text remains to its textual tradition (most scholars consider the MT the most reliable textual tradition overall to date). Since the discovery of the Dead Sea Scrolls, scholars have recognized that some of these texts are virtually identical to the MT and thus that the accuracy of this tradition was maintained for well over one thousand years. Still this does not mean that the MT has the best readings in every passage. Even the Codex Leningradensis, the earliest, most complete Hebrew manuscript we have of the MT, appears to have accumulated errors in its text (e.g., Genesis 6:16: תְּכַלֶנָּה *[těkalennâ]* instead of תְּכַלֶנָּה *[těkallennâ]*, Genesis 7:23: וַיִּשָּׁאֶר *[wayiśśā'er]* instead of וַיִּשָּׁאֶר *[wayyiśśā'er]*, Genesis 14:10: הֲשִׂדִּים *[haśiddîm]* instead of הֲשִׂדִּים *[haśśiddîm]*).

5.3.2.4 Provenance (origin/source) and purpose of the text. When weighing evidence, it is important to understand the background of a manuscript and why it was written. For example, the SP was either written or emended to confirm doctrines sacred to the Samaritans (e.g., Deuteronomy 12:5 of the SP identifies "the place which the Lord your God shall choose" as Gerizim instead of Jerusalem, as the MT suggests in later passages).

5.3.2.5 Interdependence of the witnesses. Some witnesses are interdependent and should be considered as just one witness when they agree. This principle comes into play with the LXX and the following versions that are in some way dependent on it: Peshitta (later intrusions of LXX readings), Old Latin, Vulgate, Sahidic, Bohairic, Ethiopic, Armenian and Arabic. It is still important to consult these versions since a witness may be dependent on the LXX in general and yet be at variance in specific readings. When these versions disagree with the LXX, they may reflect an original, independent reading.[8]

5.3.3 Quality of the Sources

According to these five criteria, the list of witnesses have roughly the order of importance relative to Old Testament textual criticism as shown in table 5.4.[9]

Complete or nearly complete critical editions are now available for the chief non-Hebrew versions: LXX, Peshitta, Targums and Vulgate. The critical edition of the LXX[10] is a fairly reliable source for information regarding daughter translations, such as Old Latin, Coptic, Ethiopic and Syro-Hexapla, as well as citations of the LXX by early Jewish and Christian writers.

A three-step evaluation of the various textual witnesses will enable one to

---

[8]For an example of this principle see P. Kyle McCarter, *Textual Criticism: Recovering the Text of the Hebrew Bible*, GBS:OTS (Philadelphia: Fortress, 1986), p. 65.

[9]Cf. Ernst Würthwein, *The Text of the Old Testament: An Introduction to the Biblia Hebraica*, trans. Erroll F. Rhodes, 2nd ed. (Grand Rapids: Eerdmans, 1995), pp. 114-20.

[10]Joseph Ziegler et al., eds., *Septuaginta. Vetus Testamentum Graecum auctoritate Academiae Scientarium Gottingensis editum* (Göttingen: Vandenhoeck & Ruprecht, 1931-).

Table 5.4. Quality of Old Testament Witnesses

1. MT (compare various MT witnesses)	9. Theodotion
2. Silver Amulets (only contain a few verses from the book of Numbers)	10. Targums
	11. Vulgate
3. Qumran manuscripts	12. Syriac
4. Other Hebrew manuscripts (e.g., Nash Papyrus, Masada, Murabbaʿat, Cairo Genizah)	13. Old Latin
	14. Sahidic
	15. Bohairic
5. Samaritan Pentateuch	16. Armenian
6. LXX	17. Georgian
7. Aquila	18. Ethiopic
8. Symmachus	19. Arabic

group related languages, highlight interdependence among the witnesses, and narrow down the number of readings to consider.

1. Note any divergences from the MT in the following Hebrew manuscripts:

- Ancient Hebrew manuscripts, such as Qumran manuscripts, Silver Amulets, Nash Papyrus and in manuscripts from Masada, Murabbaʿat, Cairo Genizah.

- Later Hebrew manuscripts, such as *BHS* (Leningradensis B19^A), the Aleppo Codex, Codex Cairensis, Daniel Bomberg Bible (the first Rabbinic Bible).

2. Compare the LXX and its daughter translations and note any divergent readings in the following (the Göttingen edition of the LXX often supplies the majority of this information): Old Latin, Coptic (Sahidic and Bohairic), Ethiopic, Syro-Hexapla, Armenian. At some point it will be necessary to translate the Hebrew text that gave rise to them. Because of the ambiguity and lack of precision of this procedure, various options in translation should always be noted. The concordance of the LXX by Edwin Hatch and Henry A. Redpath and the index to Hatch and Redpath compiled by Elmar C. dos Santos will be helpful for translating the Greek of the LXX back into Hebrew. The latter work indicates which Greek words have been used to translate specific Hebrew words in the MT.[11]

---

[11]Edwin Hatch and Henry A. Redpath, *A Concordance to the Septuagint and the Other Greek Versions of the Old Testament*, 3 vols. (1897-1906; reprint, Graz: Akademische Druck- u. Verlagsanstalt, 1975); Elmar C. dos Santos, *An Expanded Hebrew Index for the Hatch-Redpath Concordance to the Septuagint* (Jerusalem: Dugith, n.d.). See also Takamitsu Muraoka, *Hebrew/Aramaic Index to the Septuagint (Keyed to the Hatch-Redpath Concordance)* (Grand Rapids: Baker, 1998); Emanuel Tov, *The Text-Critical Use of the Septuagint in Biblical Research*, JBS 3 (Jerusalem: Simor, 1981), pp. 97-179; idem, "The Use of Concordances in the Reconstruction of the Vorlage of the LXX," *CBQ* 40 (1978): 29-36 (revised in Tov's *Text-Critical Use*, pp. 142-54).

3. Compare the other non-Greek translations to the MT, noting any divergent readings: Vulgate, Peshitta, Targums, Arabic. Once again, it will be necessary to translate the various languages back into Hebrew.

Example. A corruption that is not resolved merely by comparing all the sources of the MT, but requires examination of both internal and external evidence is found in Psalm 145:12-15:

$$\text{לְהוֹדִיעַ לִבְנֵי הָאָדָם גְּבוּרֹתָיו וּכְבוֹד הֲדַר מַלְכוּתוֹ}^{12}\quad \boxed{\text{ל}}$$

"To make known to the sons of man his mighty acts and the glory of the majesty of his kingdom."

$$\text{מַלְכוּתְךָ מַלְכוּת כָּל־עֹלָמִים וּמֶמְשֶׁלְתְּךָ בְּכָל־דּוֹר וָדוֹר}^{13}\quad \boxed{\text{מ}}$$

"Your kingdom is an everlasting kingdom and your rule over all generations."

[nûn verse missing] $\boxed{\text{נ}}$

$$\text{סוֹמֵךְ יְהוָה לְכָל־הַנֹּפְלִים וְזוֹקֵף לְכָל־הַכְּפוּפִים}^{14}\quad \boxed{\text{ס}}$$

"The LORD sustains all who are falling and raises up all who are bowed down."

$$\text{עֵינֵי־כֹל אֵלֶיךָ יְשַׂבֵּרוּ וְאַתָּה נוֹתֵן־לָהֶם אֶת־אָכְלָם בְּעִתּוֹ}^{15}\quad \boxed{\text{ע}}$$

"The eyes of all look to you and you are giving to them their food in its time."

Psalm 145 is an alphabetic acrostic, which means that each successive line begins with the next letter of the Hebrew alphabet; however there is no *nûn* verse in the MT. It is reasonable to expect that the author would have included the entire Hebrew alphabet; the context suggests therefore that something is missing. External evidence also points to an omission since a Dead Sea Scroll manuscript, the LXX (πιστὸς κύριος ἐν τοῖς λόγοις αὐτοῦ, καὶ ὅσιος ἐν πᾶσι τοῖς ἔργοις αὐτοῦ, "the Lord is faithful in his words, and holy in all his works") and the Syriac Peshitta each include the following line in this place: "The Lord is faithful in his words and loving in all his deeds." The verse, when translated back into Hebrew, can be constructed to begin with a *nûn:*

$$\text{נֶאֱמָן יהוה בְּכָל־דְּבָרָיו וְחָסִיד בְּכָל־מַעֲשָׂיו}$$

"The LORD is faithful in all his words and loving in all his deeds."

5.4 Determining the Most Plausible Original Reading

Once the evidence has been collected and evaluated, the next step is to determine the most plausible reading of the final form of the text. Inherent in the process is one of the most important principles in textual criticism: Which reading would most likely give rise to the others? The following steps are generally necessary to determine the most plausible reading. The three-step evaluation process on pages 121-25 can be used to organize the evidence when weighing a reading.

5.4.1 Consider the Strength of the Textual Tradition

First, one must determine which form of the MT is most reliable (step one described above). Most variants are minor and can be resolved by examining how similar forms of words or grammatical constructions are used in other parts of the book or in similar genres of the Old Testament. Pay close attention to discovering how the variations could have arisen and which reading could have given rise to the others. If at the end of this evaluation it is still unclear which reading of the MT is the most reliable, then leave open the possibilities until more evidence is available.

5.4.2 Examine Internal Evidence

Now examine the context, grammar, structure and anything else in the passage that may help determine the most plausible reading. Look for common transmissional mistakes (i.e., haplography, dittography, etc.), similar spellings, similar grammatical structures and other things that may provide evidence.

5.4.3 Examine External Evidence

Now expand your examination to include all the external evidence mentioned above. The aim of this part of your evaluation will be to determine which reading has the strongest evidence. At this point keep in mind that manuscripts must be weighed, not merely counted. Special care must be taken to determine interdependence between sources so that a particular reading is not given more weight than it deserves.

5.4.4 Evaluate the Evidence

Use the principles mentioned earlier to determine which reading is preferred for the original reading of the text.

- Determine the reading that would most likely give rise to the other readings.

- Carefully evaluate the weight of the manuscript evidence.

- Determine if the reading is a secondary reading or a gloss.

- Determine which reading is most appropriate in its context.

At times these rules may conflict with one another. For example, a secondary reading may also be the most appropriate reading in context. This is where the skill of the Old Testament text critic comes into play—one must carefully evaluate all the evidence. This evaluation process is sometimes difficult because some of the evidence may be missing. The two most important guidelines, however, are trying to determine (1) the reading that would most likely give rise to the other readings is preferable, and (2) the reading that is most appropriate in context is preferable. Common sense, caution and logic

> **VOCALIZING** דבר
>
> In Jeremiah 9:21 this word can be vocalized as
>
> דַּבֵּר, "speak,"
>
> דֶּבֶר, "plague," or
>
> דָּבָר, "a word."

must prevail—sometimes several readings are possible. In general the MT often contains the most reliable reading even though in some instances its readings can apparently be improved. It is also possible that the vocalization of the MT may not be as accurate as the consonantal text since vowel points were not added to the text until the fifth to ninth centuries A.D. Prior to this, vocalization was passed on orally from generation to generation, yet with apparent accuracy in most passages. However, there are times when the vocalization can significantly modify the meaning of the passage and must be taken into account in the weighing process (e.g., in Jer 9:21 דבר can be vocalized as דַּבֵּר, "speak," דֶּבֶר, "plague" or דָּבָר, "a word"). The chart found at table 5.5 can be used to compile and weigh the evidence.

The overall thought of the passage will not usually change significantly no matter which variant is chosen. When the difference is significant, use caution and leave open the options. Tov stresses that all variant readings have some value:

> In practical terms, the conclusion of the evaluating procedure is that some readings are often designated as "original" or "better" than others. It should, however, be remembered that when a reading is described by scholars as original, this does not imply that the other readings are worthless. First, it is possible that the assumption concerning the originality of the reading is incorrect, and that one of the other readings should nevertheless be considered the better one. Second, all ancient readings are valuable, since they contain important information, not only concerning the textual transmission, but also about the exegetical considerations of the early scribes and the first generations of those who read and interpreted the Bible, particularly their linguistic and intellectual milieu.[12]

---

[12]Tov, *Textual Criticism*, p. 295.

Table 5.5. Compiling the Evidence

PASSAGE _____

Evidence from Textual Tradition	Evidence from Manuscripts or Versions
Codex Leningradensis (BHS) Translation:	Sources in agreement with MT
Other MT readings:	Other readings:

Evaluation	
Most plausible MT readings	Other plausible readings
Most plausible reading of the text Reasons	

5.4.5 Possible Emendations

Only after every other avenue of evidence has been exhausted should the text critic resort to emending the text, and even then the emendation should remain tentative. An emendation is "an attempt to reconstruct an original reading that has not survived among extant manuscripts."[13] McCarter explains the difficulty of proposing an emendation:

> Because emendation is, at least in part, a matter of intuition, it is not possible to establish a set of rules that govern it. Perhaps the chief necessity is that the scholar should be self-critical in emending the text. A reading arising from emendation is subject to the same evaluative criteria as a transmitted reading. The critic must apply these to anything he proposes and pass judgment on it accordingly. Does the proposed emendation explain all the transmitted readings? Is it suited to its context?[14]

5.5 Specific Examples

5.5.1 1 Chronicles 6:40 (MT 25). The marginal note in the NIV for 1 Chronicles 6:40 (MT 25) indicates a variant of the name Baaseiah (בַּעֲשֵׂיָה, * baʿăśēyâ*); it says that the reading Maaseiah (מַעֲשֵׂיָה, *maʿăśēyâ*) is found in some Hebrew manuscripts, one LXX manuscript and the Peshitta. The textual note in *BHS* reads:

> 25 ᵃ l c pc Mss 𝕲 ᴮᴸ 𝕾 'מֲעַ // meaning "Read (= l) with (= c) a few manuscripts (= pc Mss), LXX (= 𝕲)(Vaticanus [= B] and Lucian recension [= L]), and the Peshitta (= 𝕾) as מַעֲשֵׂיָה (*maʿăśēyâ*).

The works of Kennicott, de Rossi and Ginsburg[15] reveal that the vast majority of Hebrew manuscripts read "Baaseiah" (בַּעֲשֵׂיָה, *baʿăśēyâ*); this reading would thus appear to be the favored textual tradition. The next step is to discover whether any other evidence would help determine which reading is most reliable.

Consider the internal and external evidence.

- *Internal evidence.* Is there any evidence of transmissional corruption? Do any parallel passages favor one of the readings? The name as it appears in 1 Chronicles 6:40 is a *hapax legomenon* (i.e., occurs only here), and there are no parallel passages. A transmissional corruption is likely since in some Dead Sea Scrolls texts the בּ (*bêt*) and מ (*mêm*) are similar, but it is still difficult to

---

[13]McCarter, *Textual Criticism*, p. 76.
[14]Ibid., p. 75.
[15]Benjamin Kennicott, *Vetus Testamentum Hebraicum cum variis lectionibus*, 2 vols. (Oxford: Clarendon, 1776-1780); Giovanni B. de Rossi, *Variae Lectiones Veteris Testamenti*, 4 vols. (Parma: Regio typographeo, 1784-1788); and Christian D. Ginsburg, *The Old Testament: Diligently Revised According to the Massorah and the Early Editions with the Various Readings from MSS and the Ancient Versions*, 4 vols. (London: Trinitarian Bible Society, 1926).

know which is the preferred reading of this name.

- *External evidence.* The only significant evidence from the versions is that Codex Vaticanus (a fourth-century A.D. Greek manuscript), Lucian's (d. A.D. 312) Greek recension and the Peshitta (probably about the third century A.D.) support "Maaseiah" (מַעֲשֵׂיָה [ma'ăśēyâ]); the rest support "Baaseiah" (בַּעֲשֵׂיָה [ba'ăśēyâ]). Based on evidence found in these early Greek and Syriac manuscripts, the editors of *BHS* suggest that the text should be changed to read "Maaseiah" (מַעֲשֵׂיָה [ma'ăśēyâ]). It is difficult to know if the Syriac Peshitta is influenced by later intrusions from the Septuagint. In the books of Chronicles, but since the MT tradition and many of the Greek manuscripts are fairly consistent in reading "Baaseiah," I believe that the reading בַּעֲשֵׂיָה (ba'ăśēyâ) should probably be retained.

5.5.2 *Hosea 7:14*

An interesting textual variant is recorded in the NIV of Hosea 7:14:

They do not cry out to me from their hearts (but) wail upon their beds. *They gather together* for grain and new wine but turn away from me.

The textual note in the *BHS* reads:

14 ᶜ l c nonn Mss 𝔊 (κατετέμνοντο) יִתְגּוֹדָדוּ ut 1 R 18,28 //

The note means "read with some Hebrew manuscripts (nonn Mss) and the LXX (κατετέμνοντο) all of which suggest that the text should be read as יִתְגּוֹדָדוּ (yitgôdādû, "they slash themselves") as in 1 Kings 18:28."

Most Hebrew manuscripts read "they gather together," and a careful examination of Kennicott, de Rossi and Ginsburg reveals that the MT fairly consistently reads the verb יִתְגּוֹרָרוּ (yitgôrārû, "they gather together") in this verse. However, some Hebrew manuscripts (11-20) and the LXX (κατετέμνοντο [katetemnonto, "they cut themselves"]) suggest that the reading should be יִתְגּוֹדָדוּ (yitgôdādû, "they slash themselves").

- *Internal evidence.* The context is not very helpful in determining the more plausible reading since both are feasible. The reading "they gather together" is compatible with the context since the Israelites were calling on God, though their hearts did not seem to be in it. The reading "they slash themselves" is also reasonable since during the eighth century B.C. many Israelites followed Baal and, according to 1 Kings 18:28, the prophets of Baal cut themselves as part of appeasement rituals. The structure of the verse may be of help here, for it is divided into two main parts:

And they did not cry out to me from their hearts
when they wailed upon their beds.

They slashed themselves (or gather together) concerning the grain and new wine; they turned against me.

If this is indeed the structure of the verse, then the first part describes Israel's heartless worship and the second part their turning against God. In this structure the reading "they slashed themselves" makes more sense, describing how the people had turned against God, whereas the phrase "they gather together" would seemingly require an explanatory phrase to describe what the Israelites were doing wrong (e.g., "they were gathering together with a wrong heart attitude").

- *External evidence.* The LXX clearly favors the reading "they slash themselves," though evidence from other versions varies greatly.

It is hard to believe that the Israelites would actually stoop so low to appease Baal, which may be one reason the variant entered the text. In addition the letters ד *(dālet)* and ר *(rēš)* are quite similar in both paleo-Hebrew and square script, so a scribe could have easily confused them at some point in the copying process. However, it does seem reasonable based on the internal and external evidence that "to slash themselves" is the more likely reading.

Here are some interesting passages to try your hand at Old Testament textual criticism:

Genesis 1:1, 6, 9, 20	Exodus 20:5, 10, 12	Joshua 1:1	Psalm 145:13
Genesis 2:2, 18, 23	Exodus 22:19	Joshua 2:15	Isaiah 13:16
Genesis 4:1, 8	Exodus 29:5	Judges 18:30	Jeremiah 2:11
Genesis 5:3, 20	Exodus 39:21	Ruth 1:14	Jeremiah 7:7
Genesis 6:3, 20	Leviticus 1:4	1 Samuel 2:22-23	Jeremiah 25:25
Genesis 7:17	Leviticus 5:5	2 Samuel 2:8	Jeremiah 27:19
Genesis 9:7	Leviticus 20:10	Job 2:9	Jeremiah 41:9
Genesis 18:22	Numbers 4:14	Psalm 2:11-12	Hosea 4:7
Genesis 22:13	Numbers 11:15	Psalm 22:17	Amos 6:12
Genesis 36:26	Numbers 14:34	Psalm 45:3(2)	Amos 8:11
Genesis 49:10	Numbers 32:24	Psalm 106:20	Micah 4:1

Further Reading

Ap-Thomas, Dafydd R. *A Primer of Old Testament Text Criticism.* 2nd ed. Oxford: Clarendon, 1964.

Barthélemy, Dominique. "Text, Hebrew, History of." *IDBSup.* See pp. 878-84.

Deist, Ferdinand E. *Towards the Text of the Old Testament.* 2nd ed. Pretoria: Kerkboekhandel Transvaal, 1981.

————. *Witnesses to the Old Testament: Introducing Old Testament Textual Criticism.* Literature of the Old Testament 5. Pretoria: Kerkboekhandel Transvaal, 1988.

Kennicott, Benjamin. *Vetus Testamentum Hebraicum cum variis lectionibus.* 2 vols. Oxford: Clarendon, 1776-1780.

Klein, Ralph W. *Textual Criticism of the Old Testament: The Septuagint After Qumran.* GBS:OTS. Philadelphia: Fortress, 1974. See pp. 62-75.

McCarter, P. Kyle. *Textual Criticism: Recovering the Text of the Hebrew Bible.* GBS:OTS. Philadelphia: Fortress, 1986. See pp. 62-84.

Michaelis, Johannes H. *Biblia Hebraica ex aliquot manuscriptis et compluribus impressis codicibus . . .* Halle: Magdeburg, 1720.

Orlinsky, Harry M. "The Textual Criticism of the Old Testament." In *BANE.* See pp. 113-32.

Payne, David F. "Old Testament Textual Criticism: Its Principles and Practice." *TynBul* 25 (1974): 99-112.

de Rossi, Giovanni B. *Variae lectiones Veteris Testamenti. . . .* 4 vols. Parma: Regio typographeo, 1784-1788.

Talmon, Shemaryahu. "Old Testament Text." In *CHB* 1:159-99.

————. "Synonymous Readings in the Textual Traditions of the Old Testament." *ScrHier* 8 (1961): 335-83.

Thompson, John A. "Textual Criticism, OT." *IDBSup.* See pp. 886-91.

Tov, Emanuel. "Criteria for Evaluating Textual Readings: The Limitations of Textual Rules." *HTR* 75 (1982): 429-48.

————. *The Text-Critical Use of the Septuagint in Biblical Research.* JBS 3. Jerusalem: Simor, 1981.

————. *Textual Criticism of the Hebrew Bible.* Minneapolis: Fortress, 1992. See esp. pp. 293-311.

Walton, Brian, ed. *Biblia Sacra Polyglotta, Complectentia.* London: Thomas Roycroft, 1657.

Weingreen, Jacob. *Introduction to the Critical Study of the Text of the Hebrew Bible.* New York: Oxford University Press, 1982.

Würthwein, Ernst. *The Text of the Old Testament: An Introduction to the Biblia Hebraica.* Translated by Erroll F. Rhodes. 2nd ed. Grand Rapids: Eerdmans, 1995. See esp. pp. 107-20.

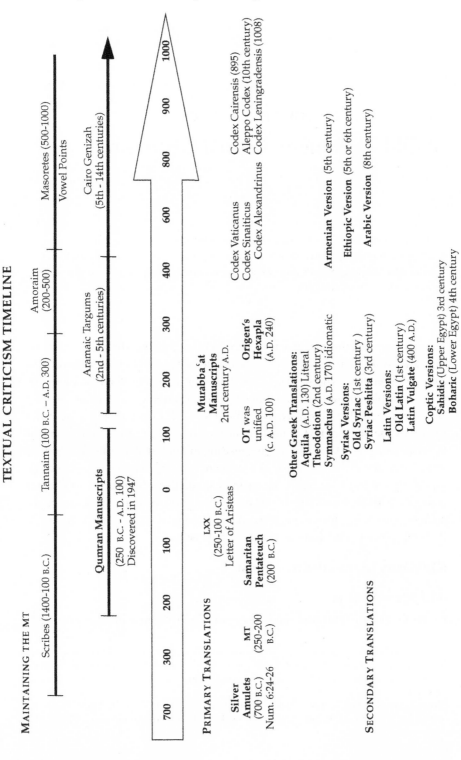

TEXTUAL CRITICISM TIMELINE

MAINTAINING THE MT

Scribes (1400-100 B.C.) | Tannaim (100 B.C. – A.D. 300) | Amoraim (200-500) | Masoretes (500-1000)

Vowel Points

Aramaic Targums (2nd - 5th centuries)

Cairo Genizah (5th - 14th centuries)

Qumran Manuscripts (250 B.C. - A.D. 100) Discovered in 1947

PRIMARY TRANSLATIONS

Silver Amulets (700 B.C.) Num. 6:24-26

MT (250-200 B.C.)

Samaritan Pentateuch (200 B.C.)

LXX (250-100 B.C.) Letter of Aristeas

OT was unified (c. A.D. 100)

Murabbaʿat Manuscripts 2nd century A.D.

Origen's Hexapla (A.D. 240)

Other Greek Translations:
Aquila (A.D. 130) Literal
Theodotion (2nd century)
Symmachus (A.D. 170) idiomatic

Syriac Versions:
Old Syriac (1st century)
Syriac Peshitta (3rd century)

Latin Versions:
Old Latin (1st century)
Latin Vulgate (400 A.D.)

Coptic Versions:
Sahidic (Upper Egypt) 3rd century
Boharic (Lower Egypt) 4th century

Codex Vaticanus
Codex Sinaiticus
Codex Alexandrinus

Codex Cairensis (895)
Aleppo Codex (10th century)
Codex Leningradensis (1008)

Armenian Version (5th century)

Ethiopic Version (5th or 6th century)

Arabic Version (8th century)

SECONDARY TRANSLATIONS

700 | 300 | 200 | 100 | 0 | 100 | 200 | 300 | 400 | 600 | 800 | 900 | 1000

6

Getting to Know the Sources
of Old Testament Textual Criticism

This chapter introduces the reader to the key source materials and their relevance
to Old Testament textual criticism. It includes primary sources such as the Silver
Amulets, Dead Sea Scrolls and Nash Papyrus, and also secondary sources such
as the SP, Targums, and LXX.

They still say that the best way to spot counterfeit money is to become very familiar with the real thing.[1] This is also true of Old Testament textual criticism—the better we know the sources, the better we will understand their purpose, possible corruptions, relationship to one another and value for Old
Testament textual criticism. Waltke states correctly: "No one source perfectly
preserves the original text of the Old Testament, and in case of disagreement
the critic must decide on the original reading in light of all the sources and his
knowledge about them."[2] The Old Testament text critic must have a thorough
knowledge of these sources in order to evaluate them properly. This chapter
provides a brief summary of the most important primary and secondary
sources, surveying the major texts in chronological order, with mention of
their relevance to Old Testament textual criticism.

6.1 Primary Sources (Hebrew Texts)

6.1.1 Silver Amulets

Currently the oldest known fragments of any Old Testament passage are the sil-

---

[1]Indigo Image, *Counterfeit Detection: A Guide to Spotting Counterfeit Currency,* "How To Spot a
Counterfeit," February 17, 2005, cited online at <www.indigoimage.com/count/
spot.html>.
[2]Bruce K. Waltke, "The Textual Criticism of the Old Testament," in *Biblical Criticism: Historical,
Literary, and Textual,* ed. Roland K. Harrison et al. (Grand Rapids: Zondervan, 1978), p. 47.

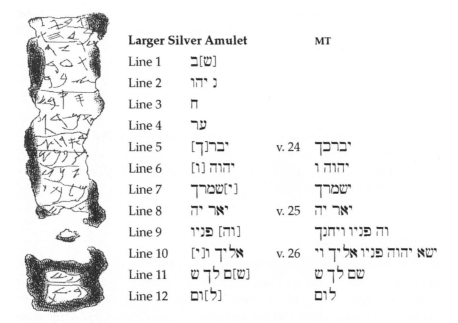

	Larger Silver Amulet	MT
Line 1	‫[שׁ]ב‬	
Line 2	‫נ יהו‬	
Line 3	‫ח‬	
Line 4	‫ער‬	
Line 5	‫יבר[נ]ך‬	v. 24 ‫יברכך‬
Line 6	‫יהוה [ו]‬	‫יהוה ו‬
Line 7	‫י[שׁמרך]‬	‫ישׁמרך‬
Line 8	‫יאר יה‬	v. 25 ‫יאר יה‬
Line 9	‫[וה] פניו‬	‫וה פניו ויחנך‬
Line 10	‫אליך ו[י]‬	v. 26 ‫ישׁא יהוה פניו אליך וי‬
Line 11	‫[שׁ]ם לך שׁ‬	‫שׁם לך שׁ‬
Line 12	‫[ל]ום‬	‫לום‬

Figure 6.1. A drawing of the larger silver amulet, discovered in 1985 in a grave near St. Andrew's Church of Scotland, Jerusalem. The paleo-Hebrew is transcribed into square script for comparison. [John C. Trever]

ver amulets, dated to the mid-seventh century B.C.[3] Part of the priestly benediction of Numbers 6:22-27 was written on two small silver sheets (when unrolled the larger is about 1 inch wide by 4 inches long and the smaller is about 1/2 inch wide by 1-1/2 inches long [see fig. 6.1]). The Silver Amulets were written in paleo-Hebrew script and have no vowel pointings or word divisions. This text is important because of its age and the close similarity of the larger amulet to the MT of Numbers 6:22-27. The differences between the larger amulet and the MT are (1) one less ‫כ‬ *(kāp)* in line 5, so that it reads "the LORD bless" instead of "the LORD bless *you*," and (2) in lines 9-10 the words ‫וִיחֻנֶּךָּ יִשָּׂא יהוה פָּנָיו אֵלֶיךָ‬ *(wiḥunnekkā yiśśāʾ yhwh pānāyw ʾēleykā,* "And be gracious unto you. The LORD lift up his face upon you") appear in the MT but not on this amulet. The smaller amulet is not as close to the text of the MT as the larger one—instead of the MT's fifteen words, there are only ten. The first four lines of the text are too damaged to translate, but the first line probably contains the owner's name (possibly

[3]Jennifer Viegas, "Rare Scrolls Reveal Early Biblical Writing," *The Daily Telegraph,* Friday, June 22, 2005. Accessed online at <http://dsc.discovery.com/news/briefs/20050718/bible.html>.

Benayahu or Shebanyahu). The rest of the text reads as follows: "The LORD bless you and keep you and make his face shine upon you and give to you peace," which may have summarized the text of the MT.

Further Reading
Primary Sources
Barkay, Gabriel. *Ketef Hinnom: A Treasure Facing Jerusalem's Walls*. Jerusalem: Israel Museum, 1986. See pp. 29-34.
Tov, Emanuel. *Textual Criticism of the Hebrew Bible*. 2nd ed. Minneapolis: Fortress, 1992. See p. 379, plate 1.

6.1.2 Dead Sea Scrolls
It is hard to believe that an Arab shepherd boy could forever change the study of Old Testament textual criticism, but in 1947 his chance discovery of several of the Dead Sea Scrolls had that effect.[4] Until then the oldest, most complete Hebrew manuscript of the Old Testament was the text of Codex Leningradensis Ms. B19[A], dated to A.D. 1008. The Dead Sea Scrolls provided texts of the Old Testament from approximately one thousand years earlier (dated from about 250 B.C. to A.D. 100). To this point eleven caves have been discovered surrounding Qumran (about seven miles south of Jericho; see map 6.1) in which manuscripts or fragments have been found of all the biblical books (usually several copies) except Esther and possibly Nehemiah. It is possible that Ezra and Nehemiah were combined into one book as in the Hebrew canon and thus only Esther is without attestation. There are 202 biblical manuscripts or fragments of the biblical books, and they are primarily written in square script; however, there are twelve fragments of biblical scrolls written in paleo-Hebrew (three of Genesis, one of Exodus, four of Leviticus, one of Numbers, two of Deuteronomy and one of Job).[5] The most common manuscripts of biblical books found at Qumran come from the Psalms (thirty-nine mss), Deuteronomy (twenty-seven mss) and Isaiah (twenty-one mss).

---

[4]Information regarding the discovery of the scrolls can be found in John M. Allegro, *The Dead Sea Scrolls* (Harmondsworth, Middlesex: Penguin, 1957), pp. 15-34; Frank M. Cross, *The Ancient Library of Qumran and Biblical Studies*, 2nd ed. (1961; reprint, Grand Rapids: Baker, 1980), pp. 3-47; Jósef T. Milik, *Ten Years of Discovery in the Wilderness of Judaea*, trans. John Strugnell, SBT 1/26 (Naperville, Ill.: Allenson, 1958), pp. 11-19; James C. VanderKam, *The Dead Sea Scrolls Today* (Grand Rapids: Eerdmans, 1994), pp. 1-27; and Yigael Yadin, *The Message of the Scrolls*, ed. James H. Charlesworth (New York: Crossroads, 1992), pp. 15-52.
[5]Emanuel Tov, *Textual Criticism of the Hebrew Bible*, 2nd ed. (Minneapolis: Fortress, 2001), pp. 104-5.

Because these biblical manuscripts were written at different times and places, they differ in textual, linguistic and scribal characteristics. There is textual diversity among the Qumran manuscripts, which are dated from the third century B.C. to the first century A.D.; the largest percentage of the texts closely follow the readings of the proto-MT (35 percent of mss). Others demonstrate some characteristics of a pre-Samaritan text (15 percent of mss; 4QpaleoExod^m, 4QNum^b, 4QDeut^n, 4Q158) or of a proto-LXX text (5 percent of mss; 4QExod^b, 4QLev^d, 4QJer^b, 4QJer^d). However, no manuscript is identical or nearly identical to the Hebrew text that gave rise to these translations.[6] Tov argues that there are two more textual groups in Qumran manuscripts: (1) texts following the Qumran practice of taking a free approach to the biblical text and resulting in unusual forms, frequent errors and numerous corrections (about 20 percent of mss),[7] and (2) nonaligned texts that are not significantly close to any other textual groups and seem to agree and disagree with them equally as many times (35 percent of mss; 2QExod^{a,b}, 4QExod-Lev^f, 11QpaleoLev^a, 4QDeut^{b,c,h,k1,k2,m}, 5QDeut, etc). While textual diversity is quite obvious among the texts from Qumran, the great number of proto-MT manuscripts almost certainly reflects its authoritative status.[8]

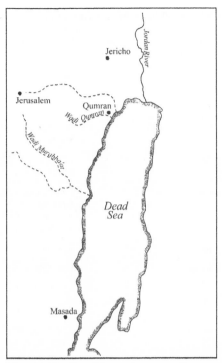

Map 6.1. The Dead Sea and surrounding area

The Dead Sea Scrolls are crucial to Old Testament textual criticism for several reasons:

- They were written during a transitional stage between unpointed texts and pointed texts; *matres lectionis* were used to indicate some of the important vowels (full vowel pointing was not added until several hundred years later; see p. 35).

---

[6]Ibid., p. 115.
[7]Ibid., p. 114.
[8]Ibid., p. 117.

Table 6.1. Biblical Manuscripts of the Dead Sea Scrolls

Biblical Books (Hebrew Order)	Number of Copies	Designations
Genesis	19	1Q1, 2Q1, 4Q1, 4Q2-7, 4Q8, 4Q8a, 4Q8c, 4Q9-10, 4Q11, 4Q12, 4QGen^n, 4Q483, 6Q1, 8Q1, Mas-Gen?, Mur 1:1-3, Mur?Genesis, Sdeir 1
Exodus	17	1Q2, 2Q2-4, 4Q1, 4Q11, 4Q13-16, 4Q17, 4Q18-21, 4Q22, Mur 1.4-5
Leviticus	13	1Q3, 2Q5, 4Q23, 4Q24, 4Q25, 4Q26, 4Q26a, 4Q26b, 11Q2, Mas1a, Mas1b, (Greek: 4Q119, 4Q120)
Numbers	12	1Q3, 2Q6, 2Q7, 2Q8, 2Q9, 4Q23, 4Q27, XHev/Se 1, XHev/Se 2, 5/6 Hev 1a, Mur 1:6-7, (Greek: 4Q121)
Deuteronomy	29	1Q4, 1Q5, 2Q10, 2Q11, 2Q12, 4Q28, 4Q29, 4Q30, 4Q31, 4Q32, 4Q33, 4Q34, 4Q35, 4Q36, 4Q37, 4Q38, 4Q38a, 4Q38b, 4Q39, 4Q40, 4Q41, 4Q42, 4Q43, 4Q44, 4Q45, 4Q46, 5Q1, 6Q3, 8Q4, Mur 2, Mas1c, XHev/Se 3, (Greek 4Q122)
Joshua	2	4Q47, 4Q48
Judges	3	1Q6, 4Q49, 4Q50
1-2 Samuel	4	1Q7, 4Q51, 4Q52, 4Q53
1-2 Kings	3	4Q54, 5Q2, 6Q4
Isaiah	22	1QIsa^a, 1Q8, 4Q55, 4Q56, 4Q57, 4Q58, 4Q59, 4Q60, 4Q61, 4Q62, 4Q62a, 4Q63, 4Q64, 4Q65, 4Q66, 4Q67, 4Q68, 4Q69, 4Q69a, 4Q69b, 5Q3, Mur 3
Jeremiah	6	2Q13, 4Q70, 4Q71, 4Q71a, 4Q71b, 4Q72
Ezekiel	7	1Q9, 3Q1, 4Q73, 4Q74, 4Q75, 11Q4, Mas1d
Twelve Prophets	8	4Q76, 4Q77, 4Q78, 4Q79, 4Q80, 4Q81, 4Q82, Mur 88, (Greek: 8Hev 1)
Psalms	39	1Q10, 1Q11, 1Q12, 2Q14, 3Q2, 4Q83, 4Q84, 4Q85, 4Q86, 4Q87, 4Q88, 4Q89, 4Q90, 4Q91, 4Q92, 4Q93, 4Q94, 4Q95, 4Q96, 4Q97, 4Q98^{a-d}, 4Q522, 4QPs^w, 5Q5, 6Q5, 8Q2, 11Q5, 11Q6, 11Q7, 11Q8, 11Q11, Mas1e, f, XHev/Se 4
Job	4	2Q15, 4Q99, 4Q100, 4Q101
Proverbs	2	4Q102, 4Q103
Ruth	4	2Q16, 2Q17, 4Q104, 4Q105
Song of Solomon	4	4Q106, 4Q107, 4Q108, 6Q6
Ecclesiastes	2	4Q109, 4Q110
Lamentations	4	3Q3, 4Q111, 5Q6, 5Q7
Esther	0	
Daniel	8	1Q71, 1Q72, 4Q112, 4Q113, 4Q114, 4Q115, 4Q116, 6Q7
Ezra	1	4Q117
Nehemiah	0	
1-2 Chronicles	1	4Q118

- They contain evidence as to how the biblical texts were read before the proto-MT became unified by the first century A.D.

- Some copies of the biblical texts also indicate how they were interpreted by this community (generally a *pesher* method of interpretation was employed, applying biblical texts directly to the contemporary situation).

- Information regarding the copying and correcting process of manuscripts can be gleaned from them, including (1) consonants that were mistakenly interchanged, (2) questionable letters that either were crossed out or around which dots were placed, (3) corrections written in the margins that could have confused later copyists, and (4) the addition of diacritical marks (marks indicating insertions, deletions or some other textual note).[9]

To get a better feel for the Dead Sea Scrolls, we will look at five significant biblical texts from the Scrolls.

6.1.2.1 The First Isaiah Scroll (1QIsa[a]). The 1QIsa[a] scroll contains the entire book of Isaiah.[10] There are about 1,375 different readings and 4,500 orthographic variants (variations in the way words are spelled) between this Isaiah Scroll (see fig. 6.2) and the MT; the latter make no difference in the reading of the text and the former alter it only slightly.[11]

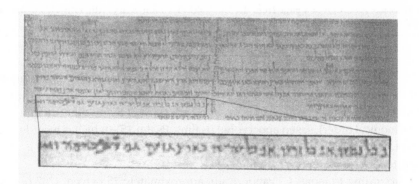

Figure 6.2. Isaiah 39-40 from the first Isaiah Scroll (1QIsa[a]) found in Cave 1 at Qumran [John C. Trever]

---

[9]For a detailed description of this process, see Malachi Martin, *The Scribal Character of the Dead Sea Scrolls*, 2 vols. (Louvain: Publications universitaires, 1958).

[10]Millar Burrows, ed., *The Dead Sea Scrolls of St. Mark's Monastery*, vol. 1, *The Isaiah Manuscript and the Habakkuk Commentary* (New Haven: American Schools of Oriental Research, 1950), plates I-XIV; John C. Trever, *Scrolls from Qumrân Cave I* (Jerusalem: Albright Institute of Archaeological Research and the Shrine of the Book, 1972), pp. 13-123.

[11]Ernst Würthwein, *The Text of the Old Testament*, trans. Erroll F. Rhodes, 2nd ed. (Grand Rapids: Eerdmans, 1995), p. 33.

6.1.2.2 The Second Isaiah Scroll (1QIsa^b). The 1QIsa^b scroll is much closer to the MT than 1QIsa^a, but it is in very poor condition; only the upper part of the last third of the scroll and a few fragments from the middle have been preserved.[12] The text contains fewer *plene* spellings than 1QIsa^a.

6.1.2.3 The Habakkuk Commentary (1QpHab). The 1QpHab scroll is a translation of and commentary on the first two chapters of Habakkuk (see fig. 6.3).[13] The sacred name Yahweh (יהוה, *yhwh*) is written in paleo-Hebrew script in this manuscript.

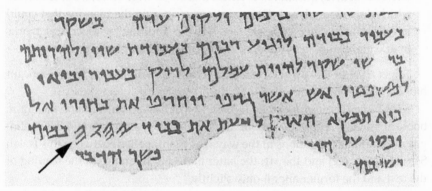

Figure 6.3. A section of a page from the Habbakkuk commentary with Yahweh's name in paleo-Hebrew [John C. Trever]

6.1.2.4 The Psalms Scroll (11QPs^a). The 11QPs^a scroll is in very good condition at the top, but the bottom is in an advanced state of decomposition.[14] It contains forty-one canonical psalms from the last third of the psalter (though not in canonical order), seven apocryphal psalms, Psalm 151 (which is recorded in the LXX) and a psalm from Sirach 51:13-20. The name Yahweh (יהוה) is also written in paleo-Hebrew script.

According to James C. VanderKam, approximately 25 percent (202 out of about 800) of the manuscripts found at Qumran are biblical texts.[15] This still leaves numerous other works, such as apocryphal books (four), pseude-

---

[12]Eleazar L. Sukenik, ed., *The Dead Sea Scrolls of the Hebrew University* (Jerusalem: Magnes, 1955), pp. 30-34, 44, figs. 18-21 and plates 1-15.

[13]Burrows, *Dead Sea Scrolls*, pp. 365-70; Géza Vermès, *The Dead Sea Scrolls in English*, 3rd ed. (Sheffield: Sheffield Academic Press, 1987), pp. 283-89; Devorah Dimant, "The Pesher on Habakkuk," in *Jewish Writings of the Second Temple Period*, ed. Michael E. Stone, CRINT 2/2 (Philadelphia: Fortress, 1984), pp. 508-10; Trever, *Scrolls from Qumrân*, pp. 149-63.

[14]James A. Sanders, *The Psalms Scroll of Qumrân Cave 11*, DJD 4 (Oxford: Clarendon, 1965).

[15]VanderKam, *Dead Sea Scrolls Today*, p. 31.

pigraphal works (three previously known and about fifty new), commentaries on biblical books (about 23), sectarian documents (some of the most important are the *Damascus Document, Manual of Discipline, Temple Scroll,* some of the *Works of the Torah* [4QMMT]) and eschatological works (*The War Scroll,* texts about the future New Jerusalem).

The Hebrew script of the Dead Sea Scrolls is similar to modern square script, making it fairly easy to compare them to the MT. The increase in *matres lectionis* is generally an insignificant variation, though the orthography (spelling) may help determine the date of the passage. For textual criticism one should note deviations of the scrolls from the MT—sometimes they will follow readings found in the LXX and SP.

Further Reading

Primary Sources

Many Qumran materials are being published in the series Discoveries in the Judaean Desert (Oxford: Clarendon).

Fitzmyer, Joseph A. *The Dead Sea Scrolls: Major Publications and Tools for Study.* Rev. ed. SBL Resources for Biblical Study 20. Missoula, Mont.: Scholars Press, 1990. See esp. bibliography.

Sukenik, Eleazer L., ed. *The Dead Sea Scrolls of the Hebrew University.* Jerusalem: Magnes, 1955.

Vermès, Géza. *The Complete Dead Sea Scrolls in English.* London/New York: Penguin, 1997.

Other Works

Allegro, John M. *The Dead Sea Scrolls.* Harmondsworth, Middlesex: Penguin, 1957.

Collins, John J. "Dead Sea Scrolls." *ABD* 2.85-101. See esp. bibliography.

Cross, Frank M. *The Ancient Library of Qumran and Biblical Studies.* 2nd ed. Grand Rapids: Baker, 1980.

———. "The History of the Biblical Text in the Light of Discoveries in the Judaean Desert." *HTR* 57 (1964): 281-99. Reprinted in *QHBT.* See pp. 177-95.

LaSor, William S. "Dead Sea Scrolls." *ISBE* 1:883-97. See esp. bibliography.

Mansoor, Menahem. *The Dead Sea Scrolls.* 2nd ed. Grand Rapids: Baker, 1983.

Mulder, Martin J. "The Transmission of the Biblical Text." In *Mikra,* pp. 96-98, edited by Martin J. Mulder. CRINT 2/1. Philadelphia: Fortress, 1988.

Skehan, Patrick W. "The Biblical Scrolls from Qumran and the Text of the Old Testament." *BA* 28 (1965): 87-100. Reprinted in *QHBT.* See pp. 264-77.

———. "The Scrolls and the Old Testament Text." In *New Directions in Biblical Archaeology,* pp. 99-112, edited by David N. Freedman and Jonas C. Greenfield. Garden City, N.Y.: Doubleday, 1971.

Talmon, Shemaryahu. "Aspects of the Textual Transmission of the Bible in the
Light of Qumran Manuscripts." *Textus* 4 (1964): 95-132. Reprinted in *QHBT*.
See pp. 226-63.

VanderKam, James C. *The Dead Sea Scrolls Today.* Grand Rapids: Eerdmans,
1994.

6.1.3 Nash Papyrus

The Nash Papyrus (see fig. 6.4) is a damaged copy of the Decalogue (Ten Commandments). William F. Albright used paleographic evidence to date this
work to the Maccabean period (169-37 B.C.). Paul Kahle dated it according to
internal evidence to before the Roman destruction of the Jerusalem temple
(A.D. 70).[16] It contains Exodus 20:2-17 (see also the parallel passage of Deuteronomy 5:6-21, from which some of the variants may derive) and the *Shema*
("Hear, O Israel, the LORD our God is one God") from Deuteronomy 6:4-5. This
combination of texts suggests that it was not part of a biblical scroll but rather
a collection of texts used for another purpose. It is interesting that the sixth and
seventh commandments are reversed and that the *Shema* is preceded by a
phrase confirmed only by the LXX:

[ואלה החק]ים והמשפטים אשר צוה
משה את [בני ישראל] במדבר בצאתם מארץ מצרים

[w'lh hḥq]ym whmšpṭym 'šr ṣwh mšh 't [bny yśr'l] bmdbr bṣ'tm m'rṣ mṣrym

"These are the ordinances and the judgments that Moses commanded the sons of
Israel in the wilderness when they went forth from the land of Egypt."

This reading suggests that the text of the Nash Papyrus is related to or at
least influenced by the LXX.

The Nash Papyrus is written in Hebrew square script (very similar to the
Qumran script) and corresponds closely to the text of the MT. It has more
matres lectionis than the MT. (These can help us date the text, though they do
not change its meaning.) It has a few minor differences from the MT that also
appear in the LXX and Vulgate.[17] Since there is a strong similarity between the
Nash Papyrus and the LXX, it is plausible that the LXX translators followed a
similar text or that the text represented in the Nash Papyrus (which appears to
be later than the LXX) was modified to correspond to the LXX.

---

[16]William F. Albright, "A Biblical Fragment from the Maccabaean Age: The Nash Papyrus,"
JBL 56 (1937): 145-76; Paul Kahle, *Die hebräischen Handschriften aus der Höhle* (Stuttgart: Kohlhammer, 1951), pp. 5-6.

[17]For example, line 10 lacks the ב (*b*, "in") of the word וביום (*wbywm*, "and in the day"), which
is found in the MT, but line 11 contains בה (*bh*, "in it") which is not found there.

Figure 6.4. The Nash Papyrus acquired in 1902 by W. L. Nash from a native dealer. He later donated it to the Cambridge University Library. It contains a damaged copy of the decalogue (Ex 20:2-17). [Cambridge University Library]

Further Reading

Primary Sources

Albright, William F. "On the Date of the Scrolls from ʿAin Feshkha and the Nash Papyrus." *BASOR* 115 (1949): 11.

Birnbaum, Shalomo A. *The Hebrew Scripts.* Vol. 1. Leiden: Brill, 1971. No. 151.

———. *The Hebrew Scripts.* Vol. 2. London: Palaeographia, 1954-1957. No. 151.

Cook, Stanley A. "A Pre-Massoretic Biblical Papyrus." *PSBA* (1903): 34-56, plates I-III.

Sukenik, Eleazer L., ed. *The Dead Sea Scrolls of the Hebrew University.* Jerusalem: Magnes, 1955. See fig. 8.

Würthwein, Ernst. *The Text of the Old Testament.* Translated by Erroll F. Rhodes. 2nd ed. Grand Rapids: Eerdmans, 1995. See pp. 34, 144-45.

Other Works

Albright, William F. "A Biblical Fragment from the Maccabean Age: The Nash Papyrus." *JBL* 56 (1937): 145-76.

Birnbaum, Shalomo A. "The Date of the Cave Scrolls." *BASOR* 115 (1949): 20-22.

Burkitt, F. Crawford. "The Hebrew Papyrus of the Ten Commandments." *JQR* 15 (1903): 392-408.

6.1.4 *Murabba'at Manuscripts*

In 1951 Bedouin from the Ta'amireh tribe discovered a piece of a leather sandal and a scroll fragment in one of four caves located in Wadi Murabba'at (or Darajeh), about eleven miles south of Cave 1 at Qumran (see map 6.1). Excavations began in January 1952 and the majority of documents come from Cave 2.

Figure 6.5. The Murabba'at caves [Israel Antiquities Authority]

Several small fragments dated to the Roman period and containing text written in Herodian script from the books of Genesis, Exodus, Numbers, Deuteronomy, Isaiah and the Minor Prophets were discovered, and the oldest papyrus document ever found in Israel. The latter is a palimpsest (a manuscript whose earlier writing was scraped off in order to be reused), the earlier writing of which is too faint to decipher fully but is dated by paleography to the eighth or seventh century B.C. Its later text, which contains a list of names with symbols and figures, is dated to the sixth century B.C. The most complete text is a scroll with ten of the twelve Minor Prophets (Mur 88; see fig. 6.6) written in Hebrew square script and dated to the second century A.D. All the manuscripts

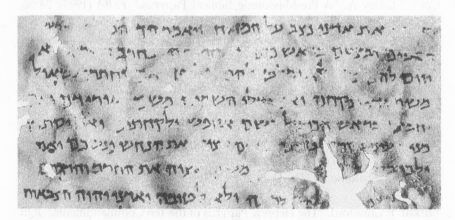

Figure 6.6. A fragment of a scroll containing the Minor Prophets (Mur 88) from Wadi Murabba'at [Israel Antiquities Authority]

found at Wadi Murabba'at are very similar to the MT (all eighteen of the additions and corrections made to the manuscripts are toward the MT)[18] and help to confirm that during the first century A.D. the MT had indeed become unified.[19]

Further Reading

Primary Sources

Benoit, Pierre, Józef T. Milik and Roland de Vaux. *Les grottes de Murabba'ât*. 2 vols. DJD 2. Oxford: Clarendon, 1961. See esp. vol. 2, plates LVI-LXXII.

Puech, Emile. "Fragment d'un rouleau de la Genèse provenant du Désert de Juda (Gen. 33,18-34,3)." *RevQ* 10, no. 38 (1980): 163-66.

Other Works

Allegro, John M. *The Dead Sea Scrolls*. Harmondsworth, Middlesex: Penguin, 1957. See pp. 168-79.

Burrows, Millar. *More Light on the Dead Sea Scrolls*. New York: Viking, 1958. See pp. 16-19, 31-33.

Cross, Frank M. *The Ancient Library of Qumran and Biblical Studies*. 2nd ed. Grand Rapids: Baker, 1980. See pp. 9-22, 120-45.

Fitzmyer, Joseph A. *The Dead Sea Scrolls: Major Publications and Tools for Study.* Rev. ed. SBL Resources for Biblical Study 20. Missoula, Mont.: Scholars Press, 1990. See pp. 41-45.

Mansoor, Menahem. *The Dead Sea Scrolls*. 2nd ed. Grand Rapids: Baker, 1983. See pp. 28-37.

Milik, Józef T. *Ten Years of Discovery in the Wilderness of Judaea,* translated by John Strugnell. SBT 1/26. Naperville, Ill.: Allenson, 1959. See pp. 135-41.

Murphy-O'Connor, Jerome. "Wadi Murabbaat: Archaeology." *ABD* 6:863-64.

O'Brien, Julia M. "Wadi Murabbaat: Texts." *ABD* 6:864.

Vermès, Géza. *Discovery in the Judean Desert.* New York: Desclee, 1956. See pp. 20-22.

Yadin, Yigael. *The Message of the Scrolls,* edited by James H. Charlesworth. New York: Crossroads, 1992. See pp. 68-72.

6.1.5 Manuscripts at Masada

Masada (which means "stronghold" or "mountain fortress" in Hebrew) is a large plateau located about two-thirds of the way down the western shore of the Dead Sea (see map 6.1). This site is a natural fortification since its sides are sheer cliffs of up to 1,300 feet in some places.

---

[18]Julia M. O'Brien, "Wadi Murabbaat: Texts," *ABD* 6:864.

[19]Moshe Greenberg, "The Stabilization of the Text of the Hebrew Bible Revised in the Light of the Biblical Materials from the Judean Desert," *JAOS* 76 (1956): 157-67 (reprinted in *CMHB*, pp. 298-326).

Figure 6.7. A photograph of Masada with an inset of the palace on the northern end of the plateau [Courtesy of Galilee College]

The Hasmoneans apparently were the first to occupy this mountain fortress, but Herod the Great (40 B.C.-A.D. 4) did most of the major construction here, including a beautiful three-tiered palace on its northern edge, from approximately 36-30 B.C. (see fig. 6.7). Later, during the First Jewish Revolt (A.D. 66-73), a group of zealots captured Masada and held it until A.D. 73, three years after the fall of Jerusalem. The Jewish zealots employed guerrilla warfare tactics to harass Roman troops and then fled to Masada for protection. In A.D. 72 Flavius Silva led the tenth legion against the zealots at Masada. He forced Jewish prisoners to build a ramp up the side of the fortress (which can still be seen in the picture), because he knew that the zealots would not kill their own countrymen. The Roman army breached the fortification in April A.D. 73, and Silva planned the final attack on Masada the following day. During the night, however, about nine hundred zealots committed suicide rather than surrender to the Romans.

Excavations at Masada in 1963-1965 uncovered the remains of fourteen scrolls, including biblical, sectarian and apocryphal texts. They date to sometime before A.D. 73, when the Romans stormed the fortress, and provide further evidence that the Hebrew text had become unified by the first century A.D. Some of the more interesting biblical texts are:

- A very fragmentary Psalms scroll containing parts of Psalms 81:3 (ET 81:2) to 85:10 (ET 85:9) (see fig. 6.8). The text of this scroll is identical to the MT in both content and spelling.

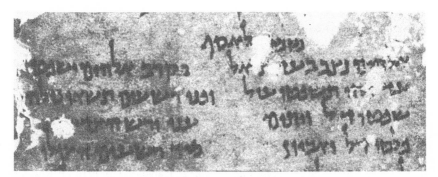

Figure 6.8. A fragment of Psalm 82 from Masada [Israel Antiquities Authority]

- A fragment of Leviticus containing the second half of eight lines from Leviticus 4:3-9. It is identical to the MT in content and spelling.

- A fragmentary Leviticus scroll containing Leviticus 8—12. The text of this document is identical to the MT even in respect to the traditional divisions of the "open" (where the line is left open after a Hebrew sentence) and "closed" (where another Hebrew sentence finishes up the line) sections.

- A scroll of Ezekiel and one containing the final two chapters of Deuteronomy. These texts largely reflect the traditional MT, but a few readings in the Ezekiel scroll differ slightly from the MT.[20]

- A copy of Psalm 150, seemingly at the end of a manuscript, which suggests that the Psalms at Masada may have been ordered similarly to the canonical psalter.

The Masada manuscripts are written in Hebrew square script and are virtually identical to the MT (in wording as well as the divisions of the lines), except for slight differences in the Ezekiel text.

Further Reading

Primary Sources

Yadin, Yigael. *The Ben Sira Scroll from Masada: With Introduction, Emendations and Commentary.* Jerusalem: Israel Exploration Society, 1965.

———. "The Excavation of Masada 1963/64: Preliminary Report." *IEJ* 15 (1965): 81-82, 103-5; plates 19-20.

———. *Masada: Herod's Fortress and the Zealots' Last Stand.* Translated by Moshe Pearlman. New York: Random House, 1966. See pp. 179, 187-89.

---

[20]Yigael Yadin, *Masada: Herod's Fortress and the Zealots' Last Stand*, trans. Moshe Pearlman (New York: Random House, 1967), pp. 168-79, 187.

Other Works

Fitzmyer, Joseph A. *The Dead Sea Scrolls: Major Publications and Tools for Study.* Rev. ed. SBL Resources for Biblical Study 20. Missoula, Mont.: Scholars Press, 1990. See p. 40.

Netzer, Ehud. "Masada." *ABD* 4:586-87.

Mansoor, Menahem. *The Dead Sea Scrolls.* 2nd ed. Grand Rapids: Baker, 1983. See pp. 204-14.

Sanders, James A. "Pre-Masoretic Psalter Texts." In *The Dead Sea Psalms Scroll.* Ithaca, N.Y.: Cornell University Press, 1967. See pp. 143-49, 152.

Würthwein, Ernst. *The Text of the Old Testament,* translated by Erroll F. Rhodes. 2nd ed. Grand Rapids: Eerdmans, 1995. See p. 32.

Yadin, Yigael. *Masada: The Yigael Yadin Excavations, 1963-1965: Final Reports.* 3 vols. Jerusalem: Israel Exploration Society, 1989-1991.

6.1.6 Naḥal Ḥever Manuscripts

Naḥal Ḥever (Wadi Ḥabra) is located about one mile south of Ein Gedi on the western shore of the Dead Sea (see map 6.1). There, in 1952, several fragmentary Hebrew manuscripts of Genesis, Numbers, Deuteronomy and Psalms were discovered. The most complete discovery, however, was a Greek manuscript of the Minor Prophets (8ḤevXIIgr, see fig. 6.9), dated between 50 B.C.-

Figure 6.9. A fragment of Zechariah 1:14a in Greek from the scroll of the Minor Prophets found at Naḥal Ḥever. The name Yahweh is in paleo-Hebrew script (see arrows). [Israel Antiquities Authority]

A.D. 50. It appears to come from a *Vorlage* very close to the MT.[21] All the biblical texts, along with a Hebrew phylactery fragment of Exodus 13:2-10, 11-16, are dated to about A.D. 130 and their translations are virtually identical to the MT.

Further Reading

Primary Sources

Barthélemy, Dominique. *Les devanciers d'Aquila.* VTSup 10. Leiden: Brill, 1963. See pp. 163-78.

Lifshitz, Baruch. "The Greek Documents from the Cave of Horror." *IEJ* 12 (1962): 201-7.

Yadin, Yigael. *The Documents from the Bar Kokhba Period in the Cave of Letters.* Jerusalem: Israel Exploration Society, 1989. See plates 1-40.

―――."Expedition D." *IEJ* 11 (1961): 40.

―――. "Expedition D: The Cave of Letters." *IEJ* 12 (1962): 229. See plate 48.

Other Works

Aharoni, Yohanan. "Expedition B: The Cave of Horror." *IEJ* 12 (1962): 186-99.

Fitzmyer, Joseph A. *The Dead Sea Scrolls: Major Publications and Tools for Study.* Rev. ed. SBL Resources for Biblical Study 20. Missoula, Mont.: Scholars Press, 1990. See esp. pp. 46-49.

Lewis, Naphtali. *The Documents from the Bar Kokhba Period in the Cave of Letters: Greek Papyri.* Jerusalem: Israel Exploration Society, 1989.

Yadin, Yigael. *Bar-Kokhba: The Rediscovery of the Legendary Hero of the Second Jewish Revolt Against Rome.* New York: Random House, 1971.

―――. *The Finds from the Bar Kokhba Period in the Cave of Letters.* Jerusalem: Israel Exploration Society, 1963.

6.1.7 Cairo Genizah Manuscripts

The Cairo Genizah is a storage room found in the 1860s in the Ben-Ezra synagogue, which was built in A.D. 1015 in Fostat or Old Cairo.[22] A *genizah* (from the Aramaic word גְּנַז, *gĕnaz*, "to hide") was a room used to store manuscripts until they could be properly disposed of so that they would not be misused or profaned since they contained the name of God. Apparently the genizah was forgotten and it was walled over and undisturbed until the 1860s. This hidden storeroom contained a great variety of materials; it has been estimated that about 200,000 fragments were deposited there (see fig. 6.10).[23] The vast majority come from about A.D. 1000 to 1400, though some date much earlier (sixth to

---

[21]Paul Kahle, *The Cairo Geniza,* 2nd ed. (New York: Praeger, 1959), p. 227.
[22]For an interesting history of the Cairo Genizah, see ibid., pp. 3-13.
[23]Ibid., p. 13.

Figure 6.10. Solomon Schechter in the Cambridge University Library with thousands of fragments from Cairo Genizah [Cambridge University Library]

eighth centuries). Several dozen manuscripts are palimpsests, about fifteen percent of which are biblical texts in Hebrew, Aramaic and Arabic. The genizah also housed materials from the Midrash, Mishnah, Talmud, liturgical texts, lists, letters and much more. Some of the most important items discovered were:

- An almost complete copy of the Wisdom of Jesus ben Sirach in Hebrew (previous to this discovery the work was known only from Greek texts).

- The *Zadokite Document* (a work closely related to the *Manual of Discipline* [1QS] from Qumran and is now generally known as the *Damascus Document* [CD = Cairo Genizah Document]).

- The most important documents for the study of textual criticism are the biblical manuscripts, some of which date back to the sixth century A.D. These show how more and more vowel pointings were gradually added in the Tiberian pointing system.[24] At present the earliest completely

---

[24]The Palestinian pointing system had been virtually lost until the discovery of several manuscripts from the Cairo Genizah with this pointing (see Oxford Ms. Heb e 30, fol. 48b). Other manuscripts show varying degrees of pointing, suggesting that there were several stages in the development of the pointing system.

pointed manuscript is the Cairo Manuscript of the Prophets from A.D. 895.[25]

Further Reading

Primary Sources

Davis, Malcolm C. *Hebrew Bible Manuscripts in the Cambridge Genizah Collections.* 2 vols. Cambridge: Cambridge University Library, 1978, 1980.

Gottheil, Richard J. H., and William H. Worrell. *Fragments of the Cairo Genizah in the Freer Collection.* New York: MacMillan, 1927.

Neubauer, Adolf, and Arthur E. Cowley. *Catalogue of Hebrew Manuscripts in the Bodleian Library.* 2 vols. Oxford: Clarendon, 1906.

Rabin, Chaim. *The Zadokite Documents.* 2nd ed. Oxford: Clarendon, 1958.

Schechter, Solomon. *Documents of Jewish Sectaries.* Vol. 1, *Fragments of a Zadokite Work.* New York: KTAV, 1970.

Other Works

Adler, Elkan N. *Catalogue of Hebrew Manuscripts in the Collection of Elkan Nathan Adler.* Cambridge: Cambridge University Library, 1921.

Davies, Philip R. "Damascus Rule (CD)." *ABD* 2:8-10.

Goshen-Gottstein, Moshe H. "Biblical Manuscripts in the United States." *Textus* 2 (1962): 35-44.

Halper, Baruch. *Descriptive Catalogue of Genizah Fragments in Philadelphia.* Philadelphia: Dropsie College for Hebrew and Cognate Learning, 1924.

Kahle, Paul. *The Cairo Geniza.* 2nd ed. Oxford: Clarendon, 1959.

Reif, Stefan C. *A Guide to the Taylor-Schechter Genizah Collection.* Cambridge: Cambridge University Library, 1973.

————. *Published Material from the Cambridge Genizah Collections, a Bibliography: 1896-1980.* Cambridge: Cambridge University Press, 1988.

Shaked, Shaul. *A Tentative Bibliography of Genizah Fragments.* Paris: Mouton, 1964.

Würthwein, Ernst. *The Text of the Old Testament.* Translated by Erroll F. Rhodes. 2nd ed. Grand Rapids: Eerdmans, 1995. See pp. 34-35.

6.1.8 Important Hebrew Manuscripts of the Old Testament

6.1.8.1 Ben Asher manuscripts. From the second half of the eighth century A.D. to the mid-tenth century A.D., the Ben Asher family played a leading role in recording and maintaining the MT at Tiberias.[26] The following are the earliest Ben Asher manuscripts, providing important examples of this tradition.

---

[25]Emanuel Tov, "The Text of the Old Testament" in *Bible Handbook*, vol. 1, *The World of the Bible*, ed. Adam S. van der Woude, trans. Sierd Woudstra (Grand Rapids: Eerdmans, 1986), p. 163.
[26]Ibid., p. 34.

- *Codex Cairensis.*[27] (This manuscript contains only the Former and Latter Prophets.) This well-preserved document appears to have been written and pointed by Moses ben Asher in A.D. 895. It has several colophons (a note at the end of a manuscript that provides information about the scribe and other matters). Kahle mentions that there are many corrections, perhaps in an effort to make it correspond to other Ben Asher manuscripts.[28]

- *Aleppo Codex.*[29] One quarter of this manuscript, dated to the first half of the tenth century, was destroyed by fire (Genesis 1:1—Deuteronomy 28:16; Song of Solomon 3:11 to the end of the Old Testament, including Ecclesiastes, Lamentations, Esther, Daniel and Ezra). Its colophon states that Aaron ben Moses ben Asher copied the pointing and the Masorah about A.D. 930 and that the consonantal text can be attributed to Shelomo ben Buya'a. This codex predates the Codex Leningradensis by over fifty years, but they are very similar. During the Crusades (July 15, 1099) it was taken as booty; about seven years later it was returned to the Karaites (a Jewish sect originating in the eighth century that denied talmudic-rabbinical tradition), who then brought it to Cairo. It is now in Jerusalem and is being used by the Hebrew University as the basis for another critical edition of the Old Testament text.

- Oriental 4445.[30] This manuscript contains 186 folios (i.e., a folded sheet of paper yielding two book pages) of the Pentateuch: Genesis 39:20—Deuteronomy 1:33. One hundred thirty-one folios are an early form of the Ben Asher text dated to about 950 and the other 55 were added by a later hand in about 1540.[31] They are written in very large, bold handwriting with full Palestinian or Western vowel points and accents but no verse dividers (called *sôp pasûq*, [:]) at the end of sentences. The Masorahs, both magna and parva, were added in the margins later than the original writing.

- *Codex Leningradensis* (Leningrad Ms. B19[A], see fig. 6.11) (L).[32] This text is a

---

[27]Paul Kahle, *Der hebräische Bibeltext seit Franz Delitzsch* (Stuttgart: Kohlhammer, 1961), figs. 1-18; David S. Loewinger, ed., *Codex Kairo of the Bible: From the Karaite Synagogue at Abbasiya. The Earliest Extant Hebrew Manuscript Written in 895 by Moshe ben Asher* (Jerusalem: Makor, 1971).

[28]Kahle, *Der hebräische Bibeltext seit Franz Delitzsch*, p. 77.

[29] Moshe H. Goshen-Gottstein, ed., *The Aleppo Codex* (Jerusalem: Hebrew University, 1976).

[30]Christian D. Ginsburg, *Introduction to the Massoretico-Critical Edition of the Hebrew Bible* (New York: KTAV, 1966), page facing pp. 469, 470-74; Tov, "Text of the Old Testament," illus. 50; Würthwein, *Text of the Old Testament*, pp. 176-77.

[31]Christian Ginsburg dates this manuscript much earlier, about A.D. 820-850 (*Introduction*, p. 469).

[32]BHK; BHS; David S. Loewinger, ed., *Pentateuch, Prophets and Hagiographia. Codex Leningrad B 19 A. The Earliest Complete Bible Manuscript* (Jerusalem: Makor, 1971); Würthwein, *Text of the Old Testament*, pp. 180-81.

very important witness to the Ben Asher family and is dated to 1008 by a colophon. Another colophon states: "Samuel ben Jacob wrote and pointed and provided with Masorah this codex of the Holy Scriptures from the corrected and annotated books prepared by Aaron ben Moses ben Asher the teacher, may he rest in the Garden of Eden! It has been corrected and properly annotated."[33] This manuscript was the main source for the most recent critical Hebrew texts (*BHK* and *BHS*), being the oldest and most complete manuscript accessible at the time (the Aleppo Codex was inaccessible and lacks one-fourth of the Old Testament).

6.1.8.2 Leningrad (Formerly Petersburg) Codex of the Prophets.[34] This manuscript, including only the Latter Prophets (Isaiah, Jeremiah, Ezekiel, the twelve Minor Prophets) and the small and large Masorahs, is dated to 916. It is the oldest dated text using the Babylonian supralinear system of vowel points and accents, a system that had been lost for centuries. The codex was discovered by Abraham Firkowitsch in 1839, apparently in the synagogue of Chufutkaleh in Crimea. Würthwein describes its importance:

> while using the Eastern signs the codex actually follows the Western tradition in its consonantal text and its pointing. Thus it stands as an impressive symbol of the victory of the Western tradition over the Eastern. . . . On several pages (212a, 221a) the Babylonian signs have been replaced by the Tiberian signs, and on folio 1b both systems stand side by side.[35]

6.1.8.3 Damascus Pentateuch.[36] This codex contains most of the Pentateuch (only Genesis 1:1—9:26 and Exodus 18:1-23a are missing) and is dated to the late ninth or early tenth century. The consonantal text is from the Tiberian school of Masoretes, with additional changes to help it conform better to the MT (e.g., in Genesis 23:17 עַל פְּנֵי מַמְרֵא, '*l pny mmr*', has been changed to the MT's לִפְנֵי מַמְרֵא, *lpny mmr*'). It was pointed according to the Ben Naphtali tradition (the other prominent family of scribes near Tiberias),[37] but in some places the accents and vowel points have been scraped off and written over with accents and vowel points from the Ben Asher tradition. All the margins surrounding the text have Masoretic notes.

---

[33]Würthwein, *Text of the Old Testament*, p. 180.

[34]Hermann L. Strack, ed., *Prophetarum posteriorum Codex Babylonicus Petropolitanus auspiciis Augustissimi Imperatoris Alexandri II* (Petropoli: Bibliothecae Publicae Imperialis, 1876).

[35]Würthwein, *Text of the Old Testament*, p. 37.

[36]David S. Loewinger, ed., *The Damascus Pentateuch*, 2 vols. (Baltimore: Johns Hopkins University Press, 1978-1982); Otto H. Lehmann, *The Damascus Pentateuch and Its Manuscript Tradition (According to Ben Naphtali)* (Oxford: Clarendon, 1962).

[37]Loewinger, *Damascus Pentateuch* 1:12.

Figure 6.11. A page from Codex Leningradensis (Genesis 28:18—29:22) [National Library of Russia]

6.1.8.4 Codex Reuchlinianus of the Prophets.[38] This manuscript is a recension of the Ben Naphtali text, dated to about 1105.

6.1.8.5 Erfurtensis Codices.[39] These three manuscripts now belong to the State Library of Prussian Cultural Properties in Berlin. E1, dated to the fourteenth century, contains the entire Old Testament, Targums and the small and large Masorahs. E2 dates to the thirteenth century and contains the entire Old Testament, Targum Onkelos and the small and large Masorahs. E3 contains the entire Old Testament, small and large Masorahs, extracts from *Okhla weOkhla*, and is the earliest of these texts, dated before 1100.

6.1.9 Important Printed Hebrew Editions

- *Soncino Bible.* Published in 1488 by Rabbi Joshua in Soncino, Italy (a small village in the vicinity of Milan). This is the first complete, printed Hebrew Bible. It includes vowel points and accents but there is no Masorah for the text. It was produced in four separate parts by different people in order to expedite its publication. The order of the biblical books is unusual—the Megilloth (i.e., five scrolls, including Esther, Song of Solomon, Ruth, Lamentations and Ecclesiastes) directly follows the Pentateuch.

- *Daniel Bomberg Bible.* Edited by Felix Pratensis, a Christian Jew (d. 1539), and published (1516-1517) by Daniel Bomberg in Venice. This is the first Rabbinic Bible. It contains the Hebrew text along with the Aramaic Targums (Onkelos, Jonathan ben Uzziel, Rabbi Joseph, Jerusalem Targum II, the second Targum on Esther) and several rabbinic commentaries (e.g., Rashi, Kimḥi). This is the first printed edition of the Old Testament to divide Samuel, Kings and Chronicles into two books each, Ezra into both Ezra and Nehemiah, and to include some *Qere* readings in the margins. Felix Pratensis dedicated his work to Pope Leo X.

- *Complutensian Polyglot Bible.* Cardinal Ximenes, archbishop of Toledo, produced this polyglot (the biblical text appears in several different languages arranged in parallel columns) in Alcala, Spain, by permission of Pope Leo X. The Old Testament comprises the MT, LXX and Vulgate versions. Prior to this time the Hebrew Scriptures had been edited and printed exclusively

---

[38]Shelomo Morag, "The Vocalization of the Codex Reuchlinianus: Is the 'Pre-Masoretic' Bible Pre-Masoretic?" *JSS* 4 (1959): 216-37; Alexander Sperber, *Codex Reuchlinianus, No. 3 of the Badische Landesbibliothek in Karlsruhe with a General Introduction: Masoretic Hebrew*, Corpus Hebraicorum Medii Aevi 2/1 (Copenhagen: E. Munksgaard, 1956); Alexander Sperber, *The Prophets According to the Codex Reuchlinianus (in a Critical Analysis)* (Leiden: Brill, 1969).

[39]Paul Kahle, *Masoreten des Westens*, Texte und Untersuchungen zur vormasoretischen Grammatik des Hebräischen 4 (Stuttgart: Kohlhammer, 1930), 2:54; Würthwein, *Text of the Old Testament*, pp. 37-38.

by Jews. Spain became a celebrated seat of Hebrew learning; the scribes at Toledo had access to some of the oldest and most reliable manuscripts. Cardinal Ximenes was the first Christian to furnish the church with a Hebrew text of the Old Testament; unfortunately, authorization for publication did not occur until 1520, after Ximenes's death. The first four volumes include the Old Testament in the same order as the Vulgate; the last two volumes contain the New Testament and a critical apparatus. The Hebrew text does not include accents, and the vowel points are unreliable, but the consonantal text is very accurate and is based in large measure on a critical examination of the manuscripts, a significant first step for textual criticism of the Old Testament.

- *Second Rabbinic Bible of Jacob ben Ḥayyim.* Published in 1524/1525 by Daniel Bomberg in Venice and edited by an orthodox rabbinic Jew from Tunis (Jacob ben Ḥayyim). This four-volume work was the standard printed text of the Old Testament until the twentieth century (see fig. 6.12). It contains the Hebrew text, an Aramaic Targum (in the Pentateuch: Targum Onkelos; in the rest: Targum Jonathan), small, large and final Masorahs, and comments by important rabbis (Rashi, Ibn Ezra, Kimḥi, etc.). This manuscript was thought to be a good representation of the Ben Asher text, but it is now viewed as a mixture of various traditions from manuscripts shortly before the time it was written.

- *Antwerp Polyglot.* Published in 1569-1572 by Christophe Plantin at Antwerp (Belgium) and paid for by King Philip II of Spain (thus it is sometimes called *Biblia Regia*). The first four volumes comprise the Old Testament, including the Hebrew text, the official Targums (except for Daniel, Ezra-Nehemiah and Chronicles) with a Latin version, the LXX (following the Complutensian text) with a Latin version, and the Vulgate. The Hebrew text of the Antwerp Polyglot derives from the Complutensian Polyglot and the Second Rabbinic Bible of Jacob ben Ḥayyim.

- *Paris Polyglot.* The cost of this polyglot was underwritten by Guy M. leJay, who from 1629 to 1645 employed two chief editors: J. Morinus edited the SP and its Targum (following the manuscript of the SP brought to Europe in 1616 by Pietro de la Valle), and Gabriel Sionita edited the Peshitta text. This too is a massive work, entailing ten volumes (vols. 1-4 reproduce the Old Testament with the same versions as the Antwerp Polyglot; vols. 5-6 comprise the New Testament, and vols. 7-10 include the SP and its Targum, the Peshitta, and an Arabic version along with a Latin translation).

- *London Polyglot Bible.* Produced from 1654 to 1657 by Brian Walton, who later became bishop of Chester, this remarkable six-volume work includes

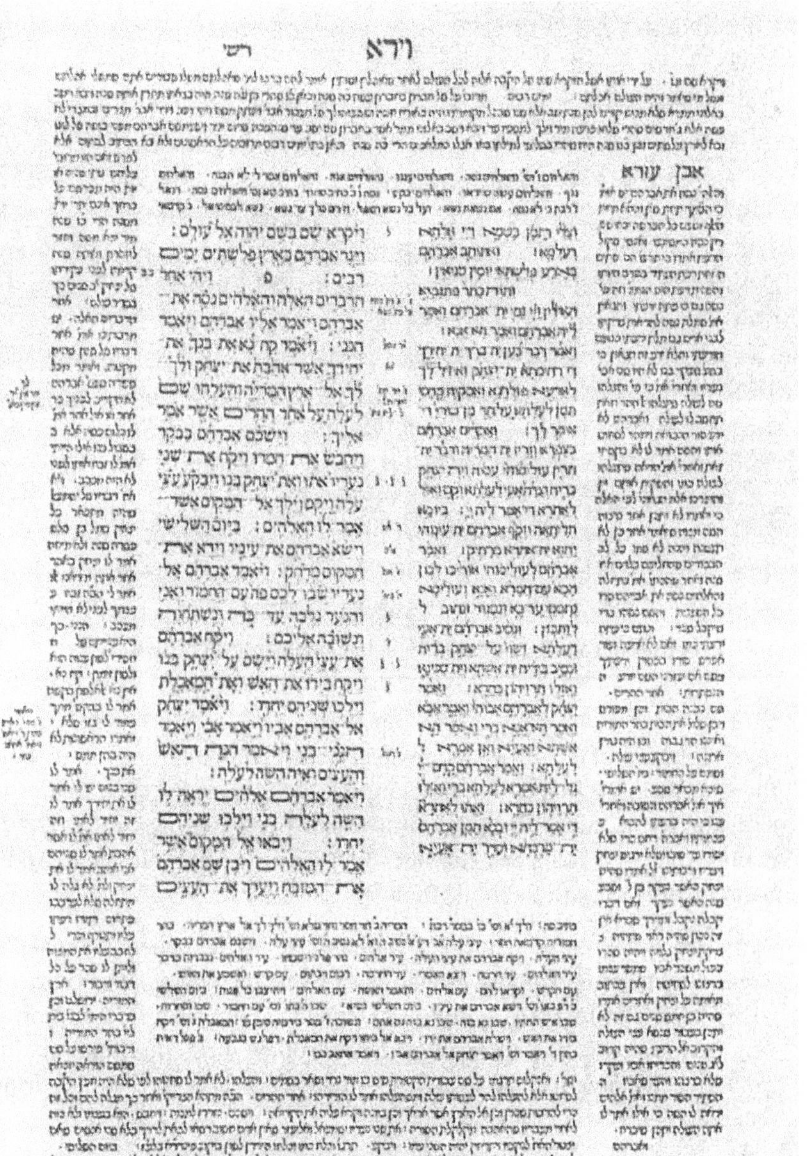

וירא רשי

אבן עזרא

Figure 6.12. A page of Genesis 21:33b—22:4a from the Second Rabbinic Bible of Jacob ben Ḥayyim [Bodleian Library, University of Oxford]

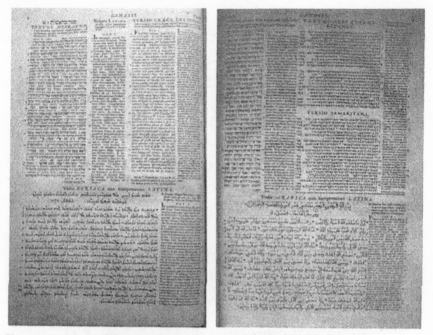

Figure 6.13. A page of Genesis 1 from the London Polyglot [Paul D. Wegner]

seven columns of texts: the Hebrew text with a Latin interlinear translation, the SP (only in the first volume), a Targum, the LXX, the Vulgate, the Peshitta and an Arabic, all with their Latin translations (see fig. 6.13). The text mainly followed Jacob ben Ḥayyim's text (Second Rabbinic Bible) and Johann Buxtorf's (Sixth Rabbinic Bible).

- *Biblia Hebraica.* Published in 1720 by Johann Heinrich Michaelis (1668-1738), a prominent German pietist, as well as a Protestant theologian and orientalist at Halle. This text largely follows Daniel E. Jablonski's 1699 edition and was the first to include a textual apparatus of the most important readings from five manuscripts at Erfurt, Germany, and nineteen other printed manuscripts.

- *Vetus Testamentum Hebraicum cum variis lectionibus.* Published from 1776-1780 by Benjamin Kennicott (1718-1783), canon of Christ Church, Oxford. This two-volume Hebrew text, with its massive textual apparatus, was printed without vowel points or accents and compiled variants from 615 manuscripts, 52 editions of the Hebrew text, and 16 manuscripts of the SP. Kennicott spent about ten years compiling readings of manuscripts from England, Italy, Germany, Switzerland and other countries.

- *Variae lectiones Veteris Testamenti.* Published from 1784 to 1788 by Giovanni B. de Rossi, an Italian scholar. This work is not a Hebrew text but rather a collection of variants of the consonantal text of the Old Testament. It contains readings from 1,475 manuscripts and editions, and is more thorough than any of its predecessors (see fig. 6.14).

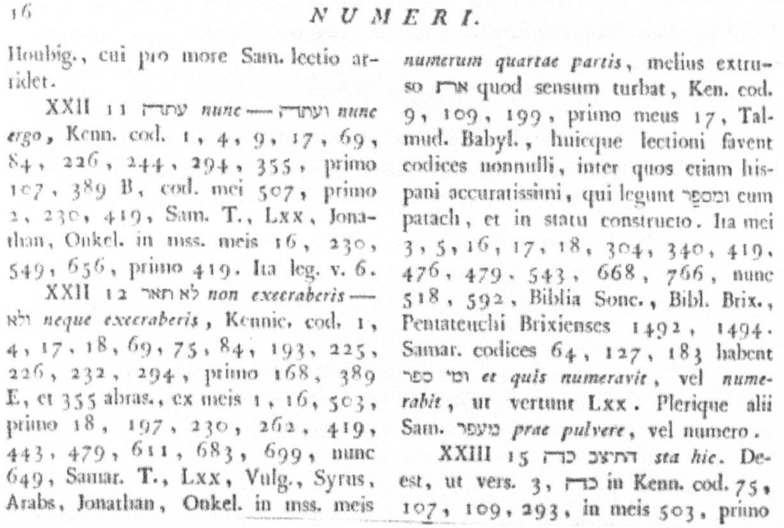

16   *N U M E R I.*

Houbig., cui pro more Sam. lectio arridet.

XXII 11 עירם *nunc* — ועירם *nunc ergo*, Kenn. cod. 1, 4, 9, 17, 69, 84, 226, 244, 294, 355, primo 107, 389 B, cod. mei 507, primo 2, 230, 419, Sam. T., Lxx, Jonathan, Onkel. in mss. meis 16, 230, 549, 656, primo 419. Ita leg. v. 6.

XXII 12 לא תאר *non exeeraberis* — לא *neque exeeraberis*, Kennic. cod. 1, 4, 17, 18, 69, 75, 84, 193, 225, 226, 232, 294, primo 168, 389 E, et 355 abras., ex meis 1, 16, 503, primo 18, 197, 230, 262, 419, 443, 479, 611, 683, 699, nunc 649, Samar. T., Lxx, Vulg., Syrus, Arabs, Jonathan, Onkel. in mss. meis

numerum quartae partis, melius extruso אר quod sensum turbat, Ken. cod. 9, 109, 199, primo meus 17, Talmud. Babyl., huicque lectioni favent codices nonnulli, inter quos etiam hispani accuratissimi, qui legunt ומספר cum patach, et in statu constructo. Ita mei 3, 5, 16, 17, 18, 304, 340, 419, 476, 479, 543, 668, 766, nunc 518, 592, Biblia Sonc., Bibl. Brix., Pentateuchi Brixienses 1492, 1494. Samar. codices 64, 127, 183 habent ומי ספר *et quis numeravit*, vel *numerabit*, ut vertunt Lxx. Plerique alii Sam. מעפר *prae pulvere*, vel numero.

XXIII 15 החרצ כה *sta hic*. Deest, ut vers. 3, כה in Kenn. cod. 75, 107, 109, 293, in meis 503, primo

Figure 6.14. A section of a page from the *Variae lectiones Veteris Testamenti* [McCormick Seminary, University of Chicago]

Further Reading

Bentzen, Aage. *Introduction to the Old Testament.* 2nd ed. 2 vols. Copenhagen: Gad, 1952. See pp. 50-60.

Darlow, Thomas H., and Horace F. Moule. *Historical Catalogue of Printed Editions of the English Bible, 1525-1961.* London: Bible House, 1903. See 2:701-37.

Eissfeldt, Otto. *The Old Testament: An Introduction.* Translated by Peter R. Ackroyd. New York: Harper & Row, 1965. See pp. 691-94.

Ginsburg, Christian D. *Introduction to the Massoretico-Critical Edition of the Hebrew Bible.* New York: KTAV, 1966. See pp. 779-956.

Kenyon, Frederic G. *Our Bible and the Ancient Manuscripts.* Edited by Arthur W. Adams. Rev. ed. New York: Harper, 1958. See esp. pp. 86-88.

Mulder, Martin J. "Transmission of the Biblical Text." In *Mikra*, pp. 116-21. Edited by Martin J. Mulder. CRINT 2/1. Philadelphia: Fortress, 1988.

Price, Ira M. *The Ancestry of Our English Bible.* 3rd ed. New York: Harper, 1956. See pp. 29-39.

Pfeiffer, Robert H. *Introduction to the Old Testament.* New York: Harper, 1941. See esp. pp. 97-101.

Roberts, Bleddyn J. *The Old Testament Text and Versions.* Cardiff: University of Wales Press, 1951. See esp. pp. 85-91.

Tasker, Randolph V. G. "The Complutensian Polyglot." *Church Quarterly Review* 154 (1953): 197-210.

Würthwein, Ernst. *The Text of the Old Testament.* Translated by Erroll F. Rhodes. 2nd ed. Grand Rapids: Eerdmans, 1995. See pp. 35-38.

6.2 Secondary Sources (Non-Hebrew Texts)

Within the last fifty years Old Testament textual criticism has experienced revolutionary changes. One of the most important is that we now have Hebrew manuscripts dated to the third or early second century B.C. Previous to this the oldest extant Hebrew manuscripts were from the ninth and tenth centuries A.D. Secondary sources (e.g., Greek translations, targums, other versions) that predated these were used extensively for Old Testament textual criticism. Tov describes this situation:

> Until recently, Old Testament textual criticism has paid much attention to the versions. This interest was justified because the oldest Hebrew manuscripts were from the Middle Ages, whereas some of the manuscripts of the Septuagint, Peshitta, and Vulgate are from the fourth and fifth centuries. This situation has now changed because the Hebrew scrolls from the Judean desert [Qumran] . . . are not only considerably older than the oldest manuscripts of the versions but also substantively more important. It is therefore likely that in the coming decades the text-critical interest will be focused more on Hebrew sources than on the versions, even though text-critically the latter remain of great importance, especially the Septuagint.[40]

There are three important concepts to remember when dealing with secondary sources. First, the process of translating a text from one language to another involves a distinct set of problems, such as the difficulties of finding equivalent words to translate the original language, and the grammatical and syntactical differences between languages. For example, the Hebrew word נָתַן (*nātan*), meaning "to give," is translated by thirty different Greek words in the LXX.[41] Conversely, one Greek word may stand for several Hebrew words.[42]

---

[40]Tov, "Text of the Old Testament," p. 172.

[41]Some of these are ἀποδίδωμι (*apodidōmi*, "to give back," 23 times), δίδωμι (*didōmi*, "to give" 1,456 times), παραδίδωμι (*paradidōmi*, "to give over, hand over," 132 times), τίθημι (*tithēmi*, "to place, set, lay down, lay aside," 139 times).

[42]In Is 13:20—14:4 of the LXX, the Greek word ἀναπαύω (*anapauō*, "to cause to rest, to give rest, refresh, or revive") is used six times in various forms to translate four different Hebrew

Second, it is not always possible to tell if divergences reconstructed from the various versions arise from discrepancies in the Hebrew text or from idiosyncrasies of the translators, who may have modified the text, either intentionally or unintentionally.[43] Despite these difficulties, suggested reconstructions of the original text from translations of the versions may provide important evidence when used carefully.[44] Third, it is important to know which translations are related so that particular readings are not given too much weight. For example, the LXX was the basis for the Old Latin, Sahidic, Ethiopic, Syro-Hexapla and Georgian versions. In addition, works such as the Vulgate are translations of an original Hebrew text and yet were heavily influenced by Greek and Old Latin versions. When related versions agree on a particular variant, they should be given the weight of only one version.

There have been some interesting changes in the study of the ancient versions and recensions, as Al Wolters points out:

> Although a substantial majority of the biblical texts discovered in the Judean desert can be classified as proto-Masoretic, it is nevertheless true that the Qumran finds have served to draw the attention of scholars to the variety of text forms current around the turn of the era. Paradoxically, the opposite is true of recent scholarship on the ancient versions. Whereas the versions had previously provided the chief evidence for readings that diverge from the MT, it is now becoming increasingly clear that the proto-Masoretic textual tradition underlies a good deal of the ancient versions, at least in certain phases of their textual transmission.[45]

---

words: 13:20, ἀναπαύσωνται *(anapausōntai)* to translate יִרְבְּצוּ *(yarbiṣû)*; 13:21, ἀναπαύσονται *(anapausontai)* to translate וְרָבְצוּ *(wĕrābṣû)*; 13:21, ἀναπαύσονται *(anapausontai)* to translate וְשָׁכְנוּ *(wĕšāknû)*; 14:1, ἀναπαύσονται *(anapausontai)* to translate וְהִנִּיחָם *(wĕhinnîḥām)*; 14:4, ἀναπέπαυται *(anapepautai)* to translate שָׁבַת *(šābat)*; 14:4, ἀναπέπαυται *(anapepautai)* to translate שָׁבְתָה *(šobtâ)* (see Walter Bauer, *A Greek-English Lexicon of the New Testament and Other Early Christian Literature,* ed. and trans. Williams F. Arndt and F. Wilbur Gingrich, 2nd ed., rev. F. Wilbur Gingrich and Frederick W. Danker [Chicago: University of Chicago Press, 1979], pp. 58-59).

[43]Tov cautions: "When a detail in a translation differs from the Massoretic text, one need not immediately assume that its *Vorlage* differed from the Massoretic text. Such differences are also caused, even in larger measure, by other factors such as exegesis, translation technique, and the transmission of the text of the versions" ("Text of the Old Testament," p. 172).

[44]See Moshe H. Goshen-Gottstein, "Theory and Practice of Textual Criticism: The Text-Critical Use of the Septuagint," *Textus* 3 (1963): 130-58; Emanuel Tov, "The Use of Concordances in the Reconstruction of the *Vorlage* of the LXX," *CBQ* 40 (1978): 29-36. This article is revised in Emanuel Tov's *Text-Critical Use of the Septuagint in Biblical Research,* JBS 3 (Jerusalem: Simor, 1981), pp. 142-54; John W. Wevers, "The Use of Versions for Text Criticism: The Septuagint," in *La Septuaginta en la investigacion contemporanea (V Congreso de la IOSCS),* ed. Natalio Fernández Marcos (Madrid: Consejo Superior de Investigaciones Científicas, 1985), pp. 15-24.

[45]Al Wolters, "The Text of the Old Testament," in *The Face of Old Testament Studies: A Survey of Contemporary Approaches,* ed. David W. Baker and Bill T. Arnold (Grand Rapids: Baker, 1999), p. 23.

Further Reading

Barr, James. *Comparative Philology and the Text of the Old Testament: With Additions and Corrections.* Winona Lake, Ind.: Eisenbrauns, 1987. See esp. pp. 238-72.

Brower, Reuben A., ed. *On Translation.* Cambridge: Cambridge University Press, 1959.

de Waarde, Jan, and Eugene A. Nida. *From One Language to Another: Functional Equivalence in Bible Translating.* Nashville: Nelson, 1986.

Goshen-Gottstein, Moshe H. "Theory and Practice of Textual Criticism: The Text-Critical Use of the Septuagint." *Textus* 3 (1963): 130-58.

Nida, Eugene A. "Theories of Translation." *ABD* 6:512-15.

———. *Toward a Science of Translating.* Leiden: Brill, 1964.

Nida, Eugene A., and Charles R. Taber. *The Theory and Practice of Translation.* Leiden: Brill, 1969.

Orlinsky, Harry M. "The Septuagint: Its Use in Textual Criticism." *BA* 9 (1946): 22-34.

Tov, Emanuel. "Text of the Old Testament." In *The World of the Bible.* Edited by Adam S. van der Woude, translated by Sierd Woudstra. Grand Rapids: Eerdmans, 1986. See pp. 172-73.

———. "The Use of Concordances in the Reconstruction of the *Vorlage* of the LXX." *CBQ* 40 (1978): 29-36. Revised in *Text-Critical Use of the Septuagint in Biblical Research.* JBS 3. Jerusalem: Simor, 1981. See pp. 142-54.

Wolters, Al. "The Text of the Old Testament." In *The Face of Old Testament Studies: A Survey of Contemporary Approaches,* pp. 19-37. Edited by David W. Baker and Bill T. Arnold. Grand Rapids: Baker, 1999.

6.2.1 Samaritan Pentateuch (SP)

Sargon II (721-705 B.C.) deported 27,290 Israelites from the Northern Kingdom to Assyria following their defeat in 721 B.C. and imported Assyrians from various parts of his empire to live in this newly defeated land. In time the Jews intermarried with the Assyrians, producing a race known as the Samaritans. The Jews living in Judah looked down on the Samaritans since they were not full Jews, and a schism developed between these two groups. The Samaritans built a temple for worship on Mt. Gerizim and accepted only the Pentateuch as authoritative Scripture, probably for theological and political reasons.[46]

---

[46]The Samaritans rejected the rest of Scripture for at least two reasons. Theologically, beginning with Joshua and Judges, Shiloh is chosen as their place of worship, not Mt. Gerizim. Politically, in the book of Joshua the land was allotted only to the Israelite tribes and thus Samaritans would be considered trespassers.

The SP[47] is a Samaritan version of the first five books of the Old Testament that developed sometime after the schism—exactly when is uncertain, but a date about 100 B.C. is probable. While little is known about the earliest period of the SP, it appears to have been accepted by the early patristic writers as a viable text, though the early rabbis rejected it largely because it was written in a form of paleo-Hebrew script and it contradicted Jewish traditions.[48] The Abisha Scroll, the most famous sacred scroll of the Samaritan community at Nablus (Shechem), is a combination of various fragments; the oldest, dated to the eleventh century A.D., contains the main part of Numbers 35 to Deuteronomy 34. Few manuscripts of the SP predate the thirteenth century A.D. and Waltke, after examining the primary manuscripts dating from the thirteenth to sixteenth centuries, concluded that the SP "is a uniform tradition drifting away from the MT through scribal error."[49]

The existing copies of the SP appear to have been revised after the proto-MT because they use more *matres lectionis* and fewer archaic endings than the MT. There are about six thousand differences between the SP and the MT, mostly minor spelling or grammatical changes.[50] However, several expansions of the text differ significantly from the MT.[51] The SP also tends toward harmonization (to bring into accord with the MT) or conflation (to combine readings from two manuscripts). After the discovery of the Qumran materials, a whole new area opened up for comparative studies. Several Qumran manuscripts show similarities to the SP primarily in the harmonistic expansions, only without the sectarian modifications (4QpaleoExod^m, 4Q158, 4QTestim, 4QNum^b, 4Q364, 4QDeut^n). This may have been the type of text used by the Samaritans to make

---

[47]Technically the SP is a recension of only part of the Old Testament and not a translation, but it can be conveniently handled with other ancient versions. Shemaryahu Talmon associates the SP with the versions and says "in this respect [the SP] falls in line with those translations, in the sense that it is a popular edition of the Pentateuch in the Hebrew language" ("The Samaritan Pentateuch," *JJS* 2 [1950-1951]: 149).

[48]See Bruce K. Waltke's interesting history of scholars' developing views of the SP in "Samaritan Pentateuch," *ABD* 5:932-33.

[49]Ibid., p. 935. Judith E. Sanderson states: "it is easy to recognize the relatively few harmonizing and clarifying expansions in the pre-Samaritan DSS [Dead Sea Scrolls] and the SP. When those are discounted, the SP agrees substantially with the text behind the MT" ("Ancient Texts and Versions of the Old Testament," in *New Interpreter's Bible* [Nashville: Abingdon, 1994], 1:299.)

[50]Several scholars argue that the SP is written in a different dialect than the Hebrew of the MT, accounting for numerous differences: Rudolf Macuch, *Grammatik des samaritanischen Hebräisch* (Berlin: de Gruyter, 1969), pp. vii-x; Alexander Sperber, "Hebrew Based upon Greek and Latin Transliterations," *HUCA* 12/13 (1937/1938): 151-53.

[51]For example, Gen 4:8; Ex 1:22; 2:21; 6:9; 7:19-20, 22, 26, 28; 14:12. See also Bruce K. Waltke, "The Samaritan Pentateuch and the Text of the Old Testament," in *New Perspectives on the Old Testament*, ed. J. Barton Payne (Waco, Tex.: Word, 1970), pp. 212-39.

their Torah.[52] The relationship among Qumran literature, the LXX and the SP is a matter of debate. Judith Sanderson has studied this relationship quite closely, and Wolters summarizes her research as follows:

> She concludes that the Hebrew textual traditions represented by the LXX, the MT, and the Samaritan Pentateuch were originally quite close, but that the first went its own way relatively early and developed an expansionist tendency, while the second and third stayed close together for some time. A century or so before the turn of the era, the pre-Samaritan tradition separated from the proto-Masoretic tradition and underwent some major expansions. Finally, the canonical form of the Samaritan Pentateuch was reached through a number of specifically sectarian expansions, especially relating to Mount Gerizim as a cultic center rather than Jerusalem.[53]

It was once thought that when the LXX and the SP agreed against the MT, the reading of the former two should be preferred. But now it is believed that a Palestinian manuscript taken into Egypt formed the basis for the LXX, so that both the SP and the LXX are actually distant members within the same family of texts (i.e., texts that are similar to one another because they derive from related texts). This explains why the SP and LXX share at least 1,600 variants from the MT.[54] It is interesting that the SP appears to be closer to the MT than some of the so-called pre-Samaritan texts found at Qumran. Waltke suggests why:

> The closer agreement of the Sam. Pent. with the MT than with some earlier mss of QL [Qumran literature] may be due to the influence of proto-MT on that collateral line of text from which the Sam. Pent. derives. Proto-MT may have been adopted by the Pharisees as early as 175 B.C., allowing time for its influence on the proto-Samaritan text-type before the emergence of the sectarian recension at 100 B.C.[55]

The SP is valuable to Old Testament textual criticism because, as Würthwein points out, "it is a very important witness to a form of the text that once enjoyed widespread use as shown by its agreements with the Qumran texts, the Septuagint, the New Testament, and some Jewish texts that escaped revision by official Judaism."[56] However, it actually turns out to be of little value for establishing original readings of the MT because of several significant limita-

---

[52]While some expansions in Qumran texts were seemingly influenced by the SP, none of the readings considered to be "sectarian" Samaritan readings appear.

[53]Wolters, "Text of the Old Testament," p. 28. See Judith E. Sanderson, *An Exodus Scroll from Qumran: 4QpaleoExod^m and the Samaritan Tradition*, HSS 30 (Atlanta: Scholars Press, 1986), p. 311.

[54]Ralph W. Klein says there are about 1,600 correlations between the LXX and SP (*Textual Criticism of the Old Testament: The Septuagint after Qumran*, GBS:OTS [Philadelphia: Fortress, 1974], p. 17), whereas Würthwein maintains there are approximately 1,900 (*Text of the Old Testament*, p. 43).

[55]Waltke, "Samaritan Pentateuch," 5:934.

[56]Würthwein, *Text of the Old Testament*, p. 46.

tions:[57] (1) it is probably a popularized revision of the text of the Old Testament; (2) no manuscripts of the SP precede the eleventh or twelfth century A.D.; and (3) it contains sectarian tendencies.[58]

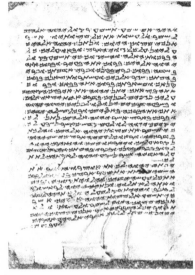

Figure 6.15. A portion of Deuteronomy 28 from the Samaritan Pentateuch (Nablus?), thirteenth century [Orlando, Fla.: The Scriptorium, VK MS 540]

Further Reading

Primary Sources

Girón-Blanc, L.-F. *Pentateuco-hebreo-samaritano, Génesis.* Madrid: Consejo Superior de Investigaciones Científicas, 1976.

leJay, Guy M., ed. *Polyglot of Paris.* Paris: Antonius Vitré, 1629-1645.

Tal, Abraham. *The Samaritan Targum of the Pentateuch.* 3 Vols. Texts and Studies in the Hebrew Language 4. Tel Aviv: Tel Aviv University Press, 1980-1983.

Tsadaqa, Avraham, and Ratson Sadaqa, eds. *The Jewish and Samaritan Version of the Pentateuch.* Tel Aviv: Rubin Mass, 1961-1965. This is a compilation from the Abisha Scroll and other medieval manuscripts.

Walton, Brian, ed. *Biblia Sacra Polyglotta, Complectentia.* London: Thomas Roycroft, 1657. This text is corrected against Pietro de la Valle's manuscript.

Other Works

Anderson, Robert T. "Samaritans." *ABD* 5:940-47. See esp. the bibliography.

Beckwith, Roger T. "Formation of the Hebrew Bible." In *Mikra,* pp. 85-86. Edited by Martin J. Mulder. CRINT 2/1. Philadelphia: Fortress, 1988.

Mulder, Martin J. "The Transmission of the Biblical Text." In *Mikra,* pp. 87-135, edited by Martin J. Mulder. CRINT 2/1. Philadelphia: Fortress, 1988. See esp. 95-96.

---

[57]Waltke states it this way: "The Sam. Pent. is of little value for establishing original readings. Out of eighty-five readings where Sanderson thought she could assign preferable readings involving the MT, LXX, Sam. Pent., and Q^m, she found no variants where the Sam. Pent. uniquely or even with LXX preserves the preferable reading (1986:85-88)" ("Samaritan Pentateuch," 5:938).

[58]For example, in Gen 22:2 the SP states that Abraham was about to offer up Isaac on Mt. Moreh near Shechem (a chief place of worship for the Samaritans) instead of Mt. Moriah, as in the MT. And in Deut 12:5 the SP identifies "the place which the Lord your God shall choose" as Gerizim, where the Samaritan temple stood, but later in the MT this place is determined to be Jerusalem.

Price, Ira M. *The Ancestry of Our English Bible: An Account of Manuscripts, Texts, and Versions of the Bible*. 3rd ed. New York: Harper & Brothers, 1956. See pp. 40-49.

Robertson, Edward. *Catalogue of the Samaritan Manuscripts in the John Rylands Library.* 2 vols. Manchester: Manchester University Press, 1938, 1962.

Sanderson, Judith E. *An Exodus Scroll from Qumran: 4QpaleoExod and the Samaritan Tradition*. Harvard Semitic Studies 30. Atlanta: Scholars Press, 1986.

Schur, Nathan. *History of the Samaritans*. Beiträge zur Erforschung des Alten Testaments und des antiken Judentums 18. Frankfurt: Peter Lang, 1989.

Skehan, Patrick W. "Qumran and the Present State of Old Testament Studies: The Massoretic Text." *JBL* 78 (1959): 21-25.

Shehadeh, Haseeb. "The Arabic Translation of the Samaritan Pentateuch: Prologomena to a Critical Edition." Ph.D. diss. Hebrew University, Jerusalem, 1977.

Waltke, Bruce K. *Prolegomena to the Samaritan Pentateuch*. Ph.D. Diss. Harvard University, 1965.

———. "Samaritan Pentateuch." *ABD* 5.932-40. See esp. the bibliography.

———. "The Samaritan Pentateuch and the Text of the Old Testament." In *New Perspectives on the Old Testament*, pp. 212-39, edited by J. Barton Payne. Waco, Tex.: Word, 1970.

6.2.2 *Aramaic Targums (or Targumim)*

Following the return from exile in 538 B.C., the Jewish people primarily spoke Aramaic (Neh 8:7-8; 13:24) and grew increasingly less familiar with Hebrew. As a result the Scripture lessons needed to be translated into Aramaic and became known as Targums. Some Targums contain a literal translation of the Hebrew text (e.g., Targum Onkelos), whereas others are paraphrastic (adding interpretive and explanatory material; e.g., Targum Neofiti).[59] Philip S. Alexander explains how these more paraphrastic translations arose: "It came to be recognized, however, that the Targum could do more than provide a simple rendering of Scripture into everyday speech: it could be a commentary as well as a translation, and impose a comprehensive interpretation on the original Hebrew."[60] At first these explanations were given extemporaneously by the scribes and teachers, it being strictly forbidden to put them into writing; thus various oral versions existed simultaneously.[61] It later became obvious

---

[59]For a good example of this see Brad H. Young, "Targum," *ISBE* 4:727-28.

[60]Philip S. Alexander, "Targum, Targumim," *ABD* 6:321.

[61]Johannes C. de Moor, "Systems of Writing and Nonbiblical Languages," in *Bible Handbook*, vol. 1, *The World of the Bible*, ed. Adam S. van der Woude, trans. Sierd Woudstra (Grand Rapids: Eerdmans, 1986), p. 116. Würthwein suggests that the Aramaic translation was to be given orally in the worship service to separate it from the sacred text (*Text of the Old Testament*, p. 79). See also Gamaliel I (mid-first century A.D.) who was not willing to recognize a targum of Job (*Shabbat* 115a; cf. *Tosefta Shabbat* 13, 2).

that to standardize these translations, they would have to be written. There are targums for every book of the Hebrew Bible except Ezra-Nehemiah and Daniel; two targums were even found at Qumran (11QtgJob; 4QtgLev).[62]

The interpretive element in the targums is clear; scribes tended to paraphrase, use explanatory phrases and reinterpret the text in order to better convey its meaning. There were two primary schools of textual study: a western school centered in Palestine at Tiberias, which existed until the end of the third century A.D. and then again from the eighth to tenth centuries A.D.; and an eastern school centered in Babylonia at Sura, Nehardea (destroyed in A.D. 259), and later at Pumbeditha.[63] Unlike the Palestinian school, the Babylonian school finally produced an official version of the targum about the fifth century A.D., but it gradually lost its influence and by the tenth or eleventh century A.D. had disappeared. Fragments of seven manuscripts of the Palestinian Targum, dating from the seventh to the ninth centuries A.D., have been found in the Cairo Genizah and greatly add to our knowledge of this targum.[64] Today only a fraction of these written Aramaic targums has survived; the major ones are listed below according to the biblical books.

6.2.2.1 Pentateuch. There are more known targums for the Pentateuch than for any other part of the Old Testament, probably because of its importance the Jewish people. Since at least the Middle Ages, Targum Onkelos has been the official Babylonian targum of the Pentateuch and has been widely accepted by the Jews as the most authoritative targum for the Pentateuch.[65]

- *Neofiti I* (Biblioteka Apostolica Vaticana, Codex Neofiti I). This targum has been in the Vatican Library since 1956 when it was given to the library as part of a collection from the Pia Domus Neophytorum in Rome. A colophon dates this manuscript to A.D. 1504, but the text that is copied may be as old as the third to fourth centuries A.D. Neofiti I is a nearly complete Palestinian targum (missing only thirty verses for various reasons); the main text appears to have been written by three different scribes. It contains numerous glosses added in the margins or between the lines. Its translation is midway between the literalness of Targum Onkelos and the paraphrastic nature of Targum Jerusalem I.

---

[62]On 11QtgJob see Johannes P. M. van der Ploeg and Adam S. van der Woude, *Le targum de Job de la grotte XI de Qumran* (Leiden: Brill, 1971); Michael Sokoloff, *The Targum to Job from Qumran Cave XI*, Bar-Ilan Studies in Near Eastern Languages and Culture (Ramat Gan: Bar-Ilan University, 1974). On 4QtgLev see Józef T. Milik, in Roland de Vaux and Józef T. Milik, *Qumrân Grotte 4. II*, DJD 6 (Oxford: Clarendon, 1977), pp. 86-89.

[63]Würthwein, *Text of the Old Testament*, p. 12.

[64]Kahle, *Masoreten des Westens*, 2:1-65.

[65]Alexander, "Targum, Targumim," 6:321.

- *Targum Jerusalem I* (sometimes erroneously called Pseudo-Jonathan). This targum is represented by two manuscripts: *editio princeps* prepared by Asher Forins, from Venice, in 1591 and the British Museum Ms. Add. 27031. Its present form dates to seventh to eighth centuries A.D. Targum Jerusalem I combines the official Targum Onkelos with much more material so that it is almost twice as long as the MT. This other material appears to come from a variety of sources, including the Palestinian Targum and other later rabbinic sources.

- *Targum Onkelos.* This targum is represented by several manuscripts housed at the Jewish Theological Seminary of America (Mss. 131, 133a, 152, 153) and Ms. Ebr. 448 at the Vatican Library. It is generally dated between the second to the fifth centuries A.D. and is also the most literal of the targums.

- *Fragment Targum* (Targum Jerusalem II). This targum is represented by Ebr. 440, Biblioteca Apostolica Vaticana; MS Hébr. 110, Bibliothèque Nationale, Paris; etc. It is dated to the seventh to the fifteenth centuries A.D. (somewhere between Neofiti and Jerusalem Targum I). Little of this work remains, but it appears to contain midrashic material from the Palestinian Targum.

- *Cairo Genizah Mss.* These include at least nine fragmentary manuscripts of Targums for the Pentateuch. They are dated anywhere from the eighth to fourteenth centuries A.D. Some of these fragments contain the full Hebrew verse, while others include only *lemmata* (i.e., the opening words of a verse). For the most part they represent the Palestinian targum, though they are not always in agreement in places where they overlap.

- *Toseftot.* Some manuscripts that contain Toseftot (or additions) are Ms. Parva 3218; Ms. Sasson 282; Ms. Heb. e. 74 (Oxford); and Ms. T-S NS 184.81 (Cambridge). The date of these additions is uncertain. Some of the manuscripts of Targum Onkelos have additional haggadic materials (rabbinic statements that illustrate the Torah) that are labeled "Tosefta Yerushalmi."

6.2.2.2 *Prophets.* Targum Jonathan was the official Babylonian targum of the Prophets and was probably translated by Rabbi Joseph ben Ḥayya (c. A.D. 270-333), head of the academy of Pumbeditha (b. *B. Bat.* 3b; *Yoma* 32b).

- *Targum Jonathan.* This targum is dated from the fourth to fifth centuries A.D. and is represented by several Yemenite manuscripts with supralinear pointing (Ms. 229 Jewish Theological Seminary of America; Mss. Or. 2210 and 2211 British Museum) and Western Ms. with Tiberian pointing (Codex Reuchlinianus). The official Babylonian Targum of the Prophets was probably translated by Rabbi Joseph ben Ḥayya (c. A.D. 270-333), head of the academy of Pumbeditha (b. *B. Bat.* 3b; *Yoma* 32b). It bears many similarities to Targum Onkelos; though not generally expansive, it includes a significant amount of *Haggadah*.

- *Toseftot.* The additions to Targum Jonathan are written in the margins or in the text itself. They may be remnants of the Palestinian Targum of the Prophets that were retained by scribes when the Babylonian Talmud began to predominate the West. About eighty additions appear in the Codex Reuchlinianus though their date is uncertain.

6.2.2.3 Writings. There is no official targum for the Writings, but the medieval writers usually quote from Targum Yerushalmi (= Jerusalem) for these books.

- *Targum Yerushalmi (= Jerusalem).* The date is uncertain. This targum for each of the books is very different and often appears in more than one recension.

Technically the targums are not translations or paraphrases but commentaries on the biblical books; most can be dated no earlier than the fifth century A.D. Nevertheless they are important to textual criticism for several reasons: (1) they may contain early traditions concerning the reading of the text; (2) they include early Jewish traditions as to the interpretation of the biblical texts; and (3) they are written in Aramaic, which is closely related to biblical Hebrew. The quality of the translation varies greatly among the targums, but on the whole they reflect the proto-MT (except a Targum of Job found at Qumran). The Palestinian targums are generally more paraphrastic in nature than the Babylonian targums, with the exception of the two Palestinian targums found at Qumran, which are quite literal.

Further Reading

Primary Texts

Díez Macho, Alejandro. *Neophyti I.* 5 vols. Madrid: Consejo Superior de Investigaciones Científicas, 1968-1978.

McNamara, Martin, et al., eds. *The Aramaic Bible: The Targums.* Wilmington, Del.: Glazier, 1987.

Sperber, Alexander. *The Bible in Aramaic Based on Old Testament Manuscripts and Printed Texts.* 4 vols. Leiden: Brill, 1959-1973.

Other Sources

Alexander, Philip S. "Targum, Targumim." *ABD* 6:320-31. See bibliography.

———. "Jewish Aramaic Translations of the Hebrew Scriptures." In *Mikra,* pp. 217-54. Edited by Martin J. Mulder. CRINT 2/1. Philadelphia: Fortress, 1988.

Bascom, Robert A. "The Targums: Ancient Reader's Helps?" *Bible Translator* 36 (1985): 301-16.

Bentzen, Aage. *Introduction to the Old Testament*. 2 vols. Copenhagen: Gad, 1952. See pp. 68-72.

Bowker, John. *The Targums and Rabbinic Literature*. Cambridge: Cambridge University Press, 1969.

Grossfeld, Bernard. "Bible: Translations: Ancient Versions: Aramaic: The Targumim." *EJ* 4:841-51.

———. *A Bibliography of Targum Literature*. Bibliographica Judaica. New York: KTAV, 1972. See pp. 41-57.

———. *A Bibliography of Targum Literature*. Bibliographica Judaica 8. Cincinnati: Hebrew Union College Press; New York: KTAV, 1972-77. See 2:31-40.

———. *A Bibliography of Targum Literature*. New York: Sepher-Hermon Press, 1990. See 3:21-30.

Levine, Étan. "The Biography of the Aramaic Bible." *ZAW* 94 (1982): 353-79.

Margolis, Max L. *The Story of the Bible Translations*. Philadelphia: Jewish Publication Society of America, 1943. See pp. 9-25.

McNamara, Martin. "Half a Century of Targum Study." *Irish Biblical Studies* 1 (1979): 157-68.

Nickelsburg, George W. E. "The Bible Rewritten and Expanded." In *Jewish Writings of the Second Temple Period*, 2:89-156. Edited by Michael E. Stone. CRINT 2. Philadelphia: Fortress, 1984.

Roberts, Bleddyn J. "The Textual Transmission of the Old Testament." In *Tradition and Interpretation*, pp. 25-30. Edited by George W. Anderson. Oxford: Clarendon, 1979.

Shin'an, Avigdor. "Live Translation: On the Nature of the Aramaic Targums to the Pentateuch." *Prooftexts* 3 (1983): 41-49.

Stenning, John F., and Harry M. Orlinsky. "Targum." *Encyclopaedia Britannica* 21:697-98.

Strack, Hermann L., and Günter Stemberger. *Introduction to the Talmud and Midrash*. Translated by Markus Bockmuehl. Edinburgh: T & T Clark; Minneapolis: Fortress, 1991.

Vermès, Géza. *Scripture and Tradition in Judaism*. 2nd ed. SPB 4. Leiden: Brill, 1973.

———. "Interpretation, History of." *IDBSup*. See pp. 438-43.

Young, Brad H. "Targum." *ISBE* 4:727-33.

6.2.3 *The Septuagint* (LXX)

The *Letter of Aristeas* (a pseudepigraphal book) purposes to give the history of the LXX, though some scholars question its veracity.[66] It states that Ptolemy Philadelphus (285-246 B.C.) wanted to assemble a great library and collect books from all over the world. Demetrius, his librarian, informed him that the Jewish Law was indeed worthy to be placed in his library, but first it would have to be translated into Greek. An Egyptian delegation was sent to Jerusalem to inform the Jewish high priest, Eleazar, of the plan. When Eleazar heard of it, he was very pleased and sent to Egypt a copy of the Hebrew Law written in gold letters, along with seventy-two rabbis (six from each of the twelve tribes) for this translation project. According to *Aristeas*, the seventy-two rabbis translated the Pentateuch in seventy-two days on the island of Pharos, and after they compared their work, the Jewish community accepted it with joy. As Ralph W. Klein points out, however:

> Later, as the story was retold in the early church, it got "better and better." According to Justin Martyr, the translation included the whole Old Testament. Later in the second century Irenaeus reports that the translators worked in isolation but came up with identical results, thanks to the inspiration of God. Finally, Epiphanius of Salmis (314-403) pushed the isolation idea to the limit. He had the translators do everything in pairs, even going by thirty-six boats each night to dine with the king. When the thirty-six independent translations were read before the king, they were found to be completely identical.[67]

The word *Septuagint* is complicated for several reasons: (1) there is no set definition, and scholars differ in the way they use it (e.g., some use *Septuagint* only for the Pentateuch, others for the entire Jewish-Greek corpus; some who realize that every extant manuscript is corrupt and thus only partially represents the original Greek translation prefer to speak of an Ur-Septuagint or proto-Septuagint);[68] (2) there is no standard LXX, for there are significant differ-

---

[66]Henry B. Swete, *An Introduction to the Old Testament in Greek*, ed. Richard R. Ottley (New York: KTAV, 1968), pp. 9-28, 533-606; Sidney Jellicoe, *The Septuagint and Modern Study* (Ann Arbor, Mich.: Eisenbrauns, 1978), esp. pp. 158-224; Robert J. H. Shutt, "Letter of Aristeas," in *The Old Testament Pseudepigrapha*, ed. James H. Charlesworth (Garden City, N.Y.: Doubleday, 1983-85), 2:7-34. Melvin K. H. Peters points out the known inconsistencies or inaccuracies in this letter: "Most notable is the mention of Demetrius of Phalerum as chief librarian—a position he never held in the court of Ptolemy II since the latter, on his accession had banished him to exile. Another error is the mention of Menedemus of Eritria as being present at the banquet held in honor of the translators when he had already been dead two years before the end of Ptolemy I Soter's reign. Several other points of detail suggest the improbability of the story being historical, among which is the matter of a Greek king being so interested in the Hebrew scriptures, to go to great lengths to secure them. In fact the idea of Greeks translating the religious scriptures of such a minority of their population is highly improbable" ("Septuagint," *ABD* 5:1096).

[67]Klein, *Textual Criticism*, pp. 1-2.

[68]Peter J. Gentry, "The Septuagint and the Text of the Old Testament," IBR lecture, San Antonio, Texas, November 20, 2004 (*Bulletin for Biblical Research*, forthcoming).

ences and corruptions in each of its Greek manuscripts; and (3) there is little agreement as to the books that are included in the LXX (i.e., biblical books, biblical and apocryphal books or biblical, apocryphal and some pseudepigraphal works). Melvin K. H. Peters, one of the leading LXX experts today, provides the following definition:

> For convenience, it is assumed throughout what follows that a single set of original translations of the Hebrew scriptures into Greek was effected in several stages, and in locations not known for sure; that the earliest parts (most likely the Torah) of the translation took place in the 3d century B.C.E. (perhaps in Egypt) and the last parts were completed by the first part of the 1st century B.C.E.; that, in the absence of "hard copy" of these translations, we can recover from the extant witnesses, texts sufficiently reliable to be considered equivalent to the originals, if carefully controlled text-critical principles are employed.[69]

This definition appears to be the standard hypothesis of the majority of Septuagintalists, but in actual fact, the situation may be much more complicated than this definition suggests, as Peters has already indicated, for it is possible that there were multiple Greek translations of the Hebrew Bible circulating contemporaneously.[70] Also the LXX may have been completed earlier than Peters indicates; the prologue to Ecclesiasticus suggests that by about 132 B.C. each of the three parts of the Hebrew Bible had already been translated into Greek:

> You are urged therefore to read with good will and attention, and to be indulgent in cases where, despite our diligent labor in translating, we may seem to have rendered some phrases imperfectly. For what was originally expressed in Hebrew does not have exactly the same sense when translated into another language. Not only this work, but even the law itself, the prophecies, and the rest of the books differ not a little as originally expressed.[71]

It is possible that Ben Sira's grandson is thinking of another Greek translation, but the LXX would be the most plausible one. There is also reliable patris-

---

[69]Peters, "Septuagint," 5:1094.

[70]Kahle, *Cairo Genizah*. See also Tov's arguments for a four-stage mediating theory: (1) original translation, (2) multiple textual traditions because of correction insertions (mainly toward the Hebrew), (3) textual stabilization in the first and second centuries A.D., and (4) creation of new textual groups and corruptions of previous ones through the influence of Origen and Lucian in the third and fourth centuries A.D. (see *The Text-Critical Use of the Septuagint in Biblical Research*, p. 42; and Peters, "Septuagint," 5:1097).

[71]*The Apocrypha of the Old Testament, Revised Standard Version*, ed. Bruce M. Metzger, The Oxford Annotated Apocrypha (New York: Oxford University Press, 1973), p. 129. See also: Robert Hanhart, "Introduction," in *The Septuagint as Christian Scripture: Its Prehistory and the Problem of its Canon*, ed. Martin Hengel (Edinburgh: T & T Clark, 2002), p. 2.

tic testimony dating it to about 280 B.C.,[72] papyri fragments of parts of the Torah that go back to the second century B.C. (Rahlfs 801, 805, 819, 957) and fragments of the Minor Prophets to late first century B.C. to early first century A.D. (Rahlfs 943).

Historically, the LXX had an important influence on both Jews and Christians. As the Greek language was disseminated throughout the ancient Near East by the conquests of Alexander the Great, it became more and more important to have the Scriptures in a language that the people could understand. Jewish immigrants living in the cosmopolitan city of Alexandria were forced by their situation to abandon their native language, but the translation of their laws into Greek was one way for them to maintain their faith. The LXX became so popular, however, that it was increasingly seen as the standard form of the Old Testament and was subsequently adopted by Christians. About 70 percent of the New Testament's quotations of the Old Testament appear to come from the LXX. By the late fourth century A.D., Augustine even demanded that Jerome use its order of the books for his translation rather than the Hebrew order.[73] The LXX was eventually rejected by the Jewish community because it was embraced by Christians as a sacred book. The more that Christians embraced the LXX and used it to argue their beliefs (e.g., Is 7:14), the further the Jewish community distanced themselves from it. Furthermore, as scribes began to accept as authoritative the MT, Jews rejected the LXX, which was not based on this text. New Greek translations were being made by Jewish scholars (e.g., Aquila, Symmachus, Theodotion) to meet their needs. Many modern scholars believe that manuscripts of the LXX derive from one original tradition, as Paul A. de Lagarde (1827-1891) argued a century ago,[74] but that text is almost impossible to recover. It is also interesting that one of the major differences between the MT and the LXX is found in the book of Jeremiah, which is approximately one-seventh shorter in the LXX. Two fragmentary Hebrew manuscripts have been found at Qumran that reflect the shorter text of the LXX (4QJer[b,d]).

At the beginning of the twentieth century, scholars used primarily the LXX for Old Testament textual criticism. In some books the LXX provides a very literal Greek translation of the Hebrew text (e.g., the Pentateuch), but in others (e.g., Jeremiah, Job and Daniel) it differs greatly from the MT. Until the discovery of the Dead Sea Scrolls there was little firm evidence to determine which

---

[72]Nina L. Collins, "281 BCE: the Year of the Translation of the Pentateuch in Greek under Ptolemy II," in *Septuagint, Scrolls, and Cognate Writings*, ed. George J. Brooke and Barnabas Lindars, SCS 33 (Atlanta: Scholars Press, 1992), pp. 403-503.

[73]Würthwein, *Text of the Old Testament*, p. 50.

[74]Paul de Lagarde, *Septuaginta Studien* (Göttingen: Dieterichsche Verlags-Buchhandlung, 1891), p. 3.

Figure 6.16. John 21:1b-25 from Codex Sinaiticus (fourth century) [British Library]

text was preferable. However, more recently there are several areas in LXX studies where scholars are finding some agreement. First, scholars now generally agree that many of the differences between the LXX and the MT are the result of a translator's free rendering or a misunderstanding of a Hebrew text and that the Hebrew *Vorlage* of the LXX is often substantially the same as the MT.[75] Second, the LXX (often called the Old Greek text) has undergone revisions that have brought it into closer conformity to the MT. (One of the texts is the so-called *kaige* recension [or "proto-Theodotion"];[76] another is the asterisked material in the LXX of Job).[77] Third, it was once common to argue that the read-

---

[75]John W. Wevers, "The Building of the Tabernacle," *JNSL* 19 (1993): 123-31 (this is a summary of his more detailed work, *Text History of the Greek Exodus*, Mitteilungen des Septuaginta-Unternehmens 21 [Göttingen: Vandenhoeck & Ruprecht, 1991]); Wolters, "Text of the Old Testament," pp. 23-24; Waltke, "The Textual Criticism of the Old Testament," 1:221-22 ; Gentry, "Septuagint," p. 5.

[76]Tov, *Textual Criticism*, pp. 25, 30; Wolters, "Text of the Old Testament," pp. 24-25.

[77]Peter J. Gentry, *The Asterisked Materials in the Greek Job*, SBLSCS 38 (Atlanta: Scholars Press, 1995), pp. 494-98. This material was asterisked in the fifth column of Origin's Hexapla, but appears to have been inserted into the LXX of Job.

ings of the LXX were older and therefore more original than the MT, but since the discoveries of the Qumran scrolls this assumption is no longer warranted because the proto-MT can be traced back at least as far, if not further, than the Old Greek (or proto-LXX) and has often been shown to be a similar Hebrew text to the MT that underlies the LXX's readings.

Peters describes some of the problems associated with finding the original text of the LXX:

> The task of the modern editor of the LXX is thus not one of picking from equals but rather of sorting and making, at every stage, critical judgments about a vast array of uneven witnesses, following well established principles which only sometimes can be clearly articulated. . . . One critical part of the editor's task is to address demonstrably Hexaplaric readings—both pluses and minuses—*en route* to determining the critical text. In this regard the readings of the early papyri are scrutinized carefully and given due consideration but not automatic preference, since they too may be corrupt.[78]

Peter Gentry summarizes current LXX studies:

> Although a multitude of apparent differences exist between the LXX and MT or other Hebrew witnesses, we must first eliminate issues arising from differences between source and target languages as codes of communication, corruption with the transmission of the Greek version, and differences which are translational and not genuinely textual. When such differences are eliminated (as more than twenty-five years of careful, patient, and painstaking comparison of the LXX and MT have shown), the first datum from this study is the high level of agreement between the two. The claim made by Gilles Dorival in his research on the text of the Greek Psalter is that the majority of differences between it and MT are translational. The same is true in Job as I concluded in my own extensive study. In Proverbs, two major recent studies conducted independently of each other concluded that the LXX is a creative re-shaping of the MT to strengthen the attribution to Solomon. . . . It is the nature of things that textual critics focus on the differences. Let us not forget that the LXX witnesses to the fact that our Hebrew text is, for the most part, ancient and pristine.[79]

---

[78]Peters, "Septuagint," 5:1100.

[79]Gentry, "Septuagint," pp. 22-23. The sources he cites within this quote are Gilles Dorival, "Septante et texte massorétique: Le cas des Psaumes," in *Congress Volume: Basel 2001*, ed. André Lemaire, VTSup 92 (Leiden: Brill, 2002), pp. 139-61; Gentry, *Asterisked Materials in the Greek of Job*; Johann Cook, *The Septuagint of Proverbs: Jewish and/or Hellenistic Proverbs? Concerning the Hellenistic Colouring of LXX Proverbs* (Leiden: Brill, 1997); and Harold C. Washington, "Wealth and Poverty in the Instruction of Amenemope and the Hebrew Proverbs: A Comparative Case Study in the Social Location and Function of Ancient Near Eastern Wisdom Literature" (Ph.D. diss., Princeton Theological Seminary, 1992), pp. 194-97.

The LXX was never intended to be a precise, scholarly translation but an early popular recension of the MT.[80]

Manuscript evidence for the text of the LXX is extensive; some of the more important manuscripts are:

Figure 6.17. A picture of Lobegott Friedrich Constantin von Tischendorf, a German Protestant theologian and text critic. He discovered Codex Sinaiticus and published more critical editions and manuscripts of the Greek New Testament than any other scholar. [Family of Constantin von Tischendorf]

- *Amherst Collection.* First acquired by Lord Amherst in Norfolk, England, and later purchased by John Pierpont Morgan and transferred to the Pierpont Library in New York. It includes portions of Genesis, Exodus, Deuteronomy, Job, Proverbs and Isaiah, dated between the fourth to ninth centuries A.D. One of its most important manuscripts is an early fourth-century A.D. fragment of Genesis 1:1-5.

- *Chester Beatty Papyri.* Sir Alfred Chester Beatty (1875-1968), an American collector, moved to Dublin in 1950 and founded a library that he bequeathed to the Irish people. The papyri, dated between the second and fourth centuries A.D., include portions of Genesis, Numbers, Deuteronomy, Psalms, Isaiah, Jeremiah, Ezekiel, Daniel, Esther, fifteen New Testament books and 1 Enoch. Important works are CBP 967-968 = Daniel (third century A.D.); CBP 961 = Genesis 9:1—44:22; CBP 962 = Genesis 8:13—9:1; and CBP 963 = portions of Numbers and Deuteronomy.

- *Oxyrhynchus Papyri.* A large collection found in Oxyrhynchus, Egypt, from about 1897 onward; housed in many museums (British Museum; Cairo Museum; Bodleian Library, Oxford; etc.). It includes portions from at least the Pentateuch, Joshua, Judges, Ruth, Psalms and the Prophets, and these date from the first to ninth centuries A.D. Its important works include Oxyrhynchus 656 = Genesis 14—15, 19—20, 24, 27.

---

[80]Würthwein, *Text of the Old Testament*, p. 66. See also Wolters, "Text of the Old Testament," p. 25.

- *Rylands Papyri.* A collection at John Rylands University Library in Manchester, England. It includes manuscripts containing portions of Genesis, Deuteronomy, Chronicles, Job and Isaiah, and dates from the second century B.C. to the fifth century A.D. Important works include Papyrus Greek 458 (Rahlfs 957) = parts of Deuteronomy, and Papyrus Greek 460 (Rahlfs 958) = parts of the later chapters of Isaiah.

- *Freer Collection.* A collection housed at the Freer Gallery of Art in the Smithsonian Institute in Washington, D.C. This collection contains manuscripts of Deuteronomy and Joshua, the Minor Prophets and Psalms, and these are dated to the third to fifth centuries A.D. Important works include Washington Greek Ms. Deuteronomy and Joshua; Washington Greek Ms. V Minor Prophets; and Washington Ms. Psalms.

- *Société Egyptienne de papyrologie.* In 1943 this society was given thirteen fragments of a papyrus scroll containing Deuteronomy 18, 20, 24—27, 31—32 dated to the late second to early first centuries B.C. It is commonly called P. Fouad Inv. 266 and is one of the oldest witnesses to the Greek Old Testament.

Some of the more important major uncials of the LXX are:

- *Codex Vaticanus* (Vatican Library Cod. Gr. 1209). This manuscript, dated to the fourth century A.D., was in the Vatican Library since at least 1481 until Napoleon took it to Paris with other manuscripts as a war prize. In 1815 it was returned to the Vatican Library. Originally it was a complete manuscript, but now several sections are missing (Genesis 1:1—46:28a; 2 Samuel 2:5-7, 10-13; Psalm 105 [106]:27—137[138]; 1-2 Maccabees; and Hebrews 9:14 to the end of the New Testament). Each page has three columns written in black ink on vellum (calfskin). There are no breaks between words, punctuation is rare, and some sacred names are abbreviated.

- *Codex Sinaiticus* (B.M. Add. 43725). Count von Tischendorf found this codex, dated to the late fourth to early fifth centuries A.D., at St. Catherine's Monastery in the Sinai Desert. Later the monks gave it as a gift to the czar of Russia, then in 1933 it was sold to the British Museum for £100,000 (≈ $500,000). It contains portions of the Old Testament, the Apocrypha and all of the New Testament. It also contains part of the *Shepherd of Hermas* and the entire *Epistle of Barnabas*. It has four columns written in black ink on vellum, without spaces between words, accents or breathing marks.

- *Codex Alexandrinus* (B.M. Royal I.D.V-VIII). Cyril Lucar, the patriarch of Constantinople, gave this codex to King James I, but it came to England in 1627 after his death. Lucar probably acquired it in Alexandria, Egypt, hence its name. The British Museum received the codex in 1757 from the royal family. It is dated to the mid-fifth century A.D. and originally it was a complete codex of the Old Testament and New Testament, as well as *1-2 Clement* and the *Psalms of Solomon*. However, the codex is now missing the following: parts of Genesis (14:14-17; 15:1-5, 16-19; 16:6-9), part of 1 Samuel (12:20—14:9), nine leaves in the Psalms (49[50]:19—79[80]:10) and some of the New Testament. This codex has two columns per page and is written in black ink on vellum without word divisions, accents or breathing marks.

- *Codex Ephraemi* (Paris, Bibliothèque Nationale Gr. 9). Housed in the national library in Paris since at least the mid-sixteenth century, this codex was first deciphered by Tischendorf, who later published it in 1845. This codex is a palimpsest, with the earliest text dating to the fifth to sixth centuries A.D. However, in the twelfth century someone erased the biblical text and wrote the sermons of Ephraem, a Syrian church father, over it. Originally it contained the entire Bible, but presently has only sixty-four leaves of the Old Testament (including portions of Proverbs, Ecclesiastes, Song of Solomon, Job), part of the apocryphal books (Wisdom of Solomon and Sirach), and 145 leaves of the New Testament. The codex is made of vellum and has one column per page without word divisions, accents or breathing marks.

The LXX is important to Old Testament textual criticism for two reasons: First, in some instances it reflects a tradition of the Hebrew text different from the MT. Second, where they agree, it provides evidence as to how the scribes at this time thought the text was to be pointed and understood. One must remember, however, that the LXX is a translation from Hebrew into Greek with the same kinds of difficulties inherent to all translations. Attempting to identify the original Hebrew *Vorlage* of the LXX is much more complicated than earlier scholars thought. Peters states it this way:

> The foregoing discussions should make clear that the Greek version, although translated from Hebrew, was not necessarily translated from a text accessible to us. The most important reason for studying the LXX then is to read and understand the thought of Jews in the pre-Christian centuries. In the process we may gain insights into the Hebrew Bible.[81]

This difficulty is represented dramatically in the LXX version of Jeremiah and Job, both of which are about one-sixth shorter than the MT. Does this mean that the translator of the LXX followed another Hebrew version of the book of Jeremiah or Job that was shorter, or that he abbreviated the text for some reason? This problem was highlighted when Hebrew texts with the shortened

---

[81]Peters, "Septuagint," 5:1102.

form of Jeremiah (4QJer[b,d]) were found at Qumran. Peter J. Gentry offers a plausible explanation for this shortening:

> The earliest Greek translation of Job is about one-sixth shorter than the Hebrew text of MT. For almost a hundred years the standard view among Septuagint scholars was that the Greek translator had used a different parent text and some thought that the MT was derivative and secondary to the Hebrew base of the Septuagint. Yet painstaking comparison of our Greek and Hebrew texts clearly showed that the differences were due to a functional equivalence approach to translation in which many of the long, windy speeches were made more manageable for a Hellenistic readership.[82]

Scholars are beginning to make a distinction between two different classes of biblical texts: (1) manuscripts that merely reproduce in a straightforward manner their *Vorlage*, and (2) manuscripts that contain a revision or updating of material to reflect contemporary circumstances.[83] This distinction may help determine why some texts are so different from others—it may not be that they reflect a different *Vorlage* but that they are written for a purpose other than simply reproducing their *Vorlage*. Our research on the book of Jeremiah found that everything missing from the LXX text of Jeremiah is found elsewhere in the book, which may suggest an intentional condensation.

Still, this does not appear to answer the question regarding the shorter text of Jeremiah in the LXX since there appear to be Hebrew texts found at Qumran dated to about 200 B.C. that have a shortened version of the book of Jeremiah (similar to that found in the LXX). Thus some manuscripts of the Hebrew text may have already been intentionally shortened or corrupted so that they contained a shorter text. Is it possible that a shorter text of Jeremiah had been maintained around Egypt and was used for the LXX, but that a longer one similar to the MT had been maintained in Babylon or Jerusalem? We still do not have a definitive answer to this dilemma.

Probably the single most important development in LXX studies for Old Testament textual criticism is the publication of critical editions that attempt to get back to the original Old Greek readings:

- *The Cambridge LXX* (smaller edition). This portable LXX text was edited by

---

[82]Gentry, "Septuagint," p. 5. For his source on the Hebrew base of the Septuagint see e.g., Edwin Hatch, "On Origen's Revision of the LXX Text of Job," in *Essays in Biblical Greek*, ed. Edwin Hatch (1889; reprint, Amsterdam: Philo Press, 1970), pp. 215-45.

[83]James A. Sanders, *Canon and Community: A Guide to Canonical Criticism* (Philadephia: Fortress, 1984), p. 22; Eugene Ulrich, *The Dead Sea Scrolls and the Origins of the Bible* (Grand Rapids: Eerdmans, 1999), 11; Bruce K. Waltke, "Old Testament Textual Criticism," in *Foundations for Biblical Interpretation*, ed. David S. Dockery, Kenneth A. Mathews and Robert B. Sloan (Nashville: Broadman & Holman, 1994), pp. 156-86; Gentry, "Septuagint," pp. 26-27.

Henry Barclay Swete between 1887 and 1894 and was the first step in preparation for the larger, more complete version of the LXX. It used Codex Vaticanus (B) as the base text, which was supplemented by two or three other uncials.

- *The Cambridge LXX* (larger edition). The earlier editions of this work were edited by Alan E. Brooke and Norman McLean, and the later ones by Henry St. John Thackeray. They also used the text of Codex Vaticanus (B) with several other witnesses in the apparatus. The apparatus generally includes citations from the versions and patristic citations, but are not always correct.[84] This project was halted in 1940 and does not appear to be resuming.

- *The Rahlfs LXX.* This very popular edition of the LXX is primarily a text based on the three major uncial manuscripts (Vaticanus, Sinaitieus and Alexandrinus) with a critical apparatus with variants from these and several other sources and was completed in 1935 just before Alfred Rahlfs died. Rahlfs followed the principles laid out by his teacher Paul de Lagarde, who believed that all the manuscripts of the LXX were mixed texts and thus the best readings should be taken from each of them. Peters explains the principles de Lagarde believed were necessary to get back to the original Greek text:

> To restore the text, one: (1) needs to be acquainted with the style of individual translators; (2) should give preference to a free translation rather than the slavishly exact one, all other things being equal; (3) should give preference to readings pointing to a Hebrew original other than the MT.[85]

By using these principles Rahlfs believed that he could work back to the original proto-LXX.

- *The Göttingen LXX.* This work basically follows the same principles established by Paul de Lagarde, and thus it is an eclectic work seeking to establish the original reading of the LXX. It is the most comprehensive and reliable critical edition of the LXX. To date thirty-one volumes have been produced by several different editors (e.g., *Exodus,* John W. Wevers; *Deuteronomium,* John W. Wevers; *Iob,* Joseph Ziegler).

Further Reading

Primary Sources

Brooke, Alan E., Norman McLean and Henry St. J. Thackeray, eds. *The Old Testament in Greek According to the Text of Codex Vaticanus.* 9 vols. Cambridge: Cambridge University Press, 1906-1940.

---

[84]Peters, "Septuagint," 5:1095.
[85]Ibid.

Rahlfs, Alfred, ed. *Septuaginta: Id est Vetus Testamentum graece iuxta* LXX *interpretes.* 2 vols. Stuttgart: Württembergische Bibelanstalt, 1935.

Swete, Henry B. *The Old Testament in Greek According to the Septuagint,* edited by Richard R. Ottley. Rev. ed. 3 vols. Cambridge: Cambridge University Press, 1914.

Ziegler, Joseph, ed. *Septuaginta. Vetus Testamentum Graecum auctoritate Academiae Scientarium Gottingensis editum.* Göttingen: Vandenhoeck & Ruprecht, 1931-.

Other Works

Eissfeldt, Otto. *The Old Testament: An Introduction.* Translated by Peter R. Ackroyd. New York: Harper & Row, 1965. See pp. 701-2, and esp. bibliography.

Jellicoe, Sidney. *The Septuagint and Modern Study.* Ann Arbor, Mich.: Eisenbrauns, 1978. See pp. 370-400, and esp. bibliography.

Kraft, Robert A. "Septuagint." *IDBSup.* See pp. 807-15.

Metzger, Bruce M. "Versions, Ancient." *IDB* 4:749-60.

Orlinsky, Harry M. "The Septuagint: Its Usage in Textual Criticism." *BA* 9 (1946): 22-34.

———. *The Septuagint: The Oldest Translation of the Bible.* Cincinnati: Publications of the Hebrew Union College, 1949.

Peters, Melvin K. H. "Septuagint." *ABD* 5:1093-1104. See esp. bibliography.

Roberts, Bleddyn J. "Text, OT." *IDB* 4:580-94.

———. *The Old Testament Text and Versions.* Cardiff, U.K.: University of Wales Press, 1951. See esp. pp. 101-87.

Soderland, Sven K. "Septuagint." *ISBE* 4:400-409. See esp. bibliography.

Swete, Henry B. *An Introduction to the Old Testament in Greek,* edited by Richard R. Ottley. Rev. ed. New York: KTAV, 1968.

Thompson, John A. "Text Criticism, OT." *IDBSup.* See pp. 886-91.

Tov, Emanuel. *The Text-Critical Use of the Septuagint in Biblical Research.* JBS 3. Jerusalem: Simor, 1981.

Wevers, John W. "Septuagint." *IDB* 4.273-78.

———. "Text History and Text Criticism of the Septuagint." In *Congress Volume: Göttingen 1977.* VTSup 29. Leiden: Brill, 1978. See pp. 392-402.

6.2.4 *Other Greek Recensions*

As Christians increasingly used the LXX as their Scriptures in defense of their faith, Jews began to distance themselves from it. For their controversies with Christians as well as for the increasing numbers of Hellenistic Jews whose primary language was Greek, Jews needed new Greek translations that corrected misinterpretations, removed Christian additions and accurately reflected the Hebrew text that had become normative in Palestine.[86]

---

[86]Ibid., 5:1097; Jellicoe, *Septuagint and Modern Study,* p. 74.

6.2.4.1 Aquila. Aquila was a Christian from Sinope (in Pontus on the Black Sea), who converted to Judaism and became a disciple of Rabbi Akiba.[87] About A.D. 130, he produced a literal Greek translation that is exceedingly helpful to Old Testament textual criticism because it so closely follows the Hebrew text— even the Hebrew definite direct object marker (אֶת, '*et*) which is usually left untranslated, is indicated by the article or by the Greek adverb σύν (*syn*, "so, with, together with") followed by the accusative case (grammatical case marking the direct object).[88] Jellicoe says that this work "was essentially a teacher's book, aimed at giving an exact rendering of the Hebrew and usable only by one who already understood that language, and its function was interpretative rather than literary."[89] And Peters states:

> The version of Aquila was respected for many years. Both Origen and Jerome were impressed with it, the latter even borrowing from the version's readings in the case of a few rare words. Aquila is considered in some circles to be identical with Onqelos, the compiler of a Targum of the Pentateuch and there is virtual unanimity in Septuagintal circles that the extant text of the Greek of Qoheleth is to be identified in some way with him.[90]

Aquila attempted to reproduce not only the meaning of the Hebrew *Vorlage*, but also its form, and since it was written after the text of the MT had been unified, it should accurately reflect the text at this time. Aquila's work has been lost, but many of its readings can be determined from the third column of Origen's Hexapla, marginal readings in some codices, patristic citations (esp. Eusebius, Theodoret and Jerome), and several sixth-century palimpsests discovered in the Cairo Genizah (141 verses of Psalms).[91]

Further Reading

Primary Sources

Burkitt, F. Crawford. *Fragments of the Books of Kings According to the Translation of Aquila.* Cambridge: Cambridge University Press, 1897.

Field, Frederick. *Origenis Hexaplorum quae supersunt; sive Veterum interpretum graecorum in totum Vetus Testamentum fragmenta.* 2 vols. Hildesheim: Olms, 1964.

Taylor, Charles. *Hebrew-Greek Cairo Geniza Palimpsests from the Taylor-Schechter Collection.* Cambridge: Cambridge University Press, 1900.

---

[87] See Dominique Barthélemy, *Les devanciers d'Aquila*, VTSup 10 (Leiden: Brill, 1963), pp. 1-30.

[88] See Jellicoe, *Septuagint and Modern Study*, p. 81.

[89] Ibid., p. 77.

[90] Peters, "Septuagint," 5:1097.

[91] See Joseph Reider, *An Index to Aquila*, ed. Nigel Turner, rev. ed., VTSup 12 (Leiden: Brill, 1966); Jellicoe, *Septuagint and Modern Study*, p. 79.

Other Works

Barthélemy, Dominique. *Les devanciers d'Aquila.* VTSup 12. Leiden: Brill, 1966.

Grabbe, Lester L. "Aquila's Translation and Rabbinic Exegesis." *JJS* 33 (1982): 527-36.

Greenspoon, Leonard J. "Aquila's Version." *ABD* 1:320-21. See bibliography.

Hyvärinen, Kyösti. *Die Übersetzung von Aquila.* ConBOT 10. Lund: Liber Läromedel-Gleerup, 1977.

Jellicoe, Sidney. *The Septuagint and Modern Study.* Ann Arbor, Mich.: Eisenbrauns, 1978. See pp. 76-83.

Kraft, Robert A. "Septuagint, Earliest Greek Versions." *IDBSup*, pp. 811-15.

Peters, Melvin K. H. "Septuagint." *ABD* 5:1097-98.

Rabinowitz, Louis I. "Aquila." *EJ* 12:1406.

Reider, Joseph. *An Index to Aquila.* 2nd ed. Edited by Nigel Turner. VTSup 12. Leiden: Brill, 1966.

Roberts, Bleddyn J. *The Old Testament Text and Versions.* Cardiff: University of Wales Press, 1951. See pp. 120-23.

Silverstone, Alec E. *Aquila and Onkelos.* Manchester: University of Manchester Press, 1931.

Swete, Henry B. *An Introduction to the Old Testament in Greek,* edited by Robert R. Ottley. 2nd ed. New York: KTAV, 1968. See pp. 31-42.

Walker, Norman. "The Writing of the Divine Name in Aquila and the Ben Asher Text." *VT* 3 (1953): 103-4.

Würthwein, Ernst. *The Text of the Old Testament.* Translated by Erroll F. Rhodes. 2nd ed. Grand Rapids: Eerdmans, 1995. See pp. 60-61.

6.2.4.2 Theodotion (see *6.2.4.6 Kaige recension*). Early church tradition says that Theodotion was a Jewish convert who lived in Ephesus during the second century A.D.[92] His Greek translation was midway between the strictly literal translation of Aquila and the literary elegance of Symmachus. Theodotion succeeded in producing a translation that retained much of its Semitic flavor and yet was readily understandable to his Greek-speaking audience. One peculiarity of his work is that he often transliterated rather than translated words, even fairly common ones.[93] It is conjectured that he was preparing this translation for Jews who, even though their primary language was Greek, were familiar with some Hebrew words.[94] Peters explains:

---

[92]Irenaeus *Adversus haereses* 3.21.1, according to Eusebius *Historia ecclesiastica* 5:8, 10. However, Jerome said he was an Ebionite (*De Vir. Ill.* 54).

[93]Frederick Field cites over one hundred, most of which are technical terms (*Origenis Hexaplorum quae supersunt; sive Veterum interpretum graecorum in totum Vetus Testamentum fragmenta* [Oxford: Clarendon, 1875], prolegomena, xl-xli).

[94]Kahle, *Cairo Geniza*, p. 254.

The text on which he worked as a reviser seems however to have been different from the standard LXX and to have been in existence since the early part of the 1st century B.C.E. For instance, NT citations from the book of Daniel, where a version generally considered to be Theodotion has supplanted the LXX in all but two mss, are drawn from the former not the latter. Early Church Fathers—Clement of Rome, Justin Martyr, Irenaeus—cite Theodotion's text of Daniel. This situation has led many scholars to postulate an Ur- or a proto-Theodotion in order to explain the presence of Theodotionic readings before the time of Theodotion.[95]

There are two other distinctives of this version: Job is one-sixth longer than in the LXX (Theodotion appears to closely follow the MT), and Daniel differs significantly (not merely a revision) from the LXX and eventually superseded the LXX version. In some books (e.g., Exodus, Joshua, Job) Theodotion's text corresponds to the sixth column of Origen's Hexapla, which he used to "correct" the then current Greek text of the Old Testament, but in other books (e.g., Minor Prophets, Psalms) his text does not reflect the sixth column.[96]

Theodotion's revision of the LXX is helpful to Old Testament textual criticism because it is a very readable translation of the Hebrew text after it had been unified. In several passages Origen considered Theodotion's revision closer to the Hebrew text than to the LXX.

Further Reading

Primary Sources

Codex Chisianus (88) (eleventh century). Chester Beatty Papyrus X (968) (third century).

Tov, Emanuel. *The Greek Minor Prophets Scroll from Naḥal Ḥever (8ḤevXIIgr). The Seiyal Collection I.* DJD VIII. Oxford: Clarendon, 1990.

Field, Frederick. *Origenis Hexaplorum quae supersunt.* 2 vols. Hildesheim: Olms, 1964.

Other Works

Barthélemy, Dominique. *Les devanciers d'Aquila.* VTSup 12. Leiden: Brill, 1966.

Cooper, Charles M. "Theodotion's Influence on the Alexandrian Text of Judges." *JBL* 67 (1948): 63-68.

Greenspoon, Leonard J. "Theodotion, Theodotion's Version." *ABD* 6:447-48. See bibliography.

Jellicoe, Sidney. *The Septuagint and Modern Study.* Ann Arbor, Mich.: Eisenbrauns, 1978. See pp. 83-94.

---

[95]Peters, "Septuagint," 5:1098.
[96]Leonard J. Greenspoon, "Theodotion, Theodotion's Version," *ABD* 6:447-48.

Kraft, Robert A. "Septuagint, Earliest Greek Versions." *IDBSup*. See pp. 811-15.

Roberts, Bleddyn J. *The Old Testament Text and Versions*. Cardiff, U.K.: University of Wales Press, 1951. See pp. 123-26.

Silverstone, Alec E. *Aquila and Onkelos*. Manchester: University of Manchester Press, 1931.

Swete, Henry B. *An Introduction to the Old Testament in Greek*, edited by Richard R. Ottley, pp. 42-49. Rev. ed. New York: KTAV, 1968.

Würthwein, Ernst. *The Text of the Old Testament*. Translated by Erroll F. Rhodes. 2nd ed. Grand Rapids: Eerdmans, 1995. See pp. 56-57.

6.2.4.3 Symmachus. It is generally agreed that Symmachus produced his Greek translation after Aquila and Theodotion. References to him or his translation are noticeably absent from sources in the late second and early third century, so that he probably dates to the early to mid-third century, shortly before Origen compiled the Hexapla.[97] According to Eusebius and Jerome, Symmachus was an Ebionite (an early Christian sect considered heretical by the early Christian fathers for observing some form of the Jewish law).[98] Jerome states that Symmachus excelled at expressing the sense of the Hebrew text as opposed to Aquila's literal translation, making it more valuable to him in preparing the Latin Vulgate.[99] Symmachus's elegant Greek style enabled him to prepare an idiomatic translation of the MT that occasionally manifests significant independence and originality. Leonard J. Greenspoon notes that "Symmachus generally preferred to supply his readers with translations (often, only guesses) for obscure or technical Hebrew terms that had remained transliterated in earlier Greek versions."[100] This freedom of style, which Symmachus used to make his translation easy to understand, also renders it less valuable for text-critical purposes.

Further Reading

Primary Sources
Field, Frederick. *Origenis Hexaplorum quae supersunt*. 2 vols. Hildesheim: Olms, 1964.

---

[97]Leonard J. Greenspoon, "Symmachus, Symmachus's Version," *ABD* 6:251.

[98]Jerome *De Viris Illustribus* 54; *Commentariorum in Habacuc* 3.13; *Praefationí in Job*; Eusebius *Historia ecclesiastica* 6.17. See Hans J. Schoeps, *Aus frühchristlicher Zeit: Religionsgeschichtliche Untersuchungen* (Tübingen: Mohr, 1950), pp. 82-119. According to Epiphanius (bishop of Constantia [Salamis], who was born in Palestine in the early fourth century), Symmachus was a Samaritan who converted to Judaism (*De mensuris et Ponderibus*, 16-17).

[99]Jellicoe, *Septuagint and Modern Study*, p. 99; Klein, *Textual Criticism*, p. 6.

[100]Greenspoon, "Symmachus," 6:251.

Other Works

Barthélemy, Dominique. *Les devanciers d'Aquila*. VTSup 12. Leiden: Brill, 1966.

————. "Qui est Symmaque?" *CBQ* 36 (1974): 451-65.

Greenspoon, Leonard J. "Symmachus, Symmachus's Version." *ABD* 6:251. See bibliography.

Jellicoe, Sidney. *The Septuagint and Modern Study*. Ann Arbor, Mich.: Eisenbrauns, 1978. See pp. 94-99.

Kraft, Robert A. "Septuagint, Earliest Greek Versions." *IDBSup*. See pp. 811-15.

Liebreich, Leon J. "Notes of the Greek Version of Symmachus." *JBL* 63 (1944): 397-403.

Luis, José G. *Le versión de Símaco a los Profetas Mayores*. Madrid: Universidad Complutense, Servicio de Reprografia, 1981.

Roberts, Bleddyn J. *The Old Testament Text and Versions*. Cardiff, U.K.: University of Wales Press, 1951. See pp. 126-27.

Salvesen, Alison. *Symmachus in the Pentateuch*. JSS Monograph 15. Manchester: University of Manchester Press, 1991.

Swete, Henry B. *An Introduction to the Old Testament in Greek*, edited by Richard R. Ottley. Rev. ed. New York: KTAV, 1968. See pp. 49-53.

Würthwein, Ernst. *The Text of the Old Testament*. Translated by Erroll F. Rhodes. 2nd ed. Grand Rapids: Eerdmans, 1995. See pp. 55-56.

6.2.4.4 *Origen's Hexapla* (c. A.D. 230-245). Origen was a Christian scholar, most likely from Alexandria, Egypt (c. 186-253/254 A.D.). His most famous work, the Hexapla, was one of the greatest achievements of textual criticism in the early church. It is a six-column compilation of the following Old Testament versions:

1. The Hebrew text

2. A Greek transliteration (a Hebrew text written in Greek letters)

3. Aquila's Greek version

4. Symmachus's Greek version

5. A revision of the LXX

6. Theodotion's Greek version (except in the Psalms and Minor Prophets)

In some books it is thought to have contained even more columns (e.g., Quinta, Sexta and Septima). Origen arranged the texts so that the reader could compare the Hebrew text to the various Greek texts.[101] He claimed in a letter to Julius Africanus (c. 240) that this work was an apologetic tool to aid Christians in their discussions with Jews and to protect them against the charge of

---

[101]Tov, *Textual Criticism*, p. 147 n. 101. See also Harry M. Orlinsky, "The Columnar Order of the Hexapla," *JQR* 27 (1936-1937): 137-49.

falsifying the biblical texts:[102] "I make it my endeavour not to be ignorant of their [LXX's] various readings, lest in my controversies with the Jews I should quote to them what is not found in their copies, and that I may make some use of what is found there, even although it should not be in our Scriptures."[103]

Origen employed particular sigla or signs, developed originally by Alexandrian classical scholarship (the Aristarchian symbols), to indicate how the LXX differed from the Hebrew text. These signs, called the obelos (—, ÷, ÷), the metobelos (/, ⫽, ╱), and the asterisk (※), were used as follows:[104]

- Words that are in the LXX but not in the original Hebrew text and should thus be deleted were placed between an obelos and a metobelos (e.g., ÷ εἰς φαῦσιν τῆς γῆς ╱, Genesis 1:14).

- Words in the original Hebrew text but not in the LXX were borrowed from another column (usually Theodotion's text) and placed between an asterisk and a metobelos (e.g., ※ " καὶ ἐγένε τὸ οὕτως ╱, Genesis 1:7).

Origen's main concern was the fifth column, which could be compared to the Hebrew text. Peters summarizes the problems with the Hexapla:

> That would have been an acceptable condition had the Hexapla been retained in its original form, or if Origen did only what he claims to have done. But he seems in fact to have adjusted his text without always indicating where he did, and also the extant witnesses to the Origenian recension do not everywhere retain the Hexaplaric signs. Equally problematic was the situation Origen faced when there was variance between the Greek and the Hebrew necessitating a choice from one of the three versions, and when those versions themselves were divergent from each other. His tendency to choose the version closest to the Hebrew meant that in effect the final form of the fifth column was conservative, mixed, and in the last analysis, not much more than a Greek version of Origen's Hebrew.[105]

This work was indeed monumental, comprising fifty volumes[106] estimated at about 6,500 pages.[107] Ironically, Origen's Hexapla, which he intended to confirm the authority of the LXX, later had the opposite effect, as Klein notes:

> The history of the LXX was adversely affected by Origen's Hexapla since it

---

[102]Sebastian P. Brock, "Origen's Aims as a Text Critic of the Old Testament," *Studia Patristica* 10 (1970): 215-18; Würthwein, *Text of the Old Testament*, p. 55.

[103]*Origen to Africanus* 5, quoted in Frederick Crombie, *Ante-Nicene Christian Library: Translations of the Writings of the Fathers down to A.D. 325*, vol. 4: *The Writings of Origen*, ed. Alexander Roberts and James Donaldson (1895; reprint, Grand Rapids: Eerdmans, 1951), p. 387. See also David C. Parker, "Hexapla of Origen, The," *ABD* 3:188-89.

[104]Würthwein, *Text of the Old Testament*, p. 56; Klein, *Textual Criticism*, p. 7.

[105]Peters, "Septuagint," 5:1099.

[106]Würthwein, *Text of the Old Testament*, 57; Parker, "Hexapla of Origen," 3:189.

[107]Peters, "Septuagint," 5:1098.

tended to obliterate the most original and distinctive features of the Old Greek, led to the neglect of some genuine Old Greek manuscripts, and led to the insertion into others of many non-genuine readings. Various church fathers consulted the Hexapla before its destruction in the seventh century, but the entire Hexapla, running to almost 6,500 pages, was never copied. Instead, it became customary to copy only the fifth column. Once removed from the Hexapla, however, the asterisks and obeli of this column would be meaningless—something like footnote numbers without footnotes.[108]

Many copies of the LXX have been corrupted because they followed the text of the Hexapla without the asterisks and obeli. These mixed texts are commonly called "hexaplaric," a term indicating that their text follows the combined readings of the Hexapla. Fortunately, some manuscripts were not affected by the "hexaplaric manuscripts," such as much of Codex Vaticanus (B) (except for small parts of the book of Isaiah). The Syro-Hexapla is also helpful for determining these readings for it is a copy of Origen's Hexapla translated into Syriac by Paul, bishop of Tella, in the early seventh century (c. 618-619). It records fairly accurately the Aristarchan signs Origen included in his text.[109]

The Hexapla presumably remained in Caesarea and was destroyed with the rest of the library during the Arab invasions in the early seventh century, but several manuscripts contain examples of the Hexapla: (1) a palimpsest in Milan contains columns 2 to 6 (column 6 is the Quinta version)[110] and is fairly extensive (35 folios of approximately 150 verses), (2) a smaller fragment contains Psalm 22 with all six columns, (3) Codex Sarravianus (G) and Codex Coislianus (M) contain the text of the Pentateuch and some of the historical books with critical symbols, and (4) the Chigi manuscripts (86 and 88) contain the Prophets and critical symbols.

The Hexapla's primary contributions to Old Testament textual criticism are its Greek translations from Aquila, Symmachus and Theodotion, and its Hebrew text from Origen's time, which was compiled after the MT had been unified.

Further Reading

Primary Sources

Cox, Claude E. *Hexaplaric Materials Preserved in the Armenian Version*. SBL Septuagint and Cognate Studies 21. Atlanta: Scholars Press, 1986.

Field, Frederick. *Origenis Hexaplorum quae supersunt*. 2 vols. Hildesheim: Olms, 1964.

---

[108]Klein, *Textual Criticism*, p. 8.

[109]See William Baars, *New Syro-Hexaplaric Texts Edited, Commented upon and Compared with the Septuagint* (Leiden: Brill, 1968).

[110]Origen had access to other Greek manuscripts for some passages, so that at times he filled in fifth, sixth and seventh columns, which are called Quinta, Sexta, and Septima, respectively. The Septima may never have been anything more than marginal notes in copies of the LXX (Klein, *Textual Criticism*, p. 7).

Mercati, Giovanni. *Psalterii Hexapli Reliquiae . . . Pars Prima. Codex rescriptus Bybliothecae Ambrosianae O 39 SVP. Phototypice Expressus et Transcriptus.* Rome: Bybliotheca Vaticana, 1958.

Taylor, Charles. *Hebrew-Greek Cairo Genizah Palimpsests.* Cambridge: Cambridge University Press, 1900.

Vööbus, Arthur. *The Pentateuch in the Version of the Syro-Hexapla: A Facsimile Edition of a Midyat MS. Discovered 1964.* CSCO 369. Louvain: Secrétariat du CSCO, 1975.

———. *The Book of Isaiah in the Version of the Syro-Hexapla.* CSCO 449. Louvain: Secrétariat du CSCO, 1983.

Other Works

Baars, William. *New Syro-Hexaplaric Texts Edited, Commented Upon and Compared with the Septuagint.* Leiden: Brill, 1968.

Crouzel, Henri. *Origen.* Translated by A. S. Worrall. San Francisco: Harper & Row, 1984.

Emerton, John A. "The Purpose of the Second Column of the Hexapla." *JTS* 7 (1956): 79-87.

Fritsch, Charles T. "The Treatment of the Hexaplaric Signs in the Syro-Hexaplar of Proverbs." *JBL* 72 (1953): 169-81.

Gentry, Peter J. *The Asterisked Materials in the Greek Job.* SBLSCS 38. Atlanta: Scholars Press, 1995.

Goshen-Gottstein, Moshe H. "The Edition of Syrohexapla Materials." *Textus* 4 (1964): 230-34.

Howorth, Henry H. "The Hexapla and Tetrapla of Origen." *PSBA* 24 (1902): 147-72.

Jellicoe, Sidney. *The Septuagint and Modern Study.* Ann Arbor, Mich.: Eisenbrauns, 1978. See pp. 100-133, 382-85.

Kahle, Paul. "The Greek Bible Manuscripts Used by Origen." *JBL* 79 (1960): 111-18.

Margolis, Max L. "Hexapla and Hexaplaric." *AJSL* 32 (1915-1916): 126-40.

Orlinsky, Harry M. "The Columnar Order of the Hexapla." *JQR* 27 (1936-1937): 137-49.

———. "Origen's Tetrapla: A Scholarly Fiction?" *PWCJS* 1 (1952): 173-82.

Parker, David C. "Hexapla of Origen, The." *ABD* 3:188-89.

Staples, William E. "The Second Column of Origen's Hexapla." *JAOS* 59 (1939): 71-80.

Swete, Henry B. *An Introduction to the Old Testament in Greek,* edited by Richard R. Ottley. Rev. ed. New York: KTAV, 1968. See pp. 59-78.

Trigg, Joseph W. "Origen." *ABD* 5:42-48.

Würthwein, Ernst. *The Text of the Old Testament.* Translated by Erroll F. Rhodes. 2nd ed. Grand Rapids: Eerdmans, 1995. See pp. 57-59.

6.2.4.5 *Other recensions of the* LXX. According to Jerome (c. A.D. 342-420), the early church used other recensions of the LXX. The following three were more prominent:

- *Origen's Palestinian recension.* It is generally believed that Origen's recension constitutes the fifth column in his Hexapla and that it is restricted to the Old Testament, unlike the recensions of Hesychius and Lucian.[111] Origen was an able scholar, well aware of the differences among the various manuscripts.[112] For example, he notes that "there are many passages through the whole of Job which, though present in the Hebrew, are lacking in our own."[113] Jellicoe summarizes the primary purpose of Origen's work:

  > His principal concern was not with the construction of a text, but rather with the presentation of the evidence, leaving the reader to make his own judgement in that light. . . . [Origen] adopts a "standard" text as his basis; lacunae are filled from what, in his judgement, was the most reliable reading; the remaining columns which constitute his *apparatus criticus* are presented quite objectively, leaving the reader in each case at liberty to draw his own conclusions.[114]

Origen's *Vorlage* was probably a "mixed text," not derived from a single text type; however, it appears to have come mainly from an Alexandrian text type, which is generally considered the earliest and most accurate.

Further Reading

Primary Sources
The extant remnants of the Hexapla are apparatuses of the Cambridge and Göttingen editions.
Rahlfs, Alfred. *Septuaginta: Id est Vetus Testamentum graece iuxta* LXX *interpretes*, 2:271-345. Stuttgart: Württembergische Bibelanstalt, 1935. The book of Job contains the critical signs (from minuscules: 248 and Codex Colbertinus [Paris], the Latin manuscripts: Bodleian 2426 and Tours 18, and the Syro-Hexapla) and can be used to derive Origen's other recension. The most important manuscripts generally associated with Origen's Palestinian recension are uncials: Codex Sarravianus (portions of Genesis to Ruth with diacritical marks); Codex Coislinianus (most of Genesis to 1 Kings with scholia [signs developed by the Alexandrian classical scholars] and hexaplaric signs in the margins); Codex Marchalianus (the text of the Prophets; while

---

[111] Jellicoe, *Septuagint and Modern Study*, p. 135.
[112] Origen *Commentary on St. Matthew* 15.14, in Migne, *PG* 13:1293-94; see also Swete, *Introduction to the Old Testament in Greek*, p. 60. See also Origen's *Letter to Africanus*.
[113] Jellicoe, *Septuagint and Modern Study*, p. 136; Migne, *PG* 13:1293.
[114] Jellicoe, *Septuagint and Modern Study*, p. 145.

the text is actually Hesychian, the copious notes and hexaplaric signs make it useful for determining Origen's readings).

Other Works

Barthélemy, Dominique. *Les devanciers d'Aquila.* VTSup 10. Leiden: Brill, 1963. See esp. p. 127.

Fritsch, Charles T. "The Treatment of the Hexaplaric Signs in the Syro-Hexaplar of Proverbs." *JBL* 72 (1953): 169-81. (He has argued that in the places where the Syro-Hexapla has recorded Origen's signs correctly, the part of a doublet that is marked by an obelos constitutes Origen's Greek text.)

Jellicoe, Sidney. *The Septuagint and Modern Study.* Ann Arbor, Mich.: Eisenbrauns, 1978. See pp. 134-46.

Orlinsky, Harry M. "Studies in the Septuagint of the Book of Job." *HUCA* 28 (1957): 53-74; 29 (1958): 229-71; 30 (1959): 153-67; 32 (1961): 239-68; 33 (1962): 119-51; 35 (1964): 57-78; 36 (1965): 37-47.

Swete, Henry B. *An Introduction to the Old Testament in Greek.* Edited by Richard R. Ottley. Rev. ed. New York: KTAV, 1968. See pp. 53-56, 65-66, 148-68.

Würthwein, Ernst. *The Text of the Old Testament.* Translated by Erroll F. Rhodes. 2nd ed. Grand Rapids: Eerdmans, 1995. See p. 55.

- *Lucian's recension.* One of the most important posthexaplaric recensions of the LXX was the work of Lucian, but it is difficult to know if a Lucianic text for the entire Old Testament ever existed.[115] Lucian was said to be a presbyter of Antioch who died as a martyr in A.D. 311/312 during the Maximilian persecution. In *Synopsis sacrae Scripturae* Pseudo-Athanasius describes Lucian and his work as follows: "Using the earlier editions [i.e., Aquila, Theodotion and Symmachus] and the Hebrew, and having accurately surveyed the expressions which fell short of or went beyond the truth, and having corrected them in their proper places, he published them for his Christian brethren."[116] His recension was most likely preserved by two Syrian church fathers, John Chrysostom (A.D. 344-407) and Theodoret (A.D. 386-457), since they often quote a Greek text (possibly Lucianic) different from the LXX.[117] There are also marginal readings that are marked with the sigla *kai lambda* (the Greek letter "l") in some Greek manuscripts and the Syriac letter

---

[115]Tov, "Text of the Old Testament," p. 176. See also Barthélemy, *Les devanciers d'Aquila,* pp. 126-27; Emanuel Tov, "Lucian and Proto-Lucian: Toward a New Solution to the Problem," *RB* 79 (1972): 101-13.

[116]Bruce M. Metzger, in Sydney Jellicoe, ed., *Studies in the Septuagint: Origins, Recensions, and Interpretations,* Library of Biblical Studies (New York: KTAV, 1974), p. 273.

[117]See Bruce M. Metzger, *Chapters in the History of New Testament Textual Criticism.* New Testament Tools and Studies 4 (Grand Rapids: Eerdmans, 1963), pp. 1-41.

"lomadh" (L) in some Syriac manuscripts, which most scholars suggest refers to Lucianic readings.[118] Lucian's text tends toward stylistic purity, regularly replacing Hellenistic forms (Greek forms after Alexander the Great) with Attic (earlier) ones. It also contains a full eclectic text, often with conflated readings.[119] The manuscripts 19, 82, 93 and 108 were identified as Lucianic by Antonio M. Ceriani, Frederick Field and Paul de Lagarde.[120] Tov suggests that there is a close agreement between the Lucianic tradition and 4QSam[a], but he admits that because of the corrupt nature of the manuscript, these findings may be misleading.[121]

An interesting debate has centered around the possibility of a so-called Ur/proto-Lucian text that appears to have readings similar to certain other Lucian texts before Lucian wrote this text. Metzger claims that proto-Lucian readings appear in certain parts of the Old Latin (c. second century A.D.), the Peshitta version of the Old Testament, a papyrus fragment of Psalm 77:1-18 (second or third century A.D.), quotations from Justin Martyr (c. mid-second century A.D.) certain New Testament quotations, some biblical quotes from Josephus of Samuel-Kings and second-century papyrus fragments of Deuteronomy.[122] Several modern scholars still question the existence of a proto-Lucianic text.[123]

Further Reading

Primary Sources
The most important manuscripts generally associated with the Lucian recension are uncials N-V, K, Y (Rahlfs 719); the following versions may have been significantly influenced by Lucian's text: Old Latin, Gothic, Slavonic, Syriac and Armenian.

Fernández Marcos, Natalio, and José R. Busto Saiz. *El texto antioqueno de la Biblia griega, II, 1-2 Reyes*. Textos y Estudios "Cardenal Cisneros" 53. Madrid: Consijo Superior de Investigaciones Científicas, 1992.

Other Works
Barthélemy, Dominique. *Les devanciers d'Aquila*. VTSup 10. Leiden: Brill, 1963. See esp. pp. 126-27. (His view that the Lucianic recension is the ancient LXX

---

[118]Peters, "Septuagint," 5:1099.
[119]Jellicoe, *Septuagint and Modern Study*, p. 159; Klein, *Textual Criticism*, p. 9. Lucian must have used Greek texts that predated his own work, as Kahle notes, "We find in the Manchester Papyrus [Greek 458] a text related to the Lucianic text of the Bible written some five hundred years before Lucian himself" (*Cairo Geniza*, p. 221).
[120]Peters, "Septuagint," 5:1009.
[121]Tov, *Textual Criticism*, p. 148.
[122]Metzger, in Jellicoe, *Studies in the Septuagint*, p. 285-88. See also Peters, "Septuagint," 5:1099.
[123]See debate in Peters, "Septuagint," 5:1099-1100.

debased and corrupted has not been widely accepted; cf. Sidney Jellicoe, "Review of *Les devanciers d'Aquila.*" *JAOS* 84 [1964]: 178-82.)

Jellicoe, Sidney. *The Septuagint and Modern Study.* Ann Arbor, Mich.: Eisenbrauns, 1978. See pp. 157-71, 385.

Moore, George F. "The Antiochian Recension of the Septuagint." *AJSL* 29 (1912-1913): 37-62.

Perkins, Larry J. "The So-called 'L' Text of Psalms 72-82." *Bulletin for the International Organization for Septuagint and Cognate Studies* 11 (1978): 44-63.

Pietersma, Albert. "Proto-Lucian and the Greek Psalter." *VT* 28 (1978): 66-72.

Swete, Henry B. *An Introduction to the Old Testament in Greek,* edited by Richard R. Ottley. Rev. ed. New York: KTAV, 1968. See pp. 81-86.

Thornhill, R. "Six or Seven Nations: A Pointer to the Lucianic Text in the Heptateuch, with Special Reference to the Old Latin Version." *JTS* 10 (1959): 233-46.

Tov, Emanuel. "Lucian and Proto-Lucian—Toward a New Solution to the Problem." *RB* 79 (1972): 101-13.

Yerkes, Royden K. "The Lucianic Version of the Old Testament as Illustrated from Jeremiah 1-3." *JBL* 37 (1918): 163-92.

- *Hesychius of Egypt (Alexandria).* Hesychius was a common name, making it difficult to identify this translator. It has been frequently suggested that he was the Egyptian bishop who coauthored a letter with Theodorus, Pachymius and Phileas, bishop of Thmuis, to Melitius, bishop of Lycopolis in Egypt, protesting what they considered to be irregular exercise of episcopal functions in their dioceses.[124] Eusebius mentions his martyrdom in the same section as that of Lucian of Antioch (*HE* 8.13.7). Peters explains its origin: "While the Hexapla was copied in Caesarea for use in Palestine, two other revisions were in circulation, so Jerome informs us, one for use in Egypt and the other in Antioch. These recensions are identified with Hesychius and Lucian respectively."[125]

Jellicoe has recently argued that the Codex Vaticanus was generally considered to represent primarily the Hesychian recension.[126] It is now generally recognized, however, that little is known about this recension; even its existence is debated.

Further Reading

Primary Sources
Uncertain, but some possibilities are uncials Vaticanus (B), Alexandrinus (A), Q and O.

---

[124]Jellicoe, *Septuagint and Modern Study,* p. 147.
[125]Peters, "Septuagint," 5:1099.
[126]Sidney Jellicoe, "The Hesychian Recension Reconsidered," *JBL* 82 (1963): 409-18; and his *Septuagint and Modern Study,* pp. 153, 155.

Other Works

Jellicoe, Sidney. "The Hesychian Recension Reconsidered." *JBL* 82 (1963): 409-18.

Swete, Henry B. *An Introduction to the Old Testament in Greek,* edited by Richard R. Ottley. Rev. ed. New York: KTAV, 1968. See pp. 78-80.

Vaccari, Alberto. "The Hesychian Recension of the Septuagint." *Bib* 46 (1965): 60-66.

Wevers, John W. "Septuagint." *IDB* 4:273-78. See esp. p. 275.

6.2.4.6 *Kaige recension* (8HevXIIIgr, Rahlfs 943): This Greek scroll found in 1953 in a cave at Naḥal Ḥever contains portions of the Minor Prophets (Jonah, Micah, Nahum, Habakkuk, Zephaniah, Zechariah and possibly also Amos). According to paleographic evidence, it dates to the first half of the first century A.D. It has a revised Old Greek text that is related to the MT but not as fully developed. Peters has summarized the characteristics of this revision identified by Barthélemy and his followers:

> (1) The use of *kaige* to translate Hebrew *gam* and *wĕgam* [this is where it gets its name]; (2) the use of *anēr* rather than *hekastos* to represent Hebrew *'iš*; (3) a tendency to use *ep/apanōthen* as a translation of the Hebrew *m'l* in contrast to LXX, which uses *apo* or *epanō*; (4) the elimination of the historical present in favor of the aorist as a translation of the Hebrew *waw*-consecutive with the imperfect in narration; (5) tendency to stress the atemporal nature of Hebrew *'ên* by translating it as *ouk estin*; (6) use of the *egō eimi* as a translation of Hebrew *'ānōki* and to distinguish it from *'ānî*; (7) avoidance of *eis apantēsin* as a translation of Hebrew *lqr't*; (8) a tendency toward transliteration, especially of unknown words; (9) a tendency to systematize the Greek equivalents of specific Hebrew words or roots. Further refinements and characteristics of this recension have also been proposed.[127]

Barthélemy says that its text is closer to the MT than to the LXX,[128] but he also questions the existence of a translator in the second century A.D. Peters explains the current situation concerning this revision:

> Some scholars have been persuaded completely by Barthélemy, and now argue that a 2d century Theodotion is no longer necessary, suggesting that Ur-/proto-/*kaige*-Theodotion was all there was, and that this reviser flourished towards the end of the 1st century B.C.E., his work being the basis for both Aquila's work and Symmachus' in light of the demonstrable similarity of all three in so many instances. Other scholars, recognizing that Barthélemy's thesis and assumptions raised as many problems as they solved, have been more cautious and maintain

---

[127]Peters, "Septuagint," 5:1098.
[128]Dominique Barthélemy, "Redécouverte d'un chaînon manquant de l'histoire de la Septante," *RB* 60 (1953): 18-29.

that the historic Theodotion may have worked as a reviser within the tradition reflected by the earlier so-called Ur-Theodotion. Questions have also been raised as to whether or not the so-called Theodotion text in Daniel is to be attributed to Theodotion, or whether the sixth column of Origen's Hexapla—traditionally considered to be Theodotion—is indeed what it has been claimed to be.[129]

The text also appears similar, if not identical, to Origen's Quinta, which is reflected in some of the citations of Justin Martyr (c. A.D. 103-165), a few readings of the Sahidic Coptic version and in the Greek Codex Washingtonensis.[130] Peters also says, "Barthélemy identified the work of the Reviser (who has been later called *kaige*-Theodotion) in other parts of LXX—Lamentations, Ruth, the B text of Judges, the Theodotionic text of Daniel, the Theodotionic supplements to LXX Jeremiah and Job, and in the Quinta of the Psalter."[131]

Further Reading

Primary Sources

See the quotations in Justin Martyr's *Dialogue with Trypho* and the Greek manuscript from Naḥal Ḥever (8HevXIIIgr).

Tov, Emanuel. *The Greek Minor Prophets Scroll from Naḥal Ḥever (8ḤevXIIgr). The Seiyal Collection I.* DJD VIII. Oxford: Clarendon, 1990.

Other Works

Barthélemy, Dominique. *Les devanciers d'Aquila.* VTSup 10. Leiden: Brill, 1963. See pp. 163-78.

Kahle, Paul. *The Cairo Geniza.* 2nd ed. Oxford: Clarendon, 1959. See esp. pp. 226-28.

———. "A Leather Scroll of the Greek Minor Prophets and the Problem of the Septuagint." In *Opera Minora.* Leiden: Brill, 1956. See esp. pp. 112-37.

———. "Problems of the Septuagint." In *Studia Patristica,* edited by Kurt Aland and Frank L. Cross. Berlin: Akademie, 1957. See 1:331-33.

Kraft, Robert A. "Septuagint, Earliest Greek Versions." *IDBSup.* See pp. 811-15.

6.2.5 Philo's Quotations of the Old Testament

Philo Judaeus (c. 20/15 B.C. to A.D. 50) was a Hellenistic Jewish philosopher who belonged to one of the wealthiest Jewish families in Alexandria, Egypt (the largest Jewish settlement outside Palestine at this time). He received an excellent and broad education at Alexandria under the Greek system, covering

---

[129]Peters, "Septuagint," 5:1098.
[130]Barthélemy, "Redécouverte d'un chaînon manquant," pp. 18-29; see also his, *Aquila,* pp. 239-45, 271.
[131]Peters, "Septuagint," 5:1098.

literature, philosophy, rhetoric, mathematics, music and logic. Robert M. Wilson summarizes Philo's importance:

> Quite apart from the influence exercised by his writings on later Christian thought and exegesis, his works are a primary source of information for the Judaism of the Dispersion, for the ideas current in NT times, for the ways in which Jews of the period could react to the thought and culture of a predominantly gentile environment, and for the extent to which it was possible to harmonize the Old Testament with Greek philosophy. At the same time, our lack of material for comparison makes it hard to say how far he is truly representative, how widely these ideas were shared.[132]

Philo was a deeply religious man and steadfastly loyal to Judaism; thus his works can be seen in some measure as a defense of Judaism, a natural response since Alexandria was a center of anti-Jewish propaganda. He wrote widely, but most valuable to Old Testament textual criticism are his quotes from a Greek version of the Old Testament. His text is often close to the LXX, but in several places it reflects more closely the readings of the Hebrew text. As Peder Borgen states:

> Many details of the textual affinities of Philo's LXX text are uncertain, particularly because he sometimes departs from the LXX readings. The reason is that in the paraphrasing expositions Philo deals with the text as an active exegete; moreover, he works exegetical traditions into his paraphrase. Thus, it is impossible to reconstruct an original LXX text on the basis of his exegesis.[133]

Philo may have used other Greek versions of the Old Testament that were being circulated at the time, because some of his readings correspond quite closely to the later translators Aquila, Symmachus and Theodotion.[134]

Further Reading

Primary Sources

Colson, Francis H. , George H. Whittaker and Ralph Marcus, eds. *Philo, with an English Translation*. 10 vols. and 2 supplementary vols. LCL. Cambridge, Mass.: Harvard University Press, 1929-1962.

Terian, Abraham, ed. *Philonis Alexandrini de Animalibus. The Armenian Text with an Introduction, Translation and Commentary*. Studies in Hellenistic Judaism (Supplements to *Studia Philonica*). Chico, Calif.: Scholars Press, 1981.

---

[132]Robert M. Wilson, "Philo Judaeus," *ISBE* 3:847.

[133]Peder Borgen, "Philo of Alexandria," *ABD* 5:336.

[134]Kahle, *Cairo Geniza*, pp. 248-49; Peter Katz, *Philo's Bible: The Aberrant Text of the Bible Quotations in Some Philonic Writings and Its Place in the Textual History of the Greek Bible* (Cambridge: Cambridge University Press, 1950), pp. 95-121.

Other Works

Borgen, Peder. "Philo of Alexandria." *ABD* 5.333-42. See Bibliography.

————. "Philo of Alexandria." In *Jewish Writings from the Second Temple Period.* Edited by Michael Stone. CRINT 2/2. Philadelphia: Fortress, 1984. See pp. 233-82.

Kahle, Paul. *The Cairo Geniza.* 2nd ed. Oxford: Clarendon, 1959. See pp. 247-49.

Katz, Peter. *Philo's Bible: The Aberrant Text of the Bible Quotations in Some Philonic Writings and Its Place in the Textual History of the Greek Bible.* Cambridge: Cambridge University Press, 1950.

Wilson, Robert M. "Philo Judaeus." *ISBE* 3:847-50.

Other Works:

Borgen, Peder. "Philo of Alexandria." ABD 5:333–42. See Bibliography.

———. "Philo of Alexandria." In Jewish Writings from the Second Temple Period. Edited by Michael Stone. CRINT 2/2. Philadelphia: Fortress, 1984. See pp. 233–82.

Kahle, Paul. The Cairo Geniza. 2nd ed. Oxford: Blackwell, 1959. See pp. 247–49.

Katz, Peter. Philo's Bible. The Aberrant Text of the Bible Quotations in Some Philonic Writings and Its Place in the Textual History of the Greek Bible. Cambridge: Cambridge University Press, 1950.

Wilson, Robert M. "Philo Judaeus." ISBE 3:847–50.

PART III

New Testament
Textual Criticism

7

A Brief History of New Testament Textual Criticism

This chapter describes the historical developments that gave rise to New Testament textual criticism beginning as early as Origen and continuing to modern eclectic texts of the New Testament.

At the beginning of the church's history, Christians could learn from eyewitnesses to Christ and the apostles and share the knowledge that they had accumulated. Papias, a second-century bishop, says he prefers this method of learning:

> but if ever anyone came who had followed the presbyters, I inquired into the words of the presbyters, what Andrew or Peter or Philip or Thomas or James or John or Matthew, or any other of the Lord's disciples, had said, and what Aristion and the presbyter John, the Lord's disciples, were saying. For I did not suppose that information from books would help me so much as the word of a living and surviving voice."[1]

However, as time went on fewer and fewer of those eyewitnesses remained, and the need arose for these sacred traditions to be recorded to safeguard their accuracy. Few individuals could afford even a portion of Scripture, so they would have had to go to their local churches to hear the reading of Scripture and its instruction. Several of Paul's letters exhort the churches to read his letters (1 Thess 5:27; 1 Tim 4:13) and even to pass them on to other churches (Col 4:16). This suggests that the letters were to be copied and sent to other churches; however, in time errors would have crept into the text.

Because the New Testament manuscripts have been hand-copied by numerous (skilled and unskilled) people throughout the life of the text, no two agree exactly

---

[1]Eusebius *HE* 3.39.3-4, quoted from Kirsopp Lake, *Eusebius: The Ecclesiastical History with an English Translation*, 2 vols. (Cambridge, Mass.: Harvard University Press, 1965), 1:292-93.

in every instance. The process of New Testament textual criticism can be traced to copyists who, in an effort to improve the text being copied, made conscious choices about its preferable reading.[2] It was these differences in manuscripts that led scholars to realize the need for textual criticism: multiple manuscripts could be compared across passages to determine the more plausible reading.

7.1 Irenaeus

While it is likely that textual criticism began earlier, one of the earliest recorded instances of New Testament textual criticism appears in the works of Irenaeus. In one example Irenaeus (c. A.D. 140-202) preferred a particular reading of Revelation 13:18 because it was "found in all the good [or weighty] and ancient copies."[3]

7.2 Origen of Alexandria/Caesarea

Origen's biblical commentaries refer to New Testament readings that were supported by "few," "many" or "most" of the biblical manuscripts available to him.[4] Origen (A.D. 185-254) complained that "the differences among the manuscripts [of the Gospels] have become great, either through the negligence of some copyists or through the perverse audacity of others; they either neglect to check over what they have transcribed, or, in the process of checking, they lengthen or shorten, as they please."[5]

7.3 Jerome

Jerome (c. 345-420) tediously sifted through numerous Old Latin manuscripts when producing the Latin Vulgate (completed between A.D. 382-405). Eldon J. Epp explained the process Jerome used to choose between readings: "Jerome . . . , who took note of variant readings, considered an older ms [manuscript] to carry more weight than a recent one, and preferred readings that best suited a passage's grammar or context."[6] Jerome even suggests that variant readings were possibly the result "of confusion of similar letters, confusion of abbreviations, accidents involving dittography and haplography, the metathesis of letters, assimilation, transpositions, and deliberate emendations by scribes."[7]

---

[2] Eldon J. Epp, "Textual Criticism (NT)," *ABD* 6:427. Bruce M. Metzger says that Theodotus, a leather merchant who was excommunicated as a heretic by Pope Victor (A.D. 187-198), was the first to use textual criticism (*The Text of the New Testament*, 3rd ed. [New York: Oxford University Press, 1992], p. 150).

[3] Eldon J. Epp, "Issues in New Testament Textual Criticism: Moving from the Nineteenth Century to the Twenty-First Century," in *Rethinking New Testament Textual Criticism*, ed. David A. Black (Grand Rapids: Baker, 2002), p. 21.

[4] Epp, "Textual Criticism," 6:427.

[5] Origen *In Matthaeum Commentarius* 15.14. See Metzger, *Text of the New Testament*, p. 152.

[6] Epp, "Textual Criticism," 6:427.

[7] Metzger, *Text of the New Testament*, p. 153.

Figure 7.1. St. Jerome (c. 345-420) painted by Jan Metsys (c. 1509-1575) on wood [Kunsthistorisches Museum, Vienna, Austria/Erich Lessing/Art Resource, NY]

Jerome lamented the great diversity of Latin manuscripts, stating that there are "almost as many forms of text as there are manuscripts."[8] This seems to suggest that the Latin texts used by Jerome were already significantly corrupted. Bruce Metzger describes Jerome's methodology:

> He used a relatively good Latin text as the basis for this revision, and compared it with some old Greek manuscripts. He emphasizes that he treated the current Latin text as conservatively as possible, and changed it only where the meaning was distorted.[9]

Jerome's comparison of manuscripts to determine the best reading of the text was textual criticism. Jerome's translation, the Latin Vulgate, reigned virtually unchallenged in Europe for over one thousand years as the New Testament text, even though in time the Vulgate text incorporated copyist errors of its own.[10]

7.4 Erasmus of Rotterdam

During the Renaissance, Erasmus of Rotterdam (c. 1466-1536) attempted at least limited textual criticism when preparing his edition of the Greek New Testament in 1516. Erasmus endeavored to complete this task as quickly as possible because another Greek text published in 1514, called the Complutensian Polyglot, could not gain sanction from Pope Leo X. In 1522 both Old and New Testaments (with Hebrew lexicon and grammar) of the polyglot were published, and

---

[8]Bruce M. Metzger, *The Bible in Translation* (Grand Rapids: Baker, 2001), p. 32.
[9]Metzger, *Text of the New Testament*, p. 76.
[10]Kurt Aland and Barbara Aland, *The Text of the New Testament*, trans. Erroll F. Rhodes, 2nd ed. (Grand Rapids: Eerdmans, 1989), p. 190.

Figure 7.2. Erasmus of Rotterdam (c. 1466-1536) painted by Holbein, Hans the younger [Galleria Nazional, Perma, Italy/Scala/Art Resource, NY]

they subsequently received the sanction of the pope. Erasmus had hoped to find reliable Greek manuscripts to prepare his Greek text, but the only manuscripts available on such short notice required significant correction before they could be sent to the printer. Metzger describes Erasmus's process of determining the text:

> Since Erasmus could not find a manuscript which contained the entire Greek Testament, he utilized several for various parts of the New Testament. For most of the text he relied on two rather inferior manuscripts from a monastic library at Basle, one of the Gospels . . . and one of the Acts and Epistles, both dating from about the twelfth century. Erasmus compared them with two or three others of the same books and entered occasional correction for the printer in the margins or between the lines of the Greek script. For the book of Revelation he had but one manuscript, dating from the twelfth century, which he had borrowed from his friend Reuchlin. Unfortunately, this manuscript lacked the final leaf, which had contained the last six verses of the book.[11]

For the last six verses of the book of Revelation and in several other places, Erasmus translated the Latin Vulgate back into Greek.

When Erasmus compared manuscripts to choose between readings, he used some of the same principles, at least in elementary form, that were developed by later text critics.[12] However, even Erasmus later admitted that his Greek text was "precipitated rather than edited."[13]

7.5 Brian Walton

The first work to systematically collect variant readings of the Greek New Testament was the London Polyglot Bible (1655-1657) by Brian Walton (1600-1661).

---

[11]Metzger, *Text of the New Testament*, p. 99.

[12]Michael W. Holmes, "Textual Criticism," in *New Testament Criticism & Interpretation*, ed. David A. Black and David S. Dockery (Grand Rapids: Zondervan, 1991), p. 109; Jerry H. Bentley, *Humanists and Holy Writ: New Testament Scholarship in the Renaissance* (Princeton: Princeton University Press, 1983), pp. 112-61.

[13]Metzger, *Text of the New Testament*, p. 99.

This work contained Robert Estienne's Greek text from the 1550 edition (better known as Stephanus's Greek text) and recorded at the bottom of the page variant readings from Codex Alexandrinus. Eldon Epp explains: "Alexandrinus, which had come to light in 1627, was assigned the symbol 'A' by Walton and was a major factor in the now increasing activity of collecting variant readings and displaying them in critical editions of the Textus Receptus."[14] In the sixth volume Walton inserted an appendix prepared by Archbishop Ussher of variant readings from fifteen different sources.[15]

Figure 7.3. Brian Walton, (1600-1661) compiler of the London Polyglot [Paul Wegner]

7.6 Other Greek Texts

Other notable works followed that compiled variant readings among Greek manuscripts. In 1675 Dr. John Fell (1625-1686), dean of Christ Church and later bishop of Oxford, edited a Greek New Testament based on the Elzevir brothers' Greek text of 1633 (the Elzevir brothers published seven editions between 1624-1678); in an apparatus Fell claims to have compared it with one hundred manuscripts and versions.

Just two weeks before he died, John Mill (1645-1707), a teaching fellow from Queen's College, Oxford, published his Greek text in which he collated evidence from manuscripts, early versions and church fathers. He asserted that there were thirty thousand variants in the few New Testament manuscripts he was familiar with. Epp summarizes Mill's work well:

> The sheer size of this body of variants raised disturbing questions about the validity of the textus receptus; beyond that, in his prolegomena and textual notes Mill enunciated several important text-critical principles, including the judgment that the more obscure a reading, the more authentic, and he implied that genealogical relationships may exist between mss. For his achievements, Mill appropriately may be called the founder of modern New Testament textual criticism.[16]

Others also collated various manuscripts and added increasingly compre-

---

[14]Epp, "Textual Criticism," 6:428.
[15]Metzger, *Text of the New Testament*, p. 107.
[16]Epp, "Textual Criticism," 6:428.

hensive critical apparatuses to the Greek text in order to correct what became commonly known as the Textus Receptus (e.g., Edward Wells, 1709-1719; Richard Bentley, 1720; Daniel Mace, 1729).

7.7 Johann Bengel

While a student at Tübingen a German scholar named Johann Bengel (1687-1752), was so disturbed by the thirty thousand variants in the Greek manuscripts published by John Mill that he devoted himself to studying the transmission of the Greek text. He collected as many editions, manuscripts and early versions as were available and carefully examined them. His work showed that there were far fewer variants than originally thought and that no variant affected any article of evangelical doctrine.[17] Bengel was the first scholar to divide the manuscripts into groups and weigh them rather than assume they were of equal value. In 1734 he published a Greek text that closely followed the Textus Receptus; in the apparatus he classified the relative value of each reading according to the following categories: α = the original reading, with full certainty; β = a reading superior to the Textus Receptus, though with less than absolute certainty; γ = a reading equally as good as the one in the text; δ = a reading not as good as the one in the text; and ϵ = an inferior reading that was to be rejected.[18] Bengel explained the principles by which this apparatus was developed; one of his key principles was "the difficult is to be preferred to the easy reading." This principle included several caveats and has since been further refined, but it remains a primary principle of textual criticism. Because his Greek text challenged the authority of the Textus Receptus, he was ostracized by some even though he was known to be a very pious man.[19]

7.8 Johann Jakob Griesbach

From 1775 until his death, Johann Griesbach (1745-1812), professor of New Testament at the University of Jena (in Germany) traveled to England, Holland and France to collate New Testament manuscripts. He also devoted much time to examining New Testament quotations in the writings of the church fathers. And he gave attention to several ancient versions that until that time had been little studied: the Gothic, Armenean and the Philoxenian Syriac versions.[20] Metzger claims that he "laid the foundations for all subsequent work on the Greek text of the New Testament."[21] Most New Testament textual critical scholars recognize the three recensions into which Griesbach divided the New Testament manu-

---

[17]Metzger, *Text of the New Testament*, p. 112.
[18]Aland and Aland, *Text of the New Testament*, p. 9; Metzger, *Text of the New Testament*, p. 112.
[19]Metzger, *Text of the New Testament*, p. 113.
[20]Ibid., p. 119.
[21]Ibid.

scripts: Alexandrian, Western and Byzantine. Some of the manuscripts of the church fathers that he placed into these recensions are as follows:

Table 7.1. Griesbach's Three Recensions

Sources	Alexandrian	Western	Byzantine
uncials	C, L, K	D	A (in the Gospels), later uncials
minuscules	1, 13, 33, 69, 106, 118		later minuscules
versions		Latin versions, Syriac Peshitta (some) Arabic (some)	
church fathers	Origen, Clement of Alexandria, Eusebius, Cyril of Alexandria, Isidore of Pelusium		later patristic quotations

Griesbach elaborated fifteen canons (or guides) for New Testament textual criticism. The first reads: "The shorter reading (unless it lacks entirely the authority of the ancient and weighty witnesses) is to be preferred to the more verbose, for scribes were much more prone to add than to omit."[22] While Griesbach sometimes would rely too heavily on a mechanical adherence to his system of recensions, by and large he was a careful and cautious scholar. He was also the first German scholar to abandon the Textus Receptus in favor of what he believed to be, by means of his principles, superior readings.

7.9 Karl Lachmann

Karl Lachmann (1793-1851), professor of classical philology at Berlin, was the first scholar to publish a Greek New Testament based entirely on textual critical principles. Although he considered it impossible to reproduce the original text, his aim was to compile a text significantly earlier than the Textus Receptus. In his own words: "Down with the late text of the Textus Receptus, and back to the text of the early fourth-century church."[23] Epp describes his method:

> His aim was to formulate the text as it had existed just prior to A.D. 400, and his bold method was to lay aside the entire established traditional text and to draw his own text from the oldest Greek uncials, the Old Latin and Vulgate, and some early fathers such as Origen, Irenaeus, and Cyprian.[24]

---

[22]Ibid., p. 120.
[23]Aland and Aland, *Text of the New Testament,* p. 11.
[24]Epp, "Textual Criticism," 6:428.

Lachmann's Greek Text (1831) indicated with brackets words that had doubtful textual support and listed passages that differed from the Textus Receptus. However, his editions of the Greek New Testament in 1831 and 1842-1850 fell short of reproducing the text of A.D. 380, partially due to his slender use of manuscript evidence. Nevertheless, his work turned New Testament textual criticism in a new direction, as Fenton J. A. Hort explains:

> A new period began in 1831, when for the first time a text was constructed directly from the ancient documents without the intervention of any printed edition, and when the first systematic attempt was made to substitute scientific method for arbitrary choice in the determination of various readings. In both respects the editor, Lachmann, rejoiced to declare that he was carrying out the principles and unfulfilled intentions of Bentley, as set forth in 1716 and 1720.[25]

7.10 Constantin von Tischendorf

Modern New Testament textual critics probably owe the most to a German Protestant theologian and textual scholar named Lobegott Friedrich Constantin von Tischendorf (1815-1874), who dedicated his life to preparing for publication as many manuscripts and fragments of the New Testament as possible (see figure 6.17). He actually produced eight editions of the New Testament (1841-1872) and nearly two dozen volumes of New Testament manuscripts.[26] In a letter to his fiancée, Tischendorf states: "I am confronted with a sacred task, the struggle to regain the original form of the New Testament."[27] During his lifetime he discovered and published more manuscripts and fragments of the New Testament than any other single scholar.[28] He relentlessly searched the libraries of Europe and the Near East in search of New Testament manuscripts. At the age of twenty-five he began the laborious task of deciphering the palimpsest codex Ephraemi; this manuscript of a fifth-century Greek text was re-used by Ephraem, a Syrian church father in the twelfth century. One of Tischendorf's most important finds was the Codex Sinaiticus at St. Catherine's Monastery, near the foot of what was believed to be Mt. Sinai. Tischendorf examined the manuscripts, versions and writings of the church fathers available in his day. Even though these sources were a fraction of what are available today, his comprehensive and accurate work paved the way for those to follow.

7.11 Brooke F. Westcott and Fenton J. A. Hort

In the latter nineteenth century two Cambridge University scholars,

---

[25]Brooke F. Westcott and Fenton J. A. Hort, *The New Testament in the Original Greek*, 2 vols. (Cambridge: Macmillan, 1881), 1:ii, 2:13; Metzger, *Text of the New Testament*, pp. 125-26.
[26]Epp, "Textual Criticism," 6:428.
[27]Metzger, *Text of the New Testament*, p. 126.
[28]Ibid.

Brooke F. Westcott (1825-1901; Regius Professor of Divinity at Cambridge, and later bishop of Durham) and Fenton J. A. Hort (1828-1892; Hulsean Professor of Divinity at Cambridge) gained renown for their studies of New Testament manuscripts and the publication of their critical edition of the New Testament. In 1881, after twenty-eight years of work, Westcott and Hort published the text of the Greek New Testament (with an introduction and appendixes) titled *The New Testament in the Original Greek.* Not being interested in simply supplying a textual apparatus with all the variant readings, they refined and applied textual principles from earlier scholars to determine what they believed to be the original Greek text, as Epp explains:

> The very title of their work, *The New Testament in the Original Greek,* shows that their goal was far more ambitious than those of Bentley or Lachmann—who wanted to establish the 3d-and 4th-century texts, respectively—for Westcott and Hort sought and claimed to be reproducing the original text itself.[29]

This was indeed an ambitious goal, but Westcott and Hort took advantage of the versions and New Testament quotations in ancient authors and the church fathers to formulate their text. Manuscripts were divided into four text types—Syrian, Western, Alexandrian and Neutral. The "Neutral text" was represented by the fourth-century uncials, namely Codex Vaticanus and Codex Sinaiticus, but could also be traced back further into the mid-second century A.D. They believed the "Neutral" text-type to be closer to the original Greek text than any of the other three text types. They considered the Syrian text type (which we now call Byzantine) to be the latest since no distinctly Syrian readings were found in any of the church fathers of the third century, whereas they are numerous in the latter fourth century, especially in the area of Antioch (Syria). Epp summarizes their conclusions:

> A major conclusion was that the Syrian text had not yet been formed by the mid-3d century and that of the other three that lay behind it, the two oldest were competing texts in the earliest traceable period: the Western and the Neutral. (The Alexandrian text, since Westcott and Hort, has generally been classified with the Neutral, though the term "Alexandrian" has been retained to describe the combined entity.)
>
> The question that remained for Westcott and Hort concerned which of these earliest pre-Syrian text types (Neutral or Western) represented the original, since both—according to them—had 2d-century claims. There was no way by which Westcott and Hort could bring their historical reconstruction to reveal—on historical grounds—which of the two was closer to the original New Testament text.[30]

---

[29]Epp, "Textual Criticism," 6:429.
[30]Ibid.

BROOKE FOSS WESTCOTT (1825-1901)

Westcott was born in Birmingham, England, on January 12, 1825, where he attended King Edward VI's School. He was greatly influenced by the

headmaster, James Prince Lee, who in Westcott's opinion was "superior . . . among the great masters of his time."[a] He attended Trinity College, Cambridge, in 1844 and became a teaching fellow in 1849. Some of his own pupils were Joseph B. Lightfoot, Edward W. Benson and Fenton J. A. Hort. In 1851 he was ordained at the parish church in Prestwich by his old teacher Dr. James P. Lee, who was then bishop of Manchester, and the next year went to teach at Harrow School as assistant master.

Figure 7.4. Brooke F. Westcott
[Paul D. Wegner]

Westcott returned to Cambridge for a brief stay in 1855 where he met the famous German textual critic Tischendorf, with whom he was unimpressed for his seemingly exclusive interest in "palimpsests and codices."[b] In 1869 Westcott was appointed canon of Peterborough and the next year was called to Cambridge University as Regius Professor of Divinity, through the instigation of Lightfoot. He was very involved in the life of the university, both in administration and pastoral concern. He helped found and organize the Cambridge Mission to Delhi and the Cambridge Clergy Training School (later called "Westcott House"). In 1875 Westcott was appointed honorary chaplain to the Queen. During this time his most noted work on New Testament textual criticism with Fenton J. A. Hort progressed, and in 1881 it was published. In 1890, at the age of sixty-six, he was appointed to succeed Lightfoot as Bishop of Durham, where he showed a deep concern for ordination candidates at Auckland Castle and for the social and industrial problems in his diocese. For the next ten years, with ever failing health, he maintained his strenuous work traveling between Durham and London until his death on July 27, 1901.

[a]Edwin H. Robertson, *Makers of the English Bible* (Cambridge: Lutterworth Press, 1990), p. 136.
[b]Ibid., p. 137.

FENTON JOHN ANTHONY HORT (1828-1892)

Hort was born in Dublin, Ireland, in April 1828. At age nine he moved with his family to Cheltenham, England, and the following year to Boulogne in the north of France, where he became interested in classics. His family later returned to Cheltenham where he continued his education and entered Rugby School in October 1841. In 1846 he attended Trinity College, Cambridge, where he became very interested in religious things and sought out evangelicals, but they seemed to him almost careless in their forms of worship. As a result, Hort continued to vacillate between the old, stable Anglican religion that he had grown up with and the new, creative ideas that were taught at Cambridge.

Figure 7.5. Fenton J. A. Hort [Paul D. Wegner]

He graduated from Cambridge with first-class honors in both moral and natural sciences and was considered one of the university's influential thinkers. Being offered a fellowship in 1852 at the same time as Joseph B. Lightfoot, he chose the field of New Testament. Hort was ordained in 1854 and retained his Cambridge fellowship until his marriage in 1857, when he moved to a country parish in Ippolyts-cum-Great Wymondley, near Hitchin, where he pastored for fifteen years. His spare time was devoted to revising the Greek New Testament. He was finally asked to return to Cambridge in 1871 to take up a fellowship and lectureship in theology at Emmanuel College, Cambridge. In 1878 he was offered the position of Hulsean Professor of Divinity and by 1881 his work with Westcott was completed. Hort continued his work at Cambridge despite failing health until his death on November 30, 1892.

7.12 Present State of New Testament Textual Criticism

Westcott and Hort evaluated the various manuscripts of the text types according to internal evidence to see which manuscripts and text types in general were more reliable and in this way attempted to determine the more accurate text types. Their text-critical principles deemphasized manuscripts that were later, read more smoothly, were harmonized or contained conflated readings, such as their so-called Syrian text type. Likewise, those texts that were early but contained paraphrase or assimilation were not favored (e.g., the Western text type). Older manuscripts that they believed contained little corruption or contamination (as the text type name "Neutral" implied) were emphasized. There is little doubt that Westcott and Hort gave too much weight to the Neutral text type, but their textual critical work provided the final blow to the Textus Receptus. These two scholars laid the groundwork for the continuing study of the text of the Greek New Testament; their classifications have been carefully refined and many of their text-critical principles remain in use today.

Several other critical editions of the Greek text appeared following Westcott and Hort: Richard F. Weymouth (1886), Bernhard Weiss (1894-1900); the British and Foreign Bible Society (1904, 1958), Alexander Souter (1910), Hermann von Soden (1911-1913); and Eberhard Nestle's Greek text, the *Novum Testamentum Graece*, published in 1898 by the Württemberg Bible Society, Stuttgart, Germany. The Nestle text went through twelve editions (1898-1923) and then was taken over first by his son, Erwin Nestle (13th-20th editions, 1927-1950), then by Kurt Aland (21st-25th editions, 1952-1963) and finally was coedited by Kurt Aland and Barbara Aland (26th-27th editions, 1979-1993).

Epp critiques the Nestle-Aland text as follows:

> As everyone knows, Nestle's edition—from its beginning and for many years to follow—was based simply on a majority vote among the texts in the editions of Tischendorf, Westcott-Hort, and Weymouth or (later) Weiss, that is, Nestle chose among competing readings by selecting the one supported by two of these three editions. Nestle's edition put forth no other principles for determining the text and certainly offered no theory of the text—both of which are prominent features of editions like those of Tischendorf and Westcott-Hort. Furthermore, the Nestle edition paid "relatively little attention to manuscripts," as the Alands admit (19). It comes as a surprise, therefore, to discover that they call the Nestle edition a "breakthrough" which represents the "conclusive battle" against the *textus receptus* (18-19).[31]

Epp goes on to say:

> It might be granted them that the Nestle text has been the dominant edition in terms of practical use down through the years, but it is difficult to see how it has been a major force at the theoretical level in our discipline, and to that extent their portrayal supports our characterization of their volume as a revisionist history of New Testament textual criticism.[32]

---

[31]Epp, "New Testament Textual Criticism," p. 217.
[32]Eldon J. Epp, "New Testament Textual Criticism Past, Present, and Future: Reflections on the Alands' *Text of the New Testament*." *HTR* 82, no. 2 (1989): 222.

In 1955 the American Bible Society, under the initiative of Eugene A. Nida, called together an international group of scholars to prepare a Greek New Testament that could be used by hundreds of Bible translation committees to revise existing Bible translations or make entirely new translations. Many missionaries, working all over the world to translate the New Testament into modern languages, needed an accurate and easy-to-use text of the Greek New Testament. The international team of scholars forming the editorial committee of this new Greek text were: Matthew Black of St. Andrews, Scotland; Bruce Metzger of Princeton; Allen Wikgren of Chicago; and Kurt Aland of Münster, Westphalia, Germany.[33] This was the beginning of the United Bible Societies' Greek text called *The Greek New Testament*. At the same time, Kurt Aland was working on a new edition of Nestle's Greek text that became known as the Nestle-Aland Greek Text.

Today two different critical Greek texts are in use, namely, *The Greek New Testament* (4th ed., 1994) and the Nestle-Aland *Novum Testamentum Graece* (27th ed., 1993); the text for both is the same even though the textual apparatuses differ as follows: (1) the textual notes of the Nestle-Aland text list more evidence (i.e., a fuller textual history), and (2) the *The Greek New Testament* (4th ed.) lists only the evidence that substantially affects the evidence of the text, but it gives graded evaluations for each textual note so that the reader can determine how certain a variant reading is.

Several ongoing issues are debated among New Testament textual critics:

- **Text types:** Most scholars subscribe to the principle that "quality is more important than quantity" (i.e., textual evidence must be weighed and not merely counted) and that manuscripts must be evaluated as to their accuracy and grouped according to textual families so that they can be reasonably weighed. There is much less agreement, however, when it comes to determining text types or groupings. Epp voices the majority opinion of textual scholars:

  > It can be argued plausibly that three textual clusters or constellations can be identified in reasonably separate groups, and that each finds its earliest representatives in papyrus mss and then carries on to one or more major uncials (cf. Epp 1989c).[34]

He goes on to give the following clusters of manuscripts:

A Text Group: $\mathfrak{P}^{84}$, $\mathfrak{P}^{68}$, $\mathfrak{P}^{42}$ ($\mathfrak{P}^{45}$), Codex Alexandrinus (Gospels)

B Text Group: $\mathfrak{P}^{75}$, $\mathfrak{P}^{66}$, Sinaiticus, L, 33, 1739

---

[33]Later, other members were added to the committee—Carlo M. Martini and since 1982 Johannes Karavidopoulos and Barbara Aland.

[34]Epp, "Textual Criticism," 6:431.

C Text Group: $\mathfrak{P}^{45}$, W (Freer Gospels), Family 13, 33, 1739

D Text Group: $\mathfrak{P}^{29}$, $\mathfrak{P}^{48}$, $\mathfrak{P}^{38}$, Codex Bezae, 1739 (Acts), 614, 383

However, it will remain debatable whether these clusters of manuscripts can be considered text types.

The Alands are strong opponents of the idea of textual traditions or text types. There has been significant discussion as to the validity of textual families before the fourth century. After examining in detail early manuscripts from mainly before the third and fourth centuries, Kurt and Barbara Aland have established the following five categories:[35]

Category I. Manuscripts of a very special quality that should always be considered in establishing the original text (e.g., the Alexandrian text belongs here). The papyri and uncials through the third to fourth centuries also belong here automatically, one may say, because they represent the text of the early period (if they offer no significant evidence, they are bracketed).

Category II. Manuscripts of a special quality but distinguished from manuscripts of category I by the presence of alien influences (particularly of the Byzantine text), and yet of importance for establishing the original text (e.g., the Egyptian text belongs here).

Category III. Manuscripts of a distinctive character with an independent text, usually important for establishing the original text but particularly important for the history of the text (e.g., f^1, f^{13}).

Category IV. Manuscripts of the D (Western) text.

Category V. Manuscripts with a purely or predominantly Byzantine text.

The Alands then categorize all the manuscripts according to the following notations:

1: agreements with the Byzantine text

1/2: agreements with the Byzantine text where it has the same reading as the original text

2: agreements with the original text

S: independent or distinctive readings (i.e., special readings, "Sonderlesarten")

This is where the Alands' research displays a measure of circular reasoning, for the original text is thought to be the Nestle-Aland's text, though not everyone would agree that it contains the most original readings in every instance, as Epp notes:

---

[35]Aland and Aland, *Text of the New Testament*, p. 106.

there is a certain measure of question-begging or circularity of argument in this schema when, for example, a MS is placed into Category I on the basis of its "incidence of agreements with the original" . . . but when—at the same time—MSS in Category I constitute those which possess "a very special quality which should always be considered in establishing the original text." In addition, there is a fair measure of prejudgment or arbitrariness if, for example, numerous MSS are automatically included in Category I merely because of their age and another MS (P^{74}) is included in that same category despite its age.[36]

- Criteria for evaluating readings. There is significant disagreement concerning the weight to be given to various canons or criteria when determining textual critical issues. This debate has occurred at two levels: (1) regarding the specific criteria used when determining a specific reading, and (2) how much weight to give internal and external evidence. This latter issue has been so hotly debated that three basic methods of criticism have emerged: historical-documentary, rigorous eclecticism, reasoned eclecticism, and Byzantine-priority (see later discussion on pp. 239-40).

I consider the balanced approach of the Reasoned Eclectic method to be preferable for resolving text-critical issues. However, the Historical-Documentary method (emphasizing external evidence) and the Rigorous Eclectic method (emphasizing internal evidence) provide a healthy counterbalance and should still be taken into account.

Further Reading

Aland, Kurt, and Barbara Aland. *The Text of the New Testament. An Introduction to the Critical Editions and to the Theory and Practice of Modern Textual Criticism.* Translated by Erroll F. Rhodes. Grand Rapids: Eerdmans, 1987.

Birdsall, J. Neville. "The New Testament Text." In *CHB* 1:308-77.

Fee, Gordon D. "The Textual Criticism of the New Testament." In *The Expositor's Bible Commentary*, 1:419-33. Edited by Frank E. Gaebelein. 12 vols. Grand Rapids: Zondervan, 1976-1992.

Finegan, Jack. *Encountering New Testament Manuscripts: A Working Introduction to Textual Criticism.* Grand Rapids: Eerdmans, 1974.

Greenlee, J. Harold *Introduction to New Testament Textual Criticism.* 2nd Edition. Peabody, Mass.: Hendrickson, 1996.

———. *Scribes, Scrolls, and Scripture. A Student's Guide to New Testament Textual Criticism.* Grand Rapids: Eerdmans, 1985.

Holmes, Michael W. "Textual Criticism." In *New Testament Criticism & Interpretation.* Edited by David A. Black and David S. Dockery. Louisville: Broad-

---

[36]Epp, "New Testament Textual Criticism," p. 226.

man & Holman, 2001. See pp. 101-36.

Metzger, Bruce M. *Chapters in the History of New Testament Textual Criticism.* New Testament Tools and Studies 4. Grand Rapids: Eerdmans, 1963.

————. *The Text of the New Testament. Its Transmission, Corruption, and Restoration.* 3rd ed. New York: Oxford University Press, 1992.

Excursus 2: *Modern Eclectic Editions of the Greek Bible*

Presently there are two common forms of the Greek text: (1) *The Greek New Testament*, 4th ed. (Stuttgart: United Bible Societies, 1994) (see figure 7.4), and (2) *Novum Testamentum Graece*, 27th ed. (Stuttgart: Deutsche Bibelgesellschaft, 1993) (Nestle-Aland text, see figure 7.5).

We will now look at each component of the United Bible Societies' critical edition to provide a foundation for those wanting to proceed to the Nestle-Aland text.

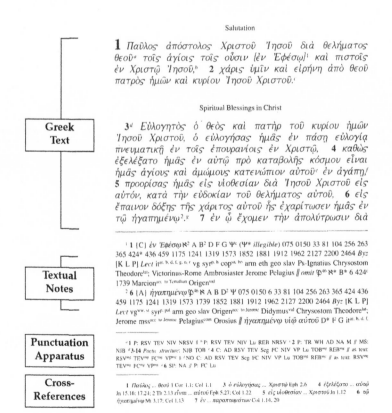

ΠΡΟΣ ΕΦΕΣΙΟΥΣ

Salutation

1 Παῦλος ἀπόστολος Χριστοῦ Ἰησοῦ διὰ θελήματος θεοῦ⁴ τοῖς ἁγίοις τοῖς οὖσιν [ἐν Ἐφέσῳ]¹ καὶ πιστοῖς ἐν Χριστῷ Ἰησοῦ,ᵇ 2 χάρις ὑμῖν καὶ εἰρήνη ἀπὸ θεοῦ πατρὸς ἡμῶν καὶ κυρίου Ἰησοῦ Χριστοῦ.ᶜ

Spiritual Blessings in Christ

Greek Text

3ᵈ Εὐλογητὸς ὁ θεὸς καὶ πατὴρ τοῦ κυρίου ἡμῶν Ἰησοῦ Χριστοῦ, ὁ εὐλογήσας ἡμᾶς ἐν πάσῃ εὐλογίᾳ πνευματικῇ ἐν τοῖς ἐπουρανίοις ἐν Χριστῷ, 4 καθὼς ἐξελέξατο ἡμᾶς ἐν αὐτῷ πρὸ καταβολῆς κόσμου εἶναι ἡμᾶς ἁγίους καὶ ἀμώμους κατενώπιον αὐτοῦᶜ ἐν ἀγάπῃ,ᶠ 5 προορίσας ἡμᾶς εἰς υἱοθεσίαν διὰ Ἰησοῦ Χριστοῦ εἰς αὐτόν, κατὰ τὴν εὐδοκίαν τοῦ θελήματος αὐτοῦ, 6 εἰς ἔπαινον δόξης τῆς χάριτος αὐτοῦ ἧς ἐχαρίτωσεν ἡμᾶς ἐν τῷ ἠγαπημένῳ².ᵍ 7 ἐν ᾧ ἔχομεν τὴν ἀπολύτρωσιν διὰ

Textual Notes

¹ 1 [C] ἐν Ἐφέσῳℵ² A B² D F G Ψᶜ (Ψ* *illegible*) 075 0150 33 81 104 256 263 365 424* 436 459 1175 1241 1319 1573 1852 1881 1912 1962 2127 2200 2464 *Byz* [K L P] *Lect* itᵃʳ·ᵇ·ᵈ·ᶠ·ᵍ·ᵒ·ʳ vg syrᵖ·ʰ copᵇᵒ·ᵇᵒ arm eth geo slav Ps-Ignatius Chrysostom Theodoreˡᵃᵗ; Victorinus-Rome Ambrosiaster Jerome Pelagius ‖ *omit* 𝔓⁴⁶ ℵ* B* 6 424ᶜ 1739 Marcionᵃᶜᶜ·ᵗᵒ ᵗᵉʳᵗᵘˡˡⁱᵃⁿ Origenᵛⁱᵈ

² 6 [A] ἠγαπημένῳ 𝔓⁴⁶ ℵ A B D² Ψ 075 0150 6 33 81 104 256 263 365 424 436 459 1175 1241 1319 1573 1739 1852 1881 1912 1962 2127 2200 2464 *Byz* [K L P] *Lect* vgᵂᵂ·ˢᵗ syrʰ·ᵖᵃˡ arm geo slav Origenᵃᶜᶜ·ᵗᵒ ʲᵉʳᵒᵐᵉ Didymusᵛⁱᵈ Chrysostom Theodoreˡᵃᵗ; Jerome mssᵃᶜᶜ·ᵗᵒ ʲᵉʳᵒᵐᵉ Pelagiusᶜᵒᵐ Orosius ‖ ἠγαπημένῳ υἱῷ αὐτοῦ D* F G itᵃʳ·ᵇ·ᵈ·ᶠ·

Punctuation Apparatus

¹ 1 P: RSV TEV NIV NRSV ‖ ^ P: RSV TEV NIV Lu REB NRSV · 2 P: TR WH AD NA M ‖ MS: NJB *⁴3-14 Poetic structure*: NJB TOB · ⁴ C: AD RSV TEV Seg FC NIV VP Lu TOBᵐᵍ REBᵐᵍ ‖ as text: RSVᵐᵍ TEVᵐᵍ FCᵐᵍ VPᵐᵍ ‖ ᶠNO C: AD RSV TEV Seg FC NIV VP Lu TOBᵐᵍ REBᵐᵍ ‖ as text: RSVᵐᵍ TEVᵐᵍ FCᵐᵍ VPᵐᵍ · ᵍ6 SP: NA ‖ P: FC Lu

Cross-References

1 Παῦλος ... θεοῦ 1 Cor 1.1; Col 1.1 3 ὁ εὐλογήσας ... Χριστῷ Eph 2.6 4 ἐξελέξατο ... αὐτῷ Jn 15.16; 17.24; 2 Th 2.13 εἶναι ... αὐτοῦ Eph 5.27; Col 1.22 5 εἰς υἱοθεσίαν ... Χριστοῦ Jn 1.12 6 τῷ ἠγαπημένῳ Mt 3.17; Col 1.13 7 ἐν ... παραπτωμάτων Col 1.14, 20

Figure E2.1. *The Greek New Testament*, 4th ed., 2001 [American Bible Society]

1 The Text

The modern Greek critical editions are a collection of the best readings from each of the approximately 5,487 manuscripts and other witnesses to the Greek text (this is called an eclectic text, whereas a diplomatic edition is primarily a text from one manuscript). In principle a compilation of the best readings for each passage provides the best Greek text of the New Testament, though some scholars would disagree (see later discussion on pp. 239-40).

2 The Textual Apparatus

A look at the following section from the current United Bible Societies' Greek text, including the textual apparatus, of Ephesians 1:1 will help to acquaint the reader with its components:

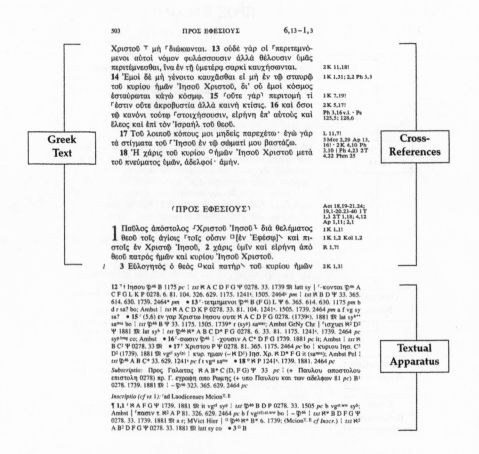

Figure E2.2. *Novum Testamentum Graece*, 27th ed. [American Bible Society]

¹ 1 {C} ἐν Ἐφέσῳ ℵ² A B² D F G Ψᶜ (Ψ* *illegible*) 075 0150 33 81 104 256 263 365 424*
436 459 1175 1241 1319 1573 1852 1881 1912 1962 2127 2200 2464 *Byz* [K L P] *Lect*
itᵃʳ, ᵇ, ᵈ, ᶠ, ᵍ, ᵒ, ʳ vg syrᵖ,ʰ copˢᵃ, ᵇᵒ arm eth geo slav Ps-Ignatius Chrysostom, Theodoreˡᵃᵗ,
Victorinus-Rome Ambrosiaster Jerome Pelagius // *omit* 𝔓⁴⁶ ℵ* B* 6 424ᶜ 1739 Mar-
cionᵃᶜᶜ. ᵗᵒ ʲᵉʳᵒᵐᵉ Origenᵛⁱᵈ

At the beginning of each textual note are two numbers. The variants of each
biblical chapter are noted by a small superscript number. The next number,
which is larger, indicates the verse number. It is possible for one verse to have
more than one variant. The textual notes provide a great deal of information
about the Greek text, generally in the following order:

2.1. A capital letter in brackets {C}. This letter system was devised by the editors
of the Greek text to give the reader some indication as to the relative certainty of
the reading. The readings are rated from A to D, depending on the evidence.

A	B	C	D
Most Certain			Least Certain

On a continuum "A" denotes those readings that the editors consider very
certain and "D" those that are least certain. In the above example from Ephe-

Table E2.1. Description of Sources in the Textual Apparatus

Category	Designation	Examples
1. Papyrus Generally the earliest writing material	lower script Gothic 𝔓 plus a superscript Arabic number	𝔓⁴⁵, 𝔓⁵², 𝔓⁷⁵
2. Uncials A type of writing most closely corresponding to our capital letters	capital letters in English, Hebrew or Greek, or a number beginning with zero	A, ℵ, Ψ, 044
3. Cursives A type of writing most closely corresponding to our cursive (including minuscules, which are smaller letters)	Arabic numbers (no initial zeros)	453, 984, 1574
4. Byzantine Lectionaries Works containing selections of biblical texts to be read in church	lower script letter ("*ℓ*") plus a superscript Arabic number	ℓ⁴⁵, ℓ⁵²⁴
5. Versions The Bible translated into other languages	common name or source	vg (Latin vulgate) syrᵖ (Syriac Peshitta)
6. Church fathers or sources Writings of church fathers or their quotations of Scripture	common name or source	Augustine, Eusebius, Jerome

sians 1:1 the footnote in verse one states that the insertion of the Greek words
ἐν Ἐφέσῳ (*en Epheso*) or "in Ephesus" into the text has a C rating (i.e., it is a
fairly uncertain reading).

2.2 *Textual evidence for each reading.* Usually the textual evidence for each
reading is given in the order and with the abbreviations (called "sigla") given
in table E2.1.

Table E2.2 is a brief description of some of the more common abbreviations
in the USB Greek New Testament textual apparatus. (The introduction to the
UBS Greek text has a complete list of abbreviations.)

Table E2.2. Common Abbreviations in the Textual Apparatus

Abbreviation	Meaning
*	the reading of the original hand of a manuscript
$X^{c,2,3}$	successive correctors of a manuscript (see fig. 6.8)
X^{mg}	textual evidence written in a margin of a manuscript
X^{gr}	the Greek text of a bilingual manuscript
X^{vid}	indicates apparent support for a given reading in a manuscript whose state of preservation makes absolute verification impossible
$X^{v.v.}$	indicates variant readings in manuscripts or other witnesses
?	indicates that a witness supports a given reading, but that there is some doubt
( )	indicates that a witness supports the reading for which it is cited, but deviates from it in minor details
cj	conjecture
X^{supp}	a portion of a manuscript supplied by a later hand where the original was missing
sic	indicates an abnormality exactly reproduced from the original
X^{txt}	The text of a manuscript when it differs from another reading given in the commentary section accompanying the text
X^{comm}	The commentary section of a manuscript where the reading differs from the accompanying Greek text

Other information about the manuscripts abbreviated in the textual apparatus, including their dates, content and where they are currently housed, appears in a list at the beginning of the United Bible Societies' Greek text (pp. 6*-
52*). Because many manuscripts do not contain the entire New Testament,
some letters are reused (e.g., two "D" *sigla* represent two different manuscripts:
[1] Bezae Cantabrigiensis—a fifth-century A.D. codex of the Gospels and Acts,
and [2] Claromontanus—a sixth-century A.D. codex of the Pauline Epistles).

The abbreviations are noted at the front of the UBS Greek text, but we must pay close attention to the contexts of the manuscripts—when working in the Gospels, for instance, make sure that the manuscript *sigla* contain that part of the text. The following symbols designate this information:

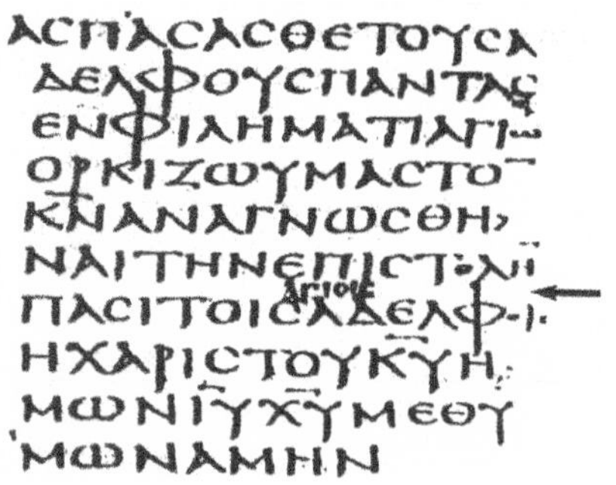

Figure E2.3. A correction to the text of 1 Thessalonians 5:27 in Codex Sinaiticus written by a later copyist [British Library]

e = Gospels

a = Acts

c = Catholic or General Epistles

p = Epistles of Paul

r = Revelation

The works are usually listed in chronological order within their catogories; the century dates of the manuscripts are noted in Roman numerals (e.g., VI = sixth century A.D.).

2.3. Two Slashed Lines (//). These slashed lines indicate the end of the textual information for the first reading, after which the note for the second reading begins in the same sequence as above.

While the textual apparatus of the UBS Greek text provides most of the information necessary to determine the most plausible original reading of a passage, the chart on p. 228 may prove helpful when collating and evaluating the evidence for various readings. The first space should be filled in with the first reading of the text you have chosen to evaluate, with its corresponding English translation. The space directly below labeled "External Evidence," should list the various Greek manuscripts, Byzantine lectionaries, versions and church fathers that include that reading of the Greek text. The next column should list similar information for the next variant and so on. Once the primary evidence has been written in the columns, you should be able to make a preliminary evaluation of the external evidence to determine which reading has the strongest evidence (see principles that can be used to evaluate the external evidence, pp. 231-38). Next, write in any internal evidence that may favor any of the readings and explain why (see later discussion of internal evidence, pp. 238-41). After a careful examination of this evidence, determine which reading is most likely the original reading of the text and explain your conclusions in the last box.

Worksheet for New Testament Textual Criticism

Passage:_____

Various Readings		
Reading 1	Reading 2	Reading 3
Meaning:	Meaning:	Meaning:
External Evidence:	External Evidence:	External Evidence:
Which one is favored and why?		
Internal Evidence:		
Conclusions:		

8

Determining the Most Plausible Reading

This chapter will help the reader understand the process of New Testament textual criticism: from gathering evidence to becoming familiar with textual families, weighing internal and external evidence and evaluating a given reading. The chapter concludes with several examples of New Testament textual criticism.

Christophe Petyt, a French artist, has turned making exact copies of masterpieces into big business. You choose the painting and for anywhere from £2,000 to £20,000 ($3,650 to $36,500) he can deliver a painting so close to the original that the original artist may have a hard time telling them apart. "Our copies are exact in every detail," says Petyt. "Sometimes we have the opportunity to put them next to the original, and it really is very, very hard to tell them apart."[1] William Langley, writer for the Telegraph, explains:

> His Paris-based company, L'Art du Faux, employs more than 80 maitres fournisseurs—painters steeped in the style of a particular artist or school. Not a brushstroke or smudge escapes them. Every work is individually commissioned and done from scratch, using new canvases and oil paints, then artificially aged by a variety of simple but ingenious techniques.[2]

Langley goes on to say, "Surprisingly, it's all legal, too—including the forging of artists' signatures."[3] Unfortunately copyists of New Testament manuscripts did not always take the same care as these painters to ensure their copies were exact.

Textual criticism is foundational to exegesis and interpretation of the text: we need to know what the wording of the text is before we can know what it

---

[1] William Langley, "Fake Art Meets Real Money," *Daily Telegraph*, Sunday, March 6, 2005, n.p. Accessed online at <http://www.telegraph.co.uk/arts/main.jhtml?xml=/arts/2003/06/30/balang30.xml>.
[2] Ibid.
[3] Ibid.

TYPES OF VARIANTS

1. The greatest number of variants are differences or errors in spelling. For example, the author of Codex Vaticanus spells "John" with only one "n" instead of the more common two ('Ιωάννης [Iōannēs]). This type of variant makes no difference in the meaning of the text.

2. The second largest group of variants arises from differences between Greek and English. For example, in Greek a person's name may or may not be preceded by an article (the); or the phrase "the good man" could also be written in Greek as "the man, the good one," whereas in English both phrases are translated as "the good man." This type of variant also makes no difference in the meaning of the text.

3. Sometimes a scribe accidentally made nonsense out of a word or phrase when copying. One scribe accidentally wrote the Greek letter π (pi) instead of φ (phi) in Luke 6:41, rendering the text, "Let me take the fruit (κάρπος [karpos]) out of your eye" instead of "Let me take the speck (κάρφος [karphos]) out of your eye." These types of errors are rare and easy to spot.

means.[4] The process of New Testament textual criticism entails two fundamental tasks: (1) the study of the extant manuscripts of the New Testament text, and (2) the evaluation of the evidence from these manuscripts.[5] The primary task of the text critic is to evaluate and critique the variants among the

---

[4]Similar types of issues arise in New Testament textual criticism as in Old Testament criticism, for Eldon J. Epp suggests that it is far too simplistic to speak of an "original text" as if we are able to determine the *ipsissima verba* ("the very words") of the original authors since the formation of the New Testament manuscripts may demand that there were multiple originals, or at least that there were several layers or levels of meaning ("Issues in New Testament Textual Criticism: Moving from the Nineteenth Century to the Twentieth Century," in *Rethinking New Testament Textual Criticism,* ed. David A. Black [Grand Rapids: Baker, 2002], pp. 70-75). I prefer Bruce M. Metzger's statement of the goal of New Testament textual criticism, namely "to ascertain from the divergent copies which form of the text should be regarded as the most nearly conforming to the original" (*The Text of the New Testament: Its Transmission, Corruption, and Restoration* [New York: Oxford University Press, 1992], p. v). While this seems to be a serious issue in the formation of Old Testament books, the multiple texts or levels do not seem to be as problematic in the formation of the New Testament books.

[5]Michael W. Holmes, "The Case for Reasoned Eclecticism," in *Rethinking New Testament Textual Criticism,* ed. David A. Black (Grand Rapids: Baker, 2002), p. 77.

New Testament manuscripts. A variant is any difference between the texts in the numerous manuscripts of the Greek New Testament (e.g., spelling differences, missing or added words, different word order). Some variants are significant; for example, the last eleven verses of the Gospel of Mark. But the vast majority have little effect on the translation of a passage and are relatively insignificant, a fact that underscores how accurate our Bibles actually are.

It is important to underscore two facts near the beginning of our discussion on New Testament textual criticism: (1) the verbal agreement between various New Testament manuscripts is closer than between many English translations of the New Testament, and (2) the percentage of variants in the New Testament is small (approximately 7 percent) and no matter of doctrine hinges on a variant reading.

8.1 Where Do We Start?

The first step is to determine where possible errors appear in the text; in New Testament textual criticism this is fairly easy. The editors of the UBS Greek text have done much of this work already for you by examining the various Greek manuscripts, ancient versions and New Testament citations in the works of the church fathers to see where variants appear. It would be almost impossible for the average student, or even scholar, to examine all of the extant Greek manuscripts, ancient versions and church fathers. At present much of this work is done at the Institute for New Testament Research in Münster/Westphalia, Germany, where a reproduction of every Greek manuscript is housed, as well as much of the evidence from church fathers and ancient versions. The most important evidence for the variants appears in the textual apparatus at the bottom of each page of the UBS Greek text. The text critic can use this information to evaluate the strength of a variant reading.

8.2 Collecting the Evidence

There are two types of evidence: internal evidence that comes from within the text itself (e.g., author's grammar or spelling habits, use of parallel passages), and external evidence that comes from outside the text (e.g., various manuscripts, versions or quotes from church fathers).

8.2.1 External Evidence

External evidence comes primarily from three different sources that are summarized below:

Each of these areas can supply valuable information to help determine the most plausible original reading.

8.2.1.1 New Testament Greek manuscripts. There are over five thousand extant New Testament manuscripts, ranging from small fragmentary manuscripts

($\mathfrak{P}^{52}$) to almost complete copies of the New Testament (Codex Alexandrinus). David A. Black states: "Even for the Book of Revelation, which is the most poorly attested writing in the New Testament, over three hundred Greek manuscripts have been preserved."[6]

The earliest manuscripts, written on papyrus, date as early as the second ($\mathfrak{P}^{52}$, $\mathfrak{P}^{46}$) or third ($\mathfrak{P}^{66}$, $\mathfrak{P}^{75}$) centuries A.D. Papyrus is made from the reedlike papyrus plant that grows along the banks of the Nile River in Egypt. The pithy centers of the stalks were sliced and layered horizontally then vertically. The papyrus sheet was then allowed to dry; the sugar in the plant caused the slices of the stalk to adhere together, forming a fairly smooth writing surface.

As a writing material, papyrus was used as early as 2400 B.C. and was very common in the first century A.D. when the biblical texts were written. Papyrus is perishable: it can easily be damaged by water or become dry and brittle when exposed to the sun, which is why there are so few papyrus manuscripts extant today, and those that do exist have primarily been found in the dry regions of Egypt. There are about 116 papyrus manuscripts known today, and every New Testament book, except 1 and 2 Timothy, is attested in at least one papyrus manuscript.[7] Christians generally used the codex format instead of scrolls as Jewish scribes did. For example, $\mathfrak{P}^{52}$, one of the earliest New Testament manuscripts, written about A.D. 125, is written on both sides of the papyrus. (Scrolls were usually written on one side.) Eventually parchment became the preferred writing material (in about the fourth century). One parchment manuscript comes from the second or third century (0189), two from the third century (0212, 0220) and two from the third or fourth century (0162, 0171), but from about the fourth century A.D. on, parchment increasingly became more popular. Parchment was a strong and durable writing surface made from animal hides, generally those of sheep and goats. The hide was first scraped clean of hair and then soaked in lime to lighten the color. It was then dried and rubbed with chalk and pumice stone to produce a smooth, fine writing surface. One hide would provide about four folios (pages) of finished manuscript, which then formed part of a codex, as the Alands describe:

> A manuscript containing a group of New Testament writings in an average format (about 200-250 folios of approximately 25 x 19 cm.) required the hides of at least fifty to sixty sheep or goats. This would mean quite a good size flock. . . .

---

[6] David A. Black, *New Testament Textual Criticism* (Grand Rapids: Baker, 1994), p. 18.

[7] Fee, "Textual Criticism of the New Testament," p. 4; Black says that every New Testament book is attested by at least one papyrus manuscript (*New Testament Textual Criticism*, p. 19).

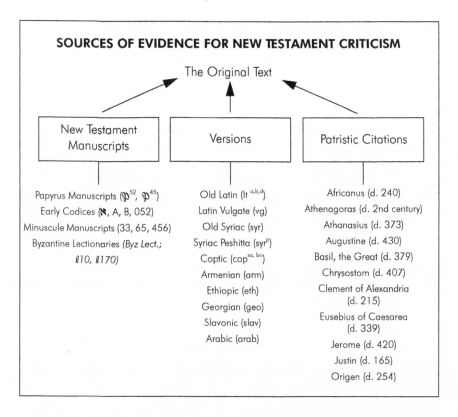

For a larger manuscript (Codex Sinaiticus was originally at least 43 x 38 cm. in size) or one of a particularly fine quality of parchment, the expense would have multiplied. In fact, a manuscript of the New Testament represented a small fortune because the preparation of the parchment was only the first step. Once it had been prepared there was still the writing of the text to be done, as well as the illumination of the initials, and frequently also the addition of miniatures by an artist.[8]

Sometimes, perhaps due to limited supply or high cost, parchment or leather was cleaned and reused—a new text written over the original writing. These manuscripts are called palimpsests ("rescraped," from the two Greek words πάλιν [*palin*, "again"] and ψάω [*psaō*, "to scrape"]. About fifty Greek New Testament manuscripts are palimpsests—the most familiar being Codex Ephraemi, a fifth-century A.D. New Testament manuscript that was erased and replaced in the twelfth century by thirty-eight sermons or treatises of Ephraem, a fourth-century Syrian church father. Parchment continued to be

---

[8]See Kurt Aland and Barbara Aland, *The Text of the New Testament*, trans. Erroll F. Rhodes, 2nd ed. (Grand Rapids: Eerdmans, 1989), p. 77.

used even into modern times, but from about the twelfth century on paper increased in popularity.

The invention of paper is commonly attributed to the Chinese in the first century A.D., but it was not until about the eighth century that it was introduced into the Western world by the Arabs. By the fifteenth century, paper had virtually replaced parchment as the common writing material, and just in time, since the invention of movable print and the printing press created a demand parchment could never have met. The Alands say that "of the 5,400 known manuscripts of the New Testament, about 1,300 are written on paper."[9]

Another way that New Testament manuscripts are distinguished is by type of writing, namely, uncial writing (similar to our printed capital letters), used from about the second to the eleventh centuries, and minuscules (similar to our cursive letters), used from about the ninth to the sixteenth centuries.[10] These categories can overlap since papyrus manuscripts were often written in uncial handwriting. Early uncial Greek texts were written without word divisions, punctuation marks and accents, which sometimes caused problems in distinguishing words.

Type of Manuscripts	Number of Manuscripts	Date of Manuscript
Uncials		
ΜΑΙΝΩΝΙΙΟΙΩ	274 manuscripts[a]	2nd to 11th centuries
Minuscules		
ϩʏλοϊλʑʏϫ ὄλεϒϲολλ	2,555 manuscripts[b]	9th to 16th centuries

[a]Black, *New Testament Textual Criticism*, p. 19.
[b]Ibid., p. 20.

There are also about 2,280 lectionary manuscripts that contain selections (or pericopes) of the New Testament that were to be read or studied in private or public worship services. There are several different types of lectionaries, the dates of which range from the fourth to sixteenth centuries.[11]

---

[9]Ibid.
[10]Ibid., p. 81.
[11]See Aland and Aland, *Text of the New Testament*, p. 81.

The lectionaries of prime importance to New Testament textual criticism are those that have Greek texts. Of lesser importance are versions, since they are translations of the Greek, and citations of the biblical text by the church fathers, since it is difficult to tell when they paraphrased or roughly translated the Greek.

8.2.1.2 Versions. Initially the New Testament was written in Greek (with a few Aramaic words), but as the church spread, people of other regions wanted the Bible in their own languages. The earliest translations of the New Testament, dating to about A.D. 180, are in Latin, Syriac and Coptic. In time other regions were evangelized and the Scriptures were then translated into Ethiopic, Armenian, Gothic and Slavonic. The early versions most useful to New Testament textual criticism are those that were translated directly from a Greek manuscript or were subsequently revised in light of Greek manuscripts. In using the versions we need to be aware of the unique difficulties in translating between particular languages (see later discussion on pp. 270-71). David A. Black underscores a second limitation:

> None of the original manuscripts of the version is extant, and therefore existing manuscripts must be subjected to textual criticism to determine the original text as nearly as possible. In addition, in certain types of variants, some versions cannot reflect what the Greek might have read. . . . However, the great benefit of versional evidence is that it can show that a particular reading was known in the place and time of the version's origin.[12]

There are about 8,000 manuscripts of the Latin Vulgate alone, not to mention all the other versions. Versions are to be evaluated by the same criteria as other manuscripts—date, accuracy and independence of sources. The following list indicates the relationship between various versions:

- *Old Latin versions* (c. mid-second century). A primary translation of the New Testament that reflects a Western text family.

- *Latin Vulgate* (c. 382-405). Apparently Old Latin texts greatly influenced this version.

- *Old Syriac versions* (c. second to fifth centuries). (1) Diatessaron (c. 170): primary translation from Greek manuscripts. (2) Syriac Peshitta (c. fifth century): primary translation from Greek manuscripts.

- *Coptic versions* (c. third to fifth centuries). Both Sahidic and Bohairic versions are primary translations from an Alexandrian text, but influence from Western texts is seen at certain points in the Gospels and Acts.

---

[12]Black, *New Testament Textual Criticism*, p. 23.

- *Gothic version* (c. fourth century). A primary, literal translation of a Byzantine text.

- *Armenian version* (c. early fifth century). Probably a primary, literal translation of Greek or Syriac manuscripts.

- *Georgian version* (c. mid-fifth century). Tertiary translation, probably from the Armenian version.

- *Ethiopic version* (c. fifth or sixth centuries). The sources of the majority of this translation are uncertain—the Catholic Epistles and Revelation appear to be primary translations, but there is evidence of subsequent influences from Coptic and Arabic.

- *Arabic versions* (c. eighth century). Influences from Greek, Old Syriac, Syriac Peshitta, Coptic and Latin versions.

- *Old Slavonic version* (c. ninth century). A primary translation from a Byzantine text family, however a significant number of Western readings.

8.2.1.3 Patristic citations. Patristic citations must be used with caution since their accuracy is difficult to judge: a text may be a direct quote of a Greek manuscript, or the author may simply allude to a text or quote loosely from memory. Church fathers sometimes used several manuscripts, so citations of a particular passage may be from different sources. The patristic citations themselves are merely copies, often very late, and not autographs. They too need to be subjected to the text-critical method in order to be given their appropriate weight. The patristic citations are extensive; it has been said that if for some reason the New Testament were destroyed, it could be completely retrieved entirely from the quotes of the early church fathers.

In spite of the difficulties and uncertainties of using patristic citations, they nevertheless have importance to New Testament textual criticism, as the Alands note:

> Establishing the New Testament text of the Church Fathers has a strategic importance for textual history and criticism. It shows us how the text appeared at particular times and in particular places: this is information we can find nowhere else. With a Greek manuscript there is no way of knowing the age of the exemplar it was copied from, nor when we know the provenance of a manuscript (as we do in exceptional instances) is there any way of knowing the provenance of its exemplar, which is even more important. . . . Many important tasks challenge us here. With more adequate information about the Church Fathers' text of the New Testament we would have firmer guidelines for a history of the text.[13]

---

[13] Aland and Aland, *Text of the New Testament*, pp. 172-73.

Modern Greek texts include important references to patristic citations. Table 8.1 lists the more prominent church fathers:

Table 8.1. Prominent Church Fathers

Marcion	c. 130-170	Rome
Justin Martyr	d. c. 165	Samaria
Tatian	c. 130- 170	Syria
Irenaeus, Bishop of Lyons	d. c. 202	Lyons, France
Clement of Alexandria	d. c. 212	Alexandria, Egypt
Tertullian of Carthage	d. after A.D. 220	Carthage, North Africa
Hippolytus	d. A.D. 235	Rome
Origen of Alexandria and Caesarea	d. 253/54	Alexandria, Egypt and Caesarea
Eusebius, bishop of Caesarea	d. 339/40	Caesarea
Hilary of Poitiers	d. 367	Poitiers, France
Lucifer of Cagliari	d. 370/71	Cagliari, Italy
Athanasius, bishop of Alexandria	d. 373	Alexandria, Egypt
Ephrem the Syrian	d. 373	Syria
Gregory of Nazianzus	d. 389/90	Cappadocia (Turkey)
Gregory of Nyssa	d. 394	Cappadocia (Turkey)
Ambrose of Milan	d. 397	Milan
Ambrosiaster (= Pseudo-Ambrose)	latter 4th century	Rome
Epiphanius, bishop of Salamis	d. 403	Salamis, Cyprus
Rufinus	d. 410	Syria
Jerome (= Hieronymos)	d. 419/20	Rome and Bethlehem
Theodore of Mopsuestia	d. 428	Mopsuestia, Cilicia (Turkey)
Augustine, bishop of Hippo	d. 430	Hippo, North Africa
Isidore of Pelusium	d. c. 435	Pelusium, Egypt
Cyril of Alexandria	d. 444	Alexandria, Egypt
Pelagius	4th-5th century	Rome

It would be unrealistically time consuming to check all the patristic primary sources for every passage. Fortunately, modern eclectic Greek New Testaments have already done much of this work for us. In addition, the Institute for New Testament Research in Münster, Westphalia, Germany, and the Ancient Biblical Manuscripts Center in Claremont, California, are dedicated to having at least a facsimile copy of all the biblical manuscripts and fragments. We are the beneficiaries of the great labor that scholars have invested in modern Greek New Testaments that include the most important information concerning variant readings of specific passages.

8.2.2 Internal Evidence

Internal evidence is collected from the text itself (e.g., the literary context; scribal habits, such as particular grammatical or spelling conventions that the author uses; and literary forms, such as parallelism or chiasm). For example, if the author of the Gospel of John always used the name "Christ" for "Jesus," but in a particular manuscript the name "Jesus" appears instead, that is a plausible corruption of the text. Internal evidence also includes common copying mistakes and intentional changes (see pp. 44-55).

Skill and familiarity with the biblical material is very useful when sorting through the different clues within a passage that point to a particular reading (e.g., parallel units, certain characteristics of an author, grammatical issues). Among commentaries that take note of internal evidence, one of the most helpful is the textual commentary on the Greek text published by the United Bible Societies.[14] This work, compiled by Bruce Metzger, explains why the committee chose specific readings for the UBS Greek text and includes the most pertinent information for these readings. There are several editions of this textual commentary, so be certain to use the one that matches your edition of the UBS Greek text. This work can help the beginning New Testament text critic understand the logic that professionals use in determining the most accurate reading of a specific passage. A section in this book explains how to use the UBS textual apparatus for the Greek text (see previous discussion on pp. 223-28).

It is helpful to ask the following questions when gathering internal evidence for determining the most plausible original reading of a text:

- Are there any spelling or grammatical characteristics that would favor one of the readings?

- Does the author of a book or passage commonly use phrases in certain ways?

- Does the near context favor one of the readings?

---

[14]Bruce M. Metzger, *A Textual Commentary on the Greek New Testament*, 2nd ed. (Stuttgart: Deutsche Bibelgesellschaft, 1994).

- Is there a probable mechanical means that disrupted the text (e.g., haplography, dittography, metathesis)?

- Are there similar phrases or wording in the same book or related books?

- Is there a figure of speech or parallel unit that may favor one of the readings?

- Is there an identifiable reason that a copyist may have changed a specific reading?

- Is there a grammatical or theological difficulty?

When examining the internal evidence, record any evidence that would favor one reading over another. Often when external evidence does not indicate a clearly superior reading, internal evidence can be used to determine the most plausible original reading of a New Testament text.

8.3 Evaluating the Evidence

Collecting the manuscript evidence is a laborious process, but it is a little more straightforward than the evaluation process. In the collection process the goal is to gather as much evidence as possible concerning various readings of a specific text. In the evaluation process the aim is to determine which reading has the best evidence for being the original reading. The evaluation process is complicated by the fact that not all scholars agree on the evaluation principles to use or the relative importance of each of them. Table 8.2 summarizes the four main methods of evaluating evidence.

Table 8.2. Four Main Methods of Evaluating Evidence

Name	Proponents	Description
reasoned eclecticism	Bruce Metzger Kurt Aland Michael Holmes Eldon Epp	balanced use of internal and external evidence
radical/thoroughgoing eclecticism	George D. Kilpatrick J. Keith Elliot	emphasizes internal evidence over external
documentary approach	Victor Dearing Phillip W. Comfort[a]	emphasizes external evidence over internal
Byzantine-priority approach	Harry A. Sturz Maurice A. Robinson Zane Hodges Arthur Farstad	emphasizes the Byzantine textual tradition

[a]Phillip W. Comfort, *The Quest for the Original Text of the New Testament* (Grand Rapids: Baker, 1992).

The method used in this book is reasoned eclecticism, wherein the New Testament text critic examines all available evidence, both external and internal, to determine the most plausible original reading of the text.[15] Michael Holmes states, "Central to this approach is a fundamental guideline: the variant most likely to be original is the one that best accounts for the origin of all competing variants in terms of both external and internal evidence."[16]

Determining the most plausible original reading of the text is a complex task that takes practice and skill. Over the course of time several principles have been developed to aid the process of evaluation; they vary somewhat from Old Testament textual principles but have similar goals and characteristics.

8.3.1 Manuscripts Must Be Weighed, Not Merely Counted

One of the most important New Testament textual principles is that manuscripts must be weighed, not merely counted. Since New Testament manuscript evidence is quite extensive, there must be some way to evaluate and rank their relative importance (e.g., an earlier manuscript should generally be more important than a later one because there was less time for the text to become corrupted). Weighing manuscripts helps to determine the parameters of a text—namely, the possible readings of a specific text and the evidence for these readings. A great place to begin is by collecting objective evidence for each of the various readings.

For example: In Matthew 1:7-8 the name Asaph (Ἀσάφ) is used instead of Asa (Ἀσά). There is good textual evidence for the first reading ($\mathfrak{P}^{1vid}$, ℵ, B, C, D[Luke], f^1, f^{13}, Harclean Syriac version [in the margin] , Coptic, etc.); but there is more evidence for the second reading, although it generally comes from a later date (L, W, P, Δ, 28, 33, 180, 565, Vulgate, etc.). In this case evidence for the first reading should be weighed more heavily because of its early date. This is not the only information that needs to be examined, but it is a good starting point.

Since there is a wealth of New Testament witnesses, it is highly unlikely that a conjectural emendation (e.g., a reading that is not supported by any textual evidence) would ever be necessary, as F. F. Bruce explains:

> It is doubtful whether there is any reading in the New Testament which requires to be conjecturally emended. The wealth of attestation is such that the true reading is almost invariably bound to be preserved by at least one of the thousands of witnesses. Sometimes what was at first put forward as a conjectureal emendation has in the course of time turned up in one of our witnesses. For example, it was long expected by a number of scholars that in John 19:29 it was not 'hyssop' (Gk. *hyssopos*) that was used to convey the sponge filled with vinegar to our Lord's

---

[15]Michael W. Holmes, "Textual Criticism," in *New Testament Criticism & Interpretation*, ed. David A. Black and David S. Dockery (Grand Rapids: Zondervan, 1991), p. 112.
[16]Holmes, "Case for Reasoned Eclecticism," p. 79.

mouth on the cross, but a soldier's javelin (Gk. *hyssos*). But more recently the reading 'javelin', which was previously a mere conjectural emendation, has been recognised in the first hand of a rather late manuscript, and it is adopted in the text of the New English Bible; but even so it is an extremely doubtful reading.[17]

The following criteria will help determine the weight given to various manuscripts:

- *Date.* The earlier the reading, the less opportunity there was for transmissional corruption. Caution must be used here, for it is possible that earlier manuscripts may have corrupt texts or that later manuscripts may preserve early readings (e.g., manuscript 1739 [tenth century] has a text very similar to $\mathfrak{P}^{46}$ [c. 200]).

- *Accuracy.* Accuracy is a function of the number of errors incorporated into a given textual tradition. By comparing specific sources within textual traditions, scholars can determine how accurate the textual traditions are (e.g., do they contain copyist mistakes, harmonizations, or secondary additions?).

- *Independence of witnesses.* Witnesses that are closely related to each other should be considered as one source (as in textual families) so that they are not given too much weight. It is advantageous to consult evidence from various geographical areas to minimize the possibility of their having been copied from the same *Vorlage* (manuscript from which a later one is copied).

It is in the evaluation process that the skill of the text critic becomes vital, for the various criteria cannot be weighed equally and sometimes specific manuscripts will be given more or less priority according to their special characteristics. Some sources will be weighted more heavily because they are older or come from more accurate text families. At this point the text critic can begin to arrange the manuscripts into groups or textual traditions. If two manuscripts are related (i.e., copied from the same *Vorlage*), they should be considered as one witness so as not to skew the evidence for that reading.

8.3.2 Examine the Textual Tradition

As manuscripts began to differ from each other in the copying process, copies of these copies began to take on similarities that can often be grouped into textual traditions or text types. J. Harold Greenlee describes this process in simple terms:

> Keeping in mind that this explanation is oversimplified, let us suppose that four copies are made from an original manuscript and that each of these copies has its own distinctive difference from the original. As further copies are made from each of the four, each further copy will contain most of the peculiarities of the copy that preceded it, although scribes might notice and correct some of the

---

[17]F. F. Bruce, *The Books and the Parchments*, 5th ed. (London: Marshall Pickering, 1991), pp. 169-70.

changes. In this way the copies made from each of the four will tend to be more like the other manuscripts of their "family" than like the manuscripts copied from the other three initial copies. All of them will contain the same basic text, but the manuscripts of each of the four families will share distinctive readings in which they differ from the manuscripts of the other three families.[18]

There has been significant discussion among New Testament text critics as to the validity and extent of using textual groups or traditions in the evaluation process, but there must be some way to indicate relationships between manuscripts so that closely related manuscripts are not given too much weight. Among early manuscripts there is little evidence of textual traditions before the fourth century A.D., primarily because all early manuscripts have been found in Egypt (except for Ms. 0212 from Dura Europos, Syria, on the Euphrates River about halfway between Aleppo and Baghdad), where the hot, dry climate allowed for their preservation.[19] But it may also be because the earliest manuscripts tend to be closer to where the New Testament originated. Either way, because most early New Testament manuscripts are from the same general region, it is difficult to speak of textual families among them.

Text types or traditions were named for the area where they were believed to have developed, the assumption being that manuscripts from near geo-

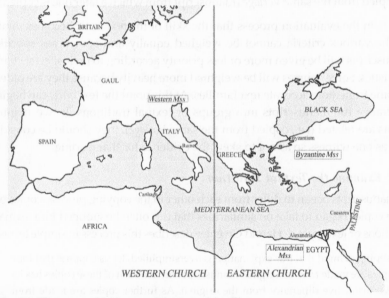

Map 8.1. The geographical areas of the textual families

---

[18] J. Harold Greenlee, *Scribes, Scrolls, & Scriptures*, Biblical Classics Library (Grand Rapids: Eerdmans, 1985), p. 39.

[19] Aland and Aland, *Text of the New Testament*, pp. 59, 64.

graphic areas may have been copied from the same *Vorlage* (see map 8.1).

However, this is now known to be far too simplistic. New Testament manuscripts traveled very quickly to various regions of the Roman Empire and influences from the known textual traditions are found in various parts of the Near Eastern area. For instance, certain Western witnesses actually originated in the East, including the Old Syriac version, Tatian's *Diatessaron* and Codex Bezae.[20] The Old Latin version arose in North Africa. Because it is doubtful that textual traditions were well-developed before the fourth century, this criterion must be used cautiously relative to earlier manuscripts. Figure 8.1 is a plausible representation of the formation of New Testament textual traditions.

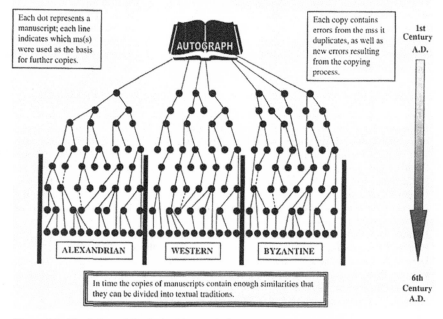

Figure 8.1. Depiction of the textual transmission process

New Testament textual critics compare manuscripts within the textual traditions to see, among other things, how accurately they have been copied, the number of new corruptions added to the texts, whether copyists tended to harmonize (bring into closer agreement) them with parallel passages. Scholars then compare textual traditions to identify their characteristics and to rank their relative accuracy. Table 8.3 summarizes the general consensus regarding the textual traditions and their accuracy.

---

[20]My thanks to Michael Holmes for this information.

Table 8.3 Characteristics of the Textual Traditions[a]

Alexandrian Group (most accurate)	Western Group	Byzantine Group (least accurate)
Most of the manuscripts from this tradition appear to come from around Alexandria, Egypt, and some are very early manuscripts. The family was once thought to be a very carefully edited, third-century recension (edition), but now is believed to be merely the result of a carefully controlled and supervised process of copying and transmission.[b]	This family has some very early manuscripts and comes from a wide geographical area, stretching from North Africa to Italy and from Gaul to Syria. It was much less controlled than the Alexandrian family, with much more variation, including harmonizing, paraphrasing and additions.[c]	This is the largest family, comprising about 80 percent of all manuscripts. While some readings may be early, there is no clear evidence for this family before about the mid-fourth century.[d] It contains the most harmonistic tendencies, paraphrasing and significant additions, most of which are believed to be secondary readings.[e]

[a] In the past it has been common to speak of a Caesarean family, especially in the Gospels; however, it is doubtful that it is a separate text type (see Bruce M. Metzger, "The Caesarean Text of the Gospels," *Chapters in the History of New Testament Textual Criticism* [Grand Rapids: Eerdmans, 1963], pp. 42-72; Larry W. Hurtado, *Text-Critical Methodology and the PreCaesarean Text: Codex W in the Gospel of Mark* [Grand Rapids: Eerdmans, 1981]; Holmes, "Textual Criticism," p. 128). There does appear to be some clear textual relatedness in the Gospel of Mark, but whether it goes beyond that is unclear (see Fee, "Textual Criticism of the New Testament," p. 8).
[b] Holmes, "Textual Criticism," pp. 106-7; Fee, "Textual Criticism of the New Testament," p. 7.
[c] Holmes, "Textual Criticism," 107; Fee, "Textual Criticism of the New Testament," p. 7.
[d] Donald A. Carson, *The King James Debate* (Grand Rapids: Baker, 1979), p. 44; Paul D. Wegner, *The Journey from Texts to Translations* (Grand Rapids: Baker, 2000), pp. 337-38; Fee, "Textual Criticism of the New Testament," p. 8.
[e] Holmes, "Textual Criticism," 107; Fee, "Textual Criticism of the New Testament," p. 8.

When manuscripts contain characteristics from more than one family, they are sometimes referred to as "mixed manuscripts." Sometimes errors in certain manuscripts may have been corrected by comparing them with other manuscripts outside their text family, but it is more likely that new errors would continue to be incorporated into later manuscripts in each successive copy.

The date and accuracy of a manuscript help to determine how much weight to give specific external evidence; for example, an early manuscript from a more accurate family would generally be given more weight when determining the most plausible original reading of a text. Table 8.4 shows the textual families the various manuscripts belong to.

Table 8.4 Textual Traditions [a]

	Alexandrian (B text)	Caesarean (C text) [b]	Western (D text)	Byzantine (A text)
Gospels	$\mathfrak{P}^1\ \mathfrak{P}^3\ \mathfrak{P}^4\ \mathfrak{P}^5\ \mathfrak{P}^7\ \mathfrak{P}^{22}$ $\mathfrak{P}^{39}\ (\mathfrak{P}^{66})\ \mathfrak{P}^{75}$	$\mathfrak{P}^{45}$	$\mathfrak{P}^{25}$	
	ℵ B C L Q T W (Lk 1—8:12; Jn) Z Δ X Ψ 054 059 060 0162	W (Mk only)	D (W Mk 1—5?) 0171	A E F G H K M S U V (W Mt Lk 8:12ff.) Γ Λ Π Ω
	20 33 164 215 376 579 718 850 892 1241 (1342 Mk)			most minuscules
	Boh (Sah) Ath, Cyr-Alex (Or)		It, [esp. k e] Sin-Syr, Cur-Syr Ter, Ir, Clem-Alex Cyp (Aug)	Goth, later versions Later church fathers
Acts	$\mathfrak{P}^8\ (\mathfrak{P}^{50})$ ℵ A B C Ψ 048 076 096		$\mathfrak{P}^{38}\ \mathfrak{P}^{41}\ \mathfrak{P}^{48}$ D E 066	H L S P
	6 33 81 104 326 1175		257 440 614 913 1108 1245 1518 1611 1739 2138 2298	most minuscules
	Boh (Sah)			
	Ath, Cyr-Alex, Clem-Alex? (Or)		It, Hark-Syr [mg]	Goth, later versions later church fathers
Catholic Epistles	$\mathfrak{P}^{20}\ \mathfrak{P}^{23}\ \mathfrak{P}^{72}$ ℵ A B C P Ψ 048 056 0142 0156		$\mathfrak{P}^{38}$ D E	H K L S
	33 81 104 323 326 424c 1175 1739 2298			most other minuscules
	Boh (Sah)			
	Ath, Cyr-Alex Clem-Alex (Or)		It, Tert, Cyp, Aug, Eph	Goth, later versions later church fathers

[a]Table 8.4 is modified from J. Harold Greenlee, *Introduction to New Testament Textual Criticism,* rev. ed. (Peabody, Mass.: Hendrickson, 1995), pp. 117-18.
[b]Epp, "Issues in New Testament Textual Criticism," p. 38.

Table 8.4 Textual Traditions (continued)

	Alexandrian (B text)	Caesarean (C text)	Western (D text)	Byzantine (A text)
Paul and Hebrews	$\mathfrak{P}^{10}$ $\mathfrak{P}^{13}$ $\mathfrak{P}^{15}$ $\mathfrak{P}^{16}$ $\mathfrak{P}^{27}$ $\mathfrak{P}^{32}$ $\mathfrak{P}^{40}$ $\mathfrak{P}^{65}$		D E F G 048 (Tit Tim Philm)	K L
	ℵ A B C H I M Ψ 048 081 088 0220			
	6 33 81 104 326 424c 1175 1739 1908		88 181 915 917 1836 1898 1912	most other minuscules
	Boh (Sah)			
			It	Goth, later versions later church fathers
Revelation	$\mathfrak{P}^{18}$ $\mathfrak{P}^{24}$ $\mathfrak{P}^{47}$			046
	ℵ A C P 0207 0169		F?	82 93 429 469 808 920 2048 most other minuscules
	61 69 94 241 1006 1175 1611 1841 1852 2040 2053 2344 2351			
			It?	Goth, later versions later church fathers

8.3.3 Determine the Reading That Would Most Likely Give Rise to the Others

Another important textual principle is to "determine the reading that would most likely give rise to the others"; this forms the basis for the other principles.

Several scholars consider this principle to be most important;[21] if the textual critic can actually determine a logical reason why certain errors occurred (e.g., haplography, dittography, metathesis), then it may explain the other variants. This principle is particularly helpful when earlier manuscripts clearly indicate one reading whereas later ones tend to favor a different reading—a later one which text critics can plausibly determine how it could have been mistakenly developed from an earlier reading. For example, manuscripts contain the following readings for Mark 1:2: (1) "as it is written in Isaiah the prophet" (ℵ, B, L, Δ, 33, etc.), and (2) "as it written in the prophets" (A, W, f[13], Vulgate ms, Herclean Syriac, Boharic ms, etc.). The first reading is clearly favored by earlier manuscripts. It is also easy to see why copyists

---

[21]Holmes, "Textual Criticism," p. 107; Black, *New Testament Textual Criticism*, p. 35; Gordon D. Fee, *New Testament Exegesis*, rev. ed. (Louisville: Westminster/John Knox, 1993), p. 89; Fee, "Textual Criticism of the New Testament," p. 14; Greenlee, *Scribes & Scrolls*, p. 56.

would be tempted to change the reading since both Isaiah and Malachi are quoted there.

8.3.4 The More Difficult Reading Is Preferable

This principle sounds contradictory—why would the more difficult reading be preferable? This means that if a reading appears to be the more difficult but on further examination of the passage it may actually be what the author is attempting to say, it should be preferred.

The reasoning behind this principle is that scribes had a tendency to simplify readings. If a scribe read something that did not seem right to him, he may have changed it without stopping to better examine the context or flow of thought. For example, Matthew 5:22 reads either "everyone who is angry with his brother shall be guilty before the court" ($\mathfrak{P}^{64}$, $\aleph^*$, B, Latin Vulgate, Ptolemy, Justin, Irenaeus[lat1/3], Tertullian[vid], Origen, etc.) or "everyone who is angry with his brother *without a cause* shall be guilty before the court" ($\aleph^2$, D, L, W, Δ, Θ, f^1, f^{13}, 28, 33, 565, 700, etc.). The external evidence seems to slightly favor the first reading, but it is reasonable that a scribe attempted to soften Jesus' statement by adding the phrase "without a cause." By contrast, it is unlikely that a scribe would purposely make Jesus' statement more difficult to live out by deleting the words "without a cause.".

8.3.5 The Shorter Reading Is Generally Preferable

This principle goes along with the one above—scribes tended to add things and not remove them. The reasoning behind this principle is that copyists generally considered the text to be the Word of God and therefore would not intentionally remove things. Rather, the tendency was to insert additions, especially with a view to making the text more understandable. This criterion must be used with caution: there are occasions when a scribe made omissions either accidentally or because the text was considered to have objectionable grammar, style or theology. For example, there are several variants of John 16:3; the more common ones read either "and these things *they will do*" (A, B, K, etc.) or "and these things *they will do to you*" (D, L, Ψ, f^1, f^{13}, etc.). In this situation there is good early support for the first reading, and it is plausible that a later copyist may have added "to you" to the text.

8.3.6 Determine Which Reading Is More Appropriate in Its Context

The last principle hinges most strongly on internal evidence: compare the author's usage of grammar, vocabulary, theology and context to help determine the most plausible original reading of the text. For example, the authenticity of Mark 16:9-20 has been questioned for several reasons, especially on the basis of grammar and context. The phrase "the first day of the week" (τῇ μιᾷ τῶν σαββάτων) in Mark 16:2 is spelled differently than in verse 9 (πρώτη σαββάτου), and Mary Magdalene is described in verse 9 even though she is mentioned earlier in verse 1.

This criterion must also be used with caution because some of these issues are not as clear-cut as others. For example, how a scribe usually spells certain words is quite clear, whereas alterations made to reflect a scribe's theology are harder to identify.[22]

While internal evidence should be weighed strongly when determining the original reading of the text, it is still subjective with few controls. The best method is to use external evidence first to determine the strength of the readings and then internal evidence to help confirm which reading is preferable in cases where external evidence is not clear. The best-case scenario is when external evidence clearly favors one reading and internal evidence tends to confirm it based on grammar, spelling and so forth. In more difficult cases we must draw on as much evidence as possible in suggesting the most likely original reading.

While these are the main principles of New Testament textual criticism, there are no across-the-board rules that dominate the text critical process. Not every one of these principles is applicable in every case, and in some cases these principles may actually oppose each other. For example, the longer reading may also be the more difficult reading, or the reading that corresponds

---

TEXTUAL CRITICAL PRINCIPLES

1. Manuscripts must be weighed, not counted.

2. Determine the reading that would most likely give rise to the others.

3. The more difficult reading is preferable.

4. The shorter reading is preferable.

5. Determine which reading is more appropriate in its context.

---

more closely to the author's theology may indicate some evidence of harmonization. Each variant must be weighed on its own merits, which is why textual criticism is an art as well as a science.

Sometimes commentaries will deal with textual variants and may be very helpful in determining the most accurate reading of a text. Several commen-

---

[22]Bart D. Ehrman, *The Orthodox Corruptions of Scripture: The Effect of Early Christological Controversies on the Text of the New Testament* (New York: Oxford University Press, 1993); cf. Bart D. Ehrman, "The Text as Window: New Testament Manuscripts and the Social History of Early Christianity," in *The Text of the New Testament in Contemporary Research,* Studies and Documents 46 (Grand Rapids: Eerdmans, 1995), pp. 361-79. See also David C. Parker, *The Living Text of the Gospels* (Cambridge: Cambridge University Press, 1997).

tary series that are especially helpful for textual critical issues are:

- Anchor Bible Commentary
- Continental Commentaries
- Hermeneia
- New International Commentary on the Old Testament
- New International Commentary on the New Testament
- Word Biblical Commentary

8.4 Specific Examples

8.4.1 *Ephesians 1:1*

Now we are ready to try our hand at evaluating the evidence found in the textual apparatus in Ephesians 1:1. The textual note on Ephesians 1:1 reads as follows:

[1] 1 {C} ἐν Ἐφέσῳ א[2] A B[2] D F G Ψ[c] (Ψ* *illegible*) 075 0150 33 81 104 256 263 365 424* 436 459 1175 1241 1319 1573 1852 1881 1912 1962 2127 2200 2464 *Byz* [K L P] *Lect* it[ar, b, d, f, g, o, r] vg syr[p,h] cop[sa, bo] arm eth geo slav Ps-Ignatius Chrysostom, Theodore[lat], Victorinus-Rome Ambrosiaster Jerome Pelagius // *omit* 𝔓[46] א* B* 6 424[c] 1739 Marcion[acc. to Tertullian] Origen[vid]

The information concerning the reading of the text will be divided according to external and internal evidence.

- External evidence. It is helpful to first record the date and family of every external witness for each reading. This detailed evidence should be noted so that each of the readings can be evaluated; see the sample worksheet for Ephesians 1:1 below.

- Conclusion. If we were to rely solely on the number of manuscripts in support of a specific reading, then the phrase "in Ephesus" would be included in this verse. A more careful examination, however, suggests that there is good evidence that this phrase should be omitted. Strong evidence from 𝔓[46] (a second-century uncial, Alexandrian text tradition), and codices Sinaiticus and Vaticanus (both fourth-century manuscripts, Alexandrian text tradition), favor omitting the phrase "in Ephesus." Evidence from Marcion (c. A.D. 170) and Origen (d. A.D. 254) also suggests that this is an early reading. The fact that Marcion was considered a heretic does not come into play since his heresies related to concepts not associated directly with this passage. It is interesting that in several sources (א, B) this phrase was added by a later corrector.

Passage: Ephesians 1:1

Various Readings	
Reading 1	**Reading 2**
Εν' Εφέσω **"in Ephesus"**	Omit reading 1
External Evidence:*	$\mathfrak{P}^{46}$ (uncial from the second
$\aleph^2$ = **Codex Sinaiticus** (uncial with a second handwriting	century; Alexandrian
from a corrector and thus must date after the fourth	family; category I)
century when the manuscript was originally written;	$\aleph$* = **Codex Sinaiticus** (uncial
Alexandrian family; Category I)	from the fourth century;
A = **Codex Alexandrinus** (uncial from the fifth century;	original handwriting;
Alexandrian family; Category III)	Alexandrian family;
B^2 = **Codex Vaticanus** (uncial with a second handwriting	category I)
and dated after the fourth century when the	B* = Codex Vaticanus (uncial
manuscript was originally written; Alexandrian	from the fourth century;
family; category I)	original handwriting;
D = **Codex Claromontanus** (uncial from the sixth century;	Alexandrian family,
Western family; Category IV)	category I)
075 (uncial from the tenth century; family uncertain;	6 (miniscule from the
category III)	thirteenth century)
0150 (uncial from the ninth century; family uncertain;	424^c (miniscule from the
category III)	eleventh century,
33 (minuscule from the ninth century; Alexandrian	Alexandrian family)
family; category I)	1739 (minuscule from the
Byzantine Lectionaries (similar to K L P dated to the ninth	tenth century;
century; Byzantine family)	Alexandrian family;
Some Old Italian manuscripts (fifth to fifteenth centuries;	category I)
Western family)	**Marcion** (second century)
Latin Vulgate (late fourth to fifth centuries; Western	quoted from Tertullian
family)	**Origen** (d. 254) "vid" means
Syriac Peshitta (fifth century)	most likely the reading,
Syriac Harclean (616)	but it cannot be
Coptic Versions Sahidic and Bohairic (third to fifth	completely verified
centuries; Alexandrian family)	
Armenian (fifth century)	
Georgian (fifth century)	
Ps-Ignatius (fourth to fifth century)	
Ambrosiaster (fourth century)	
Victorinus-Rome (d. 362)	
Chrysostom (d. 407)	
Pelagius (d. 412)	
Jerome (d. 420)	
Theodore^{lat} (d. 428)	

Passage: Ephesians 1:1

Which one is favored and why?
It appears that the omission is favored by earlier and better texts (at least the second century from good manuscripts) and that the reading ἐν Ἐφέσῳ "in Ephesus" cannot be confirmed before about the fourth or fifth century.

Internal evidence:
There is little internal evidence to help determine the correct reading, but the greeting is similar to Paul's other letters and a location would usually be included at this point, as the grammar and other greetings indicate.

Conclusion
Some scholars have argued that the document had no addressee because it was an encyclical letter sent to various churches, the church at Ephesus being the chief. By the fifth century A.D., the name "Ephesus" was inserted because tradition maintained that the letter had originally been sent there.

*Not all the external evidence needs to be included in this final worksheet, only the most important works.

The greeting of the book of Ephesians is similar to Paul's other letters and a location would usually be included at this point, as the grammar and other greetings indicate. There would be an understandable tendency to want to include a location in this spot. If one had appeared originally, it would be fairly unlikely that a copyist would have removed it. The principle of the shorter reading generally being preferable is really not applicable here since the evidence already given provides a significant rationale as to why it may have been added.

The editors of the UBS Greek text decided that the phrase "in Ephesus" was not in the original text since it is omitted in the earliest manuscripts ($\mathfrak{P}^{46}$, ℵ*, B*, Origen) and does not appear until about the fifth century A.D. (e.g., Codex Alexandrinus). It is interesting that some of Marcion's works refer to this book as "To the Laodiceans" (see Nestle-Aland text). Based on this and other evidence, they argue that the document was an encyclical letter sent to various churches, the church at Ephesus being the chief; the appropriate name was added when the letter was sent to the surrounding churches. However, by the fifth century A.D. tradition held that the letter was first sent to Ephesus, and therefore that name was placed in the letter. The final decision to leave the phrase but to put it in square brackets is explained in detail by the editors of the UBS Greek text in their commentary.[23] Notice that the editors of the UBS Greek text rate the certainty of this reading as "C." That is to say, the inclusion of the phrase "in Ephesus" is uncer-

---

[23]Metzger, *Textual Commentary on the Greek New Testament*, p. 532.

tain since they believe that it was not originally in the text; however, the idea that this is an encyclical letter cannot be proved conclusively.

8.4.2 Romans 15:7

"Therefore, accept one another, just as Christ also accepted **you** to the glory of God." This type of variant reading is quite common because the words *you* (ΥΜΑϹ) and *us* (ΗΜΑϹ) look very similar in uncial writing. The textual note reads:

[1] 7 {A} ὑμᾶς ℵ A C D^2 F G Ψ 6 33 81 256 263 365 424 436 1175 1241 1319 1573 1739 1881 1912 1962 2127* 2200 *Byz* [L] *Lect* it$^{d2, f, g, gue}$ vg syr^{p,h} cop^{bo} arm eth geo slav Origen^{lat}, Chrysostom Cyril Ambrosiaster Pelagius Speculum // ἡμᾶς B D* P 048 0150 104 459 1506 1852 2127^c ℓ 147 ℓ 590 ℓ 597 ℓ 751 ℓ 884 ℓ 1159 ℓ 1441 it$^{ar, b, d*, τ, o}$ vg^{ms} cop^{sa} Theodoret^{lem}

- External evidence

Passage: Romans 15:7

Various Readings	
Reading 1 ὑμᾶς "you"	**Reading 2** ἡμᾶς "us"
External evidence*	External evidence
ℵ = Codex Sinaiticus (uncial from the fourth century; Alexandrian family; category I) A = Codex Alexandrinus (uncial from the fifth century; Alexandrian family; category III) C = Codex Ephraemi Rescriptus (uncial from the fifth century; Alexandrian family; category II) D^2 = Codex Claromontanus (uncial from the sixth century; Western family; category IV) F (uncial from the ninth century; Western family; category II) G (uncial from the ninth century; Western family; category V) Ψ (uncial from the ninth to tenth centuries; Alexandrian family; category V) 6 (minuscule from the thirteenth century; Alexandrian family; category III) 33 (minuscule from the ninth century; Alexandrian family; category I) 81 (minuscule from 1044; Alexandrian family; category II)	B = Codex Vaticanus (uncial from the fourth century; Alexandrian family, category I) D* = Codex Claromontanus (uncial from the sixth century; Western family; category IV) P (uncial from the ninth century; uncertain family; category III) 048 (uncial from the fifth century; Alexandrian family; category II) 0150 (uncial from the ninth century; family uncertain; category III) 104 (miniscule from the eleventh century; Alexandrian family; category III) 459 (minuscule from the tenth century; probably Byzantine family; category V) **Byzantine Lectionaries** it$^{ar, b, d*, τ, o}$ Some Old Italian manuscripts (fifth to fifteenth centuries; Western family) vg^{ms} **Latin Vulgate** (late fourth to fifth centuries; Western family) cop^{sa} Sahidic (third to fifth centuries; Alexandrian family) **Theodoret**^{lem} (c. 466)

Reading 1 ὑμᾶς "you"	Reading 2 ἡμᾶς "us"
External evidence*	External evidence
Byzantine Lectionaries (similar to L dated to the ninth century; Byzantine family) **it**[d2, f, g, gue] Some Old Italian manuscripts (fifth to ninth centuries; Western family) **Latin Vulgate** (late fourth to fifth centuries; Western family) **Syriac Peshitta** (fifth century) **Syriac Harclean** (616) **Coptic Version** Bohairic (third to fifth centuries; Alexandrian family) **Armenian** (fifth century) **Ethiopic** (sixth century) **Georgian** (fifth century) **Slavonic** (ninth century) **Origen**[lat] (d. 254) **Chrysostom** (d. 407) **Cyril** (d. 444) **Ambrosiaster** (fourth century) **Pelagius** (d. 412) **Speculum** (d. fifth century)	

Which one is favored and why?
There is no strong external evidence on either side to help determine which reading is correct.

Internal evidence:
The internal evidence is not all that clear: vv. 5, 6 and 13-15 contain second-person forms, whereas vv. 1, 2, 4 and 6 have first-person forms.

Conclusion:
This is a fairly difficult decision since both readings are supported by fairly equal evidence. It seems most likely that the author would include himself in those who had been accepted by Christ, and thus the second reading makes better sense. However, it is also possible that the imperative beginning at v. 6, which implies a second person plural form, could have flavored the author's reasoning, and thus the first reading would be more likely. The second person appears to be favored grammatically, since the imperative implies a second-person form in the earlier part of the verse. Likewise, it is easy to see why someone may have changed the text into the first-person plural to include the author. I therefore consider the first reading to be the most plausible original reading. It is obvious from the evidence, however, that this should not be an "A" rating but rather at least a "B" rating, as the third edition of *The Greek New Testament* (p. 571) indicates.

- *Conclusion.* It is much more difficult to determine the original reading of the text for this textual variant than for the first one. Both readings have significant external evidence and there is not significant internal evidence to favor one reading over the other. Both forms are already used within the context, but it seems unlikely that someone would change the second-person form to the first-person if it was there initially. However, it does seem reasonable that if the second-person form was originally there, a scribe may have been tempted to include Paul with those to whom the book was written. Thus I agree with the editors of the UBS Greek text that the ὑμᾶς ("you") is probably the correct reading, but given the uncertainty of the evidence I question assigning it an "A" rating.

8.5 When Should I Use Textual Criticism?

Should textual critical problems be taught from the pulpit or in a Sunday school class? Is the modern church able to deal with this issue? Anyone who regularly preaches or teaches the Bible needs to be aware of the area of textual criticism: modern translations include just enough information to cause some people to question the accuracy of Scriptures, and the King James Bible debate is still discussed in some churches today. It is best to keep the discussion short and to the point, dealing carefully with the issues so as not to undermine people's belief in the Bible or even the translation that they are used to. It is crucial to remind people that most variants are insignificant and that no doctrine hinges on a variant text. It is also important to examine a passage carefully before you discuss it—any unresolved questions you may have will become obvious to those listening. An adult education class is often a good venue to discuss textual criticism—examining the issues can greatly increase confidence in the reliability of the Word of God. If there is no qualified person, a church can invite guest speakers who have the background to teach the principles of textual criticism and carefully explain the issues.

If you would like to try your hand at New Testament textual criticism, here are some interesting passages:

Matthew 5:22, 47	Luke 4:4	Romans 4:19	1 Thessalonians 2:3, 7
Matthew 6:4, 9, 13	Luke 15:21	Romans 5:1	1 Timothy 3:16
Matthew 14:24	John 1:18, 34	1 Corinthians 2:1	2 Peter 1:21
Matthew 17:21	John 3:13	1 Corinthians 11:29	James 2:20
Matthew 19:16, 17	John 5:3-4, 44	1 Corinthians 13:3	1 John 1:4
Mark 1:1, 2	John 7:1, 8	Ephesians 1:1	1 John 2:20
Mark 9:29; 10:40	John 7:53-8:11	Philippians 3:3	1 John 3:1
Mark 16:9-20	Acts 8:37	Colossians 1:14	Revelation 1:5

Further Reading

Aland, Kurt, and Barbara Aland. *The Text of the New Testament. An Introduction to the Critical Editions and to the Theory and Practice of Modern Textual Criticism.* Translated by Erroll F. Rhodes. Grand Rapids: Eerdmans, 1987.

Birdsall, J. Neville. "The New Testament Text." In *CHB* 1.308-77.

Black, David A. *New Testament Textual Criticism*. Grand Rapids: Baker, 1995.

Comfort, Philip W. *Early Manuscripts & Modern Translations of the New Testament*. Grand Rapids: Baker, 1990.

Fee, Gordon D. "The Textual Criticism of the New Testament." In *The Expositor's Bible Commentary*, 1:419-33. Edited by Frank E. Gaebelein. 12 vols. Grand Rapids: Zondervan, 1976-1992.

Finegan, Jack. *Encountering New Testament Manuscripts: A Working Introduction to Textual Criticism*. Grand Rapids: Eerdmans, 1974.

Greenlee, J. Harold. *Introduction to New Testament Textual Criticism*. Rev. ed. Peabody, Mass.: Hendrickson, 1996.

———. *Scribes, Scrolls, and Scripture. A Student's Guide to New Testament Textual Criticism*. Grand Rapids: Eerdmans, 1985.

Holmes, Michael W. "Textual Criticism." In *New Testament Criticism & Interpretation*. Edited by David A. Black and David S. Dockery. 2nd ed. Nashville: Broadman & Holman, 2001. See pp. 101-36.

Metzger, Bruce M. *Chapters in the History of New Testament Textual Criticism*. New Testament Tools and Studies 4. Grand Rapids: Eerdmans, 1963.

———. *The Text of the New Testament. Its Transmission, Corruption, and Restoration*. 3rd ed. New York: Oxford University Press, 1992.

———. *A Textual Commentary on the Greek New Testament*. 2nd ed. Stuttgart: Deutsche Bibelgesellschaft, 1994.

9

Getting to Know the Sources of New Testament Textual Criticism

This chapter describes some of the manuscripts most important to New Testament textual criticism, including papyrus fragments, codices and major collections.

Beginning with Brian Walton and his massive six-volume work, the London Polyglot (1655-1657), it became more and more common to list variants between the "received text" (in this case the Stephanus 1550 edition) and the other known Greek manuscripts. This came to a climax in 1707 with John Mill (1645-1707), a fellow of Queen's College, Oxford, who produced a copy of the Greek text which collected evidence from Greek manuscripts, early versions and the church fathers. In a prolegomena to his work he described thirty-two printed editions of the Greek New Testament and nearly one hundred manuscripts, as well as the important citations from early church fathers. But one of the most difficult problems to emerge with the discovery of an ever increasing number of manuscripts and other sources for the New Testament was a convenient method to record them. Initially titles and brief descriptions were assigned to each manuscript, but this proved cumbersome, and scholars often inconsistently assigned titles to the same manuscripts. Within fifty years after John Mill, a Swiss scholar, Johann Wettstein, was among the first to standardize designations in his two-volume Greek New Testament published in Amsterdam about 1751-1752. In his very simple, convenient system, uncial manuscripts were designated by capital letters and minuscules by Arabic numerals. The system was modified by Caspar René Gregory, professor at the University of Leipzig, Germany, in the latter nineteenth century, and a slightly modified form of this system is in use today. Until a few years ago Kurt Aland, New Testament scholar in Münster, Westphalia, Germany, was responsible for ascribing *sigla* to new manuscripts and fragments at the Institute for New Testament Research. This standardized system is used with great efficiency in the textual apparatus (generally at the bottom of the page) of modern Greek versions that list the manuscripts containing certain readings.

Of the approximately 5,500 extant New Testament manuscripts, about 116 are papyrus manuscripts or fragments, 274 are uncial manuscripts, 2,555 are minuscule manuscripts and 2,280 are lectionaries.

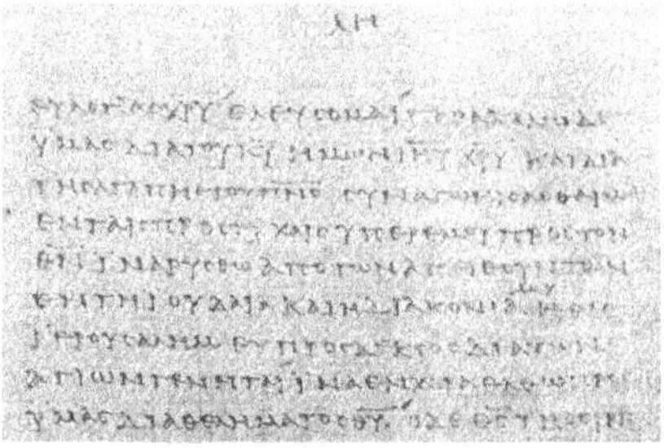

9.1 Biblical Papyri

All of the biblical papyri are fragmentary and are notated with a "$\mathfrak{P}$" followed by an Arabic number (e.g., $\mathfrak{P}^{52}$, $\mathfrak{P}^{32}$, $\mathfrak{P}^{74}$). A description of major collections follows.

Figure 9.1. $\mathfrak{P}^{46}$, from the Chester Beatty Papyrus (II) dated to about A.D. 200. This section is from Romans 15:29-33. [P. Mich. Inv. 6238, Special Collections Library, University of Michigan]

9.1.1 Chester Beatty Collection

In 1931, twelve fragments of biblical manuscripts were discovered in a Coptic graveyard in Egypt. They were sold to Chester Beatty, an American living in London, and are housed in the Beatty Museum in Dublin, Ireland. These fragments of both Old Testament and New Testament texts date to as early as A.D. 200 or 250; two of the more important fragments are $\mathfrak{P}^{45}$ and $\mathfrak{P}^{46}$:

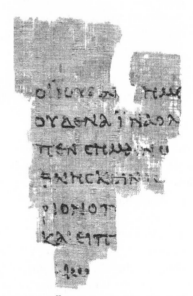

- $\mathfrak{P}^{45}$ comprises portions of thirty leaves of a papyrus codex originally about 220 leaves in length, including all four Gospels and Acts. There are two leaves from the book of Matthew, six from Mark, seven from Luke, two from John and thirteen from Acts.

- $\mathfrak{P}^{46}$ This codex contains 86 out of originally about 104 leaves from the Pauline Epistles. Portions of several of the epistles are lacking and may never have been included in the original work (see figure 9.1).

Figure 9.2. $\mathfrak{P}^{52}$ (P. Rylands 457), the earliest fragment of the New Testament. This section is from the Gospel of John 18:31-33 and is dated to the early second century. [John Rylands University Library]

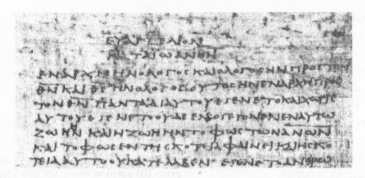

Figure 9.3. $\mathfrak{P}^{75}$, from the Bodmer collection (PB XIV, XV) dated to the early second century; the fragment pictured here is from the beginning of John. [Foundation Martin Bodmer Bibliotheque at Musée]

9.1.2 John Rylands Library

The John Rylands Library in Manchester, England, houses many notable biblical manuscripts, including:

- $\mathfrak{P}^{52}$, a small papyrus fragment (2-1/2 by 3-1/2 inches) is one of the earliest fragments of the Gospel of John (18:31-33, 37-38) dated to the first part of the second century A.D. (see figure 9.2). It was purchased in 1920 by Bernard Grenfell of the John Rylands Library, but it was not identified until 1934 by Colin Roberts.

- Rylands Papyrus Greek i.5, known as $\mathfrak{P}^{32}$, contains the text of Titus 1:11-15 and 2:4-8 and is dated to the second century A.D.

9.1.3 Bodmer Collection

Martin Bodmer from Geneva, Switzerland, founder of the Bodmer Library of World Literature at Cologne (a suburb of Geneva), came across a collection of biblical papyri in 1956, which he purchased for the library. Some of the more important biblical papyri include:

- $\mathfrak{P}^{66}$, also known as Bodmer II, contains a major portion of the Gospel of John (1:1—14:26) written about A.D. 200. The first fourteen chapters are nearly complete, but the rest are fragmentary. There are 440 alterations and corrections, most of which appear in the margins or above the text; these editorial notations were probably made by the copyist himself.

- $\mathfrak{P}^{72}$ is the earliest copy of the book of Jude; the two epistles of Peter are dated between A.D. 200-300.

Figure 9.4. The end of the Gospel of Luke and the beginning of John from the Codex Vaticanus (B; fourth century) [Bibliotheca Apostolica Vaticana]

- $\mathfrak{P}^{75}$ is another early codex containing 102 leaves out of about 144 of the books of Luke and John, dated between A.D. 175 and 225 (see figure 9.3). This is the earliest copy of Luke and one of the earliest for John.

9.2 Important Uncials

Uncials are designated by a capital letter in English, Hebrew or Greek, or by a number beginning with zero.

9.2.1 Codex Vaticanus

This codex (B in the Old Testament and 03 in the New Testament; Vatican Library, Cod. Gr. 1209) is known to have existed in the Vatican library since 1475 or 1481[1] (thus its name), but initially the Vatican discouraged work on it. At the beginning of the nineteenth century Napoleon carried off this codex to Paris with other manuscripts as a war prize, but on his death in 1815 it was

---

[1]Frederic G. Kenyon, *Handbook to the Textual Criticism of the New Testament*, 2nd ed. (London: Macmillan, 1912), p. 77. See also James H. Ropes, "Vol. III: The Text of Acts," *The Beginnings of Christianity, Part I: Acts of the Apostles*, ed. F. J. Foakes Jackson and Kirsopp Lake (London: Macmillan, 1926), p. xxxi.

returned to the Vatican library. Constantine von Tischendorf applied for and finally obtained permission to see the manuscript in order to collate difficult passages. He copied out or remembered enough of the text to be able to publish an edition of the Codex Vaticanus in 1867 (see figure 9.4). Later that century (1868-1881) the Vatican published a better copy of the codex, but in 1889-1890 a complete photographic facsimile of this manuscript superseded all earlier attempts.

9.2.2 Codex Sinaiticus

This codex (ℵ or S; B.M. Add. 43725) was discovered by Constantin von Tischendorf (1815-1874) in the middle of the nineteenth century at St. Catherine's Monastery at the foot of Mt. Sinai, hence the name Sinaiticus. Having been discovered after other Greek codices had been assigned letters of the English alphabet, it is designated by the first letter of the Hebrew alphabet, ℵ (see figure 9.5).

The history of Tischendorf's search for manuscripts is fascinating. In 1844 Tischendorf, a beginning lecturer at the University of Leipzig, was in the Near

Figure 9.5. John 21 from Codex Sinaiticus (fourth century) [British Library]

East looking for biblical manuscripts. While studying in the library of St. Catherine's Monastery, he saw a basket of stray pages written in the oldest Greek he had ever seen. On further examination they proved to be forty-three leaves of the LXX written in early Greek uncial script. The librarian said that the monks had already burned two baskets of similar material in the monastery furnace. Tischendorf was allowed to keep the forty-three leaves. In 1853 he re-visited St. Catherine's in hopes of finding more manuscripts, but without success. He returned in 1859 under the patronage of the Czar of Russia, Alexander II, official head of the Greek church, and by accident came across the manuscript called Sinaiticus, a fourth-century uncial manuscript in near perfect condition. Frederic G. Kenyon recounts the story:

> Only a few days before he was to depart, in the course of conversation with the steward of the monastery, he showed him a copy of his recently published edition of the Septuagint. Thereupon the steward remarked that he too had a copy of the Septuagint, which he would like to show to his visitor. Accordingly he took him to his room, and produced a heap of loose leaves wrapped in a cloth; and there before the astonished scholar's eyes lay the identical manuscript for which he had been longing. Not only was part of the Old Testament there, but the New Testament, complete from beginning to end. Concealing his feelings, he asked to be allowed to keep it in his room that evening to examine it; leave was given, "and that night it seemed sacrilege to sleep."[2]

After an unsuccessful attempt to purchase it, Tischendorf returned to Cairo to speak with the abbot of St. Catherine's monastery. Finally, after careful negotiations and the assistance of the Czar who, as protector of the Greek Church would help determine the next abbot of the monastery at St. Catherine's, Tischendorf received the manuscript as a gift from the monks. In 1862 Codex Sinaiticus was published for the first time by its discoverer, and on Christmas Day 1933, the British Museum bought the manuscript from the Soviet Union for £100,000 (approximately $500,000)—the Soviet government was in need of money, not Bibles. James H. Ropes describes the quality of this codex:

> Codex Sinaiticus is carelessly written, with many lapses of spelling due to the influence of dialectal and vulgar speech, and many plain errors and crude vagaries. Omissions by homeoteleuton abound, and there are many other careless omissions. All these gave a large field for the work of correctors, and the manuscript does not stand by any means on the same level of workmanship as B.[3]

---

[2]Frederick G. Kenyon, *Our Bible and the Ancient Manuscripts* (New York: Harper, 1958), p. 192.
[3]Ropes, "Vol. 3: The Text of Acts," xlviii.

Figure 9.6. The end of the Gospel of Luke from the Codex Alexandrinus (A; fifth century) [British Library]

9.2.3 *Codex Alexandrinus*

This codex (A, 02; Royal MS 1 D V-VIII) has been corrected many times in the margin, sometimes by the original hand and sometimes by a later hand, which suggests that it was compared to other manuscripts (see figure 9.6). In 1627, Cyril Lucar, patriarch of Constantinople (1621-1638), offered this manuscript to the English ambassador to Turkey, Sir Thomas Roe, as a gift to King James I. However, it came to England in 1627 after King James had died and was presented to Charles I of England. Lucar probably obtained the Codex Alexandrinus while patriarch of Alexandria (1602-1621), hence its name. The codex was housed first in the Royal Library, then in 1757 it was incorporated into the British Museum, London.

9.2.4 *Codex Ephraemi*

This fifth-century palimpsest (C) originally bore the New Testament text and was reused during the twelfth century to copy thirty-eight sermons of Ephraem, a Syrian church father. The manuscript was apparently brought first to Italy in the early sixteenth century and later to Paris by Queen Catherine de Médicis. In 1841 Tischendorf set about the difficult task of deciphering the New Testament text that had been partially erased. By 1843 he had completed the work, and it was published in 1845. Later, scholars treated the manuscript with chemicals and by use of improved photography were able to render the underneath New Testament text more readable. They found that Tischendorf had done admirably well with relatively few errors. Today the codex is one of the chief biblical treasures of the Bibliothèque nationale (National Library) in Paris.

9.2.5 Codex Bezae

In this bilingual codex (D) dating to the fifth (or possibly sixth) century A.D., the Greek text appears on the left page and the Latin text on the right (see figure 9.7). It is written in "sense lines" so that some sentences are short and others long depending on the thought in the line. The first three lines of each book are written in red ink, with one column per page. The codex includes the Gospels (in Western order; i.e., Mt, Jn, Lk, Mk), Acts and a short fragment of 3 John. It was found in 1562 at Lyons, France, by Theodore Beza, successor of John Calvin at Geneva, who presented it to Cambridge University in 1581 (thus it is sometimes called "Codex Cantabrigiensis").

Codex Bezae contains many variations from what is considered the standard New Testament text. For example, in Luke 23:53, the codex says that Joseph of Arimathea, after placing Jesus' body in the new tomb, "put before the tomb a [great] stone which twenty men could scarcely roll"; and Acts 19:9 records that Paul preached in the hall of Tyrannus "from eleven o'clock to four," an unlikely time given the heat of day.

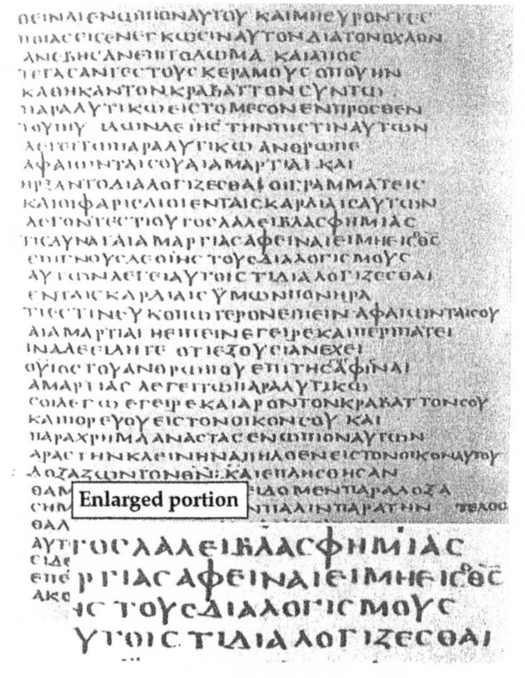

Figure 9.7. A page from Codex Bezae showing Luke 5:18-28. The enlarged portion shows a correction above the second line and the scribal abbreviation for "God" (ΘC = Θεός) [Cambridge University Library]

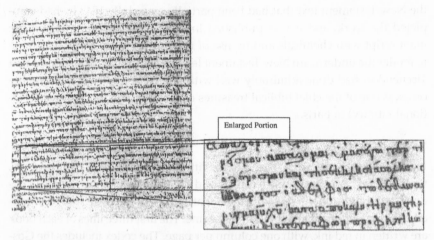

Enlarged Portion

Figure 9.8. Minuscule 33, sometimes called the "Queen of the Cursives," dates to the ninth or tenth century. This page is from the end of Romans. [Bibliotèque nationale de France]

9.3 Minuscule Manuscripts

A minuscule is denoted merely by an Arabic number. At present approximately 2,555 minuscule texts and about 2,280 lectionaries have been recorded, generally dating to a time later than the uncials. However, it does not necessarily follow that an earlier text is automatically more accurate since a later manuscript may have been copied from a better original text. For example, minuscule manuscript number 33 is very accurate even though it was copied in the ninth or tenth century A.D. Minuscule manuscripts can be grouped into families according to their similarities.

9.3.1 Ferrar Family

In 1868 Professor William Ferrar of Dublin University identified several manuscripts belonging to the same text type or family called the "Ferrar Family" (or f^{13} [Family 13] since the first minuscule is number 13). This family currently includes twelve manuscripts (13, 69, 124, 230, 346, 543, 788, 826, 828, 983, 1689 and 1709) dated between the eleventh to fifteenth centuries.[4] The story of the adulterous woman, which usually appears in John 7:53—8:11 is placed instead after Luke 21:38 in this family.

9.3.2 Lake Family

About 1902 Kirsopp Lake identified another text family, including manu-

---

[4]Bruce M. Metzger, *The Text of the New Testament* (New York: Oxford University Press, 1992), p. 61.

scripts 1, 118, 131, 209 (called the "Lake Family" or f^1 [Family 1] after manuscript 1), all dated between the twelfth to fourteenth centuries. It is now recognized that they follow a text common to Caesarea in the third and fourth centuries A.D. Manuscript 1 was one of the manuscripts Erasmus used to prepare the first Greek New Testament.

9.3.3 *Minuscule 33*

The excellent text of this manuscript (33) is very similar to that of Codex Vaticanus, and since the time of Johann G. Eichhorn in the early nineteenth century, it has been nicknamed "the Queen of the Cursives" (see figure 9.8). It includes the entire New Testament except the book of Revelation and dates to the ninth or tenth century A.D.; currently it resides in the Bibliothèque nationale, Paris.

9.3.4 *Minuscule 16*

This copy of the four Gospels in Greek and Latin, known as "16," is written in four colors: the narrative in vermilion, the words of Jesus and angels in crimson, Old Testament quotes and the words of the disciples in blue, and the words of the Pharisees, the centurion, Judas Iscariot, and Satan in black.[5] Presently the manuscript is housed in the Bibliothèque nationale, Paris.

Further Reading

Aland, Kurt, and Barbara Aland. *The Text of the New Testament. An Introduction to the Critical Editions and to the Theory and Practice of Modern Textual Criticism.* Translated by Erroll F. Rhodes. Grand Rapids: Eerdmans, 1987. See pp. 185-221.

Bruce, F. F. *The Books and the Parchments.* 5th ed. London: Marshall Pickering, 1991. See pp. 181-209.

Jellicoe, Sidney. *The Septuagint and Modern Study.* Ann Arbor, Mich. Eisenbrauns, 1978.

Metzger, Bruce M. *The Early Versions of the New Testament. Their Origin,Transmission, and Limitations.* Oxford: Clarendon, 1977.

———. *The Text of the New Testament. Its Transmission, Corruption, and Restoration.* 3rd ed. New York: Oxford University Press, 1992.

Roberts, Bleddyn J. *The Old Testament Text and Versions. The Hebrew Text in Transmission and the History of Ancient Versions.* Cardiff: University of Wales Press, 1951.

Swete, Henry B. *An Introduction to the Old Testament in Greek.* Cambridge: Cambridge University Press, 1902.

Vööbus, Arthur. "Versions." *ISBE* 4:969-83.

Würthwein, Ernst. *The Text of the Old Testament. An Introduction to the Biblia Hebraica.* Translated by Erroll F. Rhodes. 2nd ed. Grand Rapids: Eerdmans, 1995.

---

[5]See ibid., p. 66.

Additional Ancient Versions for Old and New Testament Textual Criticism

Examining the Ancient Versions

This chapter describes the early ancient versions of the Bible and notes their importance for textual critical work. The versions are divided according to the Eastern and Western church traditions and then by date.

Some of the earliest versions of the Bible were produced by missionaries desiring to spread the Gospel into new regions, among people who spoke different languages (e.g., Coptic, Syriac, Latin, Gothic).[1] Church history confirms that in areas where the Bible is not translated into the language of the common people (e.g., the Berber peoples in North Africa), persecution does a very thorough job of stamping Christianity out; but in areas such as Syria and Egypt, which had biblical translations in common languages, even the Muslim conquest in the seventh century was not able to do away with it.[2] However, by the year A.D. 600 the Gospel had been translated into only about eight languages.[3] Translating meaning from one language to another is always difficult, especially between unrelated languages. Bruce Metzger highlights several of the problems typically encountered when translating the Greek: "For example, Latin has no definite article; Syriac cannot distinguish between the Greek aorist and perfect tenses; Coptic lacks the passive voice and must use a circumlocution."[4] The problems are far worse when the translator has only a limited knowledge of Greek to begin with, as was the case, according to Augustine, in the fourth century when the Hebrew and Greek texts were translated into Latin:

> For the translations of the Scriptures from Hebrew into Greek can be counted, but the Latin translations are out of all number. For in the early days of the faith every

[1]Bruce M. Metzger, *The Text of the New Testament: Its Transmission, Corruption, and Restoration,* 3rd ed. (New York: Oxford University Press, 1992), p. 67.

[2]Paul D. Wegner, *The Journey from Texts to Translations* (Grand Rapids: Baker, 1999), p. 241.

[3]Bruce M. Metzger, *The Bible in Translation* (Grand Rapids: Baker, 2001), p. 8.

[4]Bruce M. Metzger, *The Text of the New Testament,* 3rd ed. (New York: Oxford University Press, 1992), pp. 67-68.

man who happened to get his hands upon a Greek manuscript, and who thought he had any knowledge, were it ever so little, of the two languages, ventured upon the work of translation.[5]

We must also remember that every translation is interpretative to some extent, some more so than others. Despite these difficulties, translations can still be of great help in determining the text of the New Testament. Each version provides at least one author's attempt at what he believed the New Testament text conveyed, and since some translations are very early they may provide insight into the original reading of the text.

The early church realized the importance of translating the Bible into other languages, but these translations are not all of equal importance to textual criticism. Primary translations (i.e., translated directly from the Hebrew and Greek texts) are of most importance, whereas secondary and tertiary translations have at best only a limited value.

Table 10.1 Types of Translations

Type of Translation	Definition	Example
Primary translation	a translation directly from the Greek or Hebrew texts	LXX, Latin Vulgate (for the most part)
Secondary translation	a translation of a primary translation, or a translation of a translation	Old Latin versions (translated from the LXX in the Old Testament)
Tertiary translation	a translation of a secondary translation, or a translation of a translation of a translation	Georgian version (translated from the Syriac or Armenian versions that were translated from the LXX)

The most important primary translations are the LXX, Syriac Peshitta and Latin Vulgate because they have been translated directly from some form of the Hebrew or Greek texts. Secondary translations are often helpful in determining the text they have been translated from; for example Old Latin texts are quite helpful in determining the text of the LXX since they were translated from some form of it. Tertiary translations are of much less value to textual criticism because they are quite distant from either a Greek or Hebrew text; for instance, the Georgian Version of the Old Testament appears to be a translation of the Armenian version, which is a translation of the LXX.

Some versions have greatly restricted value to textual criticism because the translators had only a limited grasp of Greek or Hebrew. Some translators may

---

[5]Augustine *On Christian Doctrine* 2.11, quoted in *The Nicene and Post-Nicene Fathers of the Christian Church*, first series, ed. Philip Schaff (Grand Rapids: Eerdmans, 1988), 2:540.

also have given quite a loose or free translation, while others a very literal one. Versions must therefore be used with care. And yet until the discovery of the Dead Sea Scrolls in 1947 the versions were the earliest witnesses to the Old Testament. The following briefly summarizes the historical background of the various versions.

Of the early translations, both the Syriac versions in the East and the Latin versions in the West are the most important for textual criticism, not only because they are so early but also because they are the basis for so many daughter translations. There is significant debate over which of these two is the earlier translation.[6]

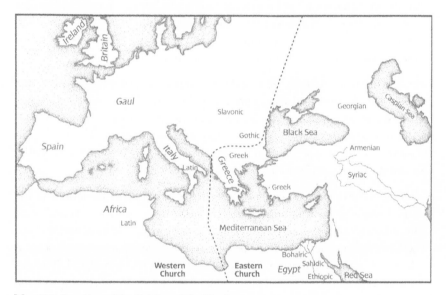

Map 10.1. Location of the Origins of the Versions

10.1 Early Eastern Versions of the Bible

10.1.1 Syriac Versions

Christ's followers were first called "Christians" in Antioch (Acts 11:26), the third largest city in the Roman Empire, and Christianity spread rapidly there. Most people knew Greek in this cosmopolitan city, but Syriac was the native language. Thus, by the latter part of the second century at least parts of the New Testament were circulated in what is commonly known as Old Syriac (see map 10.1).

---

[6]Metzger, *Bible in Translation*, p. 25.

- Tatian's Diatessaron (A.D. 170, the earliest known harmony of the Gospels). Tatian, born an Assyrian, came to Rome about A.D. 150, where he was converted to Christianity and became a pupil of Justin Martyr. However, the church later charged Tatian with heresy because of his highly ascetic beliefs. He returned to Assyria and founded a group of ascetic Christians called the Encratites (around A.D. 170). About this same time he completed his major work known as the Diatessaron, which was a harmony of the four Gospels written in Syriac. *Diatessaron* literally means "through four"; the work weaves all four Gospels into one continuous narrative. Tatian's views emerge at times in the Diatessaron; for example, because he was a vegetarian he said that John the Baptist ate "milk and honey" instead of "locusts and wild honey." His ascetic tendencies caused him to avoid any mention of marriage when speaking of Joseph and Mary (Mt 1:18-19) and to remove the phrase "when men have drunk freely" (Jn 2:10).

It is unknown whether the work was originally written at Rome in the Greek language (the word *diatessaron* is Greek)[7] or in his native language, Syriac, but it gained popularity due in large part to Ephraem, a Syrian church father from Edessa (A.D. 310-373), who wrote a commentary on it. Later the Diatessaron became so popular that it was translated into Persian, Arabic, Latin, Old Dutch, Medieval German, Old Italian and Middle English.

- Syriac Peshitta (5th century A.D.). There are two major translations of the Old Testament into classical Syriac (Eastern Aramaic): the first and most important is the Syriac Peshitta, translated from the Hebrew, and the second is the Syro-Hexapla, translated from the Greek. For centuries several Syriac translations, most of which were in Old Syriac, circulated throughout Syria and competed for superiority. Around the fifth century A.D., the Syriac Peshitta emerged over the others. Its origin is uncertain, but it may have been prepared from A.D. 411-435 by Rabbula, bishop of Edessa; some have suggested an even earlier date since the Old Syriac Gospels adapt some Old Testament quotations to the Peshitta Old Testament text.[8] The word *peshitta* probably means "simple or common," referring to the language of the common people. About A.D. 400, Theodore of Mopsuestia, an early church father, wrote concerning the Syriac Peshitta: "It has been translated into the tongue of the Syrians by someone or other, for it has not been learned up to the present day who this was."[9] With the split of

---

[7]A third-century A.D. fragment of the Greek text of the Diatessaron was discovered in 1933 at a Roman fort at Dura-Europos on the Euphrates River.

[8]Sebastian P. Brock, "Versions, Ancient (Syriac)," *ABD* 6:794.

[9]F. F. Bruce, *The Books and the Parchments*, 5th ed. (London: Marshall Pickering, 1991), p. 183.

the Syriac church into two groups in the fifth century A.D.—the Nestorians (East Syriac) and the Jacobites (West Syriac)—there arose two major recensions of the Syriac Peshitta. Some of the most important resources of the text of the Peshitta come from the writings of several early fathers of the Syriac church, such as Tatian (c. 150-190), Bardesanes (155-222), Aphraates (c. 275-345), Ephraem Syrus (c. 306-373), and Ish'odad of Merv (c. 800).

The Old Testament text of the Peshitta appears to be the work of several hands, each of which used different methods of translating.[10] The book of Chronicles seems to be much different than the rest, which Samuel R. Driver describes as "the translation of which has additions and embellishments, imparting to it quite the character of a Targum."[11] The Peshitta appears to have been translated from some form of Hebrew text and it is less clear if it was subsequently revised by the aid of the LXX.[12] The LXX's influence can be clearly seen in the word "Selah," which is rendered in the LXX as *diapsalma* (literally "through the psalm"); the Peshitta merely transliterates this Greek word into Syriac.

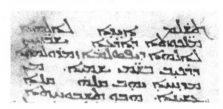

Figure 10.1. Psalm 51 in Syriac (Monastery of St. Catherine, Mt. Sinai, seventh century). [Orlando, Fla., The Scriptorium, VK MS 631, fol.1ʳ]

Syriac manuscripts vary significantly concerning the order and the books included in the Old (often included are apocryphal works—Ecclesiasticus, Judith and Susanna) and New Testaments (they do not include 2 Peter, 2 and 3 John, Jude, and Revelation).

The studies at the Leiden Peshitta Institute have provided some interesting findings concerning the transmission history of the Syriac Peshitta, which Wolters describes:

> It has become clear that this history can be divided into three stages: a first stage that ended with the sixth century A.D., a second corresponding roughly to the seventh and eighth centuries, and a third beginning in the ninth century. Most printed editions of the Peshitta reflect the third stage, which is farthest removed

---

[10]Sidney Jellicoe, *The Septuagint and Modern Study* (Ann Arbor, Mich.: Eisenbrauns, 1978), p. 246.

[11]Samuel R. Driver, *Notes on the Hebrew Text and Topography of the Books of Samuel*, 2nd ed. (Oxford: Clarendon, 1913; repr. 1960), p. lii.

[12]Ernst Würthwein, *The Text of the Old Testament*, trans. Erroll F. Rhodes (Grand Rapids: Eerdmans, 1979), p. 81. Lienhard Delekat has argued that the Peshitta is based on "oral traditions" which were first included in the LXX and later became part of the Peshitta and Targums ("Ein Septuagintatargum," *VT* 8 [1958]: 225-52).

from the MT, while the printed text of the Leiden Peshitta generally reflects manuscripts of the second stage.[13]

A new critical edition of the Syriac Peshitta was necessary since those published in the nineteenth century represented the third stage of its development and were outdated.[14] This new edition of the Leiden Peshitta is based on the Codex Ambrosianus (dating from the sixth to seventh century),[15] which is the most important manuscript of the Peshitta, but it still only goes back to the second stage of the Peshitta's development. Wolter's summary continues:

> But a small number of manuscripts preserve the text of the first stage (recorded in the second apparatus of the Leiden edition), which appears to have been quite a literal translation of a Hebrew text that was very close to the MT. It appears that the text of the Peshitta, through a process of inner-Syriac modifications, gradually moved away from a close approximation to an early stage of the MT. Consequently the divergences from the standard Hebrew text that are found in the third-stage textus receptus of the Peshitta are generally to be attributed not to a different Hebrew *Vorlage* but to developments within the Syriac tradition itself. In its earliest form the Peshitta attests to a Hebrew parent text that is already substantially that of the MT.[16]

The Syriac Peshitta is important for textual criticism because it is a fairly early version of the Old Testament from a separate Jewish tradition, and if the earlier stage can be determined, it provides significant evidence for the MT text. However, the later stages of the Peshitta text have been modified to bring it into closer harmony with the LXX and are therefore less helpful for Old Testament textual criticism.

It is significantly more valuable for New Testament textual criticism since it is a very early translation from original Greek manuscripts. Thomas Nicol states concerning the Syriac Version: "The translation of the New Testament is careful, faithful and literal, and the simplicity, directness and transparency of the style are admired by all Syriac scholars."[17] As mentioned above, the Diatessaron appeared about A.D. 70 and in time became the authoritative gospel text for the early Syriac church. F. F. Bruce describes its popularity:

> Theodoretus, bishop of Cyrrhus near the Euphrates from *c.* 423 to 457, records

---

[13] Al Wolters, "The Text of the Old Testament," in *The Face of Old Testament Studies: A Survey of Contemporary Approaches*, ed. David W. Baker and Bill T. Arnold (Grand Rapids: Baker, 1999), p. 27.

[14] See Piet B. Dirksen, "The Old Testament Peshitta," in *Mikra: Text, Translation, Reading and Interpretation of the Hebrew Bible in Ancient Judaism and Early Christianity,* ed. Martin J. Mulder (Philadelphia: Fortress, 1988), pp. 255-97.

[15] Jellicoe, *Septuagint and Modern Study,* p. 248.

[16] Wolters, "Text of the Old Testament," p. 27.

[17] Nicol, "Syriac Versions," ISBE (1915) 5:2884.

that he collected and removed more than 200 copies from the churches in his diocese, replacing them by 'the Gospels of the Four Evangelists.' This last expression probably denotes Rabbula's revision of the Gospels. Rabbula himself seems to have taken similar steps in his neighbouring diocese of Edessa; one of his directions to his clergy ran: 'The presbyters and deacons shall see to it that in all the churches a copy of the "Gospel of the separated ones" shall be available and read.'[18]

The "Gospel of the separated ones" refers to the four Gospels in contrast to the Diatessaron; by about the fifth century the latter had fallen out of favor and was being replaced by the canonical Gospels.

Modern scholars have distinguished at least five different Syriac versions of all or part of the New Testament: the Old Syriac, the Peshitta, the Philoxenian, the Harclean and the Palestinian Syriac.[19] However, the standard version in Syriac from the fifth century onward was the Syriac Peshitta. Philoxenus of Mabbug added 2 Peter, 2—3 John, Jude and Revelation into the version of the New Testament he commissioned in 507-508. More than 350 manuscripts of the Peshitta New Testament are known to exist today.

Further Reading

Primary Sources

de Boer, Pieter A. H., et al., eds. *The Old Testament in Syriac According to the Peshitta Version.* Leiden: Brill, 1972.

———. "First Supplement to the List of Old Testament Peshiṭta Manuscripts," *VT* 12 (1962): 127-28.

———. "Second Supplement to the List of Old Testament Peshiṭta Manuscripts," *VT* 12 (1962): 237-38.

———. "Third Supplement to the List of Old Testament Peshiṭta Manuscripts," *VT* 12 (1962): 351.

———. "Fourth Supplement to the List of Old Testament Peshiṭta Manuscripts," *VT* 18 (1968): 128-43.

Peshitta Institute of Leiden University, eds. *List of Old Testament Peshitta Manuscripts.* Leiden: Brill, 1961.

Other Works

Barnes, William E. *An Apparatus Criticus to Chronicles in the Peshitta Version.* Cambridge: Cambridge University Press, 1897.

———. *The Peshitta Psalter According to the West Syrian Text.* Cambridge: Cambridge University Press, 1904.

---

[18]Bruce, *Books and the Parchments*, p. 185.
[19]Metzger, *Text of the New Testament*, p. 68.

————. *Pentateuchus Syriace*. London: British and Foreign Bible Society, 1914.

Brock, Sebastian P. "Versions, Ancient (Syriac)." *ABD* 6:794-99. See bibliography.

Emerton, John A. *The Peshitta of the Wisdom of Solomon*. SPB 2. Leiden: Brill, 1959.

Jellicoe, Sidney. *The Septuagint and Modern Study*. Ann Arbor, Mich.: Eisenbrauns, 1978. See esp. pp. 246-49.

Lamsa, George M. *The Holy Bible from Ancient Eastern Manuscripts*. San Francisco: Harper & Row, 1967.

Neusner, Jacob. "The Conversion of Adiabene to Judaism: A New Perspective." *JBL* 83 (1964): 60-66.

Roberts, Bleddyn J. *The Old Testament Text and Versions. The Hebrew Text in Transmission and the History of Ancient Versions*. Cardiff: University of Wales Press, 1951. See esp. pp. 214-28.

Robinson, H. Wheeler. "The Syriac Bible." In *The Bible in Its Ancient and English Versions*. Edited by H. Wheeler Robinson. Oxford: Clarendon, 1940.

Vööbus, A. "Versions." *ISBE* 4:969-83. See bibliography.

10.1.2 Coptic Versions

From both the New Testament (Acts 2:10) and an early Greek manuscript (e.g., $\mathfrak{P}^{52}$), there is very early evidence that Christianity spread to Egypt at least by the early second century. While the Greek language had significant influence on Egypt, especially in the cosmopolitan city of Alexandria, native Egyptians would probably have spoken Coptic (a corrupted form of *Aigyptos*, meaning "Egyptian"). Coptic has at least six different dialects in the Nile Valley (due largely to the fact that the Nile River Valley stretches for approximately one thousand miles and New Testament translations have been found in at least five of them.) However, the two primary dialects are Sahidic (Upper Egypt) and Bohairic (Lower Egypt). Since Christianity spread into Egypt so soon, versions from this area may reflect early traditions (see map 10.1). The Egyptian language has a long history; originally the Egyptians used a hieroglyphic script that was then superseded by a hieratic and finally a demotic script, but at least as early as the third century Coptic was the native language of Egypt. Coptic is a combination of this common native language plus Greek loanwords, and it is written in an alphabet derived from the Greek language with seven additional characters from Demotic for sounds that did not exist in the Greek language (see figure 10.3).[20]

While little is known about the history of the early church in Egypt before A.D. 180-190, $\mathfrak{P}^{52}$ (an early Greek manuscript) indicates that at least part of the New Testament circulated there by about A.D. 125. Kurt and Barbara Aland suggest that the reason so little is known is that Gnosticism was quite promi-

---

[20]Würthwein, *Text of the Old Testament*, p. 100; Metzger, *Text of the New Testament*, p. 79.

Hieroglyphics

Demotic

Greek

Figure 10.2. Rosetta Stone. The Rosetta Stome, dated to ca 196 B.C. includes an inscription of a priestly decree affirming the royal cult of the thirteen year old, Ptolemy V. The decree is inscribed three times, first in hieroglyphics (suitable for a priestly decree), second in demotic (the native script used for daily purposes) and third in Greek (the language of government administration). [British Museum/HIP/Art Resource, NY]

nent in Egypt and thus the church there may not have been recognized by the official churches until later.[21]

- Sahidic version (upper Egypt around Thebes; at least by the third century A.D. since a manuscript of 1 Peter dates to that century). The Sahidic language (from "Es-sa'id," the Arabic name for Upper Egypt) is the oldest and in many respects the most important Coptic dialect. It was spoken from Thebes, the ancient southern capital (modern Luxor), southward. The Sahidic Old Testament is probably a translation of the Greek LXX; the New Testament, which dates to about the third century, primarily agrees with the Alexandrian text family but contains some Western readings in the Gospels and Acts.[22]

---

[21]Kurt Aland and Barbara Aland, *The Text of the New Testament*, trans. Erroll F. Rhodes (Grand Rapids: Eerdmans, 1987), p. 196.

[22]Metzger, *Text of the New Testament*, p. 79.

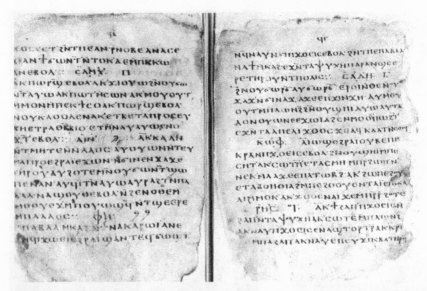

Figure 10.3. A page from the book of Jeremiah in Coptic from a folio of Jeremiah, Lamentations and Baruch (fourth century A.D.). [Orlando, Fla., The Scriptorium, VK MS 783, fols. 92ᵛ-93ʳ]

The Sahidic New Testament version has some peculiarities not found in other versions: (1) Matthew 6:13 ends with "for yours is the power and the glory forever," instead of the more common "for yours is the kingdom and the power and the glory forever." (2) In the parable of the rich man and Lazarus, Luke 16:19 records the name of the rich man as "Nineve." (3) In Acts 15 the Golden Rule is stated in the negative, i.e., "do not do unto others what you would not want them to do unto you."

- Bohairic version (lower Egypt in the Delta region; fourth or early fifth century A.D. since Papyrus Bodimer III dates to this time period). Bohairic, spoken in lower Egypt, was one of the latest and most developed dialects of the Coptic language. In time it superseded all other dialects and even shows some influence from Sahidic. It is still spoken today in the modern Coptic church centered in Cairo, Egypt, and until the eighteenth century was the only known Coptic dialect of the New Testament.[23] The Bohairic version is also an Alexandrian text and is the only completely preserved Coptic version (it is attested by several manuscripts).[24]

---

[23]Bruce M. Metzger, *The Early Versions of the New Testament* (Oxford: Clarendon, 1977), pp. 109, 121; Frederic G. Kenyon, *Our Bible and the Ancient Manuscripts* (New York: Harper, 1958), p. 234.

[24]Metzger, *Bible in Translation*, p. 36.

Egyptian Christian missionaries translated the Scriptures into Coptic in an endeavor to evangelize their non-Greek-speaking neighbors. There are a significant number of Coptic manuscripts and fragments originating from the third and fourth centuries A.D. Although they show some relationship to Old Latin versions, both the Sahidic and Bohairic versions derive from the LXX; their main contribution to Old Testament textual criticism is the light that they can shed on the LXX text. However, Willem Grossouw, in his book *Coptic Versions of the Minor Prophets*, examined the Minor Prophets and found that the Sahidic or the Achmimic (another Coptic version), and sometimes both, agreed in two hundred instances with the Hebrew against the LXX.[25] This raises two questions, neither of which has been answered satisfactorily: (1) What is the relationship between these two versions and the Hebrew text? and (2) What is the nature of the *Vorlage* (text from which they were copied) of these two translations as compared to the LXX? Take special note of readings that do not follow the LXX, since they may reflect an alternative LXX translation or some other early reading. As regards the New Testament Coptic versions, they are a primary translation of a pure Alexandrian text, but there are numerous agreements with Western texts in the Gospels and Acts.[26]

Further Reading

Primary Sources

Budge, E. A. Wallis, ed. *Coptic Biblical Texts in the Dialect of Upper Egypt.* London: Longmans, 1912.

Drescher, James, ed. *The Coptic (Sahidic) Version of Kingdoms I, II.* Louvain: Secrétariat du CSCO, 1970.

Thompson, Herbert, ed. *The Coptic (Sahidic) Version of Certain Books of the Old Testament.* London: H. Frowde, 1908.

Worrell, William H. *The Coptic Manuscripts in the Freer Collection.* New York: Macmillan, 1923.

———. *Coptic Texts in the University of Michigan Collection.* Ann Arbor, Mich.: University of Michigan Press, 1923.

Other Works

Hallock, F. Hudson. "The Coptic O.T." *AJSL* (1932/33): 325-35.

Hendley, P. L. "Three Graeco-Coptic Biblical Texts." *JTS* 35 (1934): 58-60.

Mills, Watson E. "Versions, Ancient (Coptic)." *ABD* 6: 803. See bibliography.

Roberts, Bleddyn J. *The Old Testament Text and Versions.* Cardiff: University of Wales Press, 1951. See esp. pp. 229-33.

---

[25]Monumenta Biblica et Ecclesiastica 3 (Rome: Pontifical Biblical Institute, 1938), pp. 111-12.
[26]Watson E. Mills, "Versions, Ancient (Coptic)," *ABD* 6:803.

10.1.3 Armenian Version

The Armenians lived north of Mesopotamia between the Persian and Roman empires (see map 10.1). Acts 2 mentions people from this region who were present at Pentecost (Acts 2:9 "Parthians, Medes, Elamites, and residents of Mesopotamia"). Christianity spread through Syria and into Armenia possibly as early as the first century A.D., but almost immediately would have encountered the native Armenian worship of Anahia, consort of Mithras, and Zoroastrianism.[27] Nevertheless, Armenia was the first nation to be officially declared Christian when King Tiridates III (c. 287-314), who had formerly persecuted the church, was converted by Gregory the Illuminator (c. 257-331) at the end of the third century A.D. Gregory was the son of an Armenian nobleman and studied at Caesarea in Cappadocia before returning to his native land to do missionary work. Armenia became a political and religious battleground between the Persian and Greek empires; both were determined to impose their own religions onto the Armenians, thus threatening the very existence of the young Christian nation.[28] The Armenian Christians were strongly influenced by works written in both Greek and Syriac, but they had no Scripture in their own language. The first version of the Armenian Bible was produced in the early part of the fifth century A.D. However, before the translation could be undertaken, an Armenian priest named Mesrop (c. 361-439), assisted by a Greek calligrapher named Rufanos of Samosata, developed the Armenian alphabet of thirty-six letters in about A.D. 406. Shortly afterward Mesrop collected manuscripts of the Bible from as far away as Edessa and Rome and with the help of other scholars translated them into Armenian. Mesrop was responsible for translating the New Testament and at least the book of Proverbs into Armenian; the Old Testament was finished about 410-414.[29] Determining which text was used for the original translation is still a matter of debate.

The Armenian version is one of the earlier translations of the Bible and some of its readings may go back even earlier. It has been called "the Queen of the Versions," not only because of its great number of copies, but also because it is a clear, accurate and literal rendering of the Greek New Testament. The number of extant copies of this version is second only to copies of the Latin Vulgate with over 1,244 manuscripts in whole or in part of the New Testament alone (see figure 10.4). The Armenian version contains several books outside the biblical canon. For example, the *History of Joseph and Asenath* and *The Testament of the Twelve Patriarchs* appear in the Old Testament; and the *Epistle of the Corinthians to Paul* and a *Third Epistle of Paul to the Corinthians* are included in the New Testament. More than one hundred

---

[27]Joseph M. Alexanian, "Versions, Ancient (Armenian)," *ABD* 6:805.
[28]Ibid.
[29]Metzger, *Bible in Translation*, p. 41.

copies of the Armenian New Testament stop at Mark 16:8 and leave
out the last twelve verses.[30] One
copy of the Armenian Gospels,
dated to A.D. 989, says that the last
twelve verses of Mark 16 were
added by "the presbyter Ariston"
(who is mentioned by Papias in the
early second century as one of the
disciples of the Lord).[31]

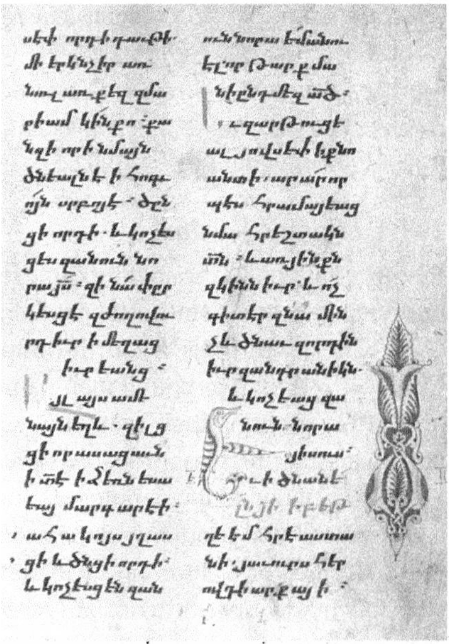

The quality of translation in
the Old Testament varies from
book to book, with significant debate as to which text was used for
the original translation. Still, it is
one of the earliest translations of
the LXX, though in places where it
does not harmonize with the LXX
it has been influenced by the
Peshitta.[32] In the Old Testament
this version depends on the LXX

Figure 10.4. Matthew 1 in Armenian
(Alt'amar, Eastern Turkey, 1420) [Orlando,
Fla., The Scriptorium, VK MS 781, fol. 9ʳ]

and the Peshitta, and in most cases should not be considered a separate witness. The New Testament, however, is a very literal translation that can be
quite helpful to textual criticism.

Further Reading

Primary Source

Cox, Claude E. *The Armenian Translation of Deuteronomy.* Chico, Calif.: Scholars
Press, 1981.

Other Works

Alexanian, Joseph M. "Versions, Ancient (Armenian)." *ABD* 6:805-8. See bibliography.

Conybeare, Frederick C. "Armenian Version." *HDB* 1:151-53.

Gehman, Henry S. "The Armenian Version of Daniel and Its Affinities." *ZAW*
7 (1930): 82-99.

———. "The Armenian Version of I. and II. Kings and Its Affinities." *JAOS* 54
(1934): 53-59.

---

[30]Ibid., p. 43.
[31]Ibid., pp. 42-43.
[32]Würthwein, *Text of the Old Testament*, p. 103.

Jellicoe, Sidney. *The Septuagint and Modern Study.* Ann Arbor, Mich.: Eisen-
    brauns, 1978. See esp. pp. 259-61.
Metzger, Bruce M. "Versions, Ancient." *IDB* 4:749-60. See bibliography.
Swete, Henry B. *An Introduction to the Old Testament in Greek.* Cambridge: Cam-
    bridge University Press, 1902. See esp. pp. 118-20.

10.1.4 Ethiopic Version

It is uncertain how Christianity came to Ethiopia (or Abyssinia, its older name);
but often scholars point to the conversion of the Ethiopian eunuch by Philip
(Acts 8:26-39). Rufinus, a fourth-century historian claimed that Ethiopia was
Christianized by two young men named Frumentius and Ædesius during the
time of Constantine the Great (about 330).[33] While each man may have had a
part, Christianity was probably spread through Ethiopia by monophysite
monks. They fled to the remote location of Ethiopia due to persecution by Byzantine rulers who condemned their view (i.e., that Christ had only one nature)
at the Council of Chalcedon in 451 (see map 10.1). The Ethiopic version was
probably made in the fifth or sixth century in connection with the activity of the
monks. There is further evidence that these monks influenced both the Coptic
and Ethiopic churches, which largely came to be monophysite. Early Ethiopic
traditions do not appear to make a clear distinction between canonical and non-
canonical books; Old Testament apocryphal books are regularly included as
well as several pseudepigraphal works (e.g., *1 Enoch, Jubilees, Ascension of Isaiah*
and *4 Baruch*).

By the fifth or sixth century A.D., portions of the Bible were translated into
Ethiopic (or Ge'ez, as Old Ethiopic is called). The Ethiopic Old Testament is
probably a translation of a Greek text that has been modified at some points
by a Hebrew original.[34] It also appears to have been significantly revised by
comparing it to an Arabic version.[35] The oldest extant copy of the Ethiopic Old
Testament dates to the thirteenth century and corresponds substantially with
the text of Codex Vaticanus (a fourth-century codex of the LXX), but it is uncertain how this corresponds to earlier Ethiopic versions). It is difficult to determine the usefulness of the Ethiopic version to Old Testament textual criticism
since it appears to have been compiled from many sources, but its major importance is the light that it sheds on a text of the LXX that has not yet been identified or one that is a mixture of various forms of the LXX. Its unique readings
must therefore be considered carefully.

---

[33]Rufinus *Ecclesiastical History* 1:9, quoted in ibid.
[34]Jellicoe, *Septuagint and Modern Study,* pp. 264-65; Arthur Vööbus, "Versions," *ISBE* 4:981;
    Bruce, *Books and the Parchments,* p. 206.
[35]Jellicoe, *Septuagint and Modern Study,* p. 265; Würthwein, *Text of the Old Testament,* p. 104.

The oldest known surviving Ethiopic text is a copy of the four Gospels from the tenth century (Abba Garima, MS. 1).[36] It is uncertain whether this translation was made from a Greek or Syriac version. According to the Alands, Acts and the Catholic Epistles were most likely translated from a Greek text; however, it is difficult to determine both the languages and the sources from which the book of Revelation came (see figure 10.5).[37]

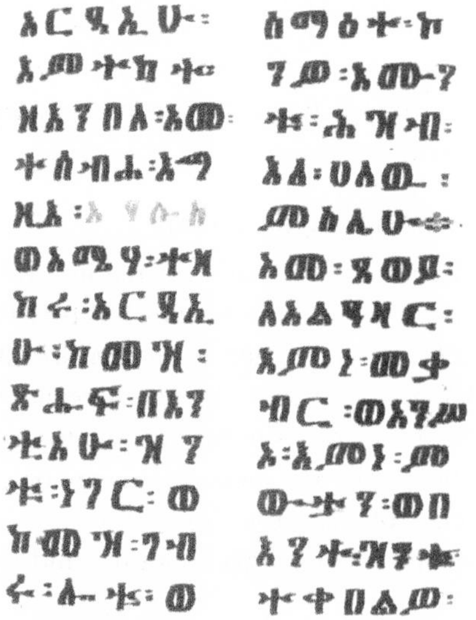

The New Testament text is not homogeneous and largely contains readings found in the Byzantine or Western text types; however, in places a Syriac influence is evident. The book of Acts, the Catholic Epistles and Revelation are most helpful since they seem to reflect some ac-

Figure 10.5. Gospels in Ethiopic (eighteenth century) [Orlando, Fla., The Scriptorium, VK MS 203]

curate, original readings. The Ethiopic New Testament also includes the two apocryphal books, *1 Enoch* and *Jubilees*.

Further Reading

Primary Sources

Boyd, James O. *The Octateuch in Ethiopic.* Pts. 1 and 2. Princeton: Princeton University Press, 1909-1911.

D'Abbadie, Antione. *Catalogue raisonné de MSS. éthiopiens.* Paris: l'Imprimerie Imperiale, 1859.

Dillmann, August. *Biblia Veteris Testamenti Aethiopicae.* 5 vols. Lipsiae: F. C. G. Vogel, 1853-1861.

Zotenberg, Herrmann. *Catalogue des MSS. éthiopiens de la Bibliothèque Nationale.* Paris: l'Imprimerie Imperiale, 1877.

Other Works

Charles, Robert H. "Ethiopic Version." *HDB* 1:791-93.

Jellicoe, Sidney. *The Septuagint and Modern Study.* Ann Arbor: Eisenbrauns,

---

[36]Metzger, *Early Versions of the New Testament,* pp. 224-25.
[37]Aland and Aland, *Text of the New Testament,* p. 209.

1978. See esp. pp. 263-66.

Swete, Henry B. *An Introduction to the Old Testament in Greek.* Edited by Richard R. Ottley. Rev. ed. New York: KTAV, 1968. See esp. pp. 109-10.

Zuurmond, Rochus. "Versions, Ancient (Ethiopic)." *ABD* 6:808-10. See bibliography.

10.1.5 Georgian Version

Georgia is north of Armenia in a rough, mountainous district known as the Caucasus mountains, which is between the Black Sea and the Caspian Sea. In antiquity the region was called Iberia; today it is part of the Confederation of Independent States (formerly Soviet Union; see map 10.1). The earliest record of Christianity's introduction into Georgia was through a slave woman named Nino, who was taken captive by Bakur, the pagan king of Georgia during the reign of Emperor Constantine.[38] But later it appears that Christianity was spread into Georgia about the mid-fourth century A.D. by both the Armenian and the Greek-speaking church.

How or when the first copies of the Bible came into Georgia is uncertain. The Georgian language is an agglutinative language, which means that it is built by combining smaller sections of meaning together. It favors the "passive construction" (e.g., "the ball was hit by me" instead of "I hit the ball"), has very few vowels, many consonants and is unrelated to languages from surrounding regions. An alphabet had to be developed before the Scriptures could be translated into Georgian (see figure 10.6).[39] Armenian tradition ascribes both the Georgian alphabet and version to Mesrop who, after finishing the Armenian

Figure 10.6. The New Testament in Georgian (Moscow: Andrew Johnson, 1743) [Orlando, Fla., The Scriptorium, VK 459, fol. 15ʳ]

---

[38]Metzger, *Early Versions of the New Testament*, p. 182.

[39]J. Neville Birdsall, "Versions, Ancient (Georgian),"*ABD* 6:811.

version, brought the gospel to his neighbors. However, according to Sidney Jellicoe, it seems most likely that a first Georgian version (fifth-sixth century A.D.) was translated from the Armenian version and was later revised by comparing it to a Greek text.[40]

A palimpsest of the Gospels is dated to the mid-fifth century A.D., so at least the Gospels were translated by this time.[41] There is some disagreement concerning which text was the basis for the Georgian version; Greek, Armenian and Syriac have all been suggested. It may have been revised several times in light of various versions.[42] The oldest Georgian manuscript (Geo[1]) is the Adysh manuscript of A.D. 897, which contains the four Gospels. But fragments of at least Genesis, Deuteronomy, Judges, Proverbs and Jeremiah are known to have existed in Georgian from between the fifth to the eighth centuries A.D. The book of Revelation was not thought to be canonical by the Georgian church, so it was not translated until about 978 by St. Euthymius (d. c. 1028).[43] The Georgian version is a tertiary translation either from the Syriac or Armenian versions, and thus its primary value to textual criticism is in corroborating Old Syriac versions.

Further Reading

Primary Source

Blake, Robert P., and Maurice Brière. *The Old Georgian Version of the Prophets.* PO 29/2-5 and 30/3. Paris: Firmin-Ditot, 1961.

Other Works

Birdsall, J. Neville. "Versions, Ancient (Georgian)." *ABD* 6:810-13. See bibliography.

Blake, Robert P. "Ancient Georgian Versions of the Old Testament." *HTR* 19 (1926): 271-97.

———. "The Athos Codex of the Georgian Old Testament." *HTR* 22 (1929): 33-56.

———. "Georgian Theological Literature." *JTS* 26 (1924-1925): 50-64.

———. "Khanmeti Palimpsest Fragments of the Old Georgian Version of Jeremiah." *HTR* 25 (1932): 225-72.

Hendly, P. L. "The Georgian Fragments of Jeremiah." *JTS* 34 (1933): 392-95.

Jellicoe, Sidney. *The Septuagint and Modern Study.* Ann Arbor, Mich.: Eisenbrauns, 1978. See esp. pp. 261-62.

---

[40]Sidney Jellicoe, *The Septuagint and Modern Study* (Oxford: Clarendon, 1968), p. 261. See also Robert P. Blake, "Georgian Theological Literature," *JTS* 26 (1924-1925): 50-64.

[41]Metzger, *Early Versions of the New Testament,* p. 190.

[42]Metzger, *Bible in Translation,* p. 43.

[43]Ibid., p. 44.

10.1.6 Arabic Versions

Arabia stretched all the way from west of Mesopotamia to south of Judea down to the Isthmus of Suez and included one of the largest desert regions, the Arabian Desert. Little is known concerning the first translation of the Bible into Arabic. The first mention of such appears in the Midrash *Siphre* on Deuteronomy 34:3, which says that the Torah was given to Israel in four languages: Hebrew, Greek, Arabic and Aramaic. The rapid spread of Islam across the southern Mediterranean area in the seventh century forced Jews and Christians who remained in the conquered lands to adopt Arabic. Since translation of the Bible into Arabic was outlawed, Jews and Christians had to translate it undercover, and therefore a number of independent versions arose.

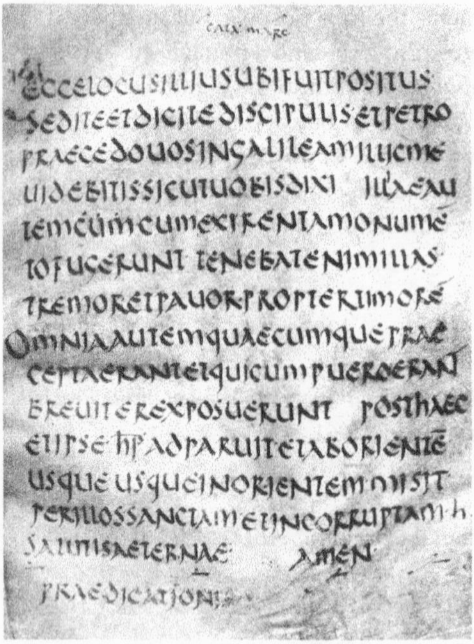

Evidence suggests that translations into Arabic are numerous and were made from Greek, the Old Syriac, Syriac Peshitta, Coptic and Latin versions. At present the oldest known manuscript of the Arabic Bible is Cod. Vaticanus arabicus 13, which contains a portion of the Gospels and the Pauline Epistles from the eighth or ninth century A.D. The Arabic translation of Saadia Gaon (A.D. 882-942) is usually regarded as the last ancient translation of the Old

Figure 10.7. A fourth- or fifth-century A.D. Old Latin manuscript (Codex Bobiensis, k) of the "shorter ending" of Mark [Biblioteca Nazionale Universitaria di Tovino]

Testament and is almost identical to the MT,[44] but most other Arabic translations are very free renderings and are a mixture of various sources (a Hebrew original, the LXX, Peshitta, and other versions).[45] The New Testament is likewise a combined text. An *agraphon* (noted in italics) is included in Matthew

---

[44]Emanuel Tov, "The Text of the Old Testament," in *The World of the Bible,* ed. Adam S. van der Woude, trans. Sierd Woudstra (Grand Rapids: Eerdmans, 1986), p. 181.

[45]Bleddyn J. Roberts, *The Old Testament Text and Versions* (Cardiff: University of Wales Press, 1951), p. 269.

6:34, where Jesus purportedly says, "sufficient unto the day is the evil thereof, *and unto the hour the pain thereof.*" Since the Arabic version was derived from a variety of sources, its greatest value to textual criticism is in the area of the history of interpretation of various texts. Spoken Arabic continues to evolve, but written Arabic has been frozen by the language of the Qur'an. Thus the Arabic versions are significantly less vernacular than other translations.

For Further Reading

Primary Sources

de Lagarde, Paul, ed. *Materialien zur Kritik und Geschichte des Pentateuchs.* Leipzig: Teubner, 1867. London Polyglott, 1652. Paris Polyglott, 1645.

Other Works

Burkitt, F. Crawford. "Arabic Versions." *HDB* 1:136-38.

Jellicoe, Sidney. *The Septuagint and Modern Study.* Ann Arbor, Mich.: Eisenbrauns, 1978. See esp. pp. 263-66.

Metzger, Bruce M. "Versions, Ancient." *IDB* 4:749-60.

Roberts, Bleddyn J. *The Old Testament Text and Versions.* Cardiff: University of Wales Press, 1951. See pp. 266-69.

Swete, Henry B. *An Introduction to the Old Testament in Greek.* Edited by Richard R. Ottley. Rev. ed. New York: KTAV, 1968. See esp. pp. 110-11.

10.2 Early Western Versions of the Bible

The Romans united their empire under a single language, paving the way for the spread of the gospel throughout; the book of Acts records how the gospel spread to this Western region. Greek prevailed over Latin in most of the Roman Empire until the third century A.D., except in southern Gaul and northern Africa, where the earliest Latin biblical texts emerged (see map 10.1). In these two areas Latin was the official language of government and trade, but indigenous peoples continued to speak their own languages. By the third century A.D., however, Latin emerged as the predominant language. Latin versions of the Bible and especially the Latin Vulgate were vital to church history.

10.2.1 Old Latin Versions

"Old Latin" is a collective term for the Latin versions in existence before the Latin Vulgate. Gradually the West became Latin speaking; by A.D. 250 Latin had become the language of Christian writers and theologians so that soon there was great need for a Latin Bible. Latin translations probably first appeared in the Roman province of Northern Africa (including present day Tunisia, Algeria and Morocco), where Carthage had especially strong ties with Roman culture. Tertullian (c. A.D. 160-220) quotes great sections from a Latin biblical text in his works, thus a Latin translation must have existed by his time. From about A.D. 180 an outbreak of persecution against Christians took place in Numidia (modern Tunisia), and during one of the trials a Christian named Speratus (from the town of Scillium) was asked what he carried in a box, to which he replied: "Books and letters of a just man, one Paul."[46]

No single manuscript contains the entire Old Latin Bible, but Old Latin manuscripts, commonly notated as "it" with a superscript letter (e.g., it^a, it^b), are fairly well attested for the New Testament, with just over one hundred fragments—about forty-six of the Gospels, nineteen of Acts, twenty of the Pauline Epistles, twelve of the Catholic Epistles and seven of the book of Revelation.[47] These fragments are by no means standardized, and they contain a variety of different readings. Generally they are very literal translations. The Gospels generally follow the Western order (e.g., Matthew, John, Luke and Mark). The Old Latin manuscripts from Africa diverge more frequently from the generally received Greek text than the Old Latin texts from Europe. It is suggested that these scribes had more freedom to incorporate their own traditions into the text rather than merely copy them.[48]

In the Old Testament, fragments exist from the Pentateuch, the Psalms and the Major and Minor Prophets; more can be gleaned from works of the church fathers.[49] The fragments were most likely translated from a copy of the LXX (Joseph Ziegler calls these "the Septuagint in Latin clothing"),[50] though some passages seem to reflect a reading closer to the Hebrew text.

The Old Latin texts of the Old Testament are secondary translations, but, as Ernst Würthwein notes, Old Latin is a "particularly important witness to the Septuagint text because it goes back to the period before the Septuagint recensions."[51] Passages in the Old Latin versions that differ from the LXX should be especially noted, for they may follow readings from an alternative LXX tradition or other early readings. In the New Testament the Old Latin texts reflect the Western text type, but some of these texts are very early and may contain original readings. These texts of the New Testament are also important in that many are a very literal (often painfully literal) rendering of the Greek text.

---

[46]Metzger, *Early Versions of the New Testament*, p. 289. See also *Acts of Scillitan Martyrs*, ed. J. Armitage Robinson (Cambridge: Cambridge University Press, 1891).
[47]Metzger, *Early Versions of the New Testament*, p. 294.
[48]Metzger, *Bible in Translation*, p. 30.
[49]For more information on Old Latin manuscripts, see Würthwein, *Text of the Old Testament*, pp. 87-90.
[50]Joseph Ziegler, "Antike und moderne lateinische Psalmenübersetzungen," *SAM* (1960): 5.
[51]Würthwein, *Text of the Old Testament*, p. 91.

Further Reading

Primary Sources

Burkitt, F. Crawford. *The Old Latin and the Itala.* Cambridge: Cambridge University Press, 1896.

Fischer, Bonifatius et al., eds. *Vetus Latina. Die Reste der altelateinischen Bibel.* Freiburg: Herder, 1949. Only Genesis.

Sabatier, Pierre. *Bibliorum Sacrorum Latinae versiones antiquae seu vetus Italica.* 3 vols. Rheims: Reginaldum Florentain, 1743-1749.

Other Works

Bogaert, Pierre-Maurice. "Versions, Ancient (Latin)." *ABD* 6:799-803. See bibliography.

Jellicoe, Sidney. *The Septuagint and Modern Study.* Ann Arbor, Mich.: Eisenbrauns, 1978. See pp. 249-51.

Kennedy, H. A. A. "Latin Versions, The Old." *HDB* 3:47-62.

Roberts, Bleddyn J. *The Old Testament Text and Versions.* Cardiff: University of Wales Press, 1951. See pp. 237-46.

Sparks, Hendly D. F. "The Latin Bible." In *The Bible in Its Ancient and English Versions.* Edited by H. Wheeler Robinson. Oxford: Clarendon, 1940. See pp. 100-110.

10.2.2 *The Latin Vulgate*

The Latin Vulgate is very important to the study of the history of the Bible on two counts: (1) it held a dominant role in Western Europe for about one thousand years, and (2) during the Reformation, when people needed the Bible in their mother tongue, the Latin Vulgate was translated into many other languages. The Latin Vulgate was translated by Jerome during the years A.D. 383 to about 405. Pope Damasus I, bishop of Rome from about A.D. 366 to 384, commissioned Jerome (Sophronius Eusebius Hieronymus, c. A.D. 345-420), his secretary, to revise and standardize the Old Latin version. There were so many differences among Old Latin texts in circulation within the Latin church that people could not be certain which text to follow. Jerome himself commented on the great diversity of manuscripts, saying that there were "almost as many forms of text as there are manuscripts."[52] Jerome, a brilliant scholar with a firm grasp of Latin, Greek and later at least some knowledge of Hebrew, was called on to rectify this problem. He considered refusing the task, knowing that people would castigate him for changing the beloved wording of the Old Latin texts, and wrote to Pope Damasus the following:

---

[52]Metzger, *Bible in Translation*, p. 32. Schaff, *Nicene and Post-Nicene Fathers*, 6:487-88.

> Is there anyone learned or unlearned, who, when he takes the volume in his hands and perceives that what he reads does not suit his settled tastes, will not break out immediately into violent language and call me a forger and profane person for having the audacity to add anything to the ancient books, or to make any changes or corrections in them?[53]

However, he later accepted the commission by the pope to undertake this important task.

His work, later known as the Latin Vulgate (*vulgate* means "common" or "plain" tongue), became the standard edition of the Bible for over one thousand years. His most important contribution was probably the Latin version of the Old Testament (390-405), which he translated from the original Hebrew text, being the only one in the Western church qualified to make such a translation.[54] He worked hard to learn Hebrew; even though his proficiency was limited, it was better than any other church father at the time. By the eighth or ninth century A.D., the Latin Vulgate had finally superseded the Old Latin version. The climax of its victory was on April 8, 1546, when the Council of Trent declared the Vulgate to be the authentic Bible of the Roman Catholic Church:

> But if any one receive not, as sacred and canonical, the said books entire with all their parts, as they have been used to be read in the Catholic Church, and as they are contained in the old Latin vulgate edition; and knowingly and deliberately contemn [condemn] the traditions aforesaid; let him be anathema (fourth session).[55]

In general, Jerome chose to translate his new work in a sense-for-sense rather than literal method.[56] He explained his procedure in a letter to the pope and claimed that he only changed the Old Latin text when it seemed absolutely necessary, and retained phrases in other cases that had become familiar to the people.[57] The text of the Vulgate is not uniform—either Jerome initially relied too heavily on the Old Latin manuscripts or perhaps he became a better translator with practice. This lack of uniformity may also indicate that Jerome was not able to translate the entire Bible; some have gone so far as to question whether he actually translated a good part of the New Testament (e.g., Pauline and Catholic Epistles, Acts and Revelation).[58] Nonetheless, Jerome used the Hebrew text as the basis for his translation of the Old

---

[53]Schaff, *Nicene and Post-Nicene Fathers*, 6:487-88.

[54]Würthwein, *Text of the Old Testament*, p. 95. See also James Barr, "St. Jerome's Appreciation of Hebrew," *BJRL* 49 (1966/1967): 281-302.

[55]Philip Schaff, *The Creeds of Christendom with a History and Critical Notes* (New York: Harper & Brothers, 1882), 2:82.

[56]Hendly D. F. Sparks, "Jerome as Biblical Translator," in *CHB* 1:523.

[57]Metzger, *Bible in Translation*, p. 33.

[58]Pierre-Maurice Bogaert, "Versions, Ancient (Latin)," *ABD* 6:801.

Testament, which was a vast improvement. But he was severely criticized for this by the church, which claimed that the LXX was inspired and therefore authoritative.[59] Some of Jerome's severest challenges came from those who wanted to include the Apocrypha; even Augustine disagreed with Jerome's Hebrew canon. The Apocrypha was finally included in the Vulgate, though Jerome did not spend much time on it. (Jerome left some apocryphal books untranslated from the Old Latin.)[60]

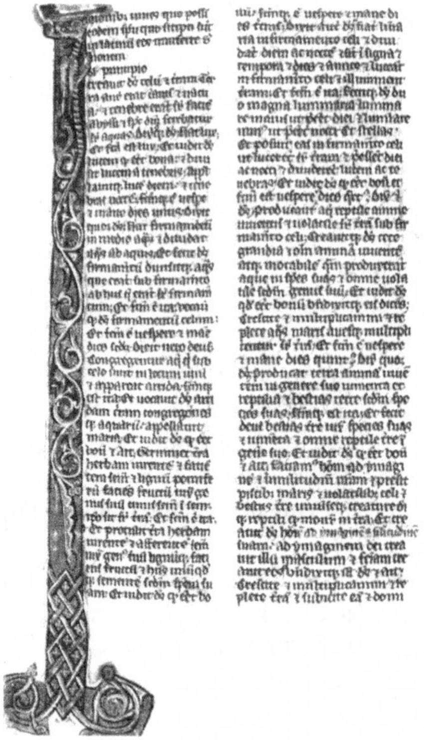

Because the Old Testament of the Latin Vulgate was translated directly from a Hebrew text, it may provide insight into the text at that time. Jerome's commentaries on the Minor Prophets, Isaiah and Jeremiah (A.D. 406-420) are important to the history of Old Testament

Figure 10.8. Genesis 1 in Latin (Paris, thirteenth century), Vulgate version [Orlando, Fla., The Scriptorium, VK MS 649, fol.1']

exegesis, showing how he interpreted the texts later. These commentaries demonstrate that Jerome used a variety of texts according to the reading that best fit his exegesis of the passage. In the New Testament it is more difficult to determine the value of the Latin Vulgate to textual criticism, since the Old Latin texts significantly influenced parts of the translation, especially in the Gospels. In some passages, however, the Greek text underlying the translation may precede the Byzantine text type and thus provide some very early readings of the text.

---

[59] Augustine, who represented a majority of people at the time, claimed that the LXX was inspired (*De Civitate Dei* 18.43), but Jerome questioned its inspiration (*Praefatio in Pentateuchum*, in *Biblia Sacra Iuxta Latinam Vulgatam Versionem*, ed. Francis Aidan Gasquet [Rome: Typis Polyglottis Vaticanis, 1926], 1:67; see also Werner Schwarz, *Principles and Problems of Biblical Translation* [Cambridge: Cambridge University Press, 1955], pp. 26-30).
[60] Metzger, *Bible in Translation*, p. 34.

Further Reading

Primary Sources

Fischer, Bonifatius et al., eds. *Biblia sacra iuxta vulgatam versionem.* 2 vols. Stuttgart: Württembergische Bibelstalt, 1969-1975.

Gasquet, Francis Aidan, ed. *Biblia sacra iuxta latinam vulgatam versionem ad vodicum fidem.* 18 vols. Rome: Typis Polyglottis Vaticanis, 1926-1978.

Other Works

Bogaert, Pierre-Maurice. "Versions, Ancient (Latin)." *ABD* 6:802-3. See bibliography.

Jellicoe, Sidney. *The Septuagint and Modern Study.* Ann Arbor, Mich.: Eisenbrauns, 1978. See esp. pp. 251-56.

Kedar-Kopfstein, Benjamin. "Textual Gleanings from the Vulgate to Jeremiah." *Textus* 7 (1969): 36-58.

———. "The Vulgate as a Translation." Ph.D. diss. Hebrew University, Jerusalem, 1968.

Loewe, Raphael. "The Medieval History of the Latin Vulgate." In *CHB* 2:102-54.

Roberts, Bleddyn J. *The Old Testament Text and Versions.* Cardiff: University of Wales Press, 1951. See pp. 247-65.

Schwarz, Werner. *Principles and Problems of Biblical Translation.* Cambridge: Cambridge University Press, 1955. See pp. 26-30.

Sparks, Hendly D. F. "The Latin Bible." In *The Bible in Its Ancient and English Versions.* Edited by H. Wheeler Robinson. Oxford: Clarendon, 1940. See pp. 110-27.

White, Henry J. "Vulgate." *HDB* 4:873-90.

Würthwein, Ernst. *The Text of the Old Testament: An Introduction to the Biblia Hebraica.* Translated by Erroll F. Rhodes. 2nd ed. Grand Rapids: Eerdmans, 1995. See pp. 95-99.

10.2.3 *The Gothic Version*

The ancient Goths (originally from Scandinavia)[61] migrated south and founded an extensive empire north of the lower Danube and the Black Sea about the third century A.D. (see map 10.1). During the fourth century the empire was split in two, one on each side of the Dniester River—on the east lived the Ostrogoths and on the west the Visigoths. During the sixth century the Ostrogoth kingdom was overthrown, and in time they lost their identity.[62] As early as the third century A.D., Gothic warriors occasionally made raids into the Roman Empire, and it was through Christian priests who were

---

[61]J. Neville Birdsall, "Versions, Ancient (Gothic)," *ABD* 6:803.

[62]Metzger, *Bible in Translation,* p. 38.

captured as prisoners that the Gothic people began to hear about salvation. There was even a Gothic bishop present at the Council of Nicea in A.D. 325.[63] When Rome was sacked by the Goths in A.D. 410, Augustine was relieved that they had already been Christianized or else Rome's fate would have been much worse.

The Gothic version probably originated with Wulfila (or possibly Ulfilas; Gothic for "Little Wolf" [311-381/83]) who began his work by developing a Gothic alphabet (about two-thirds Greek letters, one-third Latin letters, as well as elements of Old German runes [oldest known German alphabet]).[64] Wulfila was born to a Cappadocian captive and a Gothic father,[65] the latter giving him his Gothic name. However, he spent much of his early life in Constantinople, where he was converted to Christianity. He became a bishop in 341 and returned to spend the rest of his life among the Visigoths in missionary endeavors.

Evidence in the Gothic translation of Nehemiah 5—7 suggests that a version of the LXX was followed. (Some think it was the Lucianic text, but this is uncertain). In the New Testament a Byzantine text was used (see figure 10.9). Bruce Metzger notes that Wulfilas was an Arian (or semi-Arian); that is, he denied the eternality of Christ, a heresy condemned at the Council of Nicea in A.D. 325.[66] Wulfila rendered this translation for Christians who had been captured and brought into the Gothic empire during the third century A.D. Wulfila's translation reached Spain and northern Italy in the fifth century, when the Goths took over these areas; and it appears to

Figure 10.9. The ending of the Gospel of Mark in Gothic (Silver Codex) [Domkapitel Speyer]

[63]Birdsall, "Versions, Ancient (Gothic)," 6:803.
[64]Metzger, *Early Versions of the New Testament*, p. 376.
[65]Metzger, *Bible in Translation*, p. 38.
[66]Metzger, *Early Versions of the New Testament*, pp. 376-77.

have become the vernacular Bible for much of Europe.[67] According to Philostorgius, Wulfila left out Samuel and Kings when translating the Old Testament because he felt its war stories would encourage the warring Goths to continue to fight.[68] It is unknown whether Wulfila finished translating the entire Bible; only a few fragmentary pieces of the Gothic Old Testament have been preserved (i.e., references to single words or numbers in Gen 5:3-30 and Ps 52:2-3; portions of Neh 5—7), and the Gothic language is now extinct.[69] The importance of this version for Old Testament textual criticism is minimal since so little remains (about fifty-five verses). This version's primary importance to textual criticism is the light it sheds on the LXX text. There is significantly more of the New Testament that is extant (about half the Gospels and portions of the Pauline Epistles); its very literal reading of the Byzantine text from which it was translated

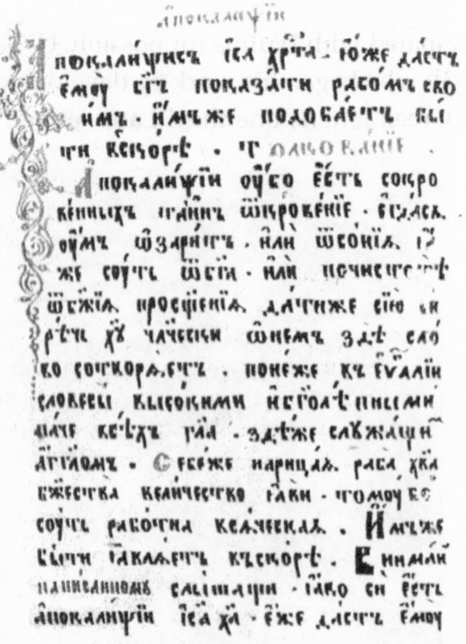

Figure 10.10. Revelation 1 in Old Slavonic (Russia, eighteenth century) [Orlando, Fla., The Scriptorium, VK MS 126, fol.1ᵛ]

has more value to New Testament textual criticism. However, its numerous Coptic readings indicate either that it was edited against a Coptic manuscript or that the Greek text used was already corrupted by Coptic translations. Wulfila translated almost word for word, even to the point of retaining the Greek order over against common Gothic idiom; the result would have been almost unintelligible to those who could not refer to the original Greek manuscripts.[70] One of the most complete manuscripts of the Gothic version is a deluxe copy of the Gospels written in silver letters on purple vellum from the sixth century A.D. It contains the complete text of Mark 16.

---

[67]Ibid., p. 377.

[68]Henry B. Swete, *An Introduction to the Old Testament in Greek* (Cambridge: Cambridge University Press, 1902), p. 117.

[69]Metzger, *Bible in Translation*, p. 39.

[70]Vööbus, "Versions," 4:982.

Further Reading

Primary Sources

Gabelentz, Hans C., and Julius Loebe. *Ulfilas: Vetus et Noues Testamenti . . . fragmenta*. Lipsiae: F. A. Brockhaus, 1843.

Other Works

Birdsall, J. Neville. "Versions, Ancient (Gothic)." *ABD* 6:803-5. See bibliography.

Jellicoe, Sidney. *The Septuagint and Modern Study*. Ann Arbor, Mich.: Eisenbrauns, 1978. See esp. pp. 258-59.

Roberts, Bleddyn J. *The Old Testament Text and Versions*. Cardiff: University of Wales Press, 1951. See p. 236.

Swete, Henry B. *An Introduction to the Old Testament in Greek*. Edited by Richard R. Ottley. Rev. ed. New York: KTAV, 1968. See esp. pp. 117-18.

10.2.4 The Old Slavonic Version

During the mid-first millennium A.D., Eastern Europe had only one Slavonic language from which all the modern dialects derive (see map 10.1). Very little is known about the early history of the Christian church in Eastern Europe, but by the ninth century Rostislav, a Moravian prince, sent a letter to Michael III, "The Drunkard" (842-867), the eastern emperor, asking for missionaries to be sent to teach his people. The emperor conceded and sent two brothers, Methodius (815-885) and Constantine (826/27-869), to evangelize this area. They later became known as the "Apostles to the Slavs." The two brothers grew up in Thessalonica, which had a large Slavic population, and thus were almost native speakers. Constantine was well educated, having completed his education at the University of Constantinople and eventually received a teaching position there in philosophy and theology. But about 863 he accompanied his brother to Moravia and began immediately to train Moravians for the clergy. Very soon afterward he devised an alphabet (Glagolitic) and began translating the Greek Scriptures into Slavonic, as well as preaching in the same language. A controversy arose over which language the church liturgy was to be sung in: Greek, Latin or Slavic. Two popes finally gave permission to use Slavic, as long as it was first read in Latin. In 864 the Byzantines evangelized the Bulgars. The Bulgars and the Slavs, now linked by both language and religion, developed Slav writing.[71] When Constantine died in 869 only the Psalms were completed from the Old Testament[72] and possibly the Gospels and Acts from the New Tes-

---

[71]Frédéric Delouche, ed., *Illustrated History of Europe* (London: Weidenfelf & Nicolson, 1992), p. 107.

[72]Jellicoe, *Septuagint and Modern Study*, p. 262.

tament.[73] Methodius and some of his helpers finished the work by the end of the ninth century, but little of the text remains except for fragments embedded in the present Slavonic Bible.[74]

There are no extant manuscripts from this earlier period, and those from the tenth or eleventh centuries (Codex Zographensis, Codex Marianus, Ostromir lectionary) display dialectical variations of the script and language (see figure 10.10). Constantine and Methodius are said to have translated the Gospels and Acts from Greek manuscripts. After Constantine's death, priests helped Methodius translate the rest of the Bible from Greek to Slavonic, omitting only the books of Maccabees. According to the *Vita Methodii (The Life of Methodius)* the translation of the rest of the Bible into Slavonic took only eight months in 884,[75] but none of it survived.

The late date of the Old Slavonic version (ninth century A.D.) means that it has little value in determining the earliest form of the text. This version is a tertiary translation and is of more help in determining the LXX text than the Hebrew. It was probably translated from a Greek text in the Byzantine text family, however it also has a significant number of earlier readings of the Western and the so-called Caesarean type.[76] This translation is of more value relative to the history of interpretation and the transmission of the text in its later stages.

Further Reading

Bebb, Llewellyn. "Versions (Georgian, Gothic, Slavonic)." *HDB* 4:861-64.

Jellicoe, Sidney. *The Septuagint and Modern Study.* Ann Arbor, Mich.: Eisenbrauns, 1978. See esp. pp. 262-63.

Roberts, Bleddyn J. *The Old Testament Text and Versions.* Cardiff: University of Wales Press, 1951. See p. 236.

Swete, Henry B. *An Introduction to the Old Testament in Greek.* Edited by Richard R. Ottley. Rev. ed. New York: KTAV, 1968. See esp. pp. 120-21.

For further discussion on the topic of ancient versions and their importance for textual criticism see the following works:

Aland, Kurt, and Barbara Aland. *The Text of the New Testament. An Introduction to the Critical Editions and to the Theory and Practice of Modern Textual Criticism.* Translated by Erroll F. Rhodes. Grand Rapids: Eerdmans, 1987. See pp. 185-221.

---

[73]Metzger, *Early Versions of the New Testament*, p. 403.
[74]Swete, *Introduction to the Old Testament*, p. 121; Jellicoe, *Septuagint and Modern Study*, p. 262.
[75]Metzger, *Early Versions of the New Testament*, p. 402.
[76]Metzger, *Text of the New Testament*, p. 85.

Bruce, F. F. *The Books and the Parchments.* 5th ed. London: Marshall Pickering, 1991. See pp. 181-209.

Jellicoe, Sidney. *The Septuagint and Modern Study.* Ann Arbor, Mich.: Eisenbrauns, 1978.

Metzger, Bruce M. *The Early Versions of the New Testament. Their Origin, Transmission, and Limitations.* Oxford: Clarendon, 1977.

———. *The Text of the New Testament: Its Transmission, Corruption, and Restoration.* 3rd ed. New York: Oxford University Press, 1992. See p. 85.

Roberts, Bleddyn J. *The Old Testament Text and Versions: The Hebrew Text in Transmission and the History of Ancient Versions.* Cardiff: University of Wales Press, 1951.

Swete, Henry B. *An Introduction to the Old Testament in Greek.* Cambridge: Cambridge University Press, 1902.

Vööbus, Arthur. "Versions." *ISBE* 4:969-83.

Würthwein, Ernst. *The Text of the Old Testament: An Introduction to the Biblia Hebraica.* Translated by Erroll F. Rhodes. 2nd ed. Grand Rapids: Eerdmans, 1995.

Conclusion

In one of my first job interviews right after graduate studies, I was asked if I believed Acts 7:14 to be incorrect in stating that there were seventy-five people who went down to Egypt with Jacob (since it appears to differ from Genesis 46:27, which says there were seventy in all). At that point I did not even know how or where to begin to answer the question, but it launched me on a journey to find answers to this and other questions of this type. If we believe that the Bible is authoritative and provides guidance for our lives, then we need to be sure of what the text says. Textual criticism is therefore crucial.

Are the modern translations an accurate reflection of the original manuscripts? Is Mark 16:9-20 really part of the New Testament canon, or was it added later? And if it was added later, was it divinely inspired and trustworthy material? Is the biblical text accurate and reliable, or has it been so corrupted in the copying process that we cannot really know with certainty what God has said? Textual criticism may not fully answer every question, but a good working knowledge of text-critical principles can help us begin. Textual criticism provides the evidence necessary to compare the many and comparatively recently discovered fragments and manuscripts to determine the most reliable reading of a text.

It is important to keep in perspective the fact that only a very small part of the text is in question—approximately 10 percent of the Old Testament and 7 percent of the New Testament. Of these, most variants make little difference to the meaning of any passage, as Douglas Stuart explains:

> It is fair to say that the verses, chapters, and books of the Bible would read largely the same, and would leave the same impressions with the reader, even if one adopted virtually every possible *alternative reading* to those now serving as the basis for current English translations.[1]

---

[1]Douglas Stuart, "Inerrancy and Textual Criticism," in *Inerrancy and Common Sense*, ed. Roger R. Nicole and J. Ramsey Michaels (Grand Rapids: Baker, 1980), p. 98. See also Shemaryahu Talmon, who says: "The scope of variation within all these textual traditions is relatively restricted. Major divergences which intrinsically affect the sense are extremely rare. A collation of variants extant, based on the synoptic study of the material available, either by a comparison of parallel passages within one Version, or of the major Versions with each other, results in the conclusion that the ancient authors, compilers, tridents and scribes enjoyed what may be termed a controlled freedom of textual variation" ("The Textual Study of the Bible—A New Outlook," in *Qumran and the History of the Biblical Text*, ed. Frank M. Cross and Shemaryahu Talmon [Cambridge, Mass.: Harvard University Press, 1975], p. 326).

This does not diminish the importance of textual criticism, for there are some variants that do change the meaning significantly. The overriding purpose for textual criticism is broader than this. It seeks to determine as accurately as possible the authoritative, final form of the biblical text, including the relatively few places where the text is in question.

At the end of the textual critical process, there is still some level of uncertainty given that the oldest, extant witnesses of the Old Testament are the Silver Amulets (c. seventh century B.C.) and certain Qumran texts (c. fourth to third century B.C.) and of the New Testament are $\mathfrak{P}^{52}$, $\mathfrak{P}^{46}$ (second century A.D.) and $\mathfrak{P}^{66}$, $\mathfrak{P}^{75}$ (third century A.D.). But what happened before our extant evidence?

1 Old Testament

Evidence for the Old Testament text seems to suggest that there was a "uniformity even among the plurality." That is to say, the scribes retained and protected the final form of the authoritative texts even though there are other forms like the LXX, SP and others that have been modified or refined from their received texts.

Tov argued for multiple authoritative texts of the Old Testament mainly because the parallel passages seem to demonstrate significant differences between them. But the evidence does not necessarily demand multiple authoritative forms of the biblical texts. The clearest example of one Old Testament text copying another is Jeremiah 26:18, which actually states that Jeremiah is quoting from Micah 3:12. Both are very similar, the only difference being the spelling for Jerusalem (וִירוּשָׁלַ‍ִם in Micah; וִירוּשָׁלַיִם in Jeremiah) which is interesting since neither of the books spell Jerusalem with the plene spelling elsewhere. Differences in the other parallel passages could reflect the author's intention to provide a rough paraphrase or to simplify or condense the narrative (see for example, the LXX text of Job or Jeremiah). There is not enough evidence to argue that there were several authoritative editions of the biblical texts in existence.

What appears more likely is that an authoritative text that varied very little (proto-MT) was maintained by the scribes, then at some point other copies were made that either differed significantly from this main text (e.g., the LXX of Jeremiah or Job) or differed little at the onset but in time departed further and further from it (e.g., proto-Theodotion, Syriac Peshitta). Following the Babylonian exile it would not have been easy to continue to maintain control over and consistency of all the copies of the Old Testament. Because of this, multiple text forms existed by the time of the Dead Sea Scrolls. Sometime during the first century, the proto-MT became the authoritative text, and deviations were not tolerated by the Jews who maintained it. It is not clear exactly how or why this happened, but the extant Hebrew manuscripts following the turn of the century clearly demonstrate a unified proto-MT. This text was then maintained by the scribes and Masoretes very accurately for over a thousand years.

2 New Testament

The New Testament transmissional process was different because there was relatively little time between the original documents and the extant copies. In a letter to the Corinthians (c. 95), Clement of Rome says, "Take up the epistle of the blessed Paul the Apostle," implying that they had in their possession an authoritative letter from Paul.[2] Polycarp, bishop of Smyrna (c. 70-160), said to the church at Philippi that Paul had written to them "letters," implying that they were aware of several biblical books.[3] The first mention of a "written" Gospel is found in the Didache (c. 100), which quotes the Lord's Prayer (Mt 6:9-11) and then exhorts Christ's followers: "And do not pray as the hypocrites, but as the Lord commanded in his Gospel."[4] At about the same time Ignatius, bishop of Antioch, states: "For I heard some men saying, 'if I find it not in the chapters of the Gospel I do not believe,' "[5] which indicates that the early Church knew of at least one authoritative Gospel. All of these quotes and many more indicate that the early church honored and revered their sacred writings and thus would have a desire to maintain them. Even though the many copies of the New Testament indicate that at least initially they were not copied by meticulous, trained scribes, the large number of manuscripts are an advantage when attempting to work back to the originals.

3 The State of Affairs Today

Since the nineteenth century when the historical-critical method came into full bloom, the accuracy of the Bible has come under constant attack. Manuscripts or fragments of manuscripts that have been discovered in the last 150 to 200 years (e.g., the Dead Sea Scrolls, the Cairo Genizah manuscripts, Codex Sinaiticus) can help answer questions regarding the accuracy of the Bible so that we can have a renewed confidence that the biblical text we have today is indeed accurate. But textual criticism cannot answer such questions as, Did the events of the Bible actually take place? Did Moses lead Israel out of Egypt and write the Pentateuch? Did the walls of Jericho fall down in Joshua's day? These are historical questions as well as questions of faith. But to begin to answer

---

[2]Clement 1 Clement 47.1, in The Apostolic Fathers with an English Translation, ed. Kirsopp Lake, LCL (Cambridge, Mass.: Harvard University Press, 1976-77), 1:88-89.
[3]Polycarp Philippians 3.2.
[4]Didache, in Lake, Apostolic Fathers, 1:32-21.
[5]Ignatius Philadelphians 8.2, in Lake, Apostolic Fathers, 1:246-47.

those questions we must first establish the reliability of the text.

It is humbling and reassuring to realize that the Old and New Testaments have been handed down through many generations as accurately and as completely as they have. Many scribes and copyists spent countless hours copying and checking their work to ensure an accurate text for later generations. All of this effort was expended because they realized just how important the Word of God is and how crucial it is to maintain an accurate record of God's revelation. Early copyists and scribes would no doubt be surprised to know that scholars in our time would uncover some of the very manuscripts they had written. But in fact, texts up to two thousand years old have been discovered. Careful examination of these manuscripts has served to strengthen our assurance that our modern Greek and Hebrew critical texts are very close to the original autographs, even though we do not have those autographs.

There is no better way to end this look at textual criticism than as we began, with the quote from Sir Frederic G. Kenyon:

> It is reassuring at the end to find that the general result of all these discoveries and all this study is to strengthen the proof of the authenticity of the Scriptures, and our conviction that we have in our hands, in substantial integrity, the veritable Word of God.[6]

---

[6]Frederic G. Kenyon, *The Story of the Bible,* 2nd ed. (Grand Rapids: Eerdmans, 1967), p. 113.

Glossary

The following definitions assume the usage of the terms within the context of biblical textual criticism.

afformative. A letter or combination of letters attached to the end of the main stem of a word.

Alexandrian family. Greek manuscripts thought to be from the region of Alexandria, Egypt.

alphabetic acrostic. A literary structure wherein each successive line begins with the next letter of the alphabet.

amulet. A charm, often inscribed with a magical incantation or symbol, to protect the wearer.

ancient translations. Translations of the biblical texts dating back to the pre-Christian and early Christian eras (e.g., LXX, Syriac Peshitta, Latin Vulgate).

aphaeresis. Absence or loss of a letter in a word.

Apocrypha. Those books (e.g., 1 Maccabees, Sirach, Tobit) regarded by some Christians as part of sacred Scripture but not found in the canon of the Hebrew Bible.

appendix. Supplemental information usually included at the end of a book.

archetype. An original manuscript of which further copies were made.

asterisk (※). Symbol used by Origen in the Hexapla to indicate whether a specific word or phrase was lacking in the Hebrew text.

author's deviation. The measure of how consistently a writer uses specific words, verb forms or other orthographic characteristics. Where an author is not consistent, the author is said to deviate from the norm.

autographs. Original manuscripts.

Bar Kochba Revolt. A Jewish revolt against the Romans led by Bar Kochba (lit. "son of the star") in A.D. 132-135.

Ben Asher. A family that played a leading role in recording and maintaining the Masoretic Text.

Ben Naphtali. A family that played a lesser role (than Ben Asher) in recording and maintaining the Masoretic Text.

bilingual. Expressed or written in two languages.

Byzantine family. Greek manuscripts thought to be derived from the region of Byzantium, the seat of the Eastern Church from the fourth century onward.

calligrapher. One who specializes in writing with pen and ink.

canon. A religious tradition's authoritative collection of books of the Bible.

chiasm. A literary structure with inverted parallel lines. In a chiastic four-line structure, the beginning and end lines and the middle two lines are parallel [a b b' a' pattern].

circulus. A small circle placed above a word in the Masoretic Text to indicate a related note in the *Masorah parva* ("little masorah") at the side of the page.

codex. A manuscript bound in book form.

colophon. A note at the end of a manuscript, usually presenting facts relating to its production.

compilation. A collection of writings.

conflated readings. Two readings that have been combined.

conjectural emendation/reading. An attempt to reconstruct the original form of a particular detail in a biblical text, usually occasioned by something missing from the extant textual witnesses or by a difficulty in the extant readings.

copyist. One who copies a manuscript.

correction/change. The conscious effort on the part of a copyist to change the text in minor or major details.

corruption. A departure from the original text due to a copyist's mistake or alteration.

critical edition. A published edition of a biblical text accompanied by a textual apparatus that allows comparison of details in the text with other textual witnesses. Usually a distinction is made between diplomatic and eclectic editions.

cursive. Manuscripts written in cursive handwriting (similar to small letter script in English).

daghesh. A dot in the middle of a Hebrew letter.

Dead Sea Scrolls. Manuscripts found at Qumran, on the western shore of the Dead Sea.

Decalogue. The Ten Commandments (lit. "ten words").

defective writing. Hebrew written without *matres lectionis*.

dialect. A regional variety of a particular language with distinct differences from the standard language.

diplomatic edition. A modern edition of a biblical text faithfully representing an early, known manuscript; in contrast with an eclectic edition, which is a compilation of the best readings from all known texts. A diplomatic edition generally includes an apparatus with variant readings.

dittography. A letter or word that has been mistakenly written twice.

Ebionites. An early Jewish Christian sect considered heretical by the early Christian fathers for, among other things, their particular adherence to Jewish law and their defective Christology, which apparently denied the preexistence of Christ.

eclectic edition. An edition of the biblical text that attempts to reconstruct the original text by combining the best readings from all known sources into one text. An eclectic edition generally also provides a critical apparatus of variants, often with editorial evaluation.

ellipsis. A missing word or phrase in a text or the three consecutive dots (. . .) used in a modern edition to indicate the omission.

emendation. A change suggested by the editors of a biblical text but not having textual support.

encyclical letter. A letter intended to be circulated among a group of churches.

euphemistic change. The substitution of a milder term for an unpleasant or offensive one.

external evidence. Evidence concerning a variant from other manuscripts or versions.

facsimile. An exact reproduction of a manuscript.

final Masorah. A collection or summary of information about the Hebrew text (i.e., how many verses are in the book, the location of its midpoint).

fission. One word that has incorrectly been separated into two.

folio. A folded sheet of paper yielding two pages in a book.

fusion. Incorrect word division that results in two words being joined into one.

genizah. A storage room in a synagogue, particularly for keeping worn and retired sacred manuscripts.

gloss. An explanatory note added to a text.

Gnosticism. A heretical teaching that emphasized that matter is evil and that special knowledge *(gnōsis)* is given only to particular people.

Haggadah. Rabbinic statements that illustrate the Hebrew Scriptures.

hapax legomenon. A word that occurs only once within the Old Testament or New Testament.

haplography. The omission of a letter or word, usually due to a similar letter or word in the context.

harmonization. Modification of a passage to make it agree with another.

harmony of the Gospels. A work that weaves all four Gospels into one continuous narrative.

Hellenism. Greek influences.

hermeneutics. The philosophy of interpreting texts, or the rules or principles used to interpret Scripture.

Hexapla. A six-column work compiled by Origen (about A.D. 230-245) and arranged so that the Hebrew text could be compared to the Greek texts known at that time.

homoioarkton. A copyist's omission caused by two words or phrases that begin similarly.

homoioteleuton. A copyist's omission caused by two phrases that end similarly.

homophony. The substitution of a word for a similar sounding word.

insertion. A word or phrase inserted into a passage.

interdependence. Texts that are related to one another.

interlinear. A translation (often literal) that lines up the translation under each word or phrase of the biblical text, or between the lines.

internal evidence. Evidence relevant to a text-critical judgment that is derived from within the text in question.

intrusion. A text that has elements of another text inserted into it.

ipsissima verba. The "actual words" (of a writer or prophet, etc.).

Karaites. A Jewish sect originating in the eighth century A.D. that denied talmudic-rabbinical tradition.

Kethib, Qere. For questionable readings of the Hebrew Bible, scribes used a *Kethib* ("that which is written") notation to designate the actual reading of the text and a *Qere* ("that which is to be read") notation to signify what the scribes believed to be the proper reading.

lacuna (pl. lacunae). A hole or gap in a manuscript.

leaf. A page (usually a folio) from a book that may be written on both front and back.

lectionary. A book or list of specific biblical passages to be read on particular dates in the church's calendar.

lemma (pl. lemmata). The biblical text (word, phrase, verse) quoted and referenced in a text-critical notation, a biblical commentary, concordance or a lexicon.

linguistics. The academic discipline of studying language.

liturgical. Pertaining to the liturgy (rites prescribed for public worship) of the church.

majority text. Using the majority of extant Greek manuscripts to determine the correct reading of the Greek text.

majuscule (uncial). A Greek manuscript (from the fourth century B.C. on) written in capital letters, or uncials.

manuscript. A handwritten text.

marginal Masorah. Notes written within the side margins of the Hebrew Bible discussing textual traditions in the biblical text.

Masada. A large flat-topped mountain along the southwestern shore of the Dead Sea where Herod built a fortress/palace. Jewish zealots took over this site in a battle with the Romans in A.D. 70.

Masorah. Literally "tradition," referring to a body of notes on the textual traditions of the Hebrew Old Testament compiled by scribes during the first millennium A.D.

Masorah magna. Textual traditions too lengthy to appear in the Hebrew Old Testament's margins and collected instead in a Masoretic handbook.

Masorah parva. Scribal notes (mainly orthographic notations) along the outside margin of the text of the Hebrew Old Testament.

Masoretes. A group of Jewish scribes from about A.D. 500 to 1000 who systematically protected the Hebrew Bible from textual corruption.

Masoretic handbook. A book with lengthier scribal textual notes than could be recorded in the margins of the Hebrew Bible.

Masoretic Text (𝔐, MT). Sometimes called the "received text," strictly speaking it is a medieval representative of a group of ancient texts of the Bible that at an early stage was accepted as the sole text by a central stream in Judaism. Earlier forms of the text type are named proto-Masoretic. In the first century A.D. the proto-Masoretic text was unified and became the standard Hebrew text.

matres lectionis. Latin for "mothers of reading"; refers to the consonants that represent certain vowel sounds that were added to the Hebrew text to aid in pronunciation before the development of vowel points.

Megilloth. The five scrolls (Esther, Song of Solomon, Ruth, Lamentations and Ecclesiastes) that were read on Jewish holidays.

metathesis. The reversal in order of two letters or words.

metobelus (/., /., /) **(pl. metobeli).** Symbol(s) in the Hexapla used by Origen to indicate whether a specific word or phrase was in the Hebrew text.

midrash. Jewish exegesis, or commentary, on Scripture.

minuscule. A manuscript written in cursive letters.

monograph. A scholarly publication on a single, well defined topic.

monophysitism. The view that Christ had only one nature—a divine one—not a human nature, even though he had a human body.

morphology. The study of the patterns of word formation in a particular language, including inflection, derivation and composition. For example, Qumran morphology includes the study of the lengthening of endings, such as independent pronouns, pronominal suffixes, second-person plurals and adverbial endings.

movable print/type. The raised letters arranged in a printing press that could be taken out and reassembled to print another page.

Naḥal Ḥever. A wadi, or dry river bed, flowing toward the Dead Sea and dotted with caves, a few of which yielded manuscripts.

obelus (—, ⸗, ÷) **(pl. obeli).** Symbol(s) in the Hexapla used by Origen to indicate whether a specific word or phrase was in the Hebrew text.

original text. The completed literary composition (commonly known as the "final form of the text") that was accepted as authoritative by the scribes.

orthography. The study of the rules and conventions of spelling. For example, Qumran orthography includes many *matres lectionis* to facilitate the reading.

ostracon. A piece of broken pottery used as writing material, much like scrap paper today.

paleo. Means "old" or "ancient."

paleo-Hebrew script. The script of Hebrew manuscripts preceding the Assyrian (square) script.

paleography. The study of ancient writing.

palimpsest. A manuscript that has been reused after earlier writing has been erased or scraped off.

papyrus (pl. papyri). Writing material made from reeds of a papyrus plant or the manuscripts written on this material.

parablepsis. "Faulty seeing" or oversight resulting in scribal error.

paraphrase. A loose translation conveying the main meaning of a text; not a literal word-for-word translation.

parchment. Writing material made from calf, goat or sheep skin.

pesher. Jewish method of interpreting Scripture by applying a biblical text directly to a current situation.

philology. The study of language, including grammar, orthography and paleography.

phylactery. Small boxes containing Scripture portions and worn by Jews on the forehead and the back of the hands. The Scripture portions themselves.

plene writing ([lit.] "full writing"). A word in which the *matres lectionis* are written.

polyglot Bible. A Bible that has several (usually ancient) versions arranged side by side in columns.

potsherd. A piece of broken pottery, occasionally used as writing material.

primary translation. A translation made directly from the Greek (New Testament) or Hebrew (Old Testament) texts.

proselyte. A convert to a religion.

provenance. The place of origin of a manuscript.

pseudepigrapha. Jewish writings from the period 200 B.C. to A.D. 200 falsely ascribed to biblical characters.

qere. A marginal note indicating a correction to the Masoretic Text.

qere perpetuum. A word that is always corrected even though marginal notes only sometimes call attention to it.

Quinta. Origen's fifth column in the Hexapla.

Qumran. An archaeological site located on the northwest side of the Dead Sea and the area where the Dead Sea Scrolls were found.

Rabbinic Bible. A copy of the Old Testament made by rabbis that generally includes masorahs, Targums and Jewish commentaries.

reading. A variant of a text.

reasoned eclecticism. The approach to textual criticism that uses a balance of internal and external evidence to determine the most plausible original reading of a text.

recension. An editorial revision of a literary work that by definition should show a conscious effort to change an earlier text systematically in a certain direction. Such characteristics include expansionistic, abbreviating, harmonizing, Judaizing or Christianizing tendencies. Some scholars argue that the Masoretic Text, Septuagint and Samaritan Pentateuch represent recensions that had reached their present form after various stages of editing and textual manipulation.

rigorous eclecticism. The approach to textual criticism that relies exclusively on internal evidence to determine the most plausible original reading of a text.

sacrosanct. To be so sacred as to be inviolable.

Samaritan Pentateuch (SP, ๗). An ancient text of the Torah written in a special form of early Hebrew script and preserved by the Samaritan community. Its basis was a Jewish text, to which the Samaritans added a thin layer of ideological and phonological changes.

Samaritans. The people who lived in Samaria, or the area of the northern kingdom of Israel, after its defeat in 722 B.C.

scribal notations. Any of the notes or aids that scribes added to the text (e.g., vowel points, accents).

scriptio continua. Continuous writing with no breaks between words.

secondary translation. A translation made from a translation of the Greek (New Testament) or Hebrew (Old Testament) text. Thus a translation of a translation.

sectarian. Relating to or characteristic of a sect.

semantics. The study of the meaning of words.

siglum (pl. sigla). Designations or symbols for specific biblical manuscripts.

sôp pasûq. Symbol signifying the end of a verse.

square script (or Assyrian script). Hebrew script in which most of the consonants have a square-like shape.

stabilize. Having to do with the standardization of the Hebrew text.

standard deviation. The degree to which an author diverges from consistently translating a specific Hebrew or Greek word into another language in the ancient versions.

standardize. To remove any variations from a text.

supralinear. Written above the line.

syntax. The way in which words are put together to form phrases, clauses or sentences.

targum (pl. targumim or targums). Aramaic translations or paraphrases of Old Testament books (lit. "interpretation").

tertiary translation. A translation of a secondary translation (or a translation of a translation of a translation).

text critic. A person who examines the variations between biblical manuscripts and versions in order to determine the most plausible original reading of a text.

texts from the Judean Desert. A broad term for Hebrew, Aramaic and Greek texts (biblical and nonbiblical) that were copied or composed between the mid-third century B.C. and A.D. 135, and discovered in the Judean Desert between 1947 and 1956. The Dead Sea Scrolls are among these texts.

textual apparatus/notes. A feature of a critical edition consisting of a collection of readings, or variants, from manuscripts or ancient versions that deviate from a central text. These variants are correlated with the text by means of a notation system.

textual criticism. The process of evaluating variations between biblical manuscripts and versions in order to determine the most plausible original reading of a text.

textual family. A group of manuscripts that are related in that they are copies from the same or similar manuscripts.

textual variant (see variant reading). The details of which texts are composed (letters, words) are "readings" and, accordingly, all readings that differ from the accepted text as central are usually called variant readings, or variants. The term is not evaluative but refers to the existence of a deviation between the accepted text and another text.

textual witness. The various sources that represent different forms of the biblical text. For the Old Testament these include the Masoretic Text, the Hebrew *Vorlage* of the Septuagint, the Samaritan Pentateuch, the texts from the Judean Desert, biblical quotations in ancient texts and other miscellaneous sources.

textus receptus. Literally "received text," a standardized form of the biblical text that has come down through the transmission process.

Tosefta. Explanatory material that was added to some copies of the Mishnah.

transmission. The process by which a text was "transmitted" over the years by repeated copying.

uncial. Uppercase, or majuscule, letter or a manuscript written in these letters.

unpointed. Hebrew writing that lacks vowel points.

Urtext. Original text.

variant reading. Any difference between two or more manuscripts of the same text.

vellum. Fine-grained writing material made of calfskin, lambskin or kidskin.

vernacular. The common language of a region or country.

version. An ancient translation of the Bible or a portion of the Bible.

Vorlage. The manuscript from which a scribe copied a text.

vowel point. A symbol representing a vowel sound that appears above or below a Hebrew consonant. These were not added to the Hebrew Bible until the period A.D. 500 to 900.

Wadi Murabbaʿat. A steep ravine with a river bed flowing from the Judean Desert to the Dead Sea. Some caves in this ravine were found to contain manuscripts.

Western family. Greek New Testament manuscripts believed to derive from the Western region of the church.

Western readings. Readings that follow the Western family of texts.

zealots. A Jewish revolutionary movement of the first century A.D.

Zoroastrianism. A Persian religion founded in the sixth century B.C. and characterized by the worship of a supreme god Ahura Mazda.

Permissions

Figures

E1.1   The *Biblia Hebraica Stuttgartensia* (1967-77, 1983). Courtesy of the American Bible Society

E1.2   Cover page from Codex Leningradensis. Courtesy of the National Library of Russia

E1.3   Marginal Parva. Courtesy of the American Bible Society

E1.4   Masorah Magna. Courtesy of the American Bible Society

E1.5   The Hebrew University Bible Project. Courtesy of Magnes Press

E1.6   *Biblia Hebraica Stuttgartensia*'s textual apparatus. Courtesy of the American Bible Society

E1.7   *Biblia Hebraica Quinta*, Ruth 1:19. Courtesy of the American Bible Society

6.1   The larger silver amulet. Courtesy of the Israel Antiquities Authority

6.2   Isaiah 39—40 from the first Isaiah Scroll (1QIsaᵃ). Courtesy of John C. Trever

6.3   A section of a page from the Habakkuk Commentary. Courtesy of John C. Trever

6.4   The Nash Papyrus containing Exodus 20:2-17. By permission of the Syndics of Cambridge University Library

6.5   The Murabba'at caves. Courtesy of the Israel Antiquities Authority

6.6   A fragment of the Minor Prophets (Mur 88). Courtesy of the Israel Antiquities Authority

6.7   Photographs of Masada. Courtesy of Galilee College

6.8   Masada fragment. Courtesy of the Israel Antiquities Authority

6.9   Naḥal Ḥever fragment. Courtesy of the Israel Antiquities Authority

6.10   Solomon Schechter. By permission by the Syndics of Cambridge University Library

6.11   A page from Codex Leningradensis (Genesis 28:18—29:22). Courtesy of the National Library of Russia

6.12   A page of Genesis 21:33b—22:4a from the second Rabbinic Bible of Jacob ben Ḥayyim. Courtesy of the Bodleian Library, University of Oxford *'Genesis' page 77, from the Rabbinic Bible, volume 1. Reference (shelfmark P. 1.8. Art Seld.)*

6.13   The London Polyglot. Paul D. Wegner

6.14   *Variae lectiones Verteris Testamenti.* Courtesy of the McCormick Library, University of Chicago

6.15   The Samaritan Pentateuch. A portion of Deuteronomy 28:1ff. from the Samaritan Pentateuch (Nablus?, 13ᵗʰ c.) Orlando, Flor., The Scriptorium VK MS 540

6.16   John 21:1b-25 from Codex Sinaiticus. By permission of the British Library

6.17   Constantin von Tischendorf. Courtesy of the Family of Constantin von Tischendorf

7.1 Jerome. Kunsthistorisches Museum, Vienna, Austria/Erich Lessing/ Art Resource, NY

7.2 Erasmus. Galleria Nazionale, Parma, Italy/Scala/Art Resource, NY

7.3 Brian Walton. Paul D. Wegner

7.4 Brooke F. Westcott. Paul D. Wegner

7.5 Fenton J. A. Hort. Paul D. Wegner

E2.1 *The Greek New Testament.* Courtesy of the American Bible Society

E2.2 *Novum Testamentum Graece.* Courtesy of the American Bible Society

E2.3 A correction in Codex Sinaiticus. By permission of the British Library

9.1 $\mathfrak{P}^{46}$, from the Chester Beatty Papyrus (II). P.Mich.Inv. 6238, Special Collections Library, University of Michigan

9.2 $\mathfrak{P}^{52}$. Reproduced by courtesy of the University Librarian and Director, John Rylands University Library of Manchester, University of Manchester

9.3 $\mathfrak{P}^{75}$, from the Bodmer Collection (PB XIV, XV). Courtesy of the Foundation Martin Bodmer Bibliothèque et Musée

9.4 Codex Vaticanus. Courtesy of the Biblioteca Apostolica Vaticana

9.5 John 21 from Codex Sinaiticus. By permission of the British Library

9.6 The end of Luke from Codex Alexandrinus. By permission of the British Library

9.7 A page from Codex Bezae. By permission of the Syndics of Cambridge University Library

9.8 Minuscule 33. Courtesy of the Bibliothèque nationale de France © BnF

10.1 Psalm 51 in Syriac. Orlando, Flor., The Scriptorium. VK MS 631, fol.1^r.

10.2 Progression of Egyptian writing. By permission of the British Museum/HIP/Art Resource, NY

10.3 A page from the book of Jeremiah in Coptic. Orlando, Flor., The Scriptorium. VK MS 783, fols. 92^v - 93^r

10.4 Matthew 1 in Armenian. Orlando, Flor., The Scriptorium. VK MS 781, fol.9^r

10.5 Gospels in Ethiopic. Orlando, Flor., The Scriptorium. VK MS 205

10.6 The New Testament in Georgian. Orlando, Flor., The Scriptorium. VK MS 459, fol.15^r

10.7 A fourth- or fifth-century A.D. Old Latin manuscript. Courtesy of the National Library of Turin

10.8 Genesis 1 in Latin. Orlando, Flor., The Scriptorium. VK MS 649, fol.1^r

10.9 The ending of the Gospel of Mark in Gothic. Courtesy of Domkapitel Speyer

10.10 Revelation 1 in Old Slavanic. Orlando, Flor., The Scriptorium. VK MS 126, fol.1^r

Names Index

Subject Index

abbreviations, 7, 13, 50, 116, 118. *See also* textual phenomena, abbreviations

Abisha ʿ scroll, 169, 171

accent(s)/accentuation, 77, 98-99, 106, 110, 112-13, 116, 122, 158-59, 161-62, 164, 183-84, 234, 308

accuracy, 19, 20, 39, 63, 71, 78-79, 96, 106-7, 129, 133, 207, 219, 235-36, 241, 243-44, 254, 300

additions. *See* textual phenomena, additions

Africanus, Sextus Julius, 95, 192-93, 196, 233

Alexandria, 237, 244, 262, 276, 302

Alexandrian family, 250, 252-53, 302

Aleppo Codex. *See* Bible, Hebrew Bible, manuscripts, Aleppo Codex

ancient versions/translations, 43-44, 61-62, 64-65, 66, 69-70, 74, 76-78, 84-85, 90, 92-93, 97, 112-13, 121-22, 126-28, 130, 133, 135, 142, 147, 151, 165, 167, 169, 176, 179, 181, 187, 198, 208, 212-15, 231, 238, 261, 265, 267, 269, 271-98, 306-9

  background, 19, 129, 254, 271

  concordances, 130, 167-68

  corruptions. *See* textual phenomena, corrupt/corruptions

  definition, 302

  free translation, 186, 271

  importance for biblical research, 19, 20, 30, 32, 34-35

  literal translations, 288

  reconstructing the Hebrew *Vorlage*. *See Vorlage; see also* Septuagint, Hebrew source

Antioch, 197, 199, 215, 271, 300

Antwerp Polygot. *See* editions, polyglot, Antwerp

Apocrypha, 178, 183, 291, 302

Apostolic Fathers, 39, 300

Apparatus. *See* critical apparatus

Arabic, Arabic translations. *See* Bible versions, Arabic

Aramaic, Aramaic translations. *See* Bible versions, Aramaic

archaic Hebrew (paleo-Hebrew), 52. *See also* script, "early Hebrew" (paleo-Hebrew)

Aristeas, letter of, 139, 176-77

Armenian, Armenian translation. *See* Bible versions, Armenian

Asia Minor, 45

Assyrian script. *See* script, Assyrian (square)

asterisk(s), 193-94, 302

Athos. *See* Bible, Hebrew Bible, manuscripts, Athos Codex

autograph(s), 23, 27, 29, 37, 39-40, 69, 79, 236, 301-2

Babylonian recension. *See* Targum(s)/ Targumim, Babylonian; Talmud, Babylonian

Babylonian vocalization. *See* vocalization, systems, Babylonian

Barnabas, Epistle of, 183

Ben Sira Scroll, 153

Bible, Greek Bible,

  Greek Bible editions

    Bengel, 11, 212

    Greek New Testament, 210, 218-19, 223, 226, 231, 233, 238, 251, 253, 255-56, 265, 280, 310

    Erasmus, 209, 210, 265

    Nestle, 218-20, 223, 251

    Soden, 218

    Souter, 218

    Tischendorf, 11, 17, 83, 182-84, 214, 216, 218, 260-63

    Wettstein, 256

    Old Greek, 93, 115, 180-81, 185, 194, 200, 209

  Greek manuscript(s)

    $\mathfrak{P}^{32}$, 79, 246, 257, 258

    $\mathfrak{P}^{42}$, 219

    $\mathfrak{P}^{45}$, 219, 220, 225, 233, 245, 257

    $\mathfrak{P}^{46}$, 16, 17, 50-51, 79, 81, 82, 225, 232, 241, 249-51, 257, 299

    $\mathfrak{P}^{47}$, 246

    $\mathfrak{P}^{48}$, 220, 245

    $\mathfrak{P}^{52}$, 16, 17, 37, 40, 79-80, 225, 232-33, 257-58, 276, 299

    $\mathfrak{P}^{64}$, 79, 247

    $\mathfrak{P}^{65}$, 246

    $\mathfrak{P}^{66}$, 47-48, 79, 82, 219, 232, 245, 258, 299

    $\mathfrak{P}^{72}$, 245, 258

    $\mathfrak{P}^{74}$, 257

  Greek Uncial manuscript(s)

    Codex Alexandrinus, 12, 17, 80, 116,

metathesis. *See* textual phenomena, unintentional changes, metathesis
midrashic elements, 174
minuscules/minuscule manuscripts, 80-82, 225, 234, 303, 306
misspelling, 54
mistaken letters. *See* textual phenomena, unintentional changes, mistaken letters
modern translations, 19, 20, 50, 56, 58, 84-85, 254-55, 298. *See* Bible versions, English
Münster, 219, 231, 238, 256
Murabbaʿat. *See* Wadi Murabbaʿat
Naḥal Ḥever, 154. *See also* Qumran; Qumran Scrolls; Masada
Naḥal Ṣeelim. *See* Qumran; Qumran Scrolls; *See also* Masada
Nash Papyrus, 10, 17, 70-71, 121, 124, 130, 140, 148-49
Nehemiah, 27, 33-34, 63, 111, 142, 144, 161-62, 173, 293
Neophyti. *See* Targum(s)/Targumim, MS Vatican Neophyti I
Nestle. *See* Bible, Greek Bible, Greek Bible editions, Nestle
Nestorians, 273
Nile, 232, 276
Numidia, 288
obelos (pl. *obeli*), 193-94, 197, 306
oldest extant text
    Greek, 79, 80, 232, 257, 258, 276, 299
    Hebrew, 89, 97, 104, 166, 299
Old Greek versions. *See* Bible, Greek Bible, Greek Bible editions, Old Greek
Old Latin versions. *See* Bible versions, Latin, Old Latin; *See also* Bible versions, Latin, Latin Vulgate
Old Syriac. *See* Bible version, Syriac, Old Syriac
omissions. *See* textual phenomena, unintentional changes, omissions
Onqelos. *See* Targum/Targumim, Targum Onqelos
open section, 153
oral tradition, 45, 106, 172, 273
Origen's Hexapla, 8, 10, 95, 124, 129, 130, 139, 167, 180, 188, 190-97, 199, 201, 272, 302, 304, 306-7
original
    reading, 9, 23, 39, 41, 54, 100, 120-21, 123, 125, 127-29, 131-33, 135, 137, 139-40, 186, 212, 227, 231, 238-40, 244, 247-48, 253, 270, 308-9
    text(s)/manuscript(s), 23, 30, 31, 38, 39,

58, 66-68, 99, 121, 128, 140, 167, 181, 213, 215, 220-21, 230, 233, 235, 239, 241, 251, 264, 298, 302-4, 306, 309
translation(s), 178, 280-81
orthography. *See also matres lectionis*
    defective/full orthography, 109, 146, 199, 303, 307
    definition, 307
    differences in orthography, 109, 128, 147
    Masorah, 109
    Masoretic Text, 64-65, 128, 147
    parallel texts, 32-33, 53, 55, 109, 117, 127, 135, 148, 243, 289, 299
    Qumran scrolls, 306
    Samaritan Pentateuch, 169
    spelling, 8, 25, 52, 55, 64, 109, 127, 147, 152-53, 169, 230-31, 238, 248, 261, 299, 306
ostracon, 16, 28, 47, 307
paleography, 33, 150, 307
paleo-Hebrew script. *See* script, "early Hebrew" (paleo-Hebrew)
Palestinian vocalization. *See* vocalization, system, Palestinian
palaeography, 79, 86
palimpsest, 82, 150, 184, 194, 214, 262, 285, 307
paper. *See* writing, writing materials, paper
papyrus, papyri, 11, 13, 17, 28, 40, 70, 79-80, 149-50, 155, 179, 181-83, 190, 198, 219-20, 225, 233-34, 256-58, 278, 307. *See also* Nash Papyrus; writing, writing materials, papyrus
parablepsis, 49, 307. *See also* textual phenomena, unintentional changes
paragraph, 74
parallel texts/sources, 32-33, 53, 55, 62, 104, 109, 117, 127, 135, 148, 161, 231, 238-39, 243, 298-99, 303. *See also* copying and transmission; readings; original, reading
paraphrase, 128, 173, 202, 218, 299, 307
parchment. *See* writing, writing materials, parchment
Paris Polygot. *See* editions, polyglot, Paris Polyglot
patristic citations, 11, 169, 186, 188, 213, 233, 236-38
Paul of Tella, 194
Pauline Epistles, 226, 257, 286, 288, 290, 294
Pelagius, 225, 237, 249-50, 252-53
persecution, 80, 82, 83, 197, 269, 282, 288
Peshitta. *See* Bible versions, Syriac, Peshitta
Peter, First, 51, 277